Complete Project Management
Office Handbook
Gerard M. Hill
0-8493-2173-5

Complex IT Project Management: 16 Steps
to Success
Peter Schulte
0-8493-1932-3

Creating Components: Object Oriented,
Concurrent, and Distributed Computing
in Java
Charles W. Kann
0-8493-1499-2

The Hands-On Project Office: Guaranteeing
and On-Time Delivery
Richard M. Kesner
0-8493-1991-9

Interpreting the CMMI®: A Process
Improvement Approach
Margaret Kulpa and Kent Johnson
0-8493-1654-5

ISO 9001:2000 for Software and Systems
Providers: An Engineering Approach
Robert Bamford and William John Deibler II
0-8493-2063-1

The Laws of Software Process:
A New Model for the Production
and Management of Software
Phillip G. Armour
0-8493-1489-5

Real Process Improvement Using
the CMMI®
Michael West
0-8493-2109-3

Six Sigma Software Development
Christine Tayntor
0-8493-1193-4

Software Architecture Design Patterns
in Java
Partha Kuchana
0-8493-2142-5

Software Configuration Management
Jessica Keyes
0-8493-1976-5

Software Engineering for Image Processing
Phillip A. Laplante
0-8493-1376-7

Software Engineering Handbook
Jessica Keyes
0-8493-1479-8

Software Engineering Measurement
John C. Munson
0-8493-1503-4

Software Metrics: A Guide to Planning,
Analysis, and Application
C.R. Pandian
0-8493-1661-8

Software Testing: A Craftsman's Approach,
Second Edition
Paul C. Jorgensen
0-8493-0809-7

Software Testing and Continuous Quality
Improvement, Second Edition
William E. Lewis
0-8493-2524-2

IS Management Handbook, 8th Edition
Carol V. Brown and Heikki Topi, Editors
0-8493-1595-9

Lightweight Enterprise Architectures
Fenix Theuerkorn
0-8493-2114-X

Outsourcing Software Development
Offshore: Making It Work
Tandy Gold
0-8493-1943-9

Maximizing ROI on Software Development
Vijay Sikka
0-8493-2312-6

Implementing the IT Balanced Scorecard
Jessica Keyes
0-8493-2621-4

AUERBACH PUBLICATIONS

www.auerbach-publications.com
To Order Call: 1-800-272-7737 • Fax: 1-800-374-3401
E-mail: orders@crcpress.com

EMBEDDED LINUX SYSTEM DESIGN AND DEVELOPMENT

EMBEDDED LINUX SYSTEM DESIGN AND DEVELOPMENT

P. Raghavan • Amol Lad • Sriram Neelakandan

Auerbach Publications
Taylor & Francis Group
Boca Raton   New York

Published in 2006 by
Auerbach Publications
Taylor & Francis Group
6000 Broken Sound Parkway NW, Suite 300
Boca Raton, FL 33487-2742

International Standard Book Number-10: 0-8493-4058-6 (Hardcover)
International Standard Book Number-13: 978-0-8493-4058-1 (Hardcover)
Library of Congress Card Number 2005048179

Library of Congress Cataloging-in-Publication Data

Raghavan, P. (Pichai), 1973-
    Embedded Linux system design and development / P. Raghavan, Amol Lad, Sriram Neelakandan.
      p. cm.
    Includes bibliographical references and index.
    ISBN 0-8493-4058-6 (alk. paper)
    1. Linux. 2. Operating systems (Computers) 3. Embedded computer systems. I. Lad, Amol. II. Neelakandan, Sriram. III. Title.

QA76.76.O63R335 2005
005.4'32--dc22
                                              2005048179

Taylor & Francis Group
is the Academic Division of T&F Informa plc.

Visit the Taylor & Francis Web site at
http://www.taylorandfrancis.com

and the Auerbach Publications Web site at
http://www.auerbach-publications.com

All source code in the book is released under GNU GPL v2. It can be used as desired under terms and conditions of GNU GPL v2.

Trademarks

- MIPS is a registered trademark and YAMON is a trademark of MIPS Technologies.
- IBM and ClearCase are registered trademarks and PowerPC is a trademark of International Business Machines Corporation.
- UNIX is a registered trademark in the United States and other countries, licensed exclusively through X/Open Company Limited.
- X11 is a trademark of Massachusetts Institute of Technology.
- NEC is a registered trademark of NEC Corporation.
- HP is a registered trademark of Hewlett-Packard Company.
- ColdFire is a registered trademark and Motorola is a trademark of Motorola, Inc.
- Microblaze is trademark of Xilinx Inc.
- Red Hat is a registered trademark and eCos and RedBoot are trademarks of Red Hat, Inc.
- uClinux is a registered trademark of Arcturus Networks Inc.
- Linux is a registered trademark of Linus Torvalds.
- GoAhead is a registered trademark of GoAhead Software, Inc.
- RTLinux is a registered trademark and FSMLabs, RTLinuxPro and RTCore are trademarks of Finite State Machine Labs, Inc.
- Debian is a registered trademark of Software in the Public Interest, Inc.
- LMBench is a trademark of BitMover, Inc.
- VRTX is a trademark of Microtech Research Inc.
- VxWorks and pSOS are registered trademarks of Wind River Systems, Inc.
- Trolltech is a registered trademark and Qt is a trademark of Trolltech in Norway, the United States and other countries.
- OpenGL is a registered trademark of Silicon Graphics, Inc.
- Perforce is a registered trademark of Perforce Software, Inc.
- Eclipse is a trademark of Eclipse Foundation, Inc.
- KDE and K Desktop Environment are trademarks of KDE.
- FFmpeg is a trademark of Fabrice Bellard, originator of the FFmpeg project.
- NVIDIA is a registered trademark of NVIDIA Corporation in the United States and other countries.
- ViewML is a registered trademark of Century Software Inc.
- QNX and Neutrino are registered trademarks of QNX Software Systems Ltd.
- Nucleus is a trademark of Accelerated Technology, Inc.
- Accelerated Technology is a registered trademark of Mentor Graphics Corporation.
- ARM and StrongARM are registered trademarks and ARM7 and ARM9 are trademarks of Advanced RISC Machines, Ltd.
- AMD is a registered trademark of Advanced Micro Devices, Inc.
- Intel and Pentium are registered trademarks and i386 and XScale are trademarks of Intel Corporation.
- Sharp is a registered trademark of Sharp Electronics Corp.
- SPARC is a registered trademark of SPARC International, Inc., and is used under license by Sun Microsystems, Inc.
- Toshiba is a registered trademark of the Toshiba Corporation.
- MontaVista is registered trademark of MontaVista Software Inc.
- LynxOS and BlueCat are registered trademarks and LynxWorks, SpyKer and VisualLynux are trademarks of LynuxWorks, Inc.
- Samsung is a registered trademark of Samsung Electronics America, Inc. and its related entities.
- Ericsson is a registered trademark of Ericsson, Inc.
- Atmel is registered trademarks of Atmel Corporation.
- TimeSys®, TimeStorm®, TimeStorm IDE™, TimeStorm LVS™, TimeStorm LDS™, TimeStorm LHD™, TimeSys Reservations™, TimeTrace®, Linux/RT™ and TimeWiz® are registered or unregistered trademarks of TimeSys Corporation in the United States and other countries.
- NeoMagic is a registered trademark of NeoMagic Corporation.
- Transmeta is a trademark of Transmeta Corporation.
- Broadcom is a registered trademark of Broadcom Corporation and/or its subsidiaries.
- SuSE is a registered trademark of SuSE AG.

- Borland is a registered trademark of Borland Software Corporation in the United States and other countries.
- Merant is a registered trademark of Merant.
- SnapGear is a registered trademark of SnapGear Inc.
- Matsushita is a trademark of the Matsushita Electric Corporation.
- I2C is a trademark of Philips Semiconductors Corporation.
- Philips® is a registered trademark of Philips Consumer Electronics Corporation.
- Cadenux is a trademark of Cadenux, LLC.
- ELinOS is a registered trademark of SYSGO AG.
- Metrowerks and CodeWarrior are trademarks of Metrowerks Corp. in the U.S. or other countries.
- FreeBSD is a registered trademark of the FreeBSD Foundation.
- IEEE and POSIX are registered trademarks of the Institute of Electrical and Electronics Engineers, Inc. in the United States.
- Xtensa is a trademark belonging to Tensilica Inc.
- Fujitsu is a registered trademark of Fujitsu, Ltd.
- Firewire is a registered trademark of Apple computer.
- SuperH is a trademark of Hitachi, Ltd.
- Windows, WinCE and Microsoft are registered trademarks and MS-DOS and DirectX are trademarks of Microsoft Corporation.
- Solaris and Java are registered trademarks and ChorusOS is a trademark of Sun Microsystems, Inc. in the U.S. or other countries.
- Symbian is a trademark of Symbian Ltd.

Dedication

Raghavan

In memory of my late father

Amol

To Lord Kṛṣṇa, my parents, my wife Parul, and my brother Amit

Sriram

To my family and all Linux enthusiasts

Contents

Appendices

Foreword

The industrial revolution appears as a knife-edge change from a rural self-employed lifestyle to a clock-punching, whistle-blowing corporate urban way of life. Being in the middle of the current revolution makes it hard to realize that in fifty years most people will consider the messy, dynamic, no-rules embedded product development environment of today as an obvious clean transition caused by technological changes.

The first embedded software project I worked on didn't use an off-the-shelf operating system—there was none. It wasn't until several years later that WindRiver introduced VxWorks®. In the mid-1990s it appeared that nothing could unseat VxWorks; yet, recently WindRiver announced a Linux-based product. Why the change? Today the most common embedded operating system used in new products is Linux.

For fourteen years I was part of a small army of firmware engineers working on the development of HP LaserJet™ printers. The printer used a homegrown operating system that as I recall was called LaserJet O.S. Usually the very best engineers worked on supporting and extending the operating system. Any LaserJet O.S. documentation that existed, engineers had created. Any test suite was similarly a burden placed on the engineer's shoulders. The effort and expense of these highly talented engineers seldom led to any features that differentiated the product from the compctitors. The most important lesson I learned from the experience was to always put your most talented engineers on the features that make your product unique and outsource the infrastructure. Embedded Linux is often the best choice for the operating system infrastructure for products needing nontrivial connectivity.

Whether you support Linux in-house or purchase a Linux board support package for your processor, you will still need to understand the overall system and at times the details of a particular subsystem. In this book the authors have done a good job fitting all the pieces together that are necessary for embedded Linux development. The book discusses topics such as board support packages, embedded storage, and real-time Linux programming in depth. Embedded graphics and uClinux are also explained with clarity. The book is a good attempt to address the concerns of an embedded Linux developer.

The rapid growth of Linux as the top choice for an embedded operating system in new products is in part due to the ease of using embedded Linux to replace homegrown operating systems. Although this book is specifically for running Linux on embedded systems it can also be used as a guide to port a system from a traditional RTOS or homegrown operating system to embedded Linux. It may be the need for TCP/IP networking, USB support, SecureDigital support, or some other standard that causes a company to dump their current operating system and switch to Linux. But it is the joy of developing with Linux that keeps the engineers promoting it for future products.

An astounding amount of Linux information is available on the Web. I suspect it is the most extensively documented software ever. How can a book about embedded Linux provide value over what is already available? First, the scope of embedded Linux and related applications is so large that getting a feel for what is available and what can be done is challenging. Seeing all the pieces separately and working together can help you make sense of the embedded Linux ecosystem. Second, there are technical reasons for needing the right information. In an embedded device, the bootloader, kernel, and file system containing the applications all need to be developed in concert for the solution to work properly. Understanding the interdependencies and getting the development environment to properly build all three images is not straightforward. Also, when you encounter a problem, understanding the tools available to debug the problem and knowing the techniques used for debugging embedded devices can save a significant amount of time and effort.

Finally, the best reason for reading this book on embedded Linux is because the technology is so fascinating. Anyone who had developed embedded products the old way, with one single executable image, will be amazed at the flexibility and power of using embedded Linux. Anyone new to embedded development will find most of the power and flexibility available on their desktop PC works the same in their embedded development environment.

Todd Fischer
President and Founder
Cadenux

Preface

When we were in college in the mid-1990s we heard of an exciting new technology called the Internet that was to have a profound impact on our lives. Along with the Internet we also heard of an open source operating system, Linux, which was being developed by hundreds of programmers around the world. Linux gave us an opportunity to understand the internals of the operating system and we quickly became Linux enthusiasts. We realized that Linux was more than an operating system; here was a movement with few parallels in human history as it was based on the concepts of human dignity, choice, and freedom. Linux gave young programmers like us the reach to the latest technology.

When we became embedded professionals Linux had yet to make a strong presence in the embedded market. However, we were hearing of some exciting improvements such as running a hard real-time kernel along with the Linux kernel and running Linux on MMU-less microcontrollers. Our happiness grew unbounded when we were asked by a customer to move our software on a MIPS-based SoC from a commercial RTOS to embedded Linux. Our experience revealed that the road to embedded Linux is not a very smooth ride. Some of the main reasons were:

1. There is undoubtedly lots of information about embedded Linux on the Internet but it is too scattered to give a consolidated view. Converting this information into a knowledge base can be a time-consuming task. Most of the product-based companies are normally short on time. Decisions need to be made quickly and executed quickly. However, a wrong decision especially on crucial issues such as licensing can prove disastrous to the company.

2. There is a gross misconception that embedded systems are all about the hardware or the operating system. As computing power increases rapidly as per Moore's law the amount of application software that goes into the embedded system has also increased at the same rate. Hence the applications have become the USP for the embedded system. So building a

Linux-based embedded system does not stop with the OS but has to do a lot with writing and building applications. And applications have their own set of issues that are different from the operating system such as licensing, toolchains, and so on.

3. Unlike a commercial RTOS, which gives a single point of support such as patches and documentation, embedded Linux takes a whole new development paradigm. Often the developers need to search for patches or for new information from the various mailing lists. And this can be very time consuming.

When we came out successfully with an embedded Linux design with a variety of applications, we decided to share some of our thoughts and experiences with the rest of the world. The result of that thought process is this book. This book contains an entire development roadmap for embedded Linux systems. Our primary aim is to make the reader aware of the various issues that arise out of embedded Linux development.

The theme of the book is twofold:

- To facilitate movement to embedded Linux from a traditional RTOS
- To explain the system design model with embedded Linux

Benefits to the Reader

The book offers solutions to problems that a developer faces when programming in an embedded Linux environment. Some of the common problems are:

- Understand the embedded Linux development model.
- Write, debug, and profile applications and drivers in embedded Linux.
- Understand embedded Linux BSP architecture.

The book offers practical solutions to the above problems.
After reading this book the reader will

- Understand the embedded Linux development environment.
- Understand and create Linux BSP for a hardware platform.
- Understand the Linux model for embedded storage and write drivers and applications for the same.
- Understand various embedded Linux drivers such as serial, I2C, and so on.
- Port applications to embedded Linux from a traditional RTOS.
- Write real-time applications in embedded Linux.
- Learn methods to find memory leaks and memory corruption in applications and drivers.
- Learn methods to profile applications and the kernel.
- Understand uCLinux architecture and its programming model.
- Understand the embedded Linux graphics subsystem.

The book is also an aid to managers in choosing an embedded Linux distribution, creating a roadmap for the transition to embedded Linux, and applying the Linux licensing model in a commercial product.

Audience

Primary Audience

- *Architects:* They are more concerned with real-time issues, performance, and porting plans.
- *Software programmers:* They need to get into the minute details of the technology.

Secondary Audience

- *Legal staff:* Because most embedded products involve intellectual property, any wrong understanding of the licensing issues can prove detrimental to the company itself.
- *Managers:* They are normally concerned about choosing the distribution, version, toolset, and vendor.
- *Testing and support team:* Because the look and feel of the product can change when moving to embedded Linux, the test and support team needs to be educated.

Background

The authors expect a basic understanding of embedded system programming in any embedded OS from the reader. The book is not a Linux kernel book. Familiarity with basic Linux kernel concepts and the user-space programming model is desirable.

The book attempts to be independent of the kernel version; however, wherever necessary the 2.4 or the 2.6 kernels are used as examples.

Downloading Source Code

Readers can download source code from the following URL: http://www.crcpress.com/e_products/downloads/download.asp?cat_no=AU0586

Acknowledgments

I thank the management of my present employer, Philips, for giving me the support to go ahead with the book. Any work of mine has always been incomplete without the blessings of my dear mother. And last but not least I would like to thank my wife, Bhargavi, for spending some cold days alone when I was busy penning down the pages for this book.

Raghavan

I would like to thank all the people who made this work possible. First my mother, who used to tell me to work for the book whenever she saw me roaming here and there, like any mother telling her kid to study. I also express thanks to my father who kept on asking me about the status of the manuscript, like a project manager. I thank my wife, Parul, for her patience during manuscript preparation. I remember when Raghav told me about this project and asked me to join. It was just two months after my marriage. I thank Parul for her encouragement and also thank her for helping me out in formatting the manuscript.

Amol

Thanks to Raghav who had the idea of writing this book. I still remember the first meeting when he instilled the confidence in me to take up this work. I thank my dad, mom, and sister for their support. Thanks to the entire "boys" gang at Bangalore who have been kind enough to share the powerful "Athlon/Audigy/ATI Radeon 9500" game PC for mean activities such as running Linux and typing sample code. They consider running a word processor on such a PC as a gross waste of computing power.

Sriram

We take this opportunity to thank Todd Fischer, president and founder, Cadenux, for giving us time from his busy schedule to write the foreword for the book. We thank David McCullogh, one of the uClinux core maintainers, and Dr. Paul Dale for reviewing the chapter on uClinux and for providing their valuable comments. We also thank Greg Haerr, CEO of Century Software and founder of the Nano-X windowing system, for his valuable review comments on the embedded graphics chapter. We thank Satish MM, director of Verismo Networks, for his valuable comments on GPL. We thank our close friend and guide, Deepak Shenoy, for coming up with the idea to write a book based on our development experience. Finally we thank all Linux kernel developers and user-space programmers for taking Linux to new heights.

Introduction

The text is divided into ten chapters and two appendices.

Chapter 1, "Introduction," gives a brief history of embedded Linux and what the benefits of embedded Linux are over other RTOSs. It discusses in detail the features of various open source and commercial embedded Linux distributions available. The chapter concludes by presenting a transition roadmap from a traditional RTOS to embedded Linux.

Chapter 2, "Getting Started," explains the architecture of embedded Linux and compares it with traditional RTOS and microkernel architectures. In brief various Linux kernel subsystems such as the hardware abstraction layer, memory management, scheduler, file system, and so on are given. A small description of the user-space Linux programming model is also given. The second half of the chapter explains the Linux start-up sequence, from bootloaders to kernel start-up and user-space start-up scripts. The last section explains the steps involved in building a GNU cross-platform toolchain.

Chapter 3, "Board Support Package," explains bootloader architecture followed by a discussion on the system memory map, both hardware and software memory maps. The second half of the chapter explains interrupt management, the PCI subsystem, timers, UART, and power management in detail.

Chapter 4, "Embedded Storage," explains the MTD subsystem architecture for accessing flash devices. The second half of the chapter discusses various embedded file systems such as RAMFS, CRAMFS, JFFS2, NFS, and so on. The chapter also discusses various methods for optimizing storage space in an embedded system, both kernel and user-space optimizations. A discussion of various applications designed for embedded Linux such as Busybox is given. Finally some steps for tuning the kernel memory are given.

Chapter 5, "Embedded Drivers," discusses in detail various embedded drivers such as the Serial driver, Ethernet driver, I2C subsystem, and USB gadgets.

Chapter 6, "Porting Applications," discusses an application porting roadmap from a traditional RTOS to embedded Linux. The rest of the chapter explains the porting roadmap in detail. First a discussion on Linux pthreads is given, then the Operating System Porting Layer (OSPL), and finally a kernel API driver.

Chapter 7, "Real-Time Linux," discusses the real-time features in Linux. It explains the various latencies involved in the kernel such as interrupt and scheduling latency and efforts that are made to improve the kernel response time such as kernel preemption and O(1) scheduler. The core of the chapter is the discussion of POSIX.1b programming interfaces in Linux. The chapter explains various POSIX.1b real-time extensions such as real-time schedulers, memory locking, message queues, semaphores, and asynchronous I/O in detail. The last section explains in brief the hard real-time approach to Linux followed by a real-time programming model in RTAI.

Chapter 8, "Building and Debugging," is divided into three sections: building, debugging, and profiling. The first section explains various mechanisms for building kernel and user-space applications. In the second section tools such as mtrace, dmalloc, and valgrind to debug memory problems are explained. Finally the last section discusses eProf, OProfile, and kernel function instrumentation profiling methods to profile user-space and kernel functions.

Chapter 9, "Embedded Graphics," explains in detail a generic frame buffer driver and how to write applications using the frame buffer interface. It also discusses in brief the X graphics subsystem and why it is not suitable for embedded devices. The last section explains the Nano-X windowing environment.

Chapter 10, "uClinux," explains the architecture and programming environment in uClinux. The first half of the chapter explains the bFLT executable file format and how programs are loaded and executed in uClinux-based systems. Next a discussion about memory management, process creation, and shared libraries in uClinux is given. The final section explains XIP and how to port applications from standard Linux to uClinux. It also explains how to build applications for uClinux.

Appendix A, "Booting Faster," explains various techniques to reduce Linux boot-up time.

Appendix B, "GPL and Embedded Linux," discusses what GPL means to embedded Linux and how proprietary software can be kept safe with embedded Linux.

Source code is available for downloading from http://www.crcpress.com/e_products/downloads/download.asp?cat_no=AU0586

About the Authors

P. Raghavan has nine years of experience in embedded software development. He has worked on a variety of embedded products ranging from graphics displays and televisions to network equipment. Other than embedded Linux he has worked on a variety of commercial operating systems such as VxWorks and Nucleus. He understands the various issues related to the software development life cycle for embedded systems. He holds an electronics engineering degree from Bangalore University, India. Presently he is employed with Philips Software, Bangalore.

Amol Lad is a computer science graduate from Motilal Nehru National Institute of Technology, Allahabad, India, one of the prestigious engineering colleges in the country. He first peeked into the Linux kernel sources in 1996 during his second year of engineering. It was his curiosity to understand how things work "under the hood" that attracted him to Linux. He started his career in 1999 as a device driver writer for satellite communication systems. His first exposure to embedded Linux was in the year 2001 when he wrote a BSP for a MIPS-based custom hardware platform. Presently he is employed by Verismo Networks as a Linux kernel engineer. He is responsible for designing systems based on embedded Linux for his company. If not busy reading kernel sources you can find him playing (or watching) cricket. He is also devoted to music. If he had not been a computer engineer he surely would have been a music composer.

Sriram Neelakandan graduated with an electronics engineering degree and started his career as a Windows device driver programmer. He likes problems that require a soldering iron and an oscilloscope to solve rather than just the keyboard. He has worked on device drivers for various technologies including ISA, PCI, USB, PCMCIA, and CF+ across platforms such as Windows, VxWorks, and Linux. His embedded Linux experience started with porting a MIPS-based System-on-Chip (SoC) networking product. Working on the product gave him the opportunity to understand various modules of Linux including the routing subsystem (fib, netlink), MTD drivers, and flash file systems (CRAMFS, JFFS2). Currently employed at Verismo Networks, India, he is part of the embedded Linux team responsible for media solutions.

Chapter 1

Introduction

An embedded system is a special-purpose computer system that is designed to perform very small sets of designated activities. Embedded systems date back as early as the late 1960s where they used to control electromechanical telephone switches. The first recognizable embedded system was the Apollo guidance computer developed by Charles Draper and his team. Later they found their way into the military, medical sciences, and the aerospace and automobile industries. Today they are widely used to serve various purposes; some examples are the following.

- Network equipment such as firewall, router, switch, and so on
- Consumer equipment such as MP3 players, cell phones, PDAs, digital cameras, camcorders, home entertainment systems, and so on
- Household appliances such as microwaves, washing machines, televisions, and so on
- Mission-critical systems such as satellites and flight control

Following are the key factors that differentiate an embedded system from a desktop computer.

- Embedded systems are usually cost sensitive.
- Most embedded systems have real-time constraints.
- There are multitudes of CPU architectures (such as ARM®, MIPS®, PowerPC™, etc.) that are used in embedded systems. Embedded systems employ application-specific processors. For example, the processor in your digital camera is specially tailored for image capturing and rendering.
- Embedded systems have (and require) very few resources in terms of RAM, ROM, or other I/O devices as compared to a desktop computer.
- Power management is an important aspect in most embedded systems.

- The development and debugging environment in an embedded system is very different from a desktop computer. Embedded systems generally have an inbuilt circuitry for debugging purposes.
- An embedded system is designed from both the hardware and software perspective, taking into account a specific application or set of applications. For example, your MP3 player may have a separate hardware MP3 decoder built inside it.

In the early days effectively no operating system was used in embedded systems. There was in-house development of all the software that directly drives the hardware with almost no or very minimal multitasking and user interaction in place. But with the passage of time, more complex embedded systems started emerging and along with that a growing list of features that an embedded system should support. All of these requirements mandated use of an operating system in embedded systems that should at least provide multitasking/multithreading, process and memory management, interprocess communication, timers, and so on. So the companies started enhancing their in-house developed software so that they could have a minimal but a full-featured operating system running on their embedded platform. Various firms started efforts to provide an operating system aimed at embedded systems.

Today we have a multitude of embedded operating systems. Apart from company in-house developed operating systems we have Wind River's VxWorks®, Microsoft® Windows® CE, QNX® Neutrino®, Accelerated Technology®'s Nucleus™, Red Hat®'s eCos™, Sun Microsystems ChorusOS™, LynuxWorks™'s LynxOS®, and embedded Linux as primary embedded operating systems.

1.1 History of Embedded Linux

Linus Benedict Torvalds at the University of Helsinki created the Linux® operating system in 1991. It was his mail in a minix development mailing list as shown in Listing 1.1 that is said to have started the Linux revolution.

Since then Linux has never looked back. Its open source development model and GNU General Public License (GPL), under which Linux is released, attracted contributions from thousands of developers worldwide. This license allowed all the Linux kernel source code to be freely available for personal or commercial use. As the Linux kernel source code is freely available, it encouraged many developers to contribute to the Linux kernel. It is because of this global pool of developers that we have a highly reliable, robust, and powerful operating system. In early 1996 Linux saw its arrival in hard real-time embedded systems as a research project of Michael Barabanov and Victor Yodaiken. This RT-Linux research project was based on using a small real-time kernel along with Linux to provide hard real-time deadline guarantees. In 1997 the uClinux® project was started with the aim of using Linux in no-MMU processors. It was released for use in the year 1998. During the years 1999 to 2004 Linux was widely used in embedded systems. The following sections mention some of the major developments in embedded Linux during this period.

Listing 1.1   The Origin of Linux

```
From: torvalds@klaava.Helsinki.FI (Linus Benedict Torvalds)
Newsgroups: comp.os.minix
Subject: What would you like to see most in minix?
Summary: small poll for my new operating system
Message-ID: <1991Aug25.205708.9541@klaava.Helsinki.FI>
Date: 25 Aug 91 20:57:08 GMT
Organization: University of Helsinki


Hello everybody out there using minix -

I'm doing a (free) operating system (just a hobby, won't be big
and Professional like gnu) for 386(486) AT clones. This has been
brewing since april, and is starting to get ready. I'd like any
feedback on things people like/dislike in minix, as my OS resembles
it somewhat(same physical layout of the file-system (due to
practical reasons)among other things).

I've currently ported bash(1.08) and gcc(1.40), and things seem to
work. This implies that I'll get something practical within a few
months, and I'd like to know what features most people would want.
Any suggestions are welcome, but I won't promise I'll implement
them :-)

Linus (torvalds@kruuna.helsinki.fi)


PS. Yes - it's free of any minix code, and it has a multi threaded
fs. It is NOT portable (uses 386 task switching etc), and it
probably never will support anything other than AT-harddisks, as
that's all I have :-(.
```

1.1.1 Year 1999

Linux started to develop its roots in the embedded systems area in the year 1999. Some of the major developments in this year were:

- At the Embedded Systems Conference (ESC) of September 1999 companies including Lineo, FSM Labs, MontaVista®, and Zentropix made announcements about embedded Linux support.
- Zentropix founded RealTimeLinux.org to discuss possibilities of real-time Linux solutions.
- Lineo announced an Embedded Advisory Board (EMLAB) for discussing the possibilities of using Linux in embedded areas.
- Rick Lehrbaum started an embedded Linux portal: Linuxdevices.com.
- RTAI was released by Paolo Mantegazza to add hard real-time support in Linux.
- BlueCat® Linux was announced by Lynx real-time systems (now LynuxWorks). It was the first commercial embedded Linux distribution.

1.1.2 Year 2000

In the year 2000 many companies adopted embedded Linux in their product lines.

- Samsung® launched Yopy, a PDA with Linux inside.
- Ericsson® launched HS210, a Linux-based cordless screen phone that combines wireless connectivity with Internet access, telephony, and e-mail functions.
- Atmel® announced a Linux-based single-chip Internet appliance, the AT75C310, that includes support for VoIP and audio.
- Agenda Computing demonstrated a Linux-based PDA at Linuxworld.

This year also saw increased awareness about real-time support in Linux.

- TimeSys® Corporation announced Linux/RT™, an embedded Linux distribution aiming to provide predictable application response times by using resource reservation technology.
- MontaVista Software started a Linux Real-Time Characterization Project to provide developers with a set of open source tools for measuring real-time responsiveness of Linux systems.
- Red Hat released EL/IX version 1.1 specifications for adding real-time support in Linux.

In this year many tools and utilities were released for use in embedded Linux.

- Busybox 0.43 was released. It was the first and most stable Busybox release.
- GoAhead® Software announced the GoAhead Web server for embedded Linux applications.
- Trolltech® launched Qt™/Embedded, a GUI application framework and windowing system for embedded Linux.
- ViewML® embedded browser was announced by Greg Haerr. ViewML is based on the Microwindows windowing system.

In this year the Embedded Linux Consortium (ELC) was founded by Rick Lehrbaum with major corporations such as Intel® and IBM® as its members. The aim of this consortium was to facilitate the use of Linux and open source software in embedded areas. ELC promoted Linux as an effective, secure, and reliable operating system for embedded systems.

OSDL (Open Source Development Lab) was also founded in this year by HP®, Intel, IBM, and NEC® with the goal of supporting enterprise Linux solutions.

1.1.3 Year 2001

The biggest announcement of the year 2001 was the release of Linux kernel 2.4, which was later adopted in many embedded Linux distributions. In this year Linux was also widely used in handheld devices and gadgets.

- Sharp® Electronics introduced Linux-based PDAs.
- Trolltech and Lisa systems announced a wireless iPAQ solution for the Compaq iPAQ palmtop computer.
- NeoMagic® also announced a Linux-based SOC platform for smart handheld devices.
- Transmeta™ Corporation released "Midori" Linux, an open source distribution targeting small devices.

Embedded Linux standardization efforts were also gaining pace in the year 2001.

- Japan Embedded Linux Consortium (EMBLIX) was founded by major corporations including Toshiba® and NEC with the aim of promoting, educating, and standardizing embedded Linux in Japan.
- TV Linux Alliance was formed to define a set of standards for using Linux in set-top boxes. Broadcom®, Motorola, and Sun Microsystems were some of its cofounders.
- The Free Standards Group (FSG) released Linux Standard Base (LSB) specification version 1.0. The goal of LSB was to develop a set of standards to increase compatibility among Linux distributions so that applications can run on any compliant Linux system. LSB is widely recognized by the enterprise Linux industry and is also considered useful for embedded Linux.

In terms of tools and utilities the following also occurred.

- First major release of uClibc, uClibc 0.9.8, was made. uClibc now is an integral part of almost all embedded Linux distributions.
- Eclipse™ consortium was formed by major corporations including IBM, SuSE®, Red Hat, QNX Software Systems, Borland®, and Merant® to provide a development environment framework for embedded systems. Today companies such as TimeSys, LynuxWorks, MontaVista, and others are using the Eclipse framework to provide IDEs for embedded Linux development.

1.1.4 Year 2002

The year 2002 saw a major advancement of Linux in embedded markets with more and more companies adopting Linux in their product designs. Real-time support in Linux was also getting better.

- Kernel preemption patch from Robert Love, low latency patches by Andrew Morton, and the O(1) scheduler by Ingo Molnar found their ways into the Linux kernel.
- RTLinux® added hard real-time capability to user space.
- The ADEOS project announced the first release of ADEOS, a hardware abstraction layer allowing a real-time kernel and a general-purpose OS to co-exist.

In terms of standardization efforts, the following occurred.

- ELC released the Embedded Linux Consortium Platform Specification (ELCPS). The ELCPS provided a standard for the API layer that increases reusability and portability of program code. The standard helps developers by decreasing time and cost to develop embedded applications in Linux.
- OSDL announced the Carrier Grade Linux (CGL) working group to promote and standardize the use of Linux in carrier grade systems. CGL released v1.x CGL requirements specifications in the same year.
- Free Standards Group announced the LSB 1.1 and LSB certification program. The aim of the LSB certification program was to employ an independent authority to verify that a Linux distribution or application adheres to LSB.

In this year Linux saw more inroads in the digital entertainment industry. Intel announced a reference design for a home digital media adapter. Trace Strategies Inc. published a research report projecting Linux as a preferred OS in devices such as digital interactive TV (ITV), set-top boxes, and so on.

In this year uClinux also gained shared library support from SnapGear® and Ridgerun. It later found its way into mainstream Linux kernel version 2.5.46.

1.1.5 Year 2003

In the year 2003 Linux saw its growth in the cell phone and SOHO markets.

- Motorola announced its A760 mobile phone handset that uses Linux as its embedded OS.
- Linux saw more penetration in gateway, routers, and wireless LANs for SOHO and consumer markets.

In this year more stress was put on standardization.

- ELC added an extension to ELCPS to add support for power management, user interface, and real-time standards.
- OSDL announced CGL v2.0 with major advances in security, high availability, and clustering.
- The Consumer Electronics Linux Forum (CELF) was formed in June 2003 to provide specifications for using Linux in CE devices and to maintain a Linux kernel source tree that has enhancements specifically for CE devices. CELF invites companies to contribute to the tree so that Linux can become a de facto operating system for CE devices. Matsushita™, Sony, Hitachi, NEC, Royal Philips® Electronics, Samsung, Sharp Corporation, and Toshiba Corporation were the founders of CELF.

The year 2003 ended with the release of the Linux 2.6.0 kernel.

1.1.6 Year 2004

Some of the highlights of the year 2004 were as follows.

- In this year LynuxWorks released the 2.6 Linux kernel-based BlueCat Linux distribution. It was the first commercial embedded Linux distribution based on the 2.6 Linux kernel.
- Sony Corporation introduced Linux-based devices for in-car navigation and infotainment systems in Japan. The devices feature 3-D map navigation technology, media players, hard drives, GPS, and PC connectivity.
- Trolltech announced a mobile phone application stack that delivers PDA-like features on smartphones.
- OSDL's CGL specifications saw wide acceptance in the telecommunications industry.
- CELF released its first specification for using Linux in CE devices. The specification is also supported by a reference implementation in the form of a patched Linux kernel source tree supporting nine target boards.
- Free Standards Group (FSG) and OSDL released LSB 2.0.

Today lots of companies are adopting embedded Linux for their new designs. More and more vendors are providing embedded Linux distribution for various hardware platforms. Today embedded Linux is a preferred operating system for embedded systems. Silicon suppliers such as AMD®, ARM, TI, Motorola™, IBM, Intel, and so on all use Linux as a preferred hardware bring-up platform. CE devices OEMs such as Sony and NEC are deploying Linux in DVDs, DVRs, and digital handsets.

1.2 Why Embedded Linux?

Any newcomer to the domain of embedded Linux is bound to be riddled with a question: "Why choose embedded Linux as an operating system in the target?" In this section we discuss some benefits of embedded Linux against proprietary embedded operating systems.

1.2.1 Vendor Independence

Selecting a proprietary OS may lock you up with the same vendor for the lifetime of your product. Bad support from the vendor can result in increased time to market of your product. You may end up waiting days or even weeks for the solution to even small problems. Changing the vendor may mean restarting the whole product life cycle.

Embedded Linux brings vendor independence. Vendors of all embedded Linux distributions have more or less the same business model. The distributions are variations of the same theme. They all have the same and common basic components such as Linux kernel, libraries, basic utilities, and the like. If at some point you feel that your embedded Linux distribution vendor is not living up to your expectations, you can switch vendors at a relatively low cost. Above all you can also decide to have no embedded OS vendor at all for your product, as the source code of the Linux kernel and associated utilities are freely available.

1.2.2 Time to Market

For embedded Linux, a rich set of toolsets and utilities is available. Most of the vendors provide preview kits for various hardware platforms that can be downloaded free of cost. It is highly likely that a Linux port for your hardware is already available. Consequently you will spend time only in writing applications without worrying about the Linux port for the hardware or device driver for a high-performance I/O card that is part of your system. With an embedded Linux system a product can be rolled out very quickly.

One advantage of using Linux in an embedded platform is reduced development time. By using a Linux-based host development environment, most of the applications that are to be run on the target hardware can be tested on a Linux host, reducing time to port applications. For example, if your target needs a DHCP client, you can very well take any open source DHCP client (meeting the size requirement for target), compile, and test on a Linux host. If it works on the host then the only effort required is to cross-compile it for your target. It should run on the target without any problems.

1.2.3 Varied Hardware Support

With the arrival of large numbers of new high-end, low-cost, and much more sophisticated microprocessors and I/O devices it's becoming increasingly difficult for the vendors of proprietary embedded OSs to support them in time. Even if the product demands high-end hardware, customers may not be able to use it because their proprietary embedded OS vendor may not support it.

Linux support for many architectures and high-end I/O devices gives you the independence to choose appropriate hardware for your system. Linux is also a preferred OS for any hardware or software innovation. It is widely accepted in universities as a research and learning tool. Linux is also a preferred bring-up platform for hardware manufacturers.

1.2.4 Low Cost

Embedded Linux brings minimal cost for development, training, and hiring needs.

Development Cost

A vendor of proprietary software may charge a huge amount for licenses of development tools. These are generally per-seat licenses and thus limit the number of users that can use the development environment. With embedded

Linux, all the tools and utilities such as compilers, linkers, libraries, shells, and the like that constitute its development environment can be downloaded for free. Good IDEs are also available at either very little cost or completely free of charge. GUI-based configuration environment and profiling tools are also available.

Training and Hiring Costs

New development environments are expensive. The manufacturing cost of your product significantly increases when your developers require retraining or if you decide to hire a specialist who understands the development process, API usage, optimization techniques, and so on in the particular proprietary OS. Linux has a UNIX®-based programming model, which is familiar to most engineers. Thus the learning curve for embedded Linux is very small.

Runtime Royalty

Finally, a runtime royalty of the proprietary embedded OS (or some other third-party component) adds to product cost. The embedded market is highly cost sensitive. These days a lot of effort is being paid to reduce the cost of the product that reaches the end user. Embedded Linux is royalty free. Most vendors of embedded Linux distribution charge no runtime royalties to their customers. Lack of runtime royalties reduces the BOM (Bill Of Materials) of the product.

1.2.5 Open Source

One of the main reasons why Linux became so popular is its open source model of development. Linux has the following advantages because of open source.

- There are thousands of developers around the world who are contributing to and enhancing the Linux kernel and other applications.
- You are assured of global support during your development. There are separate mailing lists for almost all the Linux ports whether ARM, MIPS, or no-MMU. The mailing list archives might already contain answers to most of your questions. If not, a proper reply can be expected for a genuine question posted in these lists.
- It has a rich set of features with superior software and a rich talent pool across the world reviews every feature that goes in the kernel. This makes Linux robust and reliable.
- Availability of source code facilitates better understanding of what's going under the hood, how to customize it for optimal designs, and how to fix bugs if they arise. The Linux kernel or some device driver can be tailored for achieving high performance for your platform.
- Even the tools, applications, and utilities that come with Linux have an open source nature, thus benefiting from the open source advantage.

1.2.6 Standards (POSIX®) Compliance

The idea of POSIX is to improve the portability of software written for UNIX, thus making the job of a UNIX developer much easier. It aims at providing standards that define common interfaces and features for a UNIX-like operating system. The Linux kernel provides POSIX-compliant APIs for services such as memory management, process and thread creation, interprocess communication, file systems, and TCP/IP.

It's because of these benefits that the current system software trend for an embedded system is shifting towards embedded Linux. From lower cost to rich toolset, these benefits are providing a big thrust for using Linux in embedded areas.

1.3 Embedded Linux Versus Desktop Linux

Linux is used in a variety of hardware: right from huge SMP servers to the smallest of gadgets. But it is indeed a marvel that a single code base is used for the kernel irrespective of its final destination. This was achieved by implementing a high level of modularity within the kernel and making it easily configurable to be employed across a variety of hardware. However, some distributions do provide enhancements as patches to the standard Linux kernel to "suit" it for embedded systems. But truly speaking one can simply download a stable Linux kernel source, configure it as per system requirement, cross-compile, and it should be ready for use. Features such as real-time scheduling and kernel preemption, which are suited for embedded applications, are now part of the main kernel source tree.

Following are some of the key differences.

- The way the Linux kernel is configured for embedded systems differs from its desktop counterpart. The set of device drivers and file systems that is needed differs in both. For example, an embedded system may need a flash driver and a flash file system (such as CRAMFS or JFFS2) whereas they are not needed in a desktop system.
- In embedded Linux more focus is paid to tools that are needed for development, debugging, and profiling. In embedded Linux focus is paid to a set of cross-development tools that allow developers to build applications for their target on say x86-based host systems. On the other hand, in desktop Linux more focus is paid to a set of packages that are useful for users such as word processors, e-mail, newsreaders, and so on.
- The utilities that are part of an embedded Linux distribution are different from similar ones in desktop Linux. Ash, Tinylogin, and Busybox are considered to be requirements for using with embedded Linux. Even the application libraries such as uClibc are preferred for embedded applications as opposed to its Glibc desktop counterpart.[1]
- Windowing and GUI environments that are used in embedded Linux differ from the desktop ones. The X window system, which is quite common

for desktop Linux, is not suited to embedded environments. For embedded Linux, Microwindows (nanoX) serves a similar purpose.

■ Targets deploying embedded Linux mostly run in single-user mode with almost no system administration capabilities. On the other hand, system administration plays a very important role in desktop Linux.

1.4 Frequently Asked Questions

In this section we try to answer some of the common questions regarding embedded Linux.

1.4.1 Is Linux Too Large?

Generally one tends to think that as Linux was designed to run on desktop systems, it might be bulky and unsuitable for embedded systems. But contrary to all these speculations, Linux is highly modular and it has an excellent component selection mechanism. Based on system configuration, one can keep only the components needed. For example, if no network support is needed, just disable it at Linux kernel configuration time; no file systems, just disable them too.

One may also ask about SDRAM and flash requirements of embedded Linux. A minimal working embedded Linux system with networking and file system support needs around 4 MB of SDRAM and 2 MB of flash. 16 MB or 32 MB of SDRAM and 4 MB of flash will enable one to add a rich set of applications to the platform with increased system performance

Some of the small-footprint embedded Linux efforts include the following.

■ *uClinux,* a Linux port for no-MMU platforms such as Motorola 68k, ARM7™, and so on has a full-featured version with minimum SDRAM and FLASH requirement.
■ *ELKS (Embedded Linux Kernel Subset)* plans to put embedded Linux in the Palm Pilot.
■ *ThinLinux* is yet another small-footprint distribution targeted at digital cameras, MP3 players, and similar embedded applications.

1.4.2 Is Linux Real-Time Enough?

As Linux's roots are in desktop computing, people question its usage in real-time systems. There is a lot of work going on in the embedded Linux area to enable it for real-time systems. The enhancements are either in the form of a preemptive kernel or real-time–capable scheduler. For hard real-time applications the *dual kernel* approach is used in which a real-time executive is responsible for handling time-critical jobs while preserving the Linux advantage. Today Linux is capable of satisfying the real-time needs of systems. We discuss more about Linux real-time capabilities in Chapter 7.

1.4.3 How Can I Protect My Proprietary Software?

There is lot of concern regarding GPL licensing and proprietary software. GPL licensing is seldom a problem for embedded applications. Proprietary software can always be kept safe with embedded Linux. Please refer to Appendix B for a complete discussion on GPL and its use in embedded systems.

1.4.4 Should I Buy a Commercial Embedded Linux Distribution?

This is one of the questions that you may come across when you decide to use embedded Linux for your target. With embedded Linux, it is not at all mandatory to go for any commercial distribution. You can always download free sources and then customize them for the target. But there are some disadvantages of the "on your own" approach. You may need to spend considerable time and resources to create a Linux port for your target. Even if a port is already available, lack of good support and enhanced development tools can delay the development cycle.

The authors recommend using a commercial embedded Linux distribution, unless your company has sufficient expertise in embedded Linux. There are lots of very good open source distributions available. They can also be used if they fit your requirements.

A commercial distribution comes with various advantages. Some of them are as follows.

- *Support:* This is one of the biggest advantages of going with a commercial distribution. Embedded Linux distribution firms generally have a well-trained staff and expertise in the area of system software. They can assist you with any part of your project and for a very low cost.
- *Development tools and utilities:* With commercial distribution comes a rich development environment. Most distributions have GUI-based installation, configuration, development, and debugging tools. Some provide specialized tools for profiling. Others have very user-friendly tools for downloading the image in the target. They all come with a rich set of utilities compiled for your platform. All this drastically reduces development time.
- *Kernel enhancements:* The commercial distribution generally provides some kernel enhancement either as a part of the kernel or as kernel modules. The enhancements include increased real-time response of the kernel, reduced kernel memory and flash footprint, drivers and utilities for supporting graphical or networking needs of embedded applications, and so on.

In a nutshell, a commercial embedded Linux distribution reduces effort and development time, thus reducing time to market of your product. For a company that is moving to embedded Linux with no prior Linux experience, these benefits may ease the movement.

1.4.5 Which Embedded Linux Distribution Do I Choose?

There are lots of embedded Linux distributions available. Choosing the right one is very important for the successful completion of your project. The following points should be considered before finalizing a distribution.

- *Package:* Is the distribution providing all the software necessary for your project? For example, it may have tons of utilities and drivers, but does it really have all the drivers that are needed in your target? Does the package include development, debugging, and profiling tools?
- *Documentation:* The distribution should provide documentation and sample programs for all the tools and utilities that are part of the package. It should accompany a proper reference manual explaining in detail mechanisms such as how to build the binaries and load them in the target, how to profile the system, and so on. If a distribution is accompanied by any proprietary software then that too should be properly documented.
- *Proprietary software:* Some distributions ship proprietary software either in the form of some tools or some device driver in the form of "binary only" kernel modules. You should be very careful when choosing such a distribution. You should be totally convinced that such software from the distribution is really required and there are no other alternatives. Too much dependence on proprietary software nullifies the vendor independence aspect of embedded Linux. Also check if there is any runtime royalty associated with such software.
- *Software upgrades:* An embedded Linux distribution vendor keeps enhancing the distribution either by adding more tools and utilities or using a higher version of the Linux kernel. Make sure whether they are available for free or there is extra cost involved.
- *Flexibility:* Is the distribution fitting well in short- or long-term company goals? Can you reuse the same software for the future version of your product? Can you use at least the tools provided, if not the kernel for some other product on similar lines?
- *Support:* Finally and most important is the support aspect. Do you need to sign any separate support contract? What is the cost involved? How good is the support, whether it be for some bug fixing or writing a whole new device driver? If possible, check with some existing customer of the vendor.

Choosing the right distribution is very important for the successful completion of your project. A vendor of an embedded Linux distribution should guide you in all your system software needs. But a word of caution: too much dependence on a vendor is also not recommended. A company should slowly build proper expertise in Linux. This will be a long-term benefit for the organization.

1.5 Embedded Linux Distributions

In this section we discuss various commercial and open source embedded Linux distributions available today. The idea of this section is to give readers a brief description of various embedded Linux distributions to facilitate decision making for their platform.

In this section we cover prominent distributions such as Cadenux®, Embedded Debian®, Denx, ELinOS®, RTLinux, BlueCat, Metrowerks™, MontaVista, and TimeSys. We compare distributions against the following points.

- *Features:* What are the kernel and toolchain features?
- *Development environment:* How user-friendly is the development environment?
- *Documentation:* What documentation is provided with the distribution?
- *Support:* What is the support policy?

The distributions are discussed in alphabetical order.

1.5.1 BlueCat Linux

BlueCat Embedded Linux 5.0 from LynuxWorks (www.lynuxworks.com) is a commercial distribution based on the Linux 2.6 kernel. The distribution is targeted for use in embedded systems ranging from small consumer-type devices to large-scale, multi-CPU systems.

Features

BlueCat uses Linux kernel version 2.6 thus providing

- Kernel preemption
- Low-latency fixed-time scheduler
- Improved POSIX threading support; new POSIX threads implementation based on NPTL (New POSIX Thread Library)
- POSIX timers and real-time signals

It also includes

- Enhanced GNU cross-development tools including GCC 3.2.2, GDB multithreading debugging support, and kernel debuggers
- Target support for XScale™ micro architecture, PowerPC, IA-32, ARM, MIPS, and x86 PC-compatibles
- Utilities such as Busybox, Tinylogin, uClibc, and so on
- Zebra routing protocol and enhanced network management and security features
- Embedded target tools for footprint minimization and kernel configuration

Development Environment

LynuxWorks provides a range of development tools for speedy development.

- *VisualLynux™:* Windows-based IDE. VisualLynux is a plug-in for Microsoft Visual Studio™ .NET IDE that lets developers build BlueCat Linux applications in a Windows host environment. The plug-in provides all the commands and standard GNU tools needed to streamline application development for BlueCat Linux targets in a Windows environment.
- *CodeWarrior™:* Linux- and Solaris®-based IDE. Combining an editor, code browser, compiler, linker, debugger, and intuitive GUI, the CodeWarrior

IDE speeds up Linux- and Solaris-based development for BlueCat Linux targets.

Apart from the above IDEs, LynuxWorks provides the following debugging tools.

- *TotalView:* Provides advanced debugging across multiple processors, threads, and processes
- *LynxInsure++:* For runtime error detection and analysis
- *SpyKer™ :* To monitor all the events in a system environment when some application is running

Documentation

BlueCat Linux 5.0 comes with an extensive user guide that is also available for downloading from their site.

Support

LynuxWorks provides three support packages.

- *BlueCat maintenance support:* Mainly aimed at customers who need limited support. This is competitively priced support for OS development seats and tools.
- *BlueCat priority support:* Ideal if you require short response times, unlimited access, corrections to known or observed defects, and assistance at the implementation level.
- *Block-of-time support:* Apart from all the benefits of priority support, in block-of-time support purchased support hours may be used any time during a one-year period.

1.5.2 Cadenux

Cadenux specializes in providing embedded Linux distributions for the no-MMU ARM7 and ARM9™ family of processors. Their distribution is also built around uClinux.

Features

- *Linux BSP:* Cadenux provides prebuilt board support packages based on the 2.0, 2.4, and 2.6 Linux kernels for ARM7 (TI DSC21, DSC25, DM270, etc.) and ARM9 (TI DM310, OMAP1510, etc.). It also comes with useful drivers for the above BSPs.
- *Shared library support:* Cadenux provides shared library support for no-MMU platforms. Their XFLAT shared library technology allows applications to link dynamically to libraries.

- *Compressed kernel support:* The Linux kernel can be compressed and stored in flash, thus reducing the flash requirement.
- *Real-time extensions:* These include an interrupt latency measurement tool, preemptive kernel, and real-time schedulers.
- *File mapping support:* Cadenux has implemented file mapping support into its uClinux 2.4 kernel. File mapping support allows shared program text sections. This program is like Busybox, which is large and may have numerous copies running simultaneously. These capabilities were previously available only with a file system that supports eXecute In Place (XIP) such as the ROMFS file system on a memory block driver. With file mapping, these capabilities are available using any file system or block driver.
- *Microwindows support:* This enables rich GUI applications to run on the target.

Development Environment

The Cadenux development environment consists of the GUI-based BSP configuration tool, *memconfig*. This is a one stop for building all the components of BSP such as the Linux kernel, bootloader, and file systems. Details such as target platform, SDRAM and flash types, kernel, root file system, and device details can all be configured with this tool. Cadenux BSPs ship with the rrload bootloader. Cadenux provides the uClinux toolchain modified to support XFLAT shared library support. Application libraries such as uClibc and pthreads are also provided.

Documentation

Cadenux provides extensive documentation. Some of the manuals are the following.

- Cadenux ARM board support package user's guide
- RRload bootloader manual
- Cadenux board support package configuration tool
- XFLAT shared library support

The documents are available for download from the Cadenux Web site (www.cadenux.com). These and other documents regarding device driver architecture and usage ship with Cadenux BSP.

Support

Cadenux provides support through e-mail or telephone. They offer porting services to get Linux running on your embedded hardware. They also provide other services such as driver porting, performance tuning, application development, and training for those new to embedded Linux.

1.5.3 Denx

Denx Software Engineering (www.denx.de) provides open source Linux distribution in the form of the Embedded Linux Development Kit (ELDK). The Denx ELDK provides a complete and powerful software development environment for embedded and real-time systems. At the time of this writing the latest version is ELDK 3.1.1.

Features

- Support for the PowerPC, ARM, MIPS, and Xscale processors. The PowerPC version of the ELDK runs on x86/Linux, x86/FreeBSD®, and on SPARC®/ Solaris hosts and supports a wide range of PowerPC target processors (8xx, 82xx, 7xx, 74xx, 4xx). The ARM version of the ELDK runs on x86/Linux and x86/FreeBSD hosts and supports especially the ARM920TDI target processors. Little- and big-endian MIPS processors are also supported.
- Cross-development tools (GCC 3.3.3, GDB 5.2.1, binutils 2.14-6, and glibc 2.3.1).
- Linux kernel version 2.4.25 and U-Boot Open Source boot loader for Embedded PowerPC, MIPS, ARM, and x86 Systems.
- RTAI (Real-Time Application Interface) extensions for systems requiring hard real-time responses.
- SELF (Simple Embedded Linux Framework) provides an easily extensible default configuration for embedded Linux systems.
- ELDK is available for free. Anonymous CVS access for build tools and source, installation utilities for ELDK, and Linux 2.4.x kernel sources for ARM, MIPS, and PowerPC.
- Linux STREAMS for Embedded PowerPC.
- Support for *mini_fo* overlay file system. This file system is similar to the FreeBSD union file system and serves to virtually make a read-only device writable.
- Microwindows supports for GUI-intensive applications.

Development Environment

The development environment is the standard Linux development environment under the ELDK framework.

Documentation

Denx Software Engineering provides *The DENX U-Boot and Linux Guide (DULG)*. It is an extensive document regarding

- Installation and building ELDK components
- Target image configuration, RFS building, and downloading onto the target
- U-boot and Linux kernel debugging

Support

Denx Software Engineering provides software engineering services in the area of embedded and real-time systems with a strong focus on open source software, especially Linux, but also FreeBSD, NetBSD, and so on.

They provide firmware and operating system porting services for your hardware. They also work on performance optimization and security concepts. They also provide training in software development on embedded Linux systems.

1.5.4 Embedded Debian (Emdebian)

The goal of the embedded Debian project (www.emdebian.org) is to make Debian GNU/Linux a natural choice for embedded Linux. Debian's open development process, its reputation to provide reliability and security, powerful package manager, and growing range of supported architectures provide a solid technical foundation for the realization of this goal. Emdebian comes under the category of open source embedded Linux distribution.

Features

Emdebian differs a bit from other embedded Linux distributions. Its idea is to use the Debian project in embedded systems. Debian is too large to use as is in an embedded system. Emdebian is a smaller version of Debian that retains Debian's good features such as its packaging system, the licensing, the availability of source, the build system, and so on. Emdebian is Debian optimized by size. The Debian core remains the same; only the way packages are built differs and the packaging system is enhanced to suit an embedded environment.

Today ports for Intel IA-32, Motorola m68k, Sparc, Alpha, ARM, PowerPC, MIPS, HP PA-RISC, IA64, and s390 are available. Emdebian mainly targets the PowerPC architecture.

Development Environment

Two main development environments in Emdebian are *Stag* and *Emdebsys*. Stag is a recent development in Embdebian. However Emdebsys is not currently under active maintenance.

- *Stag* is a framework to use the Debian GNU/Linux package management system for embedded development. Changes are done in debhelper and dpkg-cross tools to provide full cross-compiler support for Debian packages. The framework also comes with a fully tested cross-compiler toolchain. One of the advantages of the framework is the package dependency checks. You can select all the packages that should go in the root file system in one go. Framework then resolves all the package dependencies giving you an idea of the size of the root file system.

■ *Emdebsys* is a tool to configure and construct a minimal file system and kernel from both source and precompiled binaries. It uses Kconfig (or Configuration Menu Language 2) to define a set of dependencies, so that one doesn't need to know everything in order to get a working combination of modules, files, and binaries.

Documentation

At the time of this writing, work is going on for developing a guide to embedding Debian. This guide will cover topics such as the following.

■ Configuring and building a kernel and root file system
■ Boot and runtime kernel configuration options
■ Debugging kernel and applications
■ Setting up a build system for your target
■ Cross-compiling techniques

Support

Being an open source project, the primary means of support and communication about Emdebian is the Debian-embedded mailing list. Aleph One Ltd (UK) and Simtec Ltd (UK) also provide commercial support for Emdebian.

1.5.5 ELinOS (SYSGO)

ELinOS is a commercial embedded Linux distribution from SYSGO (www.sysgo.com). ELinOS is a development environment based on Linux for the creation of embedded systems for intelligent devices. With ELinOS the memory demand of Linux is reduced to less than 1 MB ROM and 2 MB RAM. In this manner, Linux can conform to the reduced hardware conditions of embedded systems. The core of ELinOS is a Linux kernel custom-tailored for the target.

Features

ElinOS v3.1 is the latest available at the time of this writing. It has the following features.

■ GNU cross-development toolchain (GCC 3.2.3, GDB 6.0, GLibc 2.3.2)
■ Linux kernel version 2.4.25 and 2.6.9
■ Real-time extensions such as RTAI (for hard real-time applications), Linux Trace Toolkit (LTT), Soft Real-Time Support, Real-Time Signal Extension, and so on
■ Support for migration from VxWorks or pSOS® to Linux using the emulation libraries vxworks2linux and psos2linux
■ Support for PowerPC, x86, ARM/Xscale, MIPS, and SH microprocessors

- Embedded Linux Konfigurator (ELK) 3.2: graphical user interface for the creation of directly bootable ROM images with integrated kernel and root file system
- Embedded utilities such as Busybox, thttpd, Tinylogin, and so on

Development Environment

ELinOS v3.1 is enhanced with a fully integrated development environment (IDE) with two new tools, CODEO and COGNITO.

- *CODEO:* CODEO is the Eclipse-based integrated development environment for ELinOS. It includes the ELinOS cross toolchain, the ProjectBuilder, Target Remote Debugging support, and Target View as well as plug-ins for target control and target communication.
- *COGNITO:* COGNITO is a graphical system browser for the analysis of system runtime behavior and includes the collection, storage, and display of all system parameters such as memory and system load, covering modules, processes, and system objects with measurement of response and scheduling latency.

Documentation

ELinOS v3.1 comes with extensive documentation and demo projects and examples for typical application profiles such as network, real-time, Web server, remote debugging, and so on.

Support

SYSGO offers a broad range of support services and training for ELinOS. They have the following support packages.

- *ProjectStart Package:* An ELinOS engineer sets up the project at your premises and assists with project-related queries.
- *DevelopmentSupport Package:* E-mail support for ELinOS development toolchain.
- *SolutionsSupport Package:* Assisting in development of embedded Linux applications. It is done through e-mail or telephone hotline.
- *ProjectSupport Package:* One dedicated support engineer for whole project life cycle taking care of all system software issues and who can be involved in writing device drivers.

ELinOS v3.1 comes by default with a one-year Development Support Package.

1.5.6 Metrowerks

Metrowerks (www.metrowerks.com) offers a complete end-to-end commercial embedded Linux development solution, including tools, operating system, middleware, and software stacks.

Features

- *Metrowerks Linux BSPs (BSPWerks):* Metrowerks distribution comes with in-house developed or third-party BSPs for various target platforms. They provide a custom BSP for various hardware platforms. Some of the features are Linux kernel version 2.4.21 with real-time enhancements, kernel and application debugging support, and bootloaders such as rrload, grub, lilo, uboot, and the like.
- *Metrowerks Linux applications and services:* They provide applications ranging from Web server, Busybox, Tinylogin, and so on, to debugging and network monitoring tools.
- Support x86, ARM, PowerPC, and ColdFire® architectures.

Development Environment

The development environment consists of the following.

- *CodeWarrior™ Development Studio:* It allows complete Linux development from board bring-up through application development for ARM, ColdFire, and PowerPC architectures. Some of the salient features are:
  - IDE Features: Project manager, multifunctional text editor, graphical file compare and merge, and so on
  - Debugger: Multithreading/multiprocess debugging, source- and assembly-level debugging; hardware debugging support using JTAG interface
  - Toolchain: Integrated GNU build tools, GCC, linker, and assembler
  - Host: Support on both Linux-based and Windows-based hosts
- *Platform Creation Suite (PCS):* Metrowerks' Platform Creation Suite is a tools framework into which Metrowerks Linux BSPs are integrated to provide a full target Linux OS configure, extend, build, deploy environment. Some of the utilities included in this suite are:
  - TargetWizard: Its primary purpose is to manage and build the Linux customized for the target.
  - Linux Kernel Import Tool (LKIT): LKIT gives flexibility by allowing replacing or patching of the original BSP kernel with another kernel/patch you have downloaded, produced in-house, or acquired from another Linux provider.
  - Package Editor: It provides developers with the ability to quickly add binary or build-from-source applications, services, and device drivers into Target Wizard, for subsequent build and deployment to the target.
  - GNU Tool Importer: The GNU Tool Importer gives the ability to replace or supplement the existing tool chain with a new version obtained from alternate sources such as the Internet, alternate Linux providers, or developed in-house.
- *Debugging and performance measurement tools:* Some of the debugging and monitoring tools are:
  - Graphical Remote Process Analyzer (GRPA): GRPA facilitates target debugging by displaying profiling information related to processes that are running on the target. It also provides the ability to perform remote strace.
  - *CodeTEST®:* It is a software verification tool. It delivers the least intrusive real-time embedded software analysis solution in the industry.

Documentation

They have an extensive CodeWarrior IDE SDK manual along with documentation for PCS, GRPA, and so on.

Support

Metrowerks provides 30 days of free installation e-mail support for customers purchasing CodeWarrior development tools. They also provide one year of technical support either by e-mail or telephone by signing a separate support contract.

1.5.7 MontaVista Linux

MontaVista Software (www.mvista.com) is a leading global supplier of commercial Linux-based system software and development tools for intelligent connected devices and associated infrastructure.

Features

There are three different embedded Linux distributions targeted at different market segments.

- *Montavista Linux Professional Edition (3.1):* Some of the features are:
  - Real-time support: It includes kernel preemption, O(1) real-time scheduler, high-resolution POSIX timers, NPTL POSIX thread library.
  - Rich Networking: Support for IPV4, IPV6 protocol standards, CPCI backplane networking, wireless networking, and so on.
  - Architecture support: Supports a wide range of PowerPC, ARM, MIPS, IA32, SuperH™, Xscale, and Xtensa™ architectures.
  - Host: Supports Windows-, Solaris-, and Linux-based cross-development hosts.
- *MontaVista Linux Carrier Grade Edition (3.1):*
  - Operating system features: PICMG 3.0 (ATCA platforms) support, SMP and Hyper-threading support, IPMI, OSDL Carrier Grade Linux Specification 1.1 Compliance, support for AIS CLM (Cluster Membership), API, and AIS AMF (Availability Management Framework), API, remote boot support, and logical volume management.
  - High availability: PICMG 2.12 Hot Swap, persistent device naming, watchdog timer, CPCI redundant system slot, RAID disk mirroring, Ethernet failover, and Raid multihost.
  - Hardening: Device hardening across the board.
  - Architectures: PowerPC, IA32, and PICMG 2.16 systems.
- *MontaVista Linux Consumer Electronics Edition:* This edition supports all the features mentioned in the professional edition.
  - Some other features are dynamic power management, fast boot, reduced image footprint, XIP in kernel and applications.

Development Environment

MontaVista DevRocket™ is a fully graphical IDE providing the tools and functionality to develop and deploy system software and applications built on MontaVista Linux. Some salient features are:

- It is ready to run on Windows, Solaris, and Linux host operating systems and supports integration with third-party Eclipse-based development components.
- It provides comprehensive IDE capabilities, including the latest GNU toolchains to support system software and application development.
- It includes target configuration and library optimization capabilities that are used for kernel configuration and trimming libraries.
- It provides sophisticated tracing capabilities, based on the Linux Trace Toolkit, for viewing, capturing, and analyzing system behavior.
- It supports more than 100 board-level platforms and nearly 30 processor variants across seven CPU architectures.
- It is compatible with hardware-based, source-level debugging of the Linux kernel and device drivers with BDM and JTAG-based in-circuit emulation.

Documentation

The distribution comes with extensive documented components of MontaVista Linux and IDE.

Support

MontaVista provides support for all the MontaVista Linux products. Customers can reach the MontaVista support through e-mail, phone, voicemail, or fax as specified by the purchased Product Subscription package.

1.5.8 *RTLinuxPro™*

FSMLabs™ RTLinuxPro 2.2 (www.fsmlabs.com) is a hard real-time, POSIX operating system that is based on dual-kernel architecture. The RTCore™ real-time kernel is the heart of RTLinuxPro that provides hard real-time guarantees with Linux running as an application program. More details about the dual-kernel architecture can be found in Chapter 7. It is a commercial distribution.

Features

- *Hard real-time:* With the dual-kernel architecture RTLinuxPro guarantees a hard real-time response time for applications.
- *POSIX:* Supports IEEE® 1003.13 profile 51 for real-time applications and full access to Linux for non–real-time programs. For real-time applications that get loaded under the RTcore there is a greater POSIX support, greater portability, and quicker development.

- *Quickboot:* For subsecond boot times down to 200 msec on some platforms.
- *IPC:* Faster IPC mechanism between the real-time and not real-time applications. Support for lock-free POSIX I/O provides fast IPC performance.
- *Regression suite:* For testing the validity of the RTLinuxPro system components.
- *Drivers:* Real-time drivers for serial interfaces, parallel ports, servo drivers, A/D devices, and more. These are written to be usable and also to serve as examples. The distribution comes with the 2.4.25 and 2.6 Linux kernel versions.
- *Processor reservation:* Simple processor reservation technology providing guaranteed access to CPU for real-time threads.
- *Supports:* x86, ARM, StrongARM®, MIPS, PowerPC, Alpha, and Fujitsu® FR-V processor architectures.

RTLinuxPro also has some important components.

- *PSDD:* To provide user-space hard real-time with address space protection.
- *LNet:* To provide hard real-time networking over Ethernet or Firewire®.
- *ControlKits:* Automatic process control and XML integration tools. Users can integrate easily with Web apps, spreadsheets, and more.

Development Environment

RTLinuxPro includes a full development kit for embedded Linux and also for developing real-time applications that run under RTCore. For Linux, tools are provided to simplify the task of building root file systems. The toolchain is based on GCC 3.3, which includes full C++ support.

For RTCore, a NetBSD development system with a SMP-qualified NetBSD 2.0 kernel and all the needed tools and utilities are provided. All the tools are currently BSD hosted.

Documentation

FSMLabs provide an extensive documentation for RTLinuxPro. The package comes with a 200-plus–page book with examples, explanations, and introduction to the RTCore programming environment.

Support

FSMLabs' basic support is sold by the engineering hour, which is an estimate of how much time will be needed by FSMLabs engineering staff to solve the problem. Customer support can be remote or even on-site call. Support contracts can be e-mail/telephone or e-mail depending on the level of support.

1.5.9 TimeSys Linux

TimeSys Linux 5.0 is a 2.6 kernel-based commercial embedded Linux distribution. Timesys Linux 4.0 is based on the 2.4 Linux kernel.

Features

- *Linux 2.6 kernel-based distribution:* This includes features such as kernel preemption, constant time scheduler, POSIX timers, and POSIX message queues.
- *Real-time extensions:* This includes support for high-resolution timers, priority inheritance, enhanced interrupt handling, softirq processing, periodic tasks, and other POSIX 1003.13 real-time extensions.
- *CPU reservations:* This reserves a dedicated portion of the system's processor time for most critical applications thus protecting applications against transient processor overloads. It provides simple APIs for managing CPU reservations.
- *Net reservations:* This guarantees network bandwidth for critical applications. It uses a separate network buffer pool to isolate critical applications from the rest of the system. It also provides a simple API for managing network reservations.
- *Carrier grade/high availability:* This supports Hot swap, plug-n-play, Ethernet Link Aggregation (failover), driver hardening, and IPMI (Intelligent Platform Management Interface).
- *Real-time Java:* TimeSys is in the process of developing a Java® virtual machine based on the Real-Time Specification for Java. This allows real-time system designers to benefit from Java's platform independence and object orientation.
- Network protocols such as IPSec, SSL, NAT, and the like.
- Supports a wide range of architectures from ARM, Xscale, PowerPC, MIPS, SuperH, IA32.
- Supports both Windows- and Linux-based cross-development hosts.
- Toolchain based on gcc/g++ 3.2.2, gdb 5.3, and binutils 2.13.

Development Environment

Timesys Linux comes with a set of development, debugging, and profiling tools.

- *TimeStorm IDE™:* It gives complete control over the development, editing, compiling, and debugging of C/C++/Java-embedded and real-time applications.
- *TimeStorm Linux Development Suite (LDS):* TimeStorm LDS™ delivers a complete set of tools to define, install, bring up, and develop a Linux Software Development Kit (SDK) on your target platform. As a component of TimeStorm LDS, the Target Configurator defines configurations and contents of the root file system and controls the target build.
- *TimeStorm Linux Verification Suite (LVS):* TimeStorm LVS™ comprises an automation framework of core elements required to develop, run, manage, and automate the testing and validation of a Linux SDK on the target platform.
- *TimeStorm Linux Hardware-Assisted Debugging (LHD):* TimeStorm LHD™ is a TimeSys product line of JTAG debugging tools that quickly gets Linux up and running on target hardware, reducing the time spent on hardware/software integration, initialization, and debugging.

- *TimeWiz®:* Windows-based integrated design tool for modeling, analyzing, and simulating the predicted and simulated performance and timing behavior of dynamic real-time systems.
- *TimeTrace®:* TimeTrace provides execution data from a running system and reveals the critical events happening in an application, such as context switches, timer events, scheduling events, and more, so you can pinpoint problem areas.

Documentation

The Timesys Linux development kit comes with extensive manuals for the tools shipped.

Support

Timesys provides various product maintenance and support contracts ranging from hourly, monthly, to yearly support.

In this section we have discussed some of the prominent open source and commercial embedded Linux distributions. There are many other embedded Linux distributions available. ART Linux, miniRTL, KURT, Linux/Resource Kernel, LOAF (Linux On A Floppy), RedHawk, REDICE Linux, Red Hat, and Neo Linux are some of them. You are recommended to study their features also.

1.6 Porting Roadmap

Often companies have their entire product built out of proprietary embedded OSs. When they decide to move to Linux they are confused about the porting process and its details, which often leads to wrong deadlines being set for the porting process. Hence a porting roadmap is necessary; the roadmap will identify the important milestones for the porting process. It is important that for each of the milestones you ask the right questions. Depending on the nature of the product the time needed in the porting process will change. The following path should be chosen.

- *Identify the legal issues behind the porting process:* The embedded firms have to fear more from the issues of GPL than the desktops and servers in the sense that more often a lot of intellectual property is very tied within the kernel space. This can range from ports to new architecture or architecture variants, optimization techniques, or device drivers for some proprietary hardware. Many embedded companies invest huge amounts of money in developing such components. Hence the most important step is to get the software projects evaluated by a competent legal team and to identify what pieces of software go inside the kernel. All the developers should be informed to take care of licensing issues when porting software to Linux. Appendix B talks about this in detail.

- *Choosing the kernel and an embedded Linux distribution:* Depending on the system requirements a choice has to be made about which Linux variant to use: hard real-time Linux or normal Linux. Also depending on whether your system has an MMU-based controller you need to identify whether to use uClinux or standard Linux. Depending on the system feature set you need to identify the appropriate kernel version to use (2.2, 2.4, 2.6). Kernel performance, memory requirements, and size of the distribution are other important factors that should be considered before finalizing a kernel version. Chapter 7 discusses real-time features of Linux and Chapter 10 discusses uClinux. Now the next question arises: Can we just download the entire software and tools by ourselves and use them, or do we go along with an embedded Linux distributor such as Timesys or MontaVista? This depends on the money that the company wants to spend and how confident it is of its engineering capabilities. The various distributions and their feature sets have already been discussed in this chapter. The decision regarding use of a commercial distribution should be made at this point.

- *Getting the tools:* This includes the hardware environment such as the Linux-based hosts for doing cross-development and debugging. Often proprietary embedded operating systems offer Windows-based toolkits and hence when we move to Linux-based tools, we need to have Linux-based desktops for cross-development. The cross-development environment comprises the tools such as compilers, linkers, debuggers, IDEs, and so on. If you are using help from a distributor it is very likely that they will supply you all the tools else you need to download the entire set of tools and build the development environment by yourself. In Chapter 2 we talk about how to set up a cross-development environment.

- *Porting bootloader and BSP:* If you decide to go with a distributor then there is a very good chance that the BSP for your target is already available with the distributor, or else you need to port the BSP. The BSP porting is a complicated task. It involves good understanding of the hardware, Linux kernel design, and specialized knowledge such as assembly language programming. In Chapter 3 we take a BSP porting exercise for a MIPS-based board.

- *Porting device drivers:* If your target has some proprietary hardware then you need to port drivers to Linux. If drivers are off-the-shelf hardware then they should already be part of the kernel or available on the Web or in the distribution. This book covers a variety of drivers such as storage, frame buffer, serial, Ethernet, I2C™, and USB driver.

- *Porting applications:* This task can be done in parallel with the BSP and the bootloader development as many applications can be tested on the x86-based Linux host. In Chapter 6 we discuss various strategies for porting applications to Linux.

- *Packaging:* This step is crucial if your software needs to be handed over to an OEM. This includes providing proper configuration scripts and Makefiles for the kernel and applications, keeping in mind the fact that an OEM can add his or her own applications. Chapter 8 discusses in detail building the kernel and applications.

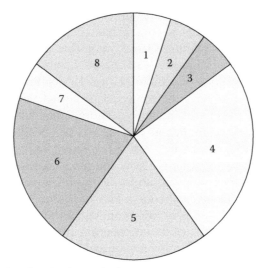

1. Identifying legal issues (5%)
2. Choosing linux kernel and embedded linux distribution (5%)
3. Getting the tools (5%)
4. Porting bootloader and BSP (25%)
5. Porting device drivers (20%)
6. Porting applications (20%)
7. Packaging (5%)
8. Optimization (15%)

Figure 1.1   Sample porting effort estimate.

■ *Tweaking for performance, memory, and size optimizations:* Once the basic software is in place then lots of tweaking has to be done so that the required performance can be obtained. This may include optimizing the code, tweaking the compiler options, and usage of profilers. Also the memory and storage size is an important factor and usually cannot be evaluated until the entire system is running with all the functionalities. The book talks about memory and storage size optimization. Appendix A talks about boot-up time reduction.

■ *Interacting with the community and getting latest updates in the kernel:* This is an important activity during the development and support phase so that the latest patches can be acquired for bugs in the kernel. Your distributor may also provide you with all the required patches.

Figure 1.1 shows an approximate porting effort estimate when migrating from another RTOS to Linux. Please note that this is a rough estimate and the numbers may differ across projects.

Notes

1. These utilities have a very small storage and memory footprint. This is the main reason why they are preferred in an embedded system although they have fewer features than their desktop peers.

Chapter 2

Getting Started

This chapter is divided into three parts. The first part takes a tour of the various embedded OS architectures and compares them to the Linux architecture. Then a brief overview of the Linux kernel and user space is given. The second part of the chapter explains the Linux start-up sequence. The final part explains the cross-development tools.

2.1 Architecture of Embedded Linux

The Linux OS is monolithic. Generally operating systems come in three flavors: real-time executive, monolithic, and microkernel. The basic reasoning behind the classification is how the OS makes use of hardware for protection.

2.1.1 Real-Time Executive

Traditional real-time executives are meant for MMU-less processors. On these operating systems, the entire address space is flat or linear with no memory protection between the kernel and applications, as shown in Figure 2.1.

Figure 2.1 shows the architecture of the real-time executive where the core kernel, kernel subsystems, and applications share the same address space. These operating systems have small memory and size footprint as both the OS and applications are bundled into a single image. As the name suggests, they are real-time in nature because there is no overhead of system calls, message passing, or copying of data. However, because the OS provides no protection, all software running on the system should be foolproof. Adding new software becomes a not-so-pleasant action because it needs to be tested thoroughly lest it bring down the entire system. Also it is very difficult to add applications or kernel modules dynamically as the system has to be brought down. Most of the proprietary and commercial RTOSs fall under this category.

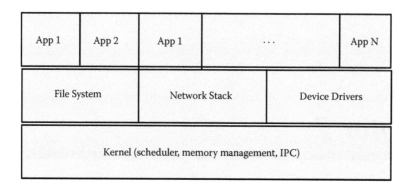

Figure 2.1   Architecture of traditional RTOS.

For the last decade, embedded systems have seen paradigm shifts with respect to architecture. The traditional embedded system model was based on having tightly controlled software running on the boards; the cost of memory and storage space further restricted the amount of software that could be run on the system. Reliability on real-time executives using the flat memory model was achieved by a rigorous testing process. However, as the prices of memory and flash dropped and computing power became cheaper, embedded systems started having more and more software on their systems. And lots of this software was not just system software (such as drivers or networking stack) but were applications. Thus software too started becoming the differentiating factor in selling the embedded systems, which were traditionally judged mainly by the hardware capabilities. Real-time executives were not suited for large-scale software integration; hence alternative models were seriously looked at with the aim of getting more software to run on the system. Two such models are the monolithic and the microkernel models for operating systems. These are suited for processors having MMU. Note that if the processor itself lacks a MMU, then the OS has no alternative but to provide the flat addressing model. (The Linux derivative uClinux that runs on the MMU-less processors provides flat address space.)

2.1.2 Monolithic Kernels

Monolithic kernels have a distinction between the user and kernel space. When software runs in the user space normally it cannot access the system hardware nor can it execute privileged instructions. Using special entry points (provided by hardware), an application can enter the kernel mode from user space. The user space programs operate on a virtual address so that they cannot corrupt another application's or the kernel's memory. However, the kernel components share the same address space; so a badly written driver or module can cause the system to crash.

Figure 2.2 shows the architecture of monolithic kernels where the kernel and kernel submodules share the same address space and where the applications each have their private address spaces.

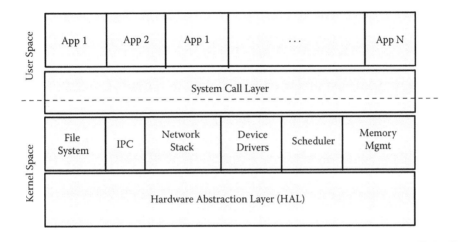

Figure 2.2   Architecture of monolithic kernel.

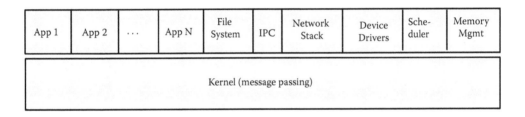

Figure 2.3   Architecture of microkernel.

Monolithic kernels can support a large application software base. Any fault in the application will cause only that application to misbehave without causing any system crash. Also applications can be added to a live system without bringing down the system. Most of the UNIX OSs are monolithic.

2.1.3 Microkernel

These kernels have been subjected to lots of research especially in the late 1980s and were considered to be the most superior with respect to OS design principles. However, translating the theory into practice caused too many bottlenecks; very few of these kernels have been successful in the marketplace. The microkernel makes use of a small OS that provides the very basic service (scheduling, interrupt handling, message passing) and the rest of the kernel (file system, device drivers, networking stack) runs as applications. On the usage of MMU, the real-time kernels form one extreme with no usage of MMU whereas the microkernels are placed on the other end by providing kernel subsystems with individual address space. The key to the microkernel is to come up with well-defined APIs for communication with the OS as well as robust message-passing schemes.

Figure 2.3 shows a microkernel architecture where kernel subsystems such as network stack and file systems have private address space similar to applications. Microkernels require robust message-passing schemes. Only if the message passing is proper are real-time and modularity ensured. Microkernels have been vigorously debated especially against the monolithic kernels. One such widely known debate was between the creator of Linux, Linus Torvalds, and Andrew Tanenbaum who was the creator of the Minix OS (a microkernel). The debate may not be of very much interest for the reader who wants to get right down into embedded Linux.

As we see, these three types of OS operate on totally different philosophies. On one end of the spectrum we have the real-time kernel that provides no memory protection; this is done to make the system more real-time but at the cost of reliability. On the other end, the microkernel provides memory protection to individual kernel subsystems at the cost of complexity. Linux takes the middle path of monolithic kernels where the entire kernel operates on a single memory space. Is this single memory space for the kernel an issue? To make sure that introduction of new kernel software does not cause any reliability issues any addition goes through a great deal of scrutiny in terms of functionality, design, and performance before it gets accepted into the mainline kernel. This examination process, which can be very trying at times, has made the Linux kernel one of the most stable pieces of software. It has allowed the kernel to be employed in a varied range of systems such as desktops, handhelds, and large servers.

There has been some confusion regarding the monolithic architecture of Linux with the introduction of dynamically loadable kernel modules. Dynamically loadable kernel modules are pieces of kernel code that are not linked (included) directly in the kernel. One compiles them separately, and can insert them into and remove them from the running kernel at almost any time. Loadable kernel modules have a separate storage and are brought into memory only when needed, thus saving memory. The point to be noted is that increasing modularization of the kernel does not make it any less monolithic because the kernel interacts with the drivers using direct function calls instead of message passing.

The next two sections present a high-level overview of the Linux kernel and user space.

2.2 Linux Kernel Architecture

Although the Linux kernel has seen major releases, the basic architecture of the Linux kernel has remained more or less unchanged. The Linux kernel can be split into the following subsystems.

- The hardware abstraction layer
- Memory manager
- Scheduler
- File system
- IO subsystem
- Networking subsystem
- IPC

We go briefly through each subsystem and detail its usage in an embedded system.

2.2.1 Hardware Abstraction Layer (HAL)

The hardware abstraction layer (HAL) virtualizes the platform hardware so that the different drivers can be ported easily on any hardware. The HAL is equivalent to the BSP provided on most of the RTOSs except that the BSP on commercial RTOSs normally has standard APIs that allow easy porting. Why does the Linux HAL not have standard APIs for hooking to the rest of the kernel? Because of legacy; because Linux was initially meant for the x86 desktop and support for other platforms was added along the way, the initial developers did not think of standardizing the HAL. However, on recent kernel versions the idea of coming up with standard APIs for hooking board-specific software is catching up. Two prominent architectures, ARM and PowerPC, have a well-described notation of data structures and APIs that make porting to a new board easier.

The following are some embedded processors (other than x86) supported on the Linux 2.6 kernel.

- MIPS
- PowerPC
- ARM
- M68K
- CRIS
- V850
- SuperH

The HAL has support for the following hardware components.

- Processor, cache, and MMU
- Setting up the memory map
- Exception and interrupt handling support
- DMA
- Timers
- System console
- Bus management
- Power management

The functions that initialize the platform are explained in more detail in Section 2.4. Chapter 3 explains in detail steps for porting Linux to a MIPS-based platform.

2.2.2 Memory Manager

The memory manager on Linux is responsible for controlling access to the hardware memory resources. The memory manager is responsible for providing dynamic memory to kernel subsystems such as drivers, file systems, and networking stack. It also implements the software necessary to provide virtual memory to user applications. Each process in the Linux subsystem operates in its separate address space called the virtual address. By using virtual address, a process can corrupt neither another process's nor the operating system's memory. Any pointer corruptions within the process are localized to the process without bringing down the system; thus it is very important for system reliability.

The Linux kernel divides the total memory available into pages. The typical size of a page is 4 KB. Though all the pages are accessible by the kernel, only some of them get used by the kernel; the rest are used by applications. Note that the pages used by the kernel are not part of the paging process; only the application pages get pulled into main memory on demand. This simplifies the kernel design. When an application needs to be executing, the entire application need not be loaded into memory; only the used pages flip between memory and storage.

The presence of separate user and kernel memory is the most radical change that a developer can expect when moving from a proprietary RTOS. For the former all the applications form a part of the same image containing the OS. Thus when this image is loaded, the applications get copied to memory too. On Linux, however, the OS and applications are compiled and built separately; each application needs its own storage instance, often referred to as the program.

2.2.3 Scheduler

The Linux scheduler provides the multitasking capabilities and is evolving over the kernel releases with the aim of providing a deterministic scheduling policy. Before going into the history of the scheduler improvements, let's understand the execution instances that are understood by the scheduler.

- *Kernel thread:* These are processes that do not have a user context. They execute in the kernel space as long as they live.
- *User process:* Each user process has its own address space thanks to the virtual memory. They enter into the kernel mode when an interrupt, exception, or a system call is executed. Note that when a process enters the kernel mode, it uses a totally different stack. This is referred to as the kernel stack and each process has its own kernel stack.
- *User thread:* The threads are different execution entities that are mapped to a single user process. The user space threads share a common text, data, and heap space. They have separate stack addresses. Other resources such as open files and signal handlers are also shared across the threads.

As Linux started becoming popular, demand for supporting real-time applications increased. As a result, the Linux scheduler saw constant improvements so that its scheduling policy became deterministic. The following are some of the important milestones in the Linux kernel evolution with respect to real-time features.

- Starting from the 1.3.55 kernel, there was support for round robin and FIFO-based scheduling along with the classic time-sharing scheduler of Linux. Also it had the facility to disable paging for selected regions of an application memory; this is referred to as memory locking (because demand paging makes the system nondeterministic).
- The 2.0 kernel provided a new function `nanosleep()` that allowed a process to sleep or delay for a very short time. Prior to this, the minimum time was around 10 msec; with `nanosleep()` a process can sleep from a few microseconds to milliseconds.
- The 2.2 kernel had support for POSIX real-time signals.
- The 2.4 kernel series saw lots of improvements with respect to real-time scheduling. Most important was the MontaVista patch for kernel preemption and Andrew Morton's low-latency patch. These were ultimately pulled in to the 2.6 kernel.
- The 2.6 kernel has a totally new scheduler referred to as the O(1) scheduler that brings determinism into the scheduling policy. Also more real-time features such as the POSIX timers were added to the 2.6 kernel.

Chapter 7 discusses the real-time policies of Linux in more detail.

2.2.4 File System

On Linux, the various file systems are managed by a layer called the VFS or the Virtual File System. The virtual file system provides a consistent view of data as stored on various devices on the system. It does this by separating the user view of file systems using standard system calls but allowing the kernel developer to implement logical file systems on any physical device. Thus it abstracts the details of the physical device and the logical file system and allows users to access files in a consistent way.

Any Linux device, whether it's an embedded system or a server, needs at least one file system. This is unlike the real-time executives that need not have any file system at all. The Linux necessity of file systems stems from two facts.

- The applications have separate program images and hence they need to have storage space in a file system.
- All low-level devices too are accessed as files.

It is necessary for every Linux system to have a master file system, the *root file system*. This gets mounted at system start-up. Later many more file systems can be mounted using this file system. If the system cannot mount the root file system over the specified device it will panic and not proceed with system start-up.

Along with disk-based file systems, Linux supports specialized file systems that are flash- and ROM-based for embedded systems. Also there is support for NFS on Linux, which allows a file system on a host to be mounted on the embedded system. Linux supports memory-based file systems, which are again useful on embedded systems. Also there is support for logical or pseudo file systems; these can be used for getting the system information as well as used as debugging tools. The following are some of the commonly used embedded file systems.

- EXT2: A classical Linux file system that has a broad user base
- CRAMFS: A compressed read-only file system
- ROMFS: A read-only file system
- RAMFS: A read-write, memory-based file system
- JFFS2: A journaling file system built specifically for storage on flash
- PROCFS: A pseudo file system used for getting system information
- DEVFS: A pseudo file system for maintaining the device files

Chapter 4 discusses these file systems in more detail.

2.2.5 IO Subsystem

The IO subsystem on Linux provides a simple and uniform interface to onboard devices. Three kinds of devices are supported by the IO subsystem.

- Character devices for supporting sequential devices.
- Block devices for supporting randomly accessible devices. Block devices are essential for implementing file systems.
- Network devices that support a variety of link layer devices.

Chapter 5 discusses the device driver architecture on Linux in more detail giving specific examples.

2.2.6 Networking Subsystems

One of the major strengths of Linux has been its robust support for various networking protocols. Table 2.1 lists the major feature set along with the kernel versions in which they are supported.

2.2.7 IPC

The interprocess communication on Linux includes signals (for asynchronous communication), pipes, and sockets as well as the System V IPC mechanisms such as shared memory, message queues, and semaphores. The 2.6 kernel has the additional support for POSIX-type message queues.

2.3 User Space

The user space on Linux is based on the following concepts.

Table 2.1   Network Stack Features for 2.2, 2.4, and 2.6 Kernel

Feature	Kernel Availability		
	2.2	2.4	2.6
Layer 2			
Support for bridging	Yes	Yes	Yes
X.25	Yes	Yes	Yes
LAPB	Experimental	Yes	Yes
PPP	Yes	Yes	Yes
SLIP	Yes	Yes	Yes
Ethernet	Yes	Yes	Yes
ATM	No	Yes	Yes
Bluetooth	No	Yes	Yes
Layer 3			
IPV4	Yes	Yes	Yes
IPV6	No	Yes	Yes
IP forwarding	Yes	Yes	Yes
IP multicasting	Yes	Yes	Yes
IP firewalling	Yes	Yes	Yes
IP tunneling	Yes	Yes	Yes
ICMP	Yes	Yes	Yes
ARP	Yes	Yes	Yes
NAT	Yes	Yes	Yes
IPSEC	No	No	Yes
Layer 4 (and above)			
UDP and TCP	Yes	Yes	Yes
BOOTP/RARP/DHCP	Yes	Yes	Yes

- *Program:* This is the image of an application. It resides on a file system. When an application needs to be run, the image is loaded into memory and run. Note that because of virtual memory the entire process image is not loaded into memory but only the required memory pages are loaded.
- *Virtual memory:* This allows each process to have its own address space. Virtual memory allows for advanced features such as shared libraries. Each process has its own memory map in the virtual address space; this is unique for any process and is totally independent of the kernel memory map.
- *System calls:* These are entry points into the kernel so that the kernel can execute services on behalf of the application.

Let's take a small example in order to understand how an application runs in Linux. Assume the following piece of code needs to run as an application on a MIPS-based target.

```
#include <stdio.h>
char str[] = "hello world";
void myfunc()
{
  printf(str);
}
main()
{
  myfunc();
  sleep(10);
}
```

The steps involved are:

1. *Compiling and making an executable program:* On an embedded system, the programs are not built on the target but require a host system with cross-development tools. More about this is discussed in Section 2.5; for now assume that you have the host and the tools to build the application, which we name `hello_world`.
2. *Getting the executable program on a file system on the target board:* Chapter 8 discusses the process of building a root file system and downloading applications on the target. Hence assume that this step is readily available to you; by some magic you are able to download `hello_world` onto `/bin` of your root file system.
3. *Running the program by executing it on the shell:* A shell is a command language interpreter; it can be used to execute files. Without going into details of how the shell works, assume that when you type the command `/bin/hello_world`, your program runs and you see the string on your console (which is normally the serial port).

For a MIPS-based target the following command is used to generate the executable.

```
#mips_fp_le-gcc hello_world.c -o hello_world
#ls -l hello_world
-rwxrwxr-x 1 raghav raghav 11782 Jul 20 13:02 hello_world
```

Four steps are involved in it: Generating preprocessed output, followed by generating assembly language output, which is followed by generating object output, and then the last stage of linking. The output file `hello_world` is a MIPS-executable file in a format called ELF (Executable Linkage Format). All executable files have two formats: binary format and script files. Executable binary formats that are most popular on embedded systems are the COFF, ELF, and the flat format. The flat format is used on MMU-less uClinux systems and is discussed in Chapter 10. COFF was the earlier default format and was replaced by the more powerful and flexible ELF format. The ELF format

Listing 2.1 Symbol Listing Using nm

```
#mips_fp_le-nm hello_world
0040157c A __bss_start
004002d0 t call_gmon_start
0040157c b completed.1
00401550 d __CTOR_END__
0040154c d __CTOR_LIST__
0040146c D __data_start
0040146c W data_start
00400414 t __do_global_ctors_aux
004002f4 t __do_global_dtors_aux
00401470 D __dso_handle
00401558 d __DTOR_END__
00401554 d __DTOR_LIST__
00401484 D _DYNAMIC
0040157c A _edata
00400468 r __EH_FRAME_BEGIN__
00401580 A _end
00400438 T _fini
0040146c A __fini_array_end
0040146c A __fini_array_start
00400454 R _fp_hw
00400330 t frame_dummy
00400468 r __FRAME_END__
00401560 D _GLOBAL_OFFSET_Table_
         w __gmon_start__
00400254 T _init
0040146c A __init_array_end
0040146c A __init_array_start
00400458 R _IO_stdin_used
0040155c d __JCR_END__
0040155c d __JCR_LIST__
         w _Jv_RegisterClasses
004003e0 T __libc_csu_fini
004003b0 T __libc_csu_init
         U __libc_start_main@@GLIBC_2.0
00400374 T main
0040035c T myfunc
00401474 d p.0
         U printf@@GLIBC_2.0
         U sleep@@GLIBC_2.0
004002ac T _start
00401478 D str
```

consists of a header followed by many sections including the text and the data. You can use the nm command to find the list of symbols in an executable as shown in Listing 2.1.

As you can see, the functions main and myfunc as well as the global data str have been assigned addresses but the printf function is undefined (specified by the "U") and is defined as printf@@GLIBC. This means that the printf is not a part of the hello_world image. Then where is this function defined and how are the addresses resolved? This function is part of a library, *libc* (C library). Libc contains a list of commonly used functions. For example, the `printf` function is used in almost all applications. Thus instead of having it reside in every application image, the library becomes a common placeholder for it. If the library is used as a shared library then not only does it optimize storage space, it optimizes memory too by making sure that only one copy of the text resides in memory. An application can have more libraries either shared or static; this can be specified at the time of linking. The list of dependencies can be found by using the following command (the shared library dependencies are the runtime dynamic linker ld.so and the C library).

```
#mips_fp_le-ldd hello_world
libc.so.6
ld-linux.so.2
```

So in effect at the time of creating the executable, all relocation and the symbol resolution have not happened. All functions and global data variables that are not part of shared libraries have been assigned addresses and their addresses resolved so that the caller knows their runtime addresses. However, the runtime address of the shared libraries is not yet known and hence their resolution (for example, from the `myfunc` function that calls `printf`) is pending. This all happens at runtime when the program is actually run from the shell.

Note that there is an alternative to using shared libraries and that is to statically link all the references. For example, the above code can be linked to a static C library `libc.a` (which is an archive of a set of object files) as shown below.

```
#mips_fp_le-gcc -static hello-world.c -o hello_world
```

If you do the symbol listing of the file as shown above, the `printf` function is given an address. Using static libraries has the disadvantage of wasting storage and memory at the cost of faster application start-up speed. Now let us run the program on the board and examine its memory map.

```
#/bin/hello_world &
[1] 4479
#cat /proc/4479/maps
00400000-00401000 r-xp 00000000 00:07 4088393    /bin/hello_world
00401000-00402000 rw-p 00001000 00:07 4088393    /bin/hello_world
2aaa8000-2aac2000 r-xp 00000000 00:07 1505291    /lib/ld-2.2.5.so
2aac2000-2aac4000 rw-p 00000000 00:00 0
2ab01000-2ab02000 rw-p 00019000 00:07 1505291    /lib/ld-2.2.5.so
2ab02000-2ac5f000 r-xp 00000000 00:07 1505859    /lib/
                                                 libc-2.2.5.so
2ac5f000-2ac9e000 ---p 0015d000 00:07 1505859    /lib/
                                                 libc-2.2.5.so
2ac9e000-2aca6000 rw-p 0015c000 00:07 1505859    /lib/
                                                 libc-2.2.5.so
2aca6000-2acaa000 rw-p 00000000 00:00 0
7ffef000-7fff8000 rwxp ffff8000 00:00 0
```

As we see along with the main program's `hello_world`, a range of the addresses is allocated to libc and the dynamic linker ld.so. The memory map of the application is created at runtime and then the symbol resolution (in our case the `printf`) is done. This is done by a series of steps. The ELF loader, which is built as a part of the kernel, scans the executable and finds out that the process has shared library dependency; hence it calls the dynamic linker ld.so. The ld.so, which is also implemented as a shared library, is a bootstrap library; it loads itself and the rest of the shared libraries (libc.so) into memory thus freezing the memory map of the application and does the rest of the symbol resolution.

This leaves us with one last question: how does the `printf` actually work? As we discussed above, any services to be done by the kernel require that an application make a system call. The `printf` too does a system call after doing all its internal work. Because the actual implementation of system calls is very hardware dependent, the C library hides all this by providing wrappers that invoke the actual system call. The list of all system calls that are done by the application can be known using an application called `strace`; for example, running `strace` on the application yields the following output a part of which is shown below.

```
#strace hello_world
...
write(1, "hello world", 11) = 11
...
```

Now that we have a basic idea of the kernel and user space, let us proceed to the Linux system start-up procedure.

2.4 Linux Start-Up Sequence

Now as we have a high-level understanding of Linux architecture, understanding the start-up sequence will give the flow of how the various kernel subsystems are started and how Linux gives control to the user space. The Linux start-up sequence describes the series of steps that happen right from the moment a Linux system is booted on until the user is presented with a log-in prompt on the console. Why do you need to understand the start-up sequence at this stage? The understanding of the start-up sequence is essential to mark milestones in the development cycle. Also once the start-up is understood, the basic pieces necessary for building a Linux system such as the boot loader and the root file system will be understood. On embedded systems the start-up time often has to be as small as possible; understanding the details will help the user to tweak the system for a faster start-up. Please refer to Appendix A for more details on fast boot-up.

The Linux start-up sequence can be split into three phases.

- *Boot loader phase:* Typically this stage does the hardware initialization and testing, loads the kernel image, and transfers control to the Linux kernel.

- *Kernel initialization phase:* This stage does the platform-specific initialization, brings up the kernel subsystems, turns on multitasking, mounts the root file system, and jumps to user space.
- *User- space initialization phase:* Typically this phase brings up the services, does network initialization, and then issues a log-in prompt.

2.4.1 Boot Loader Phase

Boot loaders are discussed in detail in Chapter 3. This section skims over the sequence of steps executed by the boot loader.

Hardware Initialization

This typically includes:

1. Configuring the CPU speed
2. Memory initialization, such as setting up the registers, clearing the memory, and determining the size of the onboard memory
3. Turning on the caches
4. Setting up the serial port for the boot console
5. Doing the hardware diagnostics or the POST (Power On Self-Test diagnostics)

Once the above steps are completed successfully, the next step is loading the Linux kernel.

Downloading Kernel Image and Initial Ram Disk

The boot loader needs to locate the kernel image, which may be on the system flash or may be on the network. In either case, the image needs to be loaded into memory. In case the image is compressed (which often is the case), the image needs to be decompressed. Also if an initial ram disk is present, the boot loader needs to load the image of the initial ram disk to the memory. Note that the memory address to where the kernel image is downloaded is decided by the boot loader by reading the ELF header of the kernel image. In case the kernel image is a raw binary dump, additional information needs to be passed to the boot loader regarding the placement of the kernel sections and the starting address.

Setting Up Arguments

Argument passing is a very powerful option supported by the Linux kernel. Linux provides a generic way to pass arguments to the kernel across all platforms. Chapter 3 explains this in detail. Typically the boot loader has to set up a memory area for argument passing, initialize it with the required data structures (that can be identified by the Linux kernel), and then fill them up with the required values.

Jumping to Kernel Entry Point

The kernel entry point is decided by the linker script when building the kernel (which is typically present in linker script in the architecture-specific directory). Once the boot loader jumps to the kernel entry point, its job is done and it is of no use. (There are exceptions to this; some platforms offer a boot PROM service that can be used by the OS for doing platform-specific operations.) If this is the case and if the boot loader executes from memory, that memory can be reclaimed by the kernel. This should be taken into account when deciding the memory map for the system.

2.4.2 Kernel Start-Up

The kernel start-up can be split into the following phases.

CPU/Platform-Specific Initialization

If you are porting Linux to your platform this section is very important as it marks the important milestones in BSP porting. The platform-specific initialization consists of the following steps.

1. *Setting up the environment for the first C routine:* The kernel entry point is an assembly language routine; the name of this entry point varies (`stext` on ARM, `kernel_entry` on MIPS, etc.). Look at the linker script to know the entry point for your platform. This function normally resides in the `arch/<name>/kernel/head.S` file. This function does the following.
   a. On machines that do not have the MMU turned on, this turns on the MMU. Most of the boot loaders do not work with the MMU so the virtual address equals the physical address. However, the kernel is compiled with the virtual address. This stub needs to turn on the MMU so that the kernel can start using the virtual address normally. This is not required on platforms such as MIPS where the MMU is turned on at power-on.
   b. Do cache initialization. This is again platform-dependent.
   c. Set up the BSS by zeroing it out (normally you cannot rely on the boot loader to do this).
   d. Set up the stack so that the first C routine can be invoked. The first C routine is the `start_kernel()` function in `init/main.c`. This function is a jumbo function that does a lot of things until it terminates in an idle task (the first task in the system having a process id of 0). This function invokes the rest of the platform initialization functions that are discussed below.
2. *The* `setup_arch()` *function:* This function does the platform- and CPU-specific initialization so that the rest of the initialization can be invoked safely. Again this is highly platform-specific; only the common functionalities are explained:
   a. Recognizing the processor. Because a CPU architecture can come in various flavors, this function recognizes the processor (such as, if you

have selected the ARM processor this finds out the ARM flavor) using hardware or information that may be passed at the time of building. Again any processor-specific fixups can be done in this code.

b. Recognizing the board. Again because the kernel supports a variety of boards this option recognizes the board and does the board-specific fixups.

c. Analysis of command-line parameters passed to the kernel.

d. Identifying the ram disk if it has been set up by the boot loader so that the kernel later can mount it as the root file system. Normally the boot loader passes the starting of the ram disk area in memory and size.

e. Calling the *bootmem* functions. Bootmem is a misnomer; it refers to the initial memory that the kernel can reserve for various purposes before the paging code grabs all the memory. For example, you can reserve a portion of a contiguous large memory that can be used for DMA by your device by calling the bootmem allocator.

f. Calling the paging initialization function, which takes the rest of the memory for setting up pages for the system.

3. *Initialization of exceptions — the* `trap_init()` *function:* This function sets the kernel-specified exception handlers. Prior to this if an exception happens, the outcome is platform-specific. (For example, on some platforms the boot loader-specified exception handlers get invoked.)

4. *Initialization of interrupt handling procedure — the* `init_IRQ()` *function:* This function initializes the interrupt controller and the interrupt descriptors (these are data structures that are used by the BSP to route interrupts; more of this in the next chapter). Note that interrupts are not enabled at this point; this is the responsibility of the individual, drivers owning the interrupt lines to enable them during their initialization which is called later. (For example, the timer initialization would make sure that the timer interrupt line is enabled.)

5. *Initialization of timers — the* `time_init()` *function:* This function initializes the timer tick hardware so that the system starts producing the periodic tick, which is the system heartbeat.

6. *Initialization of the console—the* `console_init()` *function:* This function does the initialization of the serial device as a console. Once the console is up, all the start-up messages appear on the screen. To print a message from the kernel, the `printk()` function has to be used. (`printk()` is a very powerful function as it can be called from anywhere, even from interrupt handlers.)

7. *Calculating the delay loops for the platform — the* `calibrate_delay()` *function:* This function is used to implement microdelays within the kernel using the `udelay()` function. The `udelay()` function spins for a few cycles for the microseconds specified as the argument. For `udelay` to work, the number of clock cycles per microsecond needs to be known by the kernel. This is exactly done by this function; it calibrates the number of delay loops. This makes sure that the delay loops work uniformly across all platforms. Note that the working of this depends on the timer interrupt.

Subsystem Initialization

This includes

- Scheduler initialization
- Memory manager initialization
- VFS initialization

Note that most of the subsystem initialization is done in the `start_kernel()` function. At the end of this function, the kernel creates another process, the `init` process, to do the rest of the initialization (driver initialization, initcalls, mounting the root file system, and jumping to user space) and the current process becomes the idle process with process id of 0.

Driver Initialization

The driver initialization is done after the process and memory management is up. It gets done in the context of the init process.

Mounting Root File System

Recall that the root file system is the master file system using which other file systems can be mounted. Its mounting marks an important process in the booting stage as the kernel can start its transition to user space. The block device holding the root file system can be hard-coded in the kernel (while building the kernel) or it can be passed as a command line argument from the boot loader using the boot loader tag "`root=`".

There are three kinds of root file systems that are normally used on embedded systems:

- The initial ram disk
- Network-based file system using NFS
- Flash-based file system

Note that the NFS-based root file system is mainly used for debugging builds; the other two are used for production builds. The ram disk simulates a block device using the system memory; hence it can be used to mount file systems provided a file system image is copied onto it. The ram disk can be used as a root file system; this usage of the ram disk is known as *initrd* (short form for initial ram disk). Initrd is a very powerful concept and has wide uses especially in the initial parts of embedded Linux development when you do not have a flash driver ready but your applications are ready for testing (often this is the case when you have a driver and a separate application team working in parallel). So how do you proceed without a flash-based root file system? You can use a network-based file system provided your network driver is ready; if not, the best alternative is the initrd. Creating an initial ram disk is explained in more detail in Chapter 8. This section explains how the kernel mounts an initrd as the root file system. If you want the kernel to load an initrd, you should configure the kernel during the build process with the CONFIG_BVLK_DEV_INITRD option. As previously explained, the initrd image is loaded along with the kernel image and the kernel needs to be passed the starting address and ending address of the initrd using command line arguments. Once it is known, the kernel will mount a root file system loaded on initrd. The file systems normally used are romfs and ext2 file systems.

There is more magic to initrd. Initrd is a use-and-throw root file system. It can be used to mount another root file system. Why is this necessary? Assume that your root file system is mounted on a storage device whose driver is a kernel module. So it needs to be present on a file system. This presents a chicken-and-egg problem; the module needs to be on a file system, which in turn requires that the module be loaded first. To circumvent this, the initrd can be used. The driver can be made as a module in the initrd; once the initrd is mounted then the driver module can be loaded and hence the storage device can be accessed. Then the file system on that storage device can be mounted as the actual root file system and finally the initrd can be discarded. The Linux kernel provides a way for this use-and-throw facility; it detects a file linuxrc in the root of the initrd and executes it. If this binary returns, then the kernel assumes that initrd is no longer necessary and it switches to the actual root file system (the file linuxrc can be used to load the driver modules). NFS and flash-based file systems are explained in more detail in Chapter 4.

If the root file system is not mounted, the kernel will stall execution and enter the panic mode after logging the complaint on the console:

```
Unable to mount root fs on device
```

Doing Initcall and Freeing Initial Memory

If you open the linker script for any architecture, it will have an init section. The start of this section is marked using __init_begin and the end is marked using __init_end. The idea of this section is that it contains text and data that can be thrown away after they are used once during the system start-up. Driver initialization functions are an example of the use-and-throw function. Once a driver that is statically linked to the kernel does its registration and initialization, that function will not be invoked again and hence it can be thrown away. The idea behind putting all such functions together is that the entire memory occupied by all such functions can be freed as a big chunk and hence will be available for the memory manager as free pages. Considering that memory is a scarce resource on the embedded systems, the reader is advised to use this concept effectively. A use-and-throw function or variable is declared using the __init directive. Once all the driver and subsystem initialization is done, the start-up code frees all the memory. This is done just before moving to user space.

Linux also provides a way of grouping functions that should be called at system start-up time. This can be done by declaring the function with the __initcall directive. These functions are automatically called during kernel start-up, so you need not insert them into system start-up code.

Moving to User Space

The kernel that is executing in the context of the init process jumps to the user space by overlaying itself (using execve) with the executable image of a special program also referred to as init. This executable normally resides in the root file system in the directory /sbin. Note that the user can specify the init program using a command line argument to the kernel. However, if the kernel is unable to load either the user-specified init program or the default one, it enters the panic state after logging the complaint:

```
No init found. Try passing init= option to the kernel.
```

2.4.3 User Space Initialization

User space initialization is distribution dependent. The responsibility of the kernel ends with the transition to the init process. What the init process does and how it starts the services is dependent on the distribution. We now study the generic model on Linux (which assumes that the init process is /sbin/init); the generic model is pretty similar to the initialization sequence of a UNIX variant, System V UNIX.

The /sbin/init Process and /etc/inittab

The init process is a very special process to the kernel; it has the following capabilities.

- It can never be killed. Linux offers a signal called SIGKILL that can terminate execution of any process but it cannot kill the init process.
- When a process starts another process, the latter becomes the child of the former. This parent–child relationship is important. In case the parent dies before the child then init adopts the orphaned processes.
- The kernel informs the init of special events using signals. For cxample: if you press the Ctrl-Alt-Del on your system keyboard, this makes the kernel send a signal to the init process, which typically does a system shutdown.

The init process can be configured on any system using the inittab file, which typically resides in the /etc directory. init reads the inittab file and does the actions accordingly in a sequential manner. init also decides the system state known as *run level*. A run level is a number that is passed as an argument to init. In case none is passed the default run level can be picked up by init from the inittab file. The following are the run levels that are used.

- 0 – Halt the system
- 1 – Single-user mode (used for administrative purposes)
- 2 – Multi-user mode with restricted networking capabilities
- 3 – Full multi-user mode
- 4 – Unused
- 5 – Graphics mode (X11™)
- 6 – Reboot state

The `inittab` file has a special format. It generally has the following details. (Please refer to the main page of `inittab` on your system for more information.)

- The default run level.
- The actions to be taken when `init` is moved to a run level. Typically a script `/etc/rc.d/rc` is invoked with the run level as the argument.
- The process that needs to be executed during system start-up. This is typically the file `/etc/rc.d/rc.sysinit` file.
- `init` can respawn a process if it is so configured in the `inittab` file. This feature is used for respawning the log-in process after a user has logged out from his previous log-in.
- Actions to trap special events such as `Ctrl-Alt_Del` or power failure.

The rc.sysinit File

This file does the system initialization before the services are started. Typically this file does the following on an embedded system.

- Mount special file systems such as proc, ramfs
- Create directories and links if necessary
- Set the hostname for the system
- Set up networking configuration on the system

Starting Services

As mentioned above, the script `/etc/rc.d/rc` is responsible for starting the services. A service is defined as a facility to control a system process. Using services, a process can be stopped, restarted, and its status can be queried. The services are normally organized into directories based on the run levels; depending on what run level is chosen the services are stopped or started. After performing the above steps, the `init` starts a log-in program on a TTY or runs a window manager on the graphics display (depending on the run level).

2.5 GNU Cross-Platform Toolchain

One of the initial steps in the embedded Linux movement is setting up the toolchains for building the kernel and the applications. The toolchain that is used on embedded systems is known as the cross-platform toolchain. What exactly does a cross-platform mean? Normally an x86 compiler is used to generate code for the x86 platform. However, this may not be the case in embedded systems. The target on which the application and kernel need to run may not have enough memory and disk space to house the build tools. Also in most cases the target may not have a native compiler. In such cases cross-compilation is the solution. Cross-compilation generally happens on the desktop (usually an x86-based one) by using a compiler that runs on Linux-x86 (HOST) and generates code that is executable on the embedded (TARGET) platform. This process of compiling on a HOST to generate code for the TARGET system is called *cross-compilation* and the compiler used for the purpose is called a *cross-compiler.*

Any compiler requires a lot of support libraries (such as libc) and binaries (such as assemblers and linkers). One would require a similar set of tools for cross-compilation too. This whole set of tools, binaries, and libraries is collectively called the *cross-platform toolchain.* The most reliable open source compiler toolkit available across various platforms is the GNU compiler and its accessory tools are called the GNU toolchain. These compilers are backed up by a host of developers across the Internet and tested by millions of people across the globe on various platforms.

A cross-platform toolchain has the components listed below.

- *Binutils:* Binutils are a set of programs necessary for compilation/linking/ assembling and other debugging operations.
- *GNU C compiler:* The basic C compiler used for generating object code (both kernel and applications).
- *GNU C library:* This library implements the system call APIs such as open, read, and so on, and other support functions. All applications that are developed need to be linked against this base library.

Apart from GCC and Glibc, binutils are also an important part of a toolchain. Some of the utilities that constitute binutils are the following.

- addr2line: It translates program addresses into file names and line numbers. Given an address and an executable, it uses the debugging information in the executable to figure out which file name and line number are associated with a given address.
- ar: The GNU ar program creates, modifies, and extracts from archives. An archive is a single file holding a collection of other files in a structure that makes it possible to retrieve the original individual files (called members of the archive).
- as: GNU as is a family of assemblers. If you use (or have used) the GNU assembler on one architecture, you should find a fairly similar environment when you use it on another architecture. Each version has much in common with the others, including object file formats, most assembler directives (often called pseudo-ops), and assembler syntax.
- c++filt: The c++filt program does the inverse mapping: it decodes low-level names into user-level names so that the linker can keep these overloaded functions from clashing.

- `gasp`: The GNU assembler macro preprocessor.
- `ld`: The GNU linker `ld` combines a number of object and archive files, relocates their data, and ties up symbol references. Often the last step in building a new compiled program to run is a call to `ld`.
- `nm`: GNU nm lists the symbols from object files.
- `objcopy`: The GNU `objcopy` utility copies the contents of an object file to another. `objcopy` uses the GNU BFD library to read and write the object files. It can write the destination object file in a format different from that of the source object file. The exact behavior of objcopy is controlled by command-line options.
- `objdump`: The GNU `objdump` utility displays information about one or more object files. The options control what particular information to display, such as symbol table, GOT, and the like.
- `ranlib`: `ranlib` generates an index to the contents of an archive, and stores it in the archive. The index lists each symbol defined by a member of an archive that is a relocatable object file.
- `readelf`: It interprets headers on ELF files.
- `size`: The GNU size utility lists the section sizes and the total size for each of the object files in its argument list. By default, one line of output is generated for each object file or each module in an archive.
- `strings`: GNU `strings` print the printable character sequences that are at least characters long and are followed by an unprintable character. By default, it only prints the strings from the initialized and loaded sections of object files; for other types of files, it prints the strings from the whole file.
- `strip`: GNU `strip` discards all symbols from the target object file(s). The list of object files may include archives. At least one object file must be given. `strip` modifies the files named in its argument, rather than writing modified copies under different names.

2.5.1 Building Toolchain

Building a cross-platform toolchain is slightly tricky and can get highly irritating at times when the build process fails. Hence it is advisable to download prebuilt cross-platform toolchains directly for your target platform. Note that although the binutils and the C compiler can be used for both kernel and applications build, the C library is used only by the applications.

Here is a set of links where you can pick up the latest cross-platform toolchain.

- ARM: http://www.emdebian.org/
- PPC: http:// www.emdebian.org/
- MIPS: http://www.linux-mips.org/
- M68K: http://www.uclinux.org/

Now if you are unlucky and the cross-compiler for your platform is not available off the shelf then the steps outlined below will help you in compiling a cross-platform.

1. Decide the `TARGET`.
2. Decide on the Kernel/GCC/Glibc/Binutils version combo.
3. Procure patches for all the above, if any available.
4. Decide `PREFIX` variable, where to put the image.
5. Compile binutils.
6. Obtain suitable KERNEL HEADERS for your platform.
7. Compile minimal GCC.
8. Build Glibc.
9. Recompile full-featured GCC.

Picking a Target Name

The target name decides the compiler that you are building and its output. Here are some of the basic types.

- *arm-linux:* Support for ARM processors such as armV4, armv5t, and so on.
- *mips-linux:* Support for various MIPS core such as r3000, r4000, and so on.
- *ppc-linux:* Linux/PowerPC combination with support for various PPC chips.
- *m68k-linux:* This targets Linux running on the Motorola 68k processor.

A complete list can be found at http://www.gnu.org.

Picking the Right Version Combination

This is the trickiest portion of all steps and most likely the cause of all problems. It is necessary to do some research and decide on the right version combination that will work for your target. Check up on the most active mailing list archives to guide you. For example, ARM/Kernel 2.6/GCC 2.95.1, GCC 3.3/BINUTILS 2.10.x or ARM / Kernel 2.4/GCC 2.95.1/BINUTILS 2.9.5 are known good combinations for arm-linux.

Any Patches Available?

After you decide on the version number, also be sure to search for available patches. The decision of taking up a patch or not solely depends on your requirements.

Choosing a Directory Structure and Setting Variables

Before you build the toolchain, the directory tree for storing the tools and the kernel headers must be decided. The directory tree is also exported using certain specified variables to make the job of building smoother. The following variables are used.

- TARGET: This variable represents the machine target name. For example, TARGET=mips-linux.

- PREFIX: This is the base directory containing all the other subdirectories of your toolchain; the default for the native toolchain on any system is almost always /usr. This means, you will find gcc (binary) in BINDIR = $PREFIX/bin and headers in INCLUDEDIR= $PREFIX/include. To keep from stepping on your system's native tools when you build a cross-compiler you should put your cross-development toolchain in some path other than the default /usr. For example, PREFIX=/usr/local/mips/.
- KERNEL_SOURCE_DIR: This is the place where your kernel source (or at least kernel headers) is stored. Especially if you are cross-compiling this may well be different from the native set of files. It is good practice to keep the Linux kernel files under the PREFIX/TARGET directory. For example, KERNEL_SOURCE_DIR = PREFIX/TARGET/linux (i.e., /usr/local/mips/linux).
- NATIVE: The host platform (usually x86).

Building Binutils

The first step is to build GNU binutils. Version 2.9.5 is stable but the latest release is recommended. The steps are as follows.

1. *Download and unpack:* Download the latest version from ftp://ftp.gnu.org/gnu/binutils/. Unpack the archive using the commands:

```
cd $PREFIX/src
tar -xzf binutils-2.10.1.tar.gz
```

There may be target-specific patches available for binutils that resolve various bugs; it's usually a good idea to apply these to the source, if they exist. The best place to get up-to-date information is the toolchain mailing list.

2. *Configure:* The configure script sets up a lot of compilation parameters, installed binaries, and machine configuration. The commands to cross-compile on HOST for some TARGET are:

```
./configure --target=$TARGET --prefix=$PREFIX
```

For example,

```
./configure --target=mips-linux --prefix=/usr/local/mips
```

3. *Build:* Invoke make in the binutils directory to compile binutils.
4. *Install:* Invoke make install in the binutils folder to install the toolchain. Before you install, ensure that the install path does not replace existing binutils if you already have them, unless and until you really want to force that. You'll notice your new set of tools in PREFIX/TARGET/.

Obtain Suitable Kernel Headers

The first step in building a GCC is to set up kernel headers. Cross-compiling the toolchain requires the kernel headers. The following is the list of steps that are needed to do so.

1. Download a Linux kernel from ftp.kernel.org. Unpack the tar. We suggest `$PREFIX/linux` (e.g., `/usr/local/mips/linux`).
2. Apply kernel patches if necessary.
3. Set the architecture for which you are extracting the header files. This is done by setting the `ARCH` variable in the top-level Makefile such as `ARCH=mips`.
4. Configure the kernel even though you won't necessarily want to compile from it. Issue `make menuconfig` in the top-level kernel source directory:

   ```
   make menuconfig
   ```

   This will bring up the kernel build configuration program. If you have X running on your system, you may run `make xconfig`. Select the option: `System and processor type`, and select a system consistent with the tools you're building.
5. Build dependencies (This step is only needed for 2.4 kernels). Exit the configuration program saving the changes, and then run:

   ```
   make dep
   ```

   This command actually makes the links (linking `/usr/local/mips/linux/include/asm/` to `/usr/local/mips/linux/include/asm-arm`, etc.) and ensures your kernel headers are in usable condition.

Building Minimal GCC

Minimal GCC is the compiler that has only basic C language support. Once the minimal GCC is built, the glibc can be built for the target. Glibc is then used for building full-featured GCC with C++ support. After setting up the kernel headers we can now build minimal GCC. The steps are as follows.

1. *Download and unpack:* Download the latest version of GCC from http://gcc.gnu.org. Unpack the downloaded GCC. You may then choose to apply patches if they exist.
2. *Configure:* This could be done in a similar way as done for binutils.

   ```
   ./configure --target=$TARGET --prefix=$PREFIX
   --with-headers=$KERNEL_SOURCE_DIR/include --enable-languages=c
   ```

   For example,

   ```
   ./configure --target=mips-linux --prefix=/usr/local/mips/
   --with-headers=/usr/local/mips/linux/include --enable-languages=c
   ```

The last option given to configure -enable-languages=c is necessary because the minimal GCC can support languages other than C and currently we need C language support.

3. *Build:* For compiling the minimal GCC you need to just invoke the make command. If you are compiling for the first time this may result in the following error.

```
./libgcc2.c:41: stdlib.h: No such file or directory
./libgcc2.c:42: unistd.h: No such file or directory
make[3]: *** [libgcc2.a] Error 1
```

This error can be fixed using a hack called *inhibit-libc*. The procedure is:
   a. Edit the configuration file to add the line -Dinhibit_libc and -D__gthr_ posix_h to TARGET_LIBGCC2_CFLAGS. That is, change the line TARGET_LIBGCC2_CFLAGS = -fomit-frame-pointer -fPIC to TARGET_LIBGCC2_CFLAGS = -fomit-frame-pointer -fPIC -Dinhibit_libc -D__gthr_posix_h.
   b. Rerun configure.
4. *Install:* Assuming that making the cross-compiler worked, you can now install your new cross-compiler:

```
make install
```

Building Glibc

As mentioned earlier, glibc is linked to every application. The kernel, however, does not make use of glibc (it has it own minimal C library built inside). Chapter 4 discusses alternatives to glibc basically because glibc is a heavy-weight for an embedded system. Irrespective of whether you use glibc on the target, glibc is essential to build the C compiler.

1. *Download and unpack:* Because of certain restrictions on exporting soft-ware and dependencies on external source code, glibc is split into the core glibc and a set of packages. These packages are referred to as add-ons. Along with the glibc source code, the add-ons need to be unpackaged and at the time of configuring the add-on should be enabled. Embedded systems mostly require the Linux threads add-on. Hence the downloading and unpacking involves both the core and the Linux threads. Fetch the latest glibc archive and the corresponding Linux threads archive from ftp.gnu.org/gnu/glibc. Unpack the main glibc archive somewhere handy such as $PREFIX/src/glibc. Then unpack the add-on archive inside the directory created when you unpacked the main glibc archive.
2. *Configure:* The most important thing is to set the CC system variable that prompts the build system with a compiler to be used. This is because you want to do the cross-compilation of glibc using the newly built cross-compiler. For this set the variable CC on the shell using the command:

```
export CC=$TARGET-linux-gcc
```

For example, for the mips target,

```
export CC= mips-linux-gcc
```

Run the configure command with the appropriate options.

```
./configure $TARGET --build=$NATIVE-$TARGET
--prefix=$PREFIX --enable-add-ons=linux threads, crypt
```

For example, for the mips target

```
configure mips-linux --build=i686-linux --prefix=/usr/local/
mips/ --enable-add-ons=linux threads, crypt
```

3. *Build:* Invoke make in the glibc folder to build glibc.
4. *Install:* Invoke make install in the glibc folder to install glibc.

Recompiling Full-Featured GCC

Repeat the steps for building GCC for adding extra language support. You must also remove the Dinhibit_libc hack if you had to apply it before. Also be sure to unset the CC environment variable when cross-compiling so the native compiler will be used to finish building your cross-development toolchain.

With this the entire toolchain should be available on your system. Chapter 8 explains how to build the kernel and applications using the toolchain.

2.5.2 Building Toolchain for MIPS

Following are the steps that are necessary to build a toolchain for a MIPS target. This should be used as a reference for building other targets.

Source Directory Listing

We use

```
TARGET=mips-linux
PREFIX=/usr/local/mips

binutils - /usr/local/mips/src/binutils
gcc - /usr/local/mips/src/gcc
glibc - /usr/local/mips/src/glibc
Kernel sources - /usr/local/mips/linux/
```

It is always safe to create a separate build directory and run configure from there.

```
# cd /usr/local/mips/
# mkdir build
```

```
# cd build
# mkdir binutils
# mkdir gcc
# mkdir glibc
```

Building Binutils

```
# cd /usr/local/mips/build/binutils/

# /usr/src/local/mips/src/binutils/configure
--target=mips-linux --prefix=/usr/local/mips

# make
# make install
```

Setting Kernel Headers

```
#cd /usr/local/mips/linux
```

Open Makefile and modify `ARCH:=mips`

```
#make menuconfig
```

Select a suitable MIPS target and exit with a save:

```
#make dep
```

Building Minimal GCC

```
# cd /usr/local/mips/src/gcc/gcc/config/mips
```

Open file `t-linux` and modify the line `TARGET_LIBGCC2_CFLAGS = -fomit-frame-pointer -fPIC` to `TARGET_LIBGCC2_CFLAGS = -fomit-frame-pointer -fPIC -Dinhibit_libc -D__gthr_posix_h`

```
# cd /usr/local/mips/build/gcc

#/usr/local/mips/src/gcc/configure --target=mips-linux
--host=i386-pc-linux-gnu --prefix=/usr/local/mips/
--disable-threads --enable-languages=c

#make
#make install
```

Building Glibc

```
#cd /usr/src/build/glibc/
```

```
#/usr/src/glibc/configure mips-linux --build=i386-pc-linux-gnu
--prefix=/usr/local/mips/ --enable-add-ons=linuxthreads,crypt
--with-headers=/usr/local/mips/linux/include/linux

#make
#make install
```

Building GCC with Threads and Additional Languages

```
#cd /usr/local/mips/src/gcc/gcc/config/mips
```

Open `t-linux` and revert the changes done for inhibit_libc hack. Set the `TARGET_LIBGCC2_CFLAGS` line as `TARGET_LIBGCC2_CFLAGS = -fomit-frame-pointer -fPIC`

```
#cd /usr/local/mips/build/gcc/
#rm -rf *

#/usr/local/mips/src/gcc/configure --target=mips-linux
--host=i386-pc-linux-gnu --prefix=/usr/local/mips

#make
#make install
```

Chapter 3

Board Support Package

A BSP or "Board Support Package" is the set of software used to initialize the hardware devices on the board and implement the board-specific routines that can be used by the kernel and device drivers alike. BSP is thus a hardware abstraction layer gluing hardware to the OS by hiding the details of the processor and the board. The BSP hides the board- and CPU-specific details from the rest of the OS, so portability of drivers across multiple boards and CPUs becomes extremely easy. Another term that is often used instead of BSP is the Hardware Abstraction Layer or the HAL. HAL is more famous with UNIX users whereas the RTOS developer community more often uses BSP, especially those using VxWorks. The BSP has two components:

1. *The microprocessor support:* Linux has wide support for all the leading processors in the embedded market such as MIPS, ARM, and soon the PowerPC.
2. *The board-specific routines:* A typical HAL for the board hardware will include:
   a. Bootloader support
   b. Memory map support
   c. System timers
   d. Interrupt controller support
   e. Real-Time Clock (RTC)
   f. Serial support (debug and console)
   g. Bus support (PCI/ISA)
   h. DMA support
   i. Power management

This chapter does not deal with the porting of Linux on a microprocessor or microcontroller because this is an ocean by itself; a separate book needs to be devoted to Linux porting on various processors and microcontrollers.

Rather this book assumes that the reader has a board based on one of the already supported processors. So it is devoted entirely to the board-specific issues. For making the terminology clean, we refer to the HAL as the layer that combines the board- and the processor-specific software and the BSP as the layer that has only the board-specific code. So when we talk about the MIPS HAL it means the support for the MIPS processors and the boards built with MIPS processors. When we talk about a BSP we refer to the software that does not have the processor support software but just the additional software for supporting the board. The HAL can be understood as a superset of all supported BSPs and it additionally includes the processor-specific software.

As mentioned in Chapter 2, neither the Linux HAL nor the BSP has any standard. Hence it is very difficult to explain the HAL for multiple architectures. This chapter delves into the Linux BSP and porting issues for a MIPS-based architecture; wherever necessary the discussion may spill over to other processors. For making things easier, we use a fictitious board EUREKA that is MIPS-based having the following set of hardware components.

- A 32-bit MIPS processor
- 8 MB of SDRAM
- 4 MB of flash
- A 8259-based programmable interrupt controller
- A PCI bus with some devices such as Ethernet and a sound card connected to it
- A timer chip for generating the system heartbeat
- A serial port that can be used for console and remote debugging

3.1 Inserting BSP in Kernel Build Procedure

The Linux HAL source code resides under `arch/` and `include/<asm-XXX>` (XXX = processor name such as PowerPC, MIPS) directories. Thus `arch/ppc` will contain the source files for the PPC-based board and `include/asm-ppc` will contain the header files.

Under each processor directory, all boards based on that CPU are categorized again into subdirectories. The important directories under each subdirectory are:

- *kernel:* This directory contains the CPU-specific routines for initializing, IRQ set-up, interrupts, and traps routines.
- *mm:* Contains the hardware-specific TLB set-up and exception-handling code.

For example, MIPS HAL has the two subdirectories `arch/mips/kernel` and `arch/mips/mm` that hold the above code. Along with these two directories there is a host of other subdirectories; these are the BSP directories that hold the board-specific code only. The user needs to create a subdirectory tree under the appropriate processor directory that contains the files necessary for the BSP. The next step is to integrate the BSP with the build process so that the board-specific files can be chosen when the kernel image is built. This may require that the kernel component selection process (done using the `make menuconfig` command while the kernel is built) is aware of the board. Why is this step necessary? Other than simplifying the build procedure there are added advantages to doing this.

- Jumper settings often do lots of board-specific configuration. Some examples of such settings are processor speed, UART speed, and so on. Instead of tweaking the code such as changing the header files, all such board-specific details can be made as configuration options and centrally stored in a configuration repository (such as the `.config` file used for the kernel build); this makes the process of building the kernel easier and also avoids the cluttering of source code.
- Often an OEM supplier is the buyer of an embedded solution and they may want to add their own components into a kernel. They may not be interested in choosing the kernel components for the board supplied by you; they may want it to be fixed already as a part of the build process. This is done by adding your board as a configurable item while building the kernel; when the board gets chosen all the software components required for the board automatically get pulled in. The OEM supplier need not bother about the gory details of your board and what software components are required for building it.

The above two steps can be accomplished by hooking the BSP with the configuration process. Linux kernel components are selected using the `make config` (or the `make menuconfig`/`make xconfig`) command. The heart of the configuration process is the configuration file placed under the specific processor directory. This is dealt with in more detail in Chapter 8. For example, you need to edit the file `arch/mips/config.in` (for the 2.4 kernel) or the `arch/mips/Kconfig` (for the 2.6 kernel) as shown in Figure 3.1 for including EUREKA board components in the kernel build process.

The `CONFIG_EUREKA` is the link between the configuration and the build process. For the above example, the following lines need to be added to the `arch/mips/Makefile` file.

```
ifdef CONFIG_EUREKA
LIBS        += arch/mips/eureka/eureka.o
SUBDIRS     += arch/mips/eureka
LOADADDR    := 0x80000000
endif
```

The last line, `LOADADDR`, specifies the beginning address of the kernel. The linker using the linker script pulls this in, so you can see the reference of this address again in the linker script. Thus when the user has chosen the EUREKA board at the time of configuration, the list of configurations specific to the board such as the clock speed are chosen. In addition, when the kernel is built, the build process is aware of the EUREKA-specific build options such as the subdirectories it has to traverse to build the software.

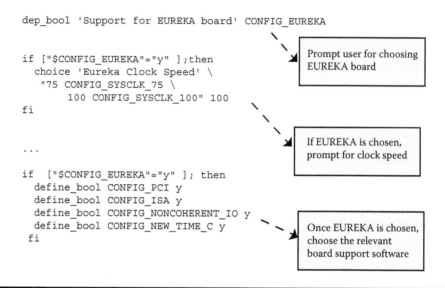

```
dep_bool 'Support for EUREKA board' CONFIG_EUREKA

if ["$CONFIG_EUREKA"="y" ];then
    choice 'Eureka Clock Speed' \
    "75 CONFIG_SYSCLK_75 \
        100 CONFIG_SYSCLK_100" 100
fi

...

if  ["$CONFIG_EUREKA"="y" ]; then
    define_bool CONFIG_PCI y
    define_bool CONFIG_ISA y
    define_bool CONFIG_NONCOHERENT_IO y
    define_bool CONFIG_NEW_TIME_C y
fi
```

Prompt user for choosing EUREKA board

If EUREKA is chosen, prompt for clock speed

Once EUREKA is chosen, choose the relevant board support software

Figure 3.1   EUREKA build options.

3.2 The Boot Loader Interface

The boot loader is the piece of software that starts executing immediately after the system is powered on. The boot loader is an important part of the development process and one of the most complicated ones too. Most of the boot-loading issues are specific to the CPU and the boards shipped out. Many CPUs such as the ARM, x86, and MIPS start execution at specific vectors at reset. Some others such as the M68K fetch the starting location from a boot ROM. Thus questions arise as to whether the first and the only image that can be loaded can be Linux itself thus eliminating the use of a boot loader. Eliminating the boot loader and flashing the kernel that bootstraps itself is an approach provided by many RTOSs including VxWorks, which provides boot initialization routines to do POST, set up chip selects, initialize RAM and memory caches, and transfer the image from ROM to RAM.

Most of the reset initialization is board-specific and normally manufacturers of boards give an onboard PROM that does the above. It is better to make use of the PROM to load either a kernel image or an intermittent boot loader and thus save the developers from the job of programming the board. Even if a PROM is not available, it is better to separate the boot process to a boot loader than let the kernel bootstrap itself. The following are the advantages with this approach.

- Other than ROM downloads, multiple methods of downloading the kernel such as serial (Kermit) or network (TFTP) can be implemented.
- It provides protection against unsafe overwrites of the kernel image in case the kernel image is stored in flash. Assume that there was a power outage when a kernel image is upgraded; then the board is in limbo. The

safer way is to burn a boot loader into some protected sectors of flash (normally called boot sectors) and leave them untouched so that there is a recovery route always available.

As a thumb rule Linux always assumes that it is executing from memory (some patches for eXecute In Place [XIP] allow Linux to execute from ROM directly; these are discussed later). Boot loaders are independent pieces of software that need to be built independently of the Linux kernel. Unless your board supports a PROM, the boot loader does the initialization of the processor and the board. Hence the boot loader is highly board- and processor-specific. The boot loader functionalities can be divided into two: the mandatory ones and the optional ones. The optional boot loader functionalities are varied and depend on the customer usage. The mandatory boot loader functionalities are:

1. *Initializing the hardware:* This includes the processor, the essential controllers such as the memory controller, and the hardware devices necessary for loading the kernel such as flash.
2. *Loading the kernel:* The necessary software to download the kernel and copy it to the appropriate memory location.

The following is the list of steps that any boot loader normally follows; these are generic steps and there can be exceptions depending on the usage. Note that the X86 processors normally are shipped with an onboard BIOS that helps with the basic power-on and loading a secondary boot loader for loading the operating system; hence the following set of steps is meant for the non-X86 processors such as MIPS and ARM.

1. *Booting:* Most boot loaders start from the flash. They do the initial processor initialization such as configuring the cache, setting up some basic registers, and verifying the onboard RAM. Also they run the POST routines to do validation of the hardware required for the boot procedure such as validating memory, flash, buses, and so on.
2. *Relocation:* The boot loaders relocate themselves to the RAM. This is because RAM is faster than flash. Also the relocation step may include decompression as the boot loaders can be kept in a compressed format to save costly storage space.
3. *Device initialization:* Next the boot loader initializes the basic devices necessary for user interaction. This usually means setting up a console so that a UI is thrown for the user. It also initializes the devices necessary for picking up the kernel (and maybe the root file system). This may include the flash, network card, USB, and so on.
4. *UI:* Next the UI is thrown for the user to select the kernel image she wishes to download onto the target. There can be a deadline set for the user to enter her choice; in case of a timeout a default image can be downloaded.
5. *Image download:* The kernel image is downloaded. In case the user has been given the choice to download a root file system using the initrd mechanism, the initrd image too gets downloaded to memory.

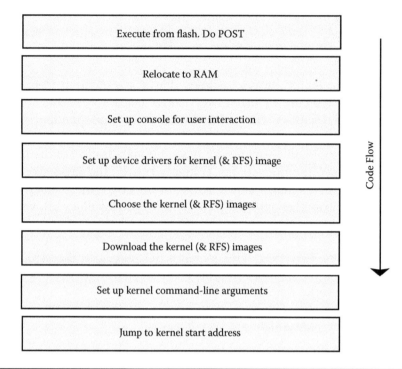

Figure 3.2 Bootloader start-up sequence.

6. *Preparing kernel boot:* Next, in case arguments need to be passed to the kernel, the command-line arguments are filled and placed at known locations to the Linux kernel.
7. *Booting kernel:* Finally the transfer is given to the kernel. Once the Linux kernel starts running, the boot loader is no longer necessary. Normally its memory is reclaimed by the kernel; the memory map set for the kernel needs to take care of this.

Figure 3.2 shows a generic boot loader start-up sequence.

There are many freely available boot loaders for Linux; the system architect can evaluate the existing ones before deciding to write a new boot loader from scratch. What are the criteria in choosing a boot loader for a given embedded platform?

- *Support for the embedded hardware:* This should be the primary criterion. There are many desktop boot loaders such as LILO that cannot be used on embedded systems because of their dependency on the PC BIOS. However there are some generic embedded boot loaders available: notably U-Boot and Redboot. The following shows some of the nongeneric boot loaders available for the most commonly used embedded processors.
  - MIPS – PMON2000, YAMON
  - ARM – Blob, Angel boot, Compaq bootldr
  - X86 – LILO, GRUB, Etherboot
  - PowerPC – PMON2000
- *Licensing issues:* These are discussed in detail in Appendix B.

- *Storage footprint:* Many boot loaders support compression to save flash space. This may be an important criterion especially when multiple kernel images are stored.
- *Support for network booting:* Network booting may be essential especially for debug builds. Most of the popular boot loaders support booting via the network and may support the popular network protocols associated with booting such as BOOTP, DHCP, and TFTP.
- *Support for flash booting:* Flash booting has two components associated with it: flash reader software and file system reader software. The latter is required in case the kernel image is stored on a file system on the flash.
- *Console UI availability:* Console UI is almost a must on most present-day boot loaders. The console UI normally provides the user the following choices.
  - Choosing the kernel image and location
  - Setting the mode of kernel download (network, serial, flash)
  - Configuring the arguments to be passed to the kernel
- *Upgrade solutions availability:* Upgrade solution requires a flash erase and flash writing software in the boot loader.

One other important area of discussion surrounding the boot loaders is the boot loader-to-kernel interface, which comprises the following components.

- *Argument passing from the boot loader to Linux kernel:* The Linux kernel like any application can be given arguments in a well-notated form, which the kernel parses and either consumes itself or passes to the concerned drivers or applications. This is a very powerful feature and can be used to implement workarounds for some hardware problems. The list of Linux kernel boot time arguments can be verified after the system is fully up by reading the proc file `/proc/cmdline`.
  - Passing boot command arguments: A boot command argument can have multiple, comma-separated values. Multiple arguments should be space separated. Once the entire set is constructed the boot loader should place them in a well-known memory address to the Linux kernel.
  - Parsing of boot command arguments: A boot command of type `foo` requires a function `foo_setup()` to be registered with the kernel. The kernel on initialization walks through each command argument and calls its appropriate registered function. If no function is registered, it is either consumed as an environment variable or is passed to the init task.

- Some important boot parameters are:
  - `root`: Specifies the device name to be used as the root file system.
  - `nfsroot`: Specifies the NFS server, directory, and options to be used as the root file system. (NFS is a very powerful step in building a Linux system in the initial stages.)
  - `mem`: Specifies the amount of memory available to the Linux kernel.
  - `debug`: Specifies the debug level for printing messages to the console.
- *Memory Map:* On many platforms, especially the Intel and PowerPC, boot loaders set up a memory map that can be picked up by the OS. This makes it easy to port the OS across multiple platforms. More on the memory map is discussed in the next section.

■ *Calling PROM routines from the kernel:* On many platforms, the boot loader that executes a PROM can be treated as a library so that calls can be made to the PROM. For example, on the MIPS-based DEC station, the PROM-based IO routines are used to implement a console.

3.3 Memory Map

The memory map defines the layout of the CPU's addressable space. Defining a memory map is one of the most crucial steps and has to be done at the beginning of the porting process. The memory map is needed for the following reasons.

■ It freezes on the address space allocated for various hardware components such as RAM, flash, and memory-mapped IO peripherals.
■ It highlights the allocation of onboard memory to various software components such as the boot loader and the kernel. This is crucial for building the software components; this information is fed normally via a linker script at the time of building.
■ It defines the virtual-to-physical address mapping for the board. This mapping is highly processor- and board-specific; the design of the various onboard memory and bus controllers on the board decides this mapping.

There are three addresses that are seen on an embedded Linux system:

■ *CPU untranslated or the physical address:* This is the address that is seen on the actual memory bus.
■ *CPU translated address or the virtual address:* This is the address range that is recognized by the CPU as the valid address range. The main kernel memory allocator kmalloc(), for example, returns a virtual address. The virtual address goes through an MMU to get translated to a physical address.
■ *Bus address:* This is the address of memory as seen by devices other than the CPU. Depending on the bus, this address may vary.

A memory map binds the memory layout of the system as seen by the CPU, the memory devices (RAM, flash, etc.), and the external devices; this map indicates how the devices having different views of the addressable space should communicate. In most of the platforms the bus address matches the physical address, but it is not mandatory. The Linux kernel provides macros to make sure that the device drivers are portable across all the platforms.

Defining the memory map requires the following understanding.

■ Understanding the memory and IO addressing of the hardware components on the board. This often requires understanding of how the memory and IO bus controllers are configured.
■ Understanding how the CPU handles memory management.

The creation of the memory map for the system can be broken down into the following tasks.

- *The processor memory map:* This is the first memory map that needs to be created. It explains the CPU's memory management policies such as how the CPU handles the different address spaces (user mode, kernel mode), what are the caching policies for the various memory regions, and so on.
- *The board memory map:* Once there is an idea of how the processor sees the various memory areas, the next step is to fit the various onboard devices into the processor memory areas. This requires an understanding of the various onboard devices and the bus controllers.
- *The software memory map:* Next a portion of the memory needs to be given for the various software components such as the boot loader and the Linux kernel. The Linux kernel sets up its own memory map and decides where the various kernel sections such as code and heap will reside.

The following sections explain each of these memory maps in detail with respect to the EUREKA board.

3.3.1 The Processor Memory Map — MIPS Memory Model

The processor address space for the MIPS 32-bit processors (4 GB) is divided into four areas as shown in Figure 3.3.

- *KSEG0:* The address range of this segment is 0x80000000 to 0x9fffffff. These addresses are mapped to the 512 MB of physical memory. The virtual-to-physical address translation happens by just knocking off the topmost bit of the virtual address. This address space goes always to the cache and it has to be generated only after the caches are properly initialized. Also this address space does not get accessed via the TLB; hence the Linux kernel makes use of this address space.
- *KSEG1:* The address range of this segment is 0xA0000000 to 0xBFFFFFFF. These addresses are mapped again to the 512 MB of physical memory; they are mapped by knocking down the last three bits of virtual address.

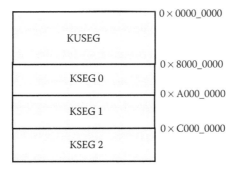

Figure 3.3   MIPS memory map.

However, the difference between KSEG0 and KSEG1 is that KSEG1 skips the cache. Hence this address space is used right after reset when the system caches are in an undefined state. (The MIPS reset vector 0xBFC00000 lies in this address range.) Also this address space is used to map IO peripherals because it bypasses the cache.

- *KUSEG:* The address range of this segment is 0x00000000 to 0x7FFFFFFF. This is the address space allocated to the user programs. They get translated via the TLB to physical addresses.
- *KSEG2:* The address range of this segment is 0xC0000000 to 0xFFFFFFFF. This is the address space that is accessible via the kernel but gets translated via the TLB.

3.3.2 Board Memory Map

The following is the memory map designed for the EUREKA board that has 8 MB of onboard SDRAM, 4 MB of flash, and IO devices that require 2 MB of memory map range.

- *0x80000000 to 0x80800000:* Used to map the 8 MB of SDRAM
- *0xBFC00000 to 0xC0000000:* Used to map the 4 MB of flash
- *0xBF400000 to 0xBF600000:* Used to map the 2 MB of IO peripherals

3.3.3 Software Memory Map

The 8 MB of SDRAM is made available for running both the boot loader and Linux kernel. Normally the boot loader is made to run from the bottom of the available memory so that once it transfers control to the Linux kernel, the Linux kernel can easily reclaim its memory. If this is not the case then you may need to employ some tricks to reclaim the boot loader memory if the boot loader memory is not contiguous with the Linux address space or if its address space lies before the kernel address space. The Linux memory map setup is divided into four stages.

- The Linux kernel layout — the linker script
- The boot memory allocator
- Creating memory and IO mappings in the virtual address space
- Creation of various memory allocator zones by the kernel

Linux Kernel Layout

The Linux kernel layout is specified at the time of building the kernel using the linker script file `ld.script`. For the MIPS architecture, the default linker script is `arch/mips/ld.script.in`; a linker script provided by the platform can override this. The linker script is written using a linker command language and it describes how the various sections of the kernel need to be packed and what addresses need to be given to them. Refer to Listing 3.1 for a sample linker script, which defines the following memory layout.

Listing 3.1   Sample Linker Script

```
OUTPUT_ARCH(mips)
ENTRY(kernel_entry)
SECTIONS
{
  /* Read-only sections, merged into text segment: */
  . = 0x80100000;
  .init       : { *(.init) } = 0

  .text       :
  {
    _ftext = . ;                /* Start of text segment */
    *(.text)
    *(.rodata)
    *(.rodata.*)
    *(.rodata1)
    /* .gnu.warning sections are handled specially by elf32.em.  */
    *(.gnu.warning)
  } =0

  .kstrtab : { *(.kstrtab) }

  . = ALIGN(16);                /* Exception table */
  __start___ex_table = .;
  __ex_table : { *(__ex_table) }
  __stop___ex_table = .;

  __start___dbe_table = .;
  __dbe_table : { *(__dbe_table) }
  __stop___dbe_table = .;

  __start___ksymtab = .;        /* Kernel symbol table */
  __ksymtab : { *(__ksymtab) }
  __stop___ksymtab = .;

  _etext = .;                   /* End of text segment */

  . = ALIGN(8192);
  .data.init_task : { *(.data.init_task)

  . = ALIGN(4096);
  __init_begin = .;             /* Start of Start-up code */
  .text.init : { *(.text.init) }
  .data.init : { *(.data.init) }

  . = ALIGN(16);
  __setup_start = .;
  .setup.init : { *(.setup.init) }
  __setup_end = .;
```

Listing 3.1   Sample Linker Script (continued)

```
  __initcall_start = .;
  .initcall.init : { *(.initcall.init) }
  __initcall_end = .;

  . = ALIGN(4096);       /* Align double page for init_task_union */
  __init_end = .;        /* End of Start-up code */


  . = .;
  .data    :
  {
    _fdata = . ;         /* Start of data segment */
    *(.data)
   /* Align the initial ramdisk image (INITRD) */
   . = ALIGN(4096);

   __rd_start = .;
   *(.initrd)
   . = ALIGN(4096);
   __rd_end = .;

    CONSTRUCTORS
  }

  .data1   : { *(.data1) }
  _gp = . + 0x8000;
  .lit8 : { *(.lit8) }
  .lit4 : { *(.lit4) }
  .ctors         : { *(.ctors)   }
  .dtors         : { *(.dtors)   }
  .got           : { *(.got.plt) *(.got) }
  .dynamic       : { *(.dynamic) }
  .sdata   : { *(.sdata) }

  . = ALIGN(4);
  _edata  = .;           /* End of data segment */
  PROVIDE (edata = .);

  __bss_start = .;       /* Start of bss segment */
  _fbss = .;
  .sbss     : { *(.sbss) *(.scommon) }
  .bss      :
  {
   *(.dynbss)
   *(.bss)
   *(COMMON)
   .   = ALIGN(4);
  _end = . ;             /* End of bss */
  PROVIDE (end = .);
  }


}
```

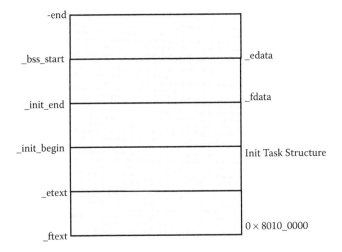

Figure 3.4   Sections of a kernel image.

- The text section starts at the address 0x8010-0000. All the other sections follow the text section continuously. The address _ftext is the beginning of the text section and the address _etext is the end of the text section.
- After _etext, a space aligned at 8 K is allocated for assigning the process descriptor and the stack for process 0, also called the swapper process.
- Following this is the space for the init section. The addresses _init_begin and _init_end denote the beginning and end of these sections, respectively.
- Following is the initialized kernel data section. The symbols _fdata and _edata denote the beginning and end of these sections, respectively.
- The last section is the uninitialized kernel data section or the BSS. Unlike the other sections, this section is not a part of the kernel image but only the space used by it is specified using the _bss_start and the _end addresses. The kernel start-up routine uses these symbols to get the BSS address range and zero the BSS space.

Figure 3.4 shows the kernel section's layout as defined by the linker script.

Boot Memory Allocators

The boot memory allocators are the kernel dynamic allocators during the early stages of the kernel (before paging is set up); once paging is set up the zone allocators are responsible for dynamic memory allocation. The bootmem allocators are invoked from the setup_arch() function. The bootmem allocator acts on the memory map of the board, which is usually passed by the boot loader; this is the normal procedure for the x86 series, which is why we look at a memory map that is passed on by the boot loader on a Pentium® PC.

```
0000000000000000 - 000000000009f800 (usable)
000000000009f800 - 00000000000a0000 (reserved)
00000000000e0000 - 0000000000100000 (reserved)
```

```
0000000000100000 - 000000001f6f0000 (usable)
000000001f6f0000 - 000000001f6fb000 (ACPI data)
000000001f6fb000 - 000000001f700000 (ACPI NVS)
000000001f700000 - 000000001f780000 (usable)
000000001f780000 - 0000000020000000 (reserved)
00000000fec00000 - 00000000fec10000 (reserved)
00000000fee00000 - 00000000fee01000 (reserved)
00000000ff800000 - 00000000ffc00000 (reserved)
00000000fffffc00 - 0000000100000000 (reserved)
```

The kernel starts using memory from the physical address of 1 MB. So the bootmem allocator reserves the following regions.

- *640 K to 1 MB:* These are reserved for the video and the extension ROMs.
- *Above 1 MB:* These are reserved for the kernel code and the data sections.

Setting Up Memory and IO Mappings

This needs to be done on processors that do not have virtual memory turned on at reset. Examples of such processors are the Intel and the PowerPC. On the other hand, MIPS live in a virtual memory environment from the reset. For the Intel and the PowerPC, the virtual memory mappings need to be set up so that they can access the memory and memory-mapped IO. For example, on the PowerPC during the early stage of kernel initialization, the virtual address is mapped one to one with the physical address. Once the memory map is known, then the virtual mapping table is set up.

Setting Up the Zone Allocators

The zone allocator divides the memory into three zones.

- *DMA zone:* This zone is for allocation of memory that can be used for DMA transfers. For the MIPS and the PowerPC platforms, all the dynamic low memory gets added to the DMA zone. However, on the i386™-based PC, this has a maximum size of 16 MB due to the memory addressing restriction on the ISA bus.
- *NORMAL zone:* The kernel memory allocators try to allocate memory from this zone, or else fall back to the DMA zone.
- *HIGHMEM zone:* Many processors cannot access all of the physical memory because of the small size of the linear address space. This zone is used to map such memory. This is not used normally on embedded systems and is used more on desktops and servers.

3.4 Interrupt Management

Every board is unique with its hardware interrupt management, mostly because of the PIC (Programmable Interrupt Controller) interface. This section details the steps involved in the programming interrupt controller in Linux. Before going into the details of programming the interrupt controller, let us evaluate the basic functionalities of a PIC.

- A microprocessor normally has a limited number of interrupts, which may be a limitation if there are many devices on the board and all of these need to interrupt the processor. The interrupt controller comes to the rescue in such a case. By allowing many interrupts to be multiplexed over a single interrupt line it expands the interrupt capability of the processor.
- PIC provides hardware priority for interrupts. This can be a useful feature in case the processor itself does not support hardware interrupt priority. When the processor is handling an interrupt of a higher priority, the PIC does not deliver a lower-priority interrupt to the processor. Also when two devices interrupt simultaneously, the PIC will look at a priority register to recognize the higher-priority interrupt and then deliver it to the CPU.
- To do trigger conversions. Hardware delivers interrupts in two ways: level and edge trigger. Edge-triggered interrupts happen on the transition of a signal from one state to another (normally from high to low); basically it is a short pulse that indicates the occurrence of an interrupt. Level-triggered interrupts on the other hand hold the interrupt line high until the processor turns it off. Edge-triggered interrupts are an older method of interrupts and used by the ISA bus architectures. However, the basic disadvantage of edge-triggered interrupts is that they do not allow interrupt sharing. Level triggers allow interrupt sharing but have to be used carefully because an improperly designed interrupt handler can cause the system to be stuck forever in the interrupt loop. Some processors allow the interrupt processing to be configured as either edge- or level-triggered whereas some processors recognize only level interrupts. If a device generating edge interrupts is connected to the latter set, then the edge interrupts will be treated as spurious interrupts because the interrupting cause will be withdrawn before the processing starts. In such a case, a PIC will be handy because a PIC can translate the edge to level interrupts by latching the input interrupt.

We take the 8259A as the example PIC for understanding the programming issues. Why 8259A? Because it is a very popular and powerful hardware and there are many variants of it used on embedded boards. Before we can understand the hooking of the 8259A into a BSP, we need a basic understanding of the 8259A. The basic features of the 8259A controller are:

- It has eight interrupt pins. Using the cascaded mode, it can be used to service up to 64 interrupts.
- It can be programmable for various modes:
  - Fully nested mode, which is entered right after initialization. In this mode priorities are unique and fixed. During this mode, a higher-priority interrupt can interrupt the CPU when it is servicing a lower-priority interrupt.
  - Automatic rotation mode to support interrupts having the same priority.
  - Specific rotation mode where interrupt priority is programmable by changing the lowest priority and thereby fixing all other priorities.

■ The PIC can be programmed for either edge- or level-triggered operation.
■ Individual interrupts can be masked.

Three registers get involved in the interrupt processing of the 8259A: the IRR or the interrupt request register, IMR or the interrupt mask register, and the ISR or the interrupt service register. When an external device needs to interrupt, the corresponding bit in IRR is set. If the interrupt is not masked depending on whether the bit in IMR is set, the interrupt is delivered to the priority arbitration logic. This looks at the contents of the ISR register to find out if a higher-priority interrupt is being serviced currently; if not, the interrupt latch is raised so that the CPU sees the interrupt. The x86 processors issue an INTA cycle so that the PIC drives the interrupt vector on the bus; however, the processors do not have this functionality in hardware; software needs to do this explicitly. The ISR bit remains set until an EOI (End Of Interrupt) is issued. If the PIC is configured for the automatic end-of-interrupt mode, then the acknowledgment of the interrupt itself causes the bit to be cleared.

A device can be directly connected to the processor in which case it interrupts the processor on one of the processor's interrupt lines; otherwise its interrupts can be routed via a PIC. But the interrupt route taken should not be the concern of the software device driver. The BSP should shield the driver from the actual interrupt routing. For example, Figure 3.5 shows an Ethernet card connected directly via a PIC to a MIPS processor (MIPS supports six input interrupts).

The Linux kernel treats all interrupts as logical interrupts; logical interrupts are directly connected to the processor or may go via a PIC. In both the cases when an interrupt is registered (via the `request_irq()` function), the device driver needs to pass an interrupt number as an argument that identifies the interrupt number; the interrupt number passed is that of the logical interrupt

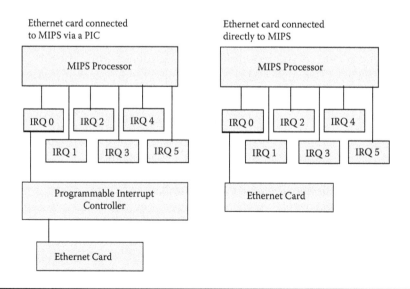

Figure 3.5   Ethernet card IRQ connections.

number. The number of logical interrupts varies across processors; for the MIPS processor it is fixed as 128. The mapping of the logical interrupts to the actual physical interrupt is the responsiblility of the BSP. So in the above example in both the cases the driver may use the same IRQ number but how the IRQ number is routed to the actual hardware is decided by the BSP; this makes portability of device drivers easier.

The core of the BSP interrupt interface is two data structures:

- *The interrupt controller descriptor* `hw_interrupt_type`: This structure is declared in `include/linux/irq.h`. Every hardware interrupt–controlling mechanism needs to implement this structure. The important fields of this data structure are:
  - `start-up`: Pointer to the function that gets invoked when interrupts are probed or when they are requested (using the `request_irq()` function)
  - `shutdown`: Pointer to the function that gets invoked when an interrupt is released (using the `free_irq()` function)
  - `enable`: Pointer to the function that enables an interrupt line
  - `disable`: Pointer to the function that disables the interrupt line
  - `ack`: Pointer to a controller-specific function used to acknowledge interrupts
  - `end`: Pointer to a function that gets invoked after the interrupt has been serviced
- *The IRQ descriptor* `irq_desc_t`: This again is declared in `include/linux/irq.h`. Every logical interrupt is defined using this structure. The important fields of this data structure are:
  - `status`: The status of the interrupting source
  - `handler`: Pointer to the interrupt controller descriptor (described above)
  - `action`: The IRQ action list

The usage of these data structures can be best explained using an example. Figure 3.6 shows interrupt architecture on the EUREKA board.

MIPS supports six hardware interrupts. On the board in Figure 3.6, five of these are connected directly to hardware devices whereas the sixth interrupt is connected to a PIC, which in turn is used to connect five more hardware devices. Thus there are ten interrupt sources on the board, which need to be mapped to ten logical interrupts for use by the device drivers for the ten devices. These are the steps that should be done by the BSP to implement the logical interrupts.

- Create an `hw_interrupt_type` for the interrupts that are directly connected to the processor. We name this the `generic_irq_hw`.
- Create an `hw_interrupt_type` for the PIC. We name this the `pic_irq_hw`.
- Define ten `irq_desc_t` structures corresponding to the ten logical interrupts. For the first five, we tie the `handler` field to `generic_irq_hw` and for the last five, we tie it to `pic_irq_hw`.

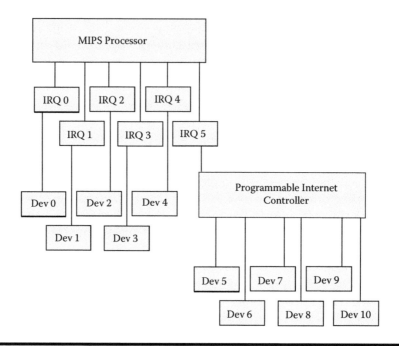

Figure 3.6   IRQ connections on EUREKA.

- Write the interrupt start-up code that gets called when the CPU is interrupted. This routine should check the MIPS interrupt status register and then the PIC status register to evaluate if the interrupt was a direct interrupt or was routed via a PIC. If the interrupt belongs to the PIC, it should read the PIC status register and find out the logical interrupt number. Then the generic IRQ handler function do_IRQ() needs to be called with the logical interrupt number. It will do the appropriate PIC handling before and after calling the actual handler.

Each interrupt controller support requires BSP hooks. The following functions are filled up in the hw_interrupt_type described above and get called during various phases of interrupt handling.

- *Initialization routine:* This needs to be called once (in the init_IRQ() function). The function issues the ICW (Initialization Command Word) commands that should be done before the 8259 can process and accept interrupt requests.
- *Start-up routine:* This function gets called when an interrupt is requested or when an interrupt is probed. On 8259 this routine just enables the interrupt by unmasking it in the PIC.
- *Shutdown routine:* It is the complement of the start-up routine; it does disabling of the interrupt.
- *Enable routine:* This routine unmasks a particular interrupt on 8259. This is called from the kernel function enable_irq().

- *Disable routine:* This routine sets the bit in the IMR. This function is called from the kernel function `disable_irq()`.
- *Acknowledgment routine:* The acknowledgment routine gets called in the initial stages of interrupt handling. When an interrupt occurs, further instances of the same interrupt are disabled before the interrupt handler is run. This is to prevent the ISR reentrancy problem. So this routine masks the IRQ that is being serviced currently. Additionally for the 8259, if the auto end of interrupt mode is not set, this routine sends the EOI command to the PIC.
- *End of interrupt routine:* This gets called at the final stages of interrupt handling. This routine has to enable the interrupt that has got disabled in the acknowledgment routine.

3.5 The PCI Subsystem

The PCI architecture on Linux has its roots with the x86 model. Linux assumes that the BIOS or the firmware is responsible for configuring every PCI device so that its resources (IO, memory, and interrupts) are allocated. By the time a device driver accesses the device, its memory and IO regions should have been mapped to the processor's address space. Many of the boards do not come with a BIOS or firmware that does PCI initialization. Even if it does, the address range offered to the devices may not exactly meet Linux requirements. Hence it becomes the responsibility of the BSP to do the probing and configuration of the PCI devices. We discuss BSP on the MIPS-based PCI devices.

3.5.1 Uniqueness of PCI Architecture

Linux identifies three PCI objects: bus, device, and function. Up to 256 buses can be on a system, each bus having 32 slots, which can host devices. Devices can be either single- or multifunctioned. Multiple PCI buses are interlinked via a PCI bridge. The connectivity of the PCI subsystem on a board can be unique; this in turn can make the PCI architecture board-specific. Some of the uniqueness can stem from the following.

Memory Map Issues

The piece of hardware that connects the processor bus to the PCI bus is called the *north bridge*. The north bridge has a memory controller built in so that it can access the processor's memory. In addition, some north bridges have the capability to make the PCI device address space part of the processor's address space; they do this by trapping the addresses on the processor's bus and issuing PCI read/write cycles. On the PC platform, the north bridge has this capability and hence the PCI address space is mapped into the processor's address space.

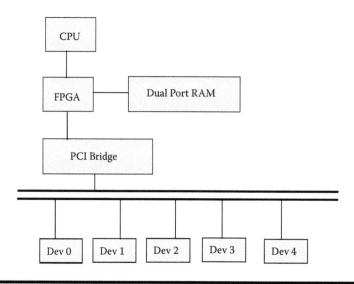

Figure 3.7   PCI via FPGA.

However, it is possible that capability to map the PCI address space into the processor's virtual address space is not available on all boards. Linux device drivers take this into account and hence none of the drivers reference PCI IO and memory via direct pointers; rather they use the inb()/outb() type of commands. These may translate to direct memory references in case PCI is mapped directly to the processor's virtual address space. Both MIPS and PowerPC allow the PCI space to be mapped to the processor address space, provided the board supports it. In such a case, the BSP needs to provide *IO base*; this is the starting address in the processor's virtual map for accessing the PCI devices. For example, consider the board layout as shown in Figure 3.7 where the PCI bridge communicates to the processor via an FPGA and a dual-port RAM. The FPGA provides specific registers for starting a configuration, memory, and IO operation. Such a board has two anomalies when compared to normal boards and hence two ramifications on the BSP.

- The PCI memory and IO address space cannot be mapped to the processor's address space directly because IO and memory operation require programming on the FPGA. So the BSP needs to provide routines to do memory and IO operations on the PCI bus.
- The dual-ported RAM is provided so that the PCI devices can do DMA to the RAM. But because the main memory is not accessible by the PCI controller, the PCI device drivers requiring DMAble memory should be supplied memory from within the dual-ported RAM area.

Configuration Space Access

Every PCI device has a configuration space that needs to be read and programmed before the device can actually be used. The processor does not

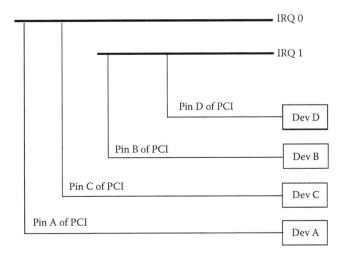

Figure 3.8   PCI IRQ routing.

have direct access to the configuration space but is dependent on the PCI controller for this. The PCI controller normally provides registers, which need to be programmed for doing device configuration. Because this is board dependent, the BSP needs to provide for these routines.

Interrupt Routing on the Board

PCI hardware provides four logical interrupts, A, B, C, and D, to be hard-coded in every PCI device. This information is stored in the *interrupt pin* field in the configuration header. How the PCI logical interrupts are actually connected to the processor interrupts is board-specific. The configuration space has another field called the *interrupt line,* which needs to be filled with the actual interrupt line that the PCI device uses. The BSP needs to scan the configuration header for the interrupt pin information and then from the interrupt routing map fill the *interrupt line* field. For example, in Figure 3.8 all pins marked A and C are connected to IRQ0 and pins marked B and D are connected to IRQ1. Hence on the interrupt line, the BSP needs to program the former set of cards (Dev-A and Dev-C) with IRQ0 and the latter with IRQ1 (Dev-B and Dev-D).

3.5.2 PCI Software Architecture

The PCI software architecture can be divided into four layers for MIPS.

- ■ *BSP:* The BSP gives the following information to the software.
  - – The IO base for accessing the PCI memory and IO regions
  - – The routines to access the PCI configuration space
  - – The interrupt routing map on the board

- *HAL:* This layer implements the BIOS functionality of assigning the PCI resources (memory and IO) to the various devices. The HAL uses the information given by the BSP to assign resources. The HAL support includes functions for scanning the bus, building the PCI device tree, and resource management. As such the BSP developer need not bother about the details of the HAL; it is a part of the MIPS HAL. The BSP developer needs to bother about the interface between the BSP and HAL. This is discussed in detail below under the PCI BSP section.
- *PCI library:* It provides APIs for the HAL and the device drivers.. The library is located in the kernel source under the directory `drivers/pci`.
- *PCI device drivers:* They make use of the functions exported by the PCI library.

In this section we discuss PCI BSP.

PCI BSP

The actual implementation of the information exchange between the BSP and the HAL is architecture-dependent. MIPS defines a PCI channel structure for this purpose; this data structure has the starting and ending of the memory and IO regions and also has a pointer to the `pci_ops` structure containing routines to access the configuration space. This data structure points to the following data structures that need to be filled in.

- `pci_ops`: This is a pointer to the structure containing the routines to access the PCI configuration space. The definition of this structure is from `include/linux/pci.h`. Because the configuration access is board-specific, the BSP needs to fill these routines so that the rest of the PCI subsystem can access the configuration space.
- `io_resource` *and* `mem_resource`: These data structures specify the starting and ending addresses of the IO and memory space that are assigned to the PCI devices. Although the HAL does the scanning and resource allocation, all the devices are assigned either memory or IO space within the address range specified by the BSP.

The definition of the PCI channel structure varies across the 2.4 and 2.6 implementation. In the 2.4 implementation, the channel is defined statically using the `mips_pci_channels`; this is picked up by the HAL. In the 2.6 implementation, the structure `pci_controller` implements the PCI channel; the BSP needs to fill in this structure and register it specifically to the HAL using the `register_pci_controller()` API.

Along with the filling in of the above structure, the PCI BSP has one more responsibility and that is of doing the various fix-ups, which are described below.

- The most important fix-up is the one that does IRQ routing. Because IRQ routing is very board-specific, the BSP has to read the interrupt pin number for every bus discovered and assign the interrupt line to that device; this is done in a standard API `pcibios_fixup_irqs()` that is called by the HAL.

■ The other set of fix-ups includes any systemwide fix-ups and device-specific fix-ups. The former needs to be implemented by the BSP using the function `pcibios_fixup()`. The device-specific fix-ups are registered in a table `pcibios_fixups[]`. When a device is discovered on the PCI bus, using its ID as the identifier, the fix-ups are applied for that particular device. This is particularly useful to undo any anomalies with respect to the PCI implementation for that particular device.

3.6 Timers

There are two timers that need to be programmed by the BSP:

■ *The Programmable Interval Timer (PIT):* This timer is hooked to the timer interrupt that provides the system pulse or ticks. The default value for a tick on an MIPS Linux system is 10 msec.
■ *The Real-Time Clock (RTC):* This is independent of the processor as it is an external chip on the board. The RTC is operated by a special battery that powers it even when the board is switched off; thus once programmed it can provide the time of day services.

The first timer is mandatory on any Linux system; the RTC on the other hand is not mandatory. The hardware implementation of the PIT again varies across hardware architectures. On the PowerPC, the decrementer register, which is a countdown register, can be used to generate a periodic interrupt; hence it can be used as the PIT. However, similar counter registers are not available on all MIPS processors and hence they need to rely on external hardware. On the MIPS, `board_timer_setup()` is used for setting and enabling the timer interrupt handler.

3.7 UART

The serial port on your board can be used for three purposes:

■ The system console for displaying all the boot messages
■ Standard TTY device
■ The kernel debugger KGDB interface

3.7.1 Implementing the Console

The console is set up in the function `console_init()` in file `init/main.c`. This is done during the initial stages of system bring-up so that it can be used as an early debugging tool. All the kernel prints happen via the `printk()`

function; this function can take in a variable number of arguments (such as printf()). The first argument to printk() can be a priority to the string that needs to be printed; the lower the number is, the higher the priority of the string. Priority number 0 is used for printing emergency statements whereas 7 (which is the highest) is used to spew out debug-level messages. printk() compares the string priority against the console priority set using the syslog() function; if the string priority is less than or equal to the console priority then the messages are printed.

printk() keeps the list of messages that need to be printed in a circular log buffer and calls a list of registered console device handlers to print the queued-up messages. Registration of the console happens using the register_console() function, which is taken in the console data structure; this is the heart of the console subsystem. Any device such as the UART, printer, or network can use this data structure to interface with the console and capture the output from printk().

The console is implemented as a data structure; its definition can be found from the header file include/linux/console.h. Important members of the structure are:

- name: Name of the console device.
- write(): This is the main function; it gets called by the printk() to spew out the messages. The printk function can be called from any part of the kernel including the interrupt handlers, so you should be careful in designing the write handler so that it does not sleep. Normally the write handler is a simple routine that makes use of polling to transmit characters to the device (UART, printer, etc.).
- device(): This function returns the device number for the underlying TTY device that is currently acting as a console.
- unblank(): This function, if defined, is used to unblank the screen.
- setup(): This function is called when the console= command-line argument matches the name for this console structure.

3.7.2 The KGDB Interface

KGDB is the kernel source-level debugger. It makes use of GDB for source-level debugging of the kernel; because GDB is a widely used protocol, KGDB is a very popular kernel debugging tool. More information on the actual usage of KGDB is presented in Chapter 8. KGDB is used mainly over the serial interface (there are some patches available for using KGDB over an Ethernet interface). The KGDB architecture can be split into two portions: the GDB stub and the serial driver. The GDB stub is available in the kernel HAL layer; it implements the GDB protocol and fixes the exception handlers. Binding the serial interface to the GDB stub is the responsibility of the BSP; the BSP needs to implement two simple functions for sending and receiving characters over the serial interface.

3.8 Power Management

Many types of embedded devices have different power requirements depending on their usage. For example, network routers need to have minimal energy consumption to avoid heating, especially when used under rugged conditions. Devices such as PDAs and cell phones need to consume less energy so that battery life is not cut short. This section explains the power management schemes available under Linux for embedded systems and the power management framework on Linux, which spans across the BSP, drivers, and application layers. But before that we discuss the nexus between hardware design and power management.

3.8.1 Hardware and Power Management

In order to understand how an embedded system consumes power, it is very useful to find out the power consumption of the various hardware devices constituting it. Let's consider a handheld device that consists of the following components.

- A processor such as MIPS or StrongArm
- Memory (both DRAM and flash memory)
- A network card such as a wireless card
- A sound card
- An LCD-based display unit

Typically the LCD display unit would be the biggest power consumer in the system; followed by the CPU; followed by the sound card, memory, and the network card. Once the units that display maximum power can be identified, then techniques to maintain the devices in their low-power modes can be studied. Many hardware devices available on the market today have different operation modes to satisfy varying power requirements; they have the capability to work with very low power when not under use and switch to normal power usage mode when they are normally used. The device drivers for such devices need to take the power management into account. Of the various hardware devices the most important is the CPU. Many CPUs for the embedded market provide robust power-saving schemes, which we analyze now.

The basis of power management of the CPU lies in the following two facts.

- Power consumed by a processor is directly proportional to the clock frequency.
- Power consumed by a processor is directly proportional to the square of the voltage.

New embedded processors take these into account and offer two schemes: *dynamic frequency scaling* and *dynamic voltage scaling*. An example of a processor that supports dynamic frequency scaling is the SA1110 and an example of a processor that supports dynamic voltage scaling is Transmeta's Crusoe processor. The modes offered by the CPUs are controlled typically by the OS, which can deduce the mode depending on the system load. Typically embedded systems are event-driven systems and the processor spends a lot of time waiting for events from the user or from the external world. The OS running on these systems can tune the processor's power consumption depending on the system load. In case the processor is idling waiting for user events, it would be attending to minimal tasks necessary for the system such as servicing timer interrupts. If a processor supports idle mode, then the OS can put the CPU into the idle mode under such conditions. The idle mode is the mode where the various processor clocks are stopped (the clocks to the peripherals may be still active). Some processors go still further and offer another mode called the *sleep mode* wherein the power to the CPU and most of the peripherals is turned off. This is the lowest power-consumption mode; however, making use of this mode is very tricky and the OS needs to consider the following factors to use the sleep mode.

- The state of the system such as the CPU and the peripherals needs to be saved in memory so that the saved context can be restored when the system returns from the sleep condition.
- The time to come out of the sleep state should be fast enough so that real-time characteristics of the system are met (both from a hardware and software perspective).
- The events that need to awaken the system must be evaluated and appropriately incorporated in the software.
- Keeping track of the time when the system goes to sleep is a very tricky part. Other than the fact that the system should not lose track of the time when going to sleep, the system should also consider the fact that there may be tasks that are sleeping and need to be awakened after the system goes to sleep. Usually there may be an external hardware clock (such as the RTC) that does not get shut down in the sleep mode; the RTC can be programmed to awaken the system for waking tasks. The RTC can also be used to maintain the external time, which the system can sync up to after returning from the sleep state.

The operating system plays a very important role in implementing the power management framework. The role of the OS is multi-faceted:

- As discussed above, it makes decisions as to when the processor can go into various modes such as idle mode and sleep mode. Also the appropriate wake-up mechanisms need to be devised by the OS.
- Provides support for dynamically scaling the frequency and voltage depending on the system load.
- Provides a driver framework so that the various device drivers can be written to exploit the power-saving modes of the peripherals.
- Exports the power management framework to specific applications. This step is a very important one because the power requirements of every embedded device are very unique and hence it is very difficult to put in

the policies in the OS to suit a variety of embedded devices. Rather the OS should just build the framework but leave the policies to applications, which can configure the framework depending on requirements.

We will show how Linux offers each of these to the embedded developers but before that we need to understand the standards that are available with respect to power management.

3.8.2 Power Management Standards

There are two power management standards supported by Linux: the APM and the ACPI standard. Both these standards have their roots in the x86 architecture. The basic difference between these two standards is that ACPI allows for more control within the OS whereas APM is more dependent on the BIOS for doing power management. Power management is built in the kernel by choosing the CONFIG_PM option during kernel configuration; the user will be prompted to choose either APM or the ACPI standard. Depending on the option chosen within the kernel, the corresponding user-space applications should be chosen; for example, if APM was chosen as the power management standard within the kernel, then the application apmd should also be chosen.

The APM standard introduced by Microsoft and Intel allocated most of the power management control to the BIOS. The BIOS monitors the list of devices it knows to deduce system inactivity to put the system into low-power modes. The decision to let the BIOS do the control had many disadvantages:

- The BIOS may choose to put a system into low-power mode when the system is actually involved in a computationally intensive task. This is because the BIOS assumes the system state by just looking at the activity on the IO ports such as the keyboard. So in the middle of a huge compilation task where the activity on the keyboard may be nil, the BIOS may choose to put the system in low-power mode.
- The BIOS detects activity only on devices that are residing on the motherboard. Devices not on the motherboard such as those plugged into the USB bus cannot participate in power management.
- Because the APM was dependent on the BIOS and each BIOS had its own set of limitations and interfaces (and bugs!), getting the power management working across all systems was too difficult.

When it was realized that APM was not the ideal power management standard, a new standard called ACPI was developed. The rationale behind APCI was that most of the power management policies should be handled by the OS because it can make the best judgment with respect to the system load and hence it can manage the power of the CPU and the peripherals. The ACPI standard makes the system still dependent on the BIOS but to a lesser degree. By using an interpreted language called AML (ACPI Machine Language), an OS can operate on the devices without knowing much about the devices.

3.8.3 Supporting Processor's Power-Saving Modes

One of the earliest things that happened in the Linux kernel with respect to power management was the integration of the processor idle state in the idle loop. The idle loop of the Linux kernel is the task with process ID 0; this task gets scheduled when the CPU is idling and waiting for an interrupt to occur. Entering the idle state during the loop and being awakened when an external interrupt happens lowers the power consumption because the clocks are stopped.

The next major thing that happened with respect to power management was support for the APM model in Linux. This was followed by support for the ACPI. Now a question arises: as these power management models are mainly for the x86 architecture and dependent on the BIOS, could they be used for other processors? The usage of these standards will ensure that the set of interfaces is readily available even on non-x86 platforms; hence the power management applications can be used directly. The method chosen on non-x86 platforms was to introduce a hack within the Linux kernel to expose APM/ACPI type interfaces to the user land by distributing the job of the x86 BIOS to the kernel and the boot loader. Let us look at how a platform based on the StrongArm processor can do this.

- The StrongArm BSP on Linux provides routines for suspending and resuming the entire system software; this is the job of the BIOS on the x86 platforms (routines `sa1100_cpu_suspend()` and `sa1100_cpu_resume()` in file `arch/arm/mach-sa1100/sleep.S`). These routines are used in a handler that is registered with the power management code on Linux and get invoked when the system goes to sleep. However, before going to sleep, a wake-up source is selected (such as activity on the GPIO pin or an alarm from the RTC).
- Before the system goes into the sleep mode, the memory is put in a self-refresh mode to make sure the contents of the memory are preserved across suspends/wake-ups. The memory needs to be put out of the self-refresh mode when the system is awakened. The boot loader does this. If the boot loader was invoked because of a wake-up from a sleep event, it puts the memory out of the self-refresh mode and jumps to an address stored in a register (the PSPR register, which gets saved across sleep mode). This address is provided by the kernel and contains a routine to bootstrap the kernel out of the sleep mode by restoring the context and continuing from where the kernel had suspended itself.

The 2.6 kernel has an integrated framework to do frequency scaling. The framework provides a method for changing the frequency dynamically on the supported architectures. However the kernel does not implement the policies; rather they are left to applications that use the framework to drive the frequency. This is because the frequency scaling policies depend on the nature of the system usage. A generic solution is not possible; hence the implementation of the policy is left to user land applications or daemons. The following are the important features of the frequency scaling mechanism.

- The frequency scaling software inside the kernel is divided into two components: the scalar core and the frequency driver. The frequency scalar core is implemented in the file `linux/kernel/cpufreq.c`. The core is the generic piece of code that implements the framework that is independent of the hardware. However the actual job of controlling the hardware to do frequency transitions is left to the frequency drivers, which are platform dependent.

- The core does the important job of updating the important system variable `loops_per_jiffy`, which is dependent on the CPU frequency. This variable is used by various hardware devices to do small but timed pauses using the kernel function `udelay()`. At system start-up time this variable is set using the function `calibrate_delay()`. However, whenever the system frequency changes later, this variable has to be updated. The core does this.

- The changes in the clock frequency may affect the hardware components, which are dependent on the CPU frequency. All the corresponding device drivers need to be notified of the frequency changes so that they can control the hardware accordingly. The core implements a driver notify mechanism; a driver that is interested in receiving frequency change events needs to register to the core.

- The frequency settings can be controlled from user land using the proc interface. This can be used by applications to change the clock frequency.

- Various applications and tools are available in the user space to control the frequency depending on the system load. For example, the `cpufreqd` application monitors battery level, AC state, and running programs, and adjusts the frequency governor according to a set of rules specified in the configuration file.

3.8.4 Unified Driver Framework for Power Management

The device drivers are a central piece in the power management software; it is important to ensure their cooperation especially if the power consumption of the devices they control adds up to a significant portion of the power consumption. Similar to the technique employed by the frequency scaling mechanism, the kernel separates the device drivers from the actual power management software in the kernel by allowing the device drivers to register themselves before they participate in the power management. This is done using the `pm_register()` call; one of the arguments to this function is a callback function. The kernel maintains a list of all drivers that are registered with the power management; whenever there is an event associated with the power management the driver callbacks are invoked.

If the device driver participates in power management, it is necessary that no operations on the device are done unless the device is in the running state. For this Linux offers an interface `pmaccess`; a device driver needs to call this interface before it operates on the hardware. An additional interface `pm_dev_idle` is provided to identify idle devices so that they can be put to sleep.

An important issue in implementing power management to enable drivers is the issue of ordering. When a device is dependent on another device, they should be turned on and off in the right order. The classic case for this is the PCI subsystem. When all the PCI devices on a PCI bus are turned off, then the PCI bus itself can be turned off. But if the bus is turned off while the devices are still alive or if any device is awakened before the bus itself then it can prove disastrous. The same holds true when the PCI buses are chained. The PCI subsystem takes care of this by recursing through the PCI buses bottom up and making sure that the devices are turned off before the bus is turned off on every bus encountered. Upon resuming from the sleep the bus is recursed top down to make sure that the bus is restored before the devices on that bus are awakened.

3.8.5 Power Management Applications

As mentioned earlier, the Linux kernel provides mechanisms to implement power management but leaves the decision making to user land. Both APM and ACPI come with applications that are used to initiate system suspend/standby transition. The `apmd` daemon for APM uses the `/proc/apm` interface to check if there is support for APM in the Linux kernel; along with initiating standby it does logging of the various PM events. The ACPI daemon `acpid` listens on a file (`/proc/acpi/event`) and when an event occurs, executes programs to handle the event. More information about these daemons can be found from

- `apmd`: http://worldvisions.ca/
- `acpid`: http://acpid.sf.net/

Chapter 4

Embedded Storage

Traditional storage on embedded systems was done using a ROM for storage of read-only code and a NVRAM for storage for the read-write data. However, they were replaced by flash technology, which provides high-density nonvolatile storage. These advantages combined with the low cost of flash have dramatically increased their usage in embedded systems. This chapter discusses the storage systems primarily around flash devices and the various file systems available on Linux meant for embedded systems. The chapter is divided into four parts.

- Flash maps for embedded Linux.
- Understanding the MTD (Memory Technology Drivers) subsystem meant primarily for flash devices.
- Understanding the file systems associated with embedded systems. There are specialized file systems on flash and onboard memory for embedded systems.
- Tweaking for more storage space: techniques to squeeze more programs onto your flash.

4.1 Flash Map

On an embedded Linux system, a flash will be generally used for:

- Storing the boot loader
- Storing the OS image
- Storing the applications and application library images
- Storing the read-write files (having configuration data)

Of the four, the first three are read-only for most of the system execution time (except at upgrade times). It is inherent that if you use a boot loader you should have at least two partitions: one having the boot loader and the other holding the root file system. The division of the flash can be described as the flash map. It is very advisable that at the beginning of your project you come up with a flash map. A flash map like the memory map fixes on how you plan to partition the flash for storage of the above data and how you plan to access the data.

The following are various design issues that will come up when you try to freeze on a flash map.

- How would you like to partition the flash? You can have the OS, applications, and read-write files in a single partition but that increases the risk of corrupting the entire system data because the entire partition is read-write. On the other hand you can put the read-only data in a separate partition and the read-write in a separate partition so that the read-only data is safe from any corruptions; but then you would need to fix a size on each partition making sure that the partition size will not be exceeded at any point in the future.
- How would you like to access the partitions, as raw or would you like to use a file system? Raw partitions can be useful for the boot loader because you will not be requiring a file system; you can mark a flash sector for holding boot configuration data and the rest of the sectors for holding boot code. However, for partitions holding Linux data, it is safer to go via file systems. What file system you choose for the data also plays a crucial role in fixing the flash map.
- How would you like to do upgrades? Upgrades on an embedded system can be done on a running system or from the boot. In case your upgrades involve changing only the read-only data (as is usually the case) it is better to partition the flash into read-only and read-write partitions so that you will not have to do any backup and restore of read-write data.

Figure 4.1 shows the flash map on a 4 MB flash holding a boot loader, OS images, and applications. As you see, the read-only data is kept in a CRAMFS file system, which is a read-only file system, and the read-write data is kept in the JFFS2 file system, which is a read-write file system.

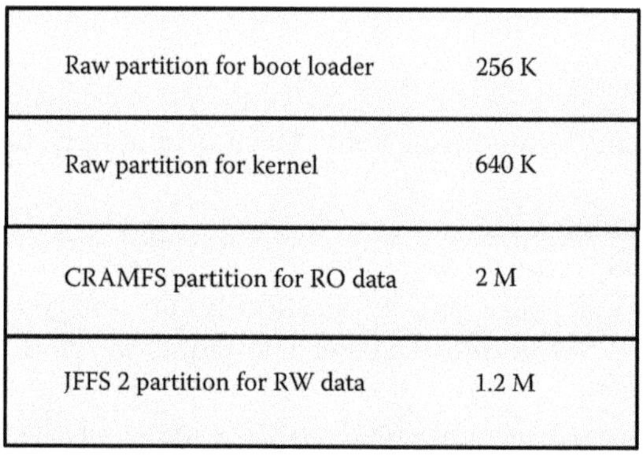

Raw partition for boot loader	256 K
Raw partition for kernel	640 K
CRAMFS partition for RO data	2 M
JFFS 2 partition for RW data	1.2 M

Figure 4.1   Flash map for 4-MB flash.

4.2 MTD—Memory Technology Device

MTD stands for Memory Technology Device and is the subsystem used to handle onboard storage devices. Is MTD a separate class of driver set like a character or block? The simple answer is no. Then what exactly is the job of MTD and when and how do you include flash devices under an MTD subsystem? How will you put file systems on an MTD device? The following subsections answer these questions.

4.2.1 *The MTD Model*

Although flash devices are storage devices like hard disks, there are some fundamental differences between them.

- Normally hard disks have a sector that divides a page size (generally 4096 bytes). The standard value is 512 bytes. The Linux file system model, especially the buffer cache (a memory cache between the file system and block device layer), is based upon this assumption. Flash chips on the other hand have large sector sizes; the standard size is 64 K.
- Flash sectors normally have to be erased before writing to them; the write and the erase operations can be independent depending on the software using the flash.
- Flash chips have a limited lifetime which is defined in terms of the number of times a sector is erased. So if a particular sector is getting written very often the lifespan gets shortened. To prevent this, the writes to a flash need to be distributed to all the sectors. This is called wear leveling and is not supported by the block devices.
- Normal file systems cannot be used on top of a flash because these go through the buffer cache. Normal disk IO is slow; to speed it up a cache in memory called the buffer cache stores the IO data to the disk. Unless this data gets flushed back to the disk, the file system is in an inconsistent state. (This is the reason why you need to shut down your OS on the PC before switching it off.) However, embedded systems can be powered off without proper shutdown and still have consistent data; so normal file systems and the block device model do not go well with embedded systems.

The traditional method to access flash used to be via the FTL, that is, the Flash Translation Layer. This layer emulates a block device behavior on a flash to get regular file systems to work on flash devices. However, getting a new file system or a new flash driver working with the FTL is cumbersome and this is the reason why the MTD subsystem was invented. (David Woodhouse is the owner of the MTD subsystem and the developments regarding MTD can be obtained on the Web site http://www.linux-mtd.infradead.org/. The MTD subsystem was made a part of the 2.4 mainstream kernel.) MTD's solution to the above problems is simple: treat memory devices as memory devices and not like disks. So instead of changing the low-level drivers or introducing a translation layer, change the application to use memory devices as they are.

MTD is very much tied to the applications; the MTD subsystem is divided into two parts: drivers and the applications.

The MTD subsystem does not implement a new kind of driver but rather it maps any device to both a character and a block device driver. When the driver is registered with the MTD subsystem, it exports the device in both these driver flavors. Why is it done this way? The character device can let the memory device be accessed directly using standard `open/read/write/ioctl` calls. But in case you want to mount a regular file system on the memory device using the traditional method, you can still mount it using the block driver.

We go through each layer in Figure 4.1 but before that let's understand two devices that are presently supported by MTD: flash chips and flash disks.

4.2.2 Flash Chips

We look at the variety of flash chips supported by the MTD subsystem. Flash devices come in two flavors: NAND and NOR flash. Although both of them came around the same time (NOR was introduced by Intel and NAND by Toshiba in the late 1980s), NOR caught up fast with the embedded world because of its ease to use. However when embedded systems evolved to have large storage (like media players and digital cameras), NAND flash became popular for data storage applications. The MTD layer also evolved initially around the NOR flash but the support for NAND was added later. Table 4.1 compares the two kinds of flashes.

NOR chips come in two flavors: older non-CFI chips and the newer CFI compliant. CFI stands for Common Flash Interface and is an industry standard for ensuring compatibility among flash chips coming from the same vendor. Flash chips like any other memory device are always in a stage of evolution with new chips replacing the older ones very quickly; this would involve rewriting the flash drivers. Often these changes would be configuration changes such as erase timeouts, block sizes, and the like. To circumvent this effort, CFI standards were introduced that enable the flash vendors to allow the configuration data to be read from the flash devices. So system software could interrogate the flash devices and reconfigure itself. MTD supports the CFI command sets from Intel and AMD.

NAND flash support was added in the late 2.4 series; along with the NFTL (NAND Flash Translation Layer) it can mount regular file systems, but support for JFFS2 was added only for the 2.6 kernel. The 2.6 kernel can be considered a good port for using NAND flash.

4.2.3 Flash Disks

Flash disks were introduced for mass storage applications. As their name suggests, flash disks mean local disks on a system based on flash technology. Flash disks again come in two flavors: ATA-based and linear.

Table 4.1   NOR versus NAND Flash

	NOR	NAND
Access to data	The data can be accessed at random like SRAM. The operations on the flash can be: *Read routine:* Read the contents of the flash. *Erase routine:* Erase is the process of making all the bits on a flash 1. Erase on the NOR chips happens in terms of blocks (referred to as erase regions). *Write routine:* Write is the process of converting a 1 to 0 on the flash. Once a bit is made 0, it cannot be written into until the block is erased, which sets all the bits in a block to 1.	The NAND chips divide the storage into blocks, which are divided into pages again. Each page is divided into regular data and out-of-band data. The out-of-band data is used for storing metadata such as ECC (Error-Correction Code) data and bad block information. The NAND flash like the NOR flash has three basic operations: `read`, `erase`, and `write`. However, unlike NOR which can access data randomly, the NAND reads and writes are done in terms of pages whereas erases happen in terms of blocks.
Interface to the board	These are connected like the normal SRAM device to the processor address and data bus.	There are multiple ways of connecting the NAND flash to the CPU varying across vendors. Raw NAND access is done by connecting the data and command lines to the usually 8 IO lines on the flash chip.
Execution of code	Code can be executed directly from NOR because it is directly connected to the address/data bus.	If code is in NAND flash it needs to be copied to memory for execution.
Performance	NOR flash is characterized by slow erase, slow write, and fast read.	NAND flash is characterized by fast erase, fast write, and fast read.
Bad blocks	NOR flash chips are not expected to have bad blocks because they have been designed to hold system data.	These flashes have been designed as basically media storage devices at lower prices, so expect that they have bad blocks. Normally these flash chips come with the bad sectors marked in them. Also NAND flash sectors suffer more the problem of bit flipping where a bit gets flipped when being written to; this is detected by error-correcting algorithms called ECC/EDC, which are done either in hardware or in software.

Table 4.1   NOR versus NAND Flash (continued)

	NOR	NAND
Usage	These are basically used for code execution. Boot loaders can exist on the NOR flashes because the code from these flashes can be directly executed. These flashes are pretty expensive and they provide lesser memory densities and have a relatively shorter life span (around 100,000 erase cycles).	These are used mainly as storage devices for embedded systems such as set-top boxes and MP3 players. If you plan to use a board with only NAND, you may have to put in an additional boot ROM. They offer high densities at lower prices and have a longer life span (around 10 to the power of 6 erase cycles).

ATA-based flash disks use the standard disk interface for interfacing on the motherboard, so they appear as IDE disks on the system. A controller sits on the same silicon as the flash but does the FTL implementation to map the flash to sectors. In addition, it implements the disk protocol so that the flash appears as a normal disk to the system. This was the approach taken by the CompactFlash designers. The main advantage of using this approach was software compatibility but the disadvantage was that it was more expensive because the total solution was done in hardware. Linux treats these devices as regular IDE devices and the driver for these devices can be found in the `drivers/ide` directory.

The linear flash disk is the mechanism that is employed by the M2000 systems. These are NAND-based devices that have boot capabilities (it has a boot ROM that is recognized as a BIOS extension), a thin controller that employs error-correction algorithms, and the trueFFFS software that does the FTL emulation. Thus these devices can be used for directly booting the system and can be used for running regular file systems on a blocklike device. These are less expensive when compared to the compact flashes but at the same time give all the features required as a block device. Because the access to these flash devices is similar to a memory device access, Linux implements the drivers for these under the MTD model.

4.3 MTD Architecture

The following two questions are generally asked when getting Linux to work on a flash-based device.

- Does Linux support my flash driver; if not, how do I port the driver?
- If Linux supports my flash driver, how do I make it detect the flash on my board and get its driver automatically installed?

Understanding the MTD architecture answers these questions. The MTD architecture is divided into the following components.

- *MTD core:* This provides the interface between the low-level flash drivers and the applications. It implements the character and block device mode.
- *Low-level flash drivers:* This section talks about NOR- and NAND-based flash chips only.
- *BSP for flash:* A flash can be uniquely connected on a board. For example, a NOR flash can be connected directly on the processor bus or may be connected to an external PCI bus. The access to the flash also can be unique depending on the processor type. The BSP layer makes the flash driver work with any board/processor. The user has to provide the details of how the flash is mapped on the board; we refer to this piece of the code as the *flash mapping-driver.*
- *MTD applications:* This can be either kernel submodules such as JFFS2 or NFTL, or user-space applications such as upgrade manager.

Figure 4.2 shows how these components interact with each other and the rest of the kernel.

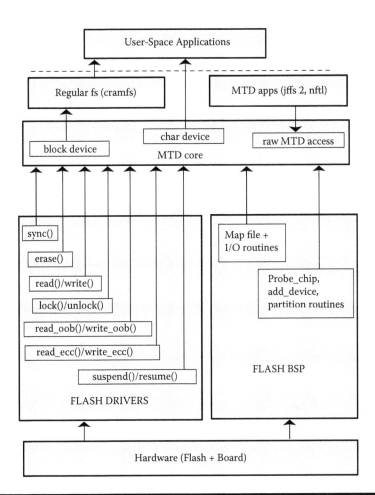

Figure 4.2   MTD architecture.

4.3.1 `mtd_info` *Data Structure*

`mtd_info` is the heart of the MTD software. It is defined in the file `include/linux/mtd/mtd.h`. The software driver on detecting a particular flash fills up this structure with the pointers to all the required routines (such as `erase`, `read`, `write`, etc.) that are used by the MTD core and the MTD applications. The list of the `mtd_info` structures for all devices added is kept in a table called the `mtd_table[]`.

4.3.2 Interface Between MTD Core and Low-Level Flash Drivers

As mentioned above, the low-level flash driver exports the following functions to the MTD core.

- Functions common to both the NAND and NOR flash chips
  - `read()/write()`
  - `erase()`
  - `lock()/unlock()`
  - `sync()`
  - `suspend()/resume()`
- Functions for NAND chips only
  - `read_ecc()/write_ecc()`
  - `read_oob()/write_oob()`

If you have a CFI-enabled NOR flash or a standard IO device-mapped 8-bit NAND chip, then your driver is already ready. Otherwise you need to implement the MTD driver. Some of the routines may require hardware support; so you need to check your flash data sheet to implement the functions. The following section gives the description of routines other than the `read()`, `write()`, and `erase()` routines.

- `lock()` and `unlock()`: These are used to implement flash locking; a portion of the flash can be write or erase protected to prevent accidental overwriting of images. For example, you can lock all the partitions on which you have read-only file systems for most of the system execution except when upgrades are done. These are exported to the user applications using the ioctls `MEMLOCK` and `MEMUNLOCK`.
- `sync()`: This gets called when a device gets closed or released and it makes sure that the flash is in a safe state.
- `suspend()` and `resume()`: These are useful only when you turn on the `CONFIG_PM` option on building the kernel.
- `read_ecc()` and `write_ecc()`: These routines apply for NAND flash only. ECC is the error-correction code that is used to detect any bad bits in a page. These routines behave as the normal `read()/write()` except that a separate buffer containing the ECC is also read or written along with the data.
- `read_oob()` and `write_oob()`: These routines apply for NAND flash only. Every NAND flash is divided into either 256- or 512-byte pages; each

of these pages contains an additional 8- or 16-byte spare area called out-of-band data, which stores the ECC, bad block information, and any file system–dependent data. These functions are used to access the out-of-band data.

4.4 Sample MTD Driver for NOR Flash

We now go into the details of a NOR flash driver for Linux. The file `mtd.c` contains the code for a simple NOR flash based on the following assumptions.

- The flash device has a single erase region so that all sectors have the same size. (An erase region is defined as an area of a chip that contains the sectors of the same size.)
- The flash chip is accessed using a 4-byte bus width.
- There are no locking, unlocking, suspend, and resume functionalities.

For simplicity's sake we assume that the following information is available to us as macros or as functions.

- `DUMMY_FLASH_ERASE_SIZE`: The flash erase sector size
- `DUMMY_FLASH_SIZE`: The flash size
- `PROBE_FLASH()`: The function that probes if the NOR flash is present at the specified address
- `WRITE_FLASH_ONE_WORD`: The function/macro to write a word at a specified address
- `ERASE_FLASH_SECTOR`: The function to erase a given sector
- `DUMMY_FLASH_ERASE_TIME`: Per-sector erase time in jiffies

First let us put all the header files we want for our flash driver.

```
/* mtd.c */
#include <linux/kernel.h>
#include <linux/module.h>
#include <linux/types.h>
#include <linux/sched.h>
#include <linux/errno.h>
#include <linux/interrupt.h>
#include <linux/mtd/map.h>
#include <linux/mtd/mtd.h>
#include <linux/mtd/cfi.h>
#include <linux/delay.h>
```

Now we put all the APIs/macros that we expect the user to define.

```
#define DUMMY_FLASH_ERASE_SIZE
#define PROBE_FLASH(map)
#define WRITE_FLASH_ONE_WORD(map, start, addr, data)
#define ERASE_FLASH_SECTOR(map, start, addr)
```

```
#define DUMMY_FLASH_ERASE_TIME
#define DUMMY_FLASH_SIZE
```

A brief explanation of the arguments that are passed to the above APIs is as follows.

- `map`: This is a pointer to a structure `map_info` declared in the header file `include/linux/mtd/map.h`. This structure is explained in more detail in Section 4.5.
- `start`: This is the start address of the NOR flash chip. This address is normally used for programming the flash with the command to erase or write data.
- `addr`: This is the offset from the chip's starting address to where data needs to be written or the sector needs to be erased.
- `data`: This argument for the write API is a 32-bit word that specifies what needs to be written at the specified address.

Next we define a structure that contains the information private to this flash.

```
struct dummy_private_info_struct
{
  int number_of_chips; /* Number of flash chips */
  int chipshift; /* Size of each flash */
  struct flchip *chips;
} ;
```

A brief explanation of each of the structure fields is as follows.

- `number_of_chips`: As the name suggests, this specifies how many consecutive chips can be found at the probe address. The API `PROBE_FLASH()` is required to return this number to the driver code.
- `chipshift`: It is the total number of address bits for the device, which is used to calculate address offsets and the total number of bytes of which the device is capable.
- `chips`: The `struct flchip` can be found in `include/linux/mtd/flashchip.h`. More of it is explained in the `dummy_probe()` function.

Next is the list of the static functions that need to be declared.

```
static struct mtd_info * dummy_probe(struct map_info *);
static void dummy_destroy(struct mtd_info *);
static int dummy_flash_read(struct mtd_info *, loff_t , size_t ,
                        size_t *, u_char *);
static int dummy_flash_erase(struct mtd_info *,
                        struct erase_info *);
static int dummy_flash_write(struct mtd_info *, loff_t ,
                        size_t , size_t *, const u_char *);
static void dummy_flash_sync(struct mtd_info *);
```

The structure `mtd_chip_driver` is used by the initialization routine `dummy_flash_init()` and the exit function `dummy_flash_exit()`. The most important field is the `.probe` that is called to detect if a flash of a particular type is present at a specified address on the board. The MTD layer maintains a list of these structures. The probe routines are accessed when the routine `do_map_probe()` is invoked by the flash-mapping driver.

```
static struct mtd_chip_driver dummy_chipdrv =
{
  .probe    = dummy_probe,
  .destroy  = dummy_destroy,
  .name     = "dummy_probe",
  .module   = THIS_MODULE
};
```

Now we define the probe routine. This function validates if a flash can be found at the address `map->virt`, which is filled by the mapping driver. If it is able to detect a flash, then it allocates the `mtd` structure and the `dummy_private_info` structure. The `mtd` structure is filled with the various driver routines such as read, write, erase, and so on. The `dummy_private_info` structure is filled with the flash-specific information. Refer to Listing 4.1 for implementation of the probe routine.

The most interesting data structures that are initialized in the probe function are the wait queue and the mutex. These are used to prevent concurrent accesses to the flash, which is a requirement for almost all flash devices. Thus whenever an operation such as read or write needs to be performed, the driver needs to check if the flash is not already in use. This is done using the state field, which is set to `FL_READY` at initialization time. If the flash is being used, then the process needs to block on the wait queue until it is awakened. The mutex (spinlock) is used to prevent race problems on SMP machines or in case preemption is enabled.

Next we go to the read routines. The read routine registered with the MTD core is `dummy_flash_read()`, which is called to read `len` number of bytes from the flash offset `from`. Because the writes can span multiple chips, the function `dummy_flash_read_one_chip()` gets called internally to read data from a single chip. Refer to Listing 4.2 for their implementation.

Now we go to the write routines. The routine registered with the MTD core is `dummy_flash_write()`. Because the write can start from unaligned addresses, the function makes sure that it buffers data in such cases and in turn calls the function `dummy_flash_write_oneword()` to write 32-bit data to 32-bit aligned addresses. Refer to Listing 4.3 for their implementation.

The erase function registered to the MTD core is `dummy_flash_erase()`. This function needs to make sure that the erase address specified is sector aligned and the number of bytes to be erased is a multiple of the sector size. The function `dummy_flash_erase_one_block()` is called internally; this erases one sector at a given address. Because the sector erase is time consuming,

Listing 4.1   Dummy Probe Function

```
static struct mtd_info *dummy_probe(struct map_info *map)
{
  struct mtd_info * mtd = kmalloc(sizeof(*mtd), GFP_KERNEL);
  unsigned int i;
  unsigned long size;
  struct dummy_private_info_struct * dummy_private_info =
        kmalloc(sizeof(struct dummy_private_info_struct), GFP_KERNEL);

  if(!dummy_private_info)
  {
    return NULL;
  }
  memset(dummy_private_info, 0, sizeof(*dummy_private_info));

  /* The probe function returns the number of chips identified */
  dummy_private_info->number_of_chips = PROBE_FLASH(map);
  if(!dummy_private_info->number_of_chips)
  {
    kfree(mtd);
    return NULL;
  }

  /* Initialize mtd structure */
  memset(mtd, 0, sizeof(*mtd));
  mtd->erasesize = DUMMY_FLASH_ERASE_SIZE;
  mtd->size = dummy_private_info->number_of_chips * DUMMY_FLASH_SIZE;
  for(size = mtd->size; size > 1; size >>= 1)
    dummy_private_info->chipshift++;
  mtd->priv = map;
  mtd->type = MTD_NORFLASH;
  mtd->flags = MTD_CAP_NORFLASH;
  mtd->name = "DUMMY";
  mtd->erase = dummy_flash_erase;
  mtd->read = dummy_flash_read;
  mtd->write = dummy_flash_write;
  mtd->sync = dummy_flash_sync;

  dummy_private_info->chips = kmalloc(sizeof(struct flchip) *
          dummy_private_info->number_of_chips, GFP_KERNEL);
  memset(dummy_private_info->chips, 0,
        sizeof(*(dummy_private_info->chips)));
  for(i=0; i < dummy_private_info->number_of_chips; i++)
  {
    dummy_private_info->chips[i].start = (DUMMY_FLASH_SIZE * i);
    dummy_private_info->chips[i].state = FL_READY;
    dummy_private_info->chips[i].mutex =
                      &dummy_private_info->chips[i]._spinlock;
    init_waitqueue_head(&dummy_private_info->chips[i].wq);
    spin_lock_init(&dummy_private_info->chips[i]._spinlock);
    dummy_private_info->chips[i].erase_time = DUMMY_FLASH_ERASE_TIME;
  }

  map->fldrv = &dummy_chipdrv;
  map->fldrv_priv = dummy_private_info;

  printk("Probed and found the dummy flash chip\n");
  return mtd;
}
```

Listing 4.2 Dummy Read Routines

```
static inline int dummy_flash_read_one_chip(struct map_info *map,
        struct flchip *chip, loff_t addr, size_t len, u_char *buf)
{
  DECLARE_WAITQUEUE(wait, current);

again:
  spin_lock(chip->mutex);

  if(chip->state != FL_READY)
  {
    set_current_state(TASK_UNINTERRUPTIBLE);
    add_wait_queue(&chip->wq, &wait);
    spin_unlock(chip->mutex);
    schedule();
    remove_wait_queue(&chip->wq, &wait);
    if(signal_pending(current))
      return -EINTR;
    goto again;
  }

  addr += chip->start;
  chip->state = FL_READY;
  map_copy_from(map, buf, addr, len);
  wake_up(&chip->wq);
  spin_unlock(chip->mutex);
  return 0;
}

static int  dummy_flash_read(struct mtd_info *mtd, loff_t from,
                        size_t len,size_t *retlen, u_char *buf)
{
  struct map_info *map = mtd->priv;
  struct dummy_private_info_struct *priv = map->fldrv_priv;
  int chipnum = 0;
  int ret = 0;
  unsigned int ofs;
  *retlen = 0;

  /* Find the chip number and offset for the first chip */
  chipnum = (from >> priv->chipshift);
  ofs = from & ((1 << priv->chipshift) - 1);
  while(len)
  {
    unsigned long to_read;
    if(chipnum >= priv->number_of_chips)
      break;

    /* Check whether the read spills over to the next chip */
    if( (len + ofs - 1) >> priv->chipshift)
      to_read = (1 << priv->chipshift) - ofs;
    else
      to_read = len;
    if( (ret = dummy_flash_read_one_chip(map, &priv->chips[chipnum],
                                    ofs, to_read, buf)))
      break;
```

Listing 4.2   Dummy Read Routines (continued)

```
    *retlen += to_read;
    len -= to_read;
    buf += to_read;
    ofs=0;
    chipnum++;
  }
  return ret;
}
```

this function preempts the calling task making it sleep for DUMMY_FLASH_
ERASE_TIME jiffies. At the end of the erase, the MTD core is signaled that
the erase is finished by setting the erase state to MTD_ERASE_DONE and then
any erase callbacks that are registered get invoked before returning. Refer to
Listing 4.4 for the implementation of erase routines.

The sync function is invoked when the flash device is closed. This function
has to make sure that none of the flash chips are in use at the time of closing;
if they are then the function makes the calling process wait until all the chips
go into the unused state. Refer to Listing 4.5 for dummy flash sync function
implementation.

The function dummy_destroy is invoked in case the flash driver is loaded
as a module. When the module is unloaded, the function dummy_destroy()
does all the cleanup.

```
static void dummy_destroy(struct mtd_info *mtd)
{
  struct dummy_private_info_struct *priv =
                  ((struct map_info *)mtd->priv)->fldrv_priv;
  kfree(priv->chips);
}
```

The following are the initialization and exit functions.

```
int __init dummy_flash_init(void)
{
  register_mtd_chip_driver(&dummy_chipdrv);
  return 0;
}

void __exit dummy_flash_exit(void)
{
  unregister_mtd_chip_driver(&dummy_chipdrv);
}

module_init(dummy_flash_init);
module_exit(dummy_flash_exit);

MODULE_LICENSE("GPL");
MODULE_AUTHOR("Embedded Linux book");
MODULE_DESCRIPTION("Sample MTD driver");
```

Listing 4.3   Dummy Write Routines

```
static inline int dummy_flash_write_oneword(struct map_info *map,
                    struct flchip *chip, loff_t addr, __u32 datum)
{
  DECLARE_WAITQUEUE(wait, current);

again:
  spin_lock(chip->mutex);

  if(chip->state != FL_READY)
  {
    set_current_state(TASK_UNINTERRUPTIBLE);
    add_wait_queue(&chip->wq, &wait);
    spin_unlock(chip->mutex);
    schedule();
    remove_wait_queue(&chip->wq, &wait);
    if(signal_pending(current))
      return -EINTR;
    goto again;
  }

  addr += chip->start;
  chip->state = FL_WRITING;
  WRITE_FLASH_ONE_WORD(map, chip->start, addr, datum);
  chip->state = FL_READY;
  wake_up(&chip->wq);
  spin_unlock(chip->mutex);
  return 0;
}

static int  dummy_flash_write(struct mtd_info *mtd, loff_t from,
                    size_t len,size_t *retlen, const u_char *buf)
{
  struct map_info *map = mtd->priv;
  struct dummy_private_info_struct *priv = map->fldrv_priv;
  int chipnum = 0;
  union {
    unsigned int idata;
    char cdata[4]; }
  wbuf;
  unsigned int ofs;
  int ret;

  *retlen = 0;
  chipnum = (from >> priv->chipshift);
  ofs = from & ((1 << priv->chipshift) - 1);

  /* First check if the first word to be written is aligned */
  if(ofs & 3)
  {
    unsigned int from_offset = ofs & (~3);
    unsigned int orig_copy_num = ofs - from_offset;
    unsigned int to_copy_num = (4 - orig_copy_num);
    unsigned int i, len;

    map_copy_from(map, wbuf.cdata, from_offset +
                  priv->chips[chipnum].start, 4);
```

Listing 4.3   Dummy Write Routines (continued)

```
    /* Overwrite with the new contents from buf[] */
    for(i=0; i < to_copy_num; i++)
      wbuf.cdata[orig_copy_num + i] = buf[i];

    if((ret = dummy_flash_write_oneword(map, &priv->chips[chipnum],
                                   from_offset, wbuf.idata)) < 0)
      return ret;

    ofs += i;
    buf += i;
    *retlen += i;
    len -= i;
    if(ofs >> priv->chipshift)
    {
      chipnum++;
      ofs = 0;
    }
  }

  /* Now write all the aligned words */
  while(len / 4)
  {
    memcpy(wbuf.cdata, buf, 4);
    if((ret = dummy_flash_write_oneword(map, &priv->chips[chipnum],
                                   ofs, wbuf.idata)) < 0)
      return ret;

    ofs += 4;
    buf += 4;
    *retlen += 4;
    len -= 4;
    if(ofs >> priv->chipshift)
    {
      chipnum++;
      ofs = 0;
    }
  }

  /* Write the last word */
  if(len)
  {
    unsigned int i=0;

    map_copy_from(map, wbuf.cdata, ofs + priv->chips[chipnum].start,
                  4);
    for(; i<len; i++)
      wbuf.cdata[i] = buf[i];

    if((ret = dummy_flash_write_oneword(map, &priv->chips[chipnum],
                                   ofs, wbuf.idata)) < 0)
      return ret;
    *retlen += i;
  }

  return 0;
}
```

Listing 4.4   Dummy Erase Routines

```
static int dummy_flash_erase_one_block(struct map_info *map,
                    struct flchip *chip,  unsigned long addr)
{
  DECLARE_WAITQUEUE(wait, current);
again:
  spin_lock(chip->mutex);

  if(chip->state != FL_READY)
  {
    set_current_state(TASK_UNINTERRUPTIBLE);
    add_wait_queue(&chip->wq, &wait);
    spin_unlock(chip->mutex);
    schedule();
    remove_wait_queue(&chip->wq, &wait);
    if(signal_pending(current))
      return -EINTR;
    goto again;
  }

  chip->state = FL_ERASING;
  addr += chip->start;
  ERASE_FLASH_SECTOR(map, chip->start, addr);

  spin_unlock(chip->mutex);
  schedule_timeout(chip->erase_time);
  if(signal_pending(current))
    return -EINTR;

  /* We have been woken after the timeout. Take the mutex to proceed */
  spin_lock(chip->mutex);

  /* Add any error checks if the flash sector has not been erased. */

  /* We assume that here the flash erase has been completed */
  chip->state = FL_READY;
  wake_up(&chip->wq);
  spin_unlock(chip->mutex);
  return 0;
}

static int dummy_flash_erase(struct mtd_info *mtd,
                        struct erase_info *instr)
{
  struct map_info *map = mtd->priv;
  struct dummy_private_info_struct *priv = map->fldrv_priv;
  int chipnum = 0;
  unsigned long addr;
  int len;
  int ret;

  /* Some error checkings initially */
  if( (instr->addr > mtd->size) ||
      ((instr->addr + instr->len) > mtd->size) ||
      instr->addr & (mtd->erasesize -1)))
    return -EINVAL;
```

Listing 4.4   Dummy Erase Routines (continued)

```
  /* Find the chip number for the first chip */
  chipnum = (instr->addr >> priv->chipshift);
  addr = instr->addr & ((1 << priv->chipshift) - 1);
  len = instr->len;
  while(len)
  {
    if( (ret = dummy_flash_erase_one_block(map, &priv-
>chips[chipnum], addr)) < 0)
      return ret;
    addr += mtd->erasesize;
    len -= mtd->erasesize;
    if(addr >> priv->chipshift)
    {
      addr = 0;
      chipnum++;
    }
  }

  instr->state = MTD_ERASE_DONE;
  if(instr->callback)
    instr->callback(instr);
  return 0;
}
```

4.5 The Flash-Mapping Drivers

Irrespective of the type of device (NAND or NOR), the basis of the mapping-driver operations is to get the `mtd_info` structure populated (by calling the appropriate probe routines) and then register with the MTD core. The `mtd_info` will have different function pointers depending on the device type. The `mtd_info` structures are placed in an array `mtd_table[]`. A maximum of 16 such devices can be stored in this table. How the entries in the `mtd_table` are exported as character and block devices is explained later. The process of flash-mapping driver can be split into:

- Creating and populating the `mtd_info` structure
- Registering `mtd_info` with the MTD core

4.5.1 Filling up `mtd_info` for NOR Flash Chip

The low-level NOR hardware is dependent on the board regarding the following things in case your flash is connected directly on the processor hardware bus (as is the case normally).

- The address to which the flash is memory mapped
- The size of the flash
- The bus width; this can be an 8-, 16-, or 32-bit bus
- Routines to do 8-,16-, and 32-bit read and write
- Routines to do bulk copy

Listing 4.5   Dummy Sync Routine

```
static void dummy_flash_sync(struct mtd_info *mtd)
{
  struct map_info *map = mtd->priv;
  struct dummy_private_info_struct *priv = map->fldrv_priv;
  struct flchip *chip;
  int i;

  DECLARE_WAITQUEUE(wait, current);

  for(i=0; i< priv->number_of_chips;i++)
  {
    chip = &priv->chips[i];
again:
    spin_lock(chip->mutex);

    switch(chip->state)
    {
      case FL_READY:
      case FL_STATUS:
        chip->oldstate = chip->state;
        chip->state = FL_SYNCING;
        break;
      case FL_SYNCING:
        spin_unlock(chip->mutex);
        break;
      default:
        add_wait_queue(&chip->wq, &wait);
        spin_unlock(chip->mutex);
        schedule();
        remove_wait_queue(&chip->wq, &wait);
        goto again;
    }
  }

  for(i--; i >=0; i--)
  {
    chip = &priv->chips[i];
    spin_lock(chip->mutex);
    if(chip->state == FL_SYNCING)
    {
      chip->state = chip->oldstate;
      wake_up(&chip->wq);
    }
    spin_unlock(chip->mutex);
  }
}
```

The NOR flash map is defined in the `map_info` data structure and the database for the various board configurations is found in the `drivers/mtd/maps` directory. Once the `map_info` structure is filled, then the function `do_map_probe()` is invoked with the `map_info` as an argument. This function returns a pointer to the `mtd_info` structure filled with the function pointers for operating on the flash chip.

Table 4.2   ALE and CLE Pins Usage

ALE	CLE	Register
0	0	Data register
0	1	Command register
1	0	Address register

4.5.2 *Filling up* mtd_info *for NAND Flash Chip*

As mentioned earlier, the NAND flash access is done by connecting the data and command lines to the processor IO lines. The following are the important pins found on a NAND flash chip.

- CE (Chip Enable) pin: When this pin is asserted low the NAND flash chip is selected.
- WE (Write Enable) pin: When this pin is asserted low, the NAND flash chip accepts data from the processor.
- RE (Read Enable) pin: When this pin is asserted low, the NAND flash chip sends out data to the processor.
- CLE (Command Latch Enable) pin and ALE (Address Latch Enable) pin.

These pins determine the destination of the operations on the NAND chip. Table 4.2 explains how these pins are used.

- WP (Write Protect) pin: This pin can be used for write protection.
- RB (Ready Busy) pin: This is used in data-transfer phases to indicate that the chip is in use.
- IO pins: This is used for data transfer.

Unlike the NOR flash chip that calls the do_map_probe() to allocate the mtd_info structure, a NAND-based mapping driver needs to allocate the mtd_info structure. The key to this is a structure nand_chip, which is filled by the NAND mapping driver. The following steps are done by the NAND mapping driver.

- Allocate the mtd_info structure.
- Allocate a nand_chip structure and fill up the required fields.
- Make the mtd_info's priv field point to the nand_chip structure.
- Call the function nand_scan(), which will probe for the NAND chip, and fill the mtd_info structure with the functions for NAND operation.
- Register the mtd_info structure with the MTD core.

The parameters for the NAND that are stored in the nand_chip structure can be classified into:

- Mandatory parameters:
  - IO_ADDR_R, IO_ADDR_W: These are the addresses for accessing the IO lines of the NAND chip.
  - hwcontrol(): This function implements the board-specific mechanism for setting and clearing the CLE, ALE, and the CE pins.
  - eccmode: This is used to denote the ECC type for the NAND flash. These include no ECC at all, software ECC, and hardware ECC.
- Mandatory parameters if hardware does ECC. Some hardware provides ECC generation; in that case the following functions need to be implemented. In case of software ECC, the NAND driver by default provides the following functions.
  - calculate_ecc(): Function to generate the ECC
  - correct_data(): Function for ECC correction
  - enable_hwecc(): Function to enable HW ECC generation
- Nonmandatory parameters. The driver provides default functions/values for the following parameters. However they can be overridden by the mapping driver:
  - dev_ready(): This function is used to find the state of the flash.
  - cmdfunc(): This function is for sending commands to the flash.
  - waitfunc(): This function is invoked after a write or erase is done. The default function provided by the NAND driver is a polling function; in case the board can hook the RB pin to an interrupt line, this function can be converted to an interrupt-driven function.
  - chip_delay: This is the delay for transferring data from the NAND array to its registers; the default value is 20 us.

4.5.3 *Registering* mtd_info

The following steps are generic and apply to both NAND and NOR flashes. The basis of the registration is the function add_mtd_device() function, which adds the device to the mtd_table[] array. However in most of the cases you would not use this function directly because you want to create partitions on the chip.

Partitioning

Partitioning allows multiple partitions on a flash to be created and to be added into different slots in the mtd_table[] array. Thus the partitions will be exported as multiple devices to the application. The various partitions share the same functions for accessing the array. For example, you would want to divide the 4-MB flash into a 1-MB and 3-MB partition as shown in Figure 4.3.

The key to partitioning is the mtd_partition data structure. You would define an array of this data structure to export the partition.

```
struct mtd_partition partition_info[] =
{
  { .name="part1", .offset=0, .size= 1*1024*1024},
```

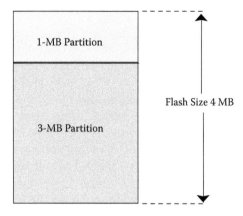

Figure 4.3   Flash partitioned into two halves.

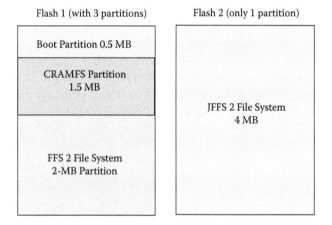

Figure 4.4   Multipartition flash.

```
    { .name="part2", .offset=1*1024*1024, .size= 3*1024*1024}
    }
```

The partitions are added using the `add_mtd_partition()` function. More details of this may be found in the mapping driver example in Section 4.5.4.

Concatenation

This is a powerful technique that allows multiple devices to merge separate devices into a single device. Assume that you have two flash devices on the system. Figure 4.4 shows one flash having three partitions and the other flash having a single partition.

As the file system needs to span across two flash chips, normally you would need to create two file systems on each of the chips. This is a cumbersome technique because you would need to maintain two file systems.

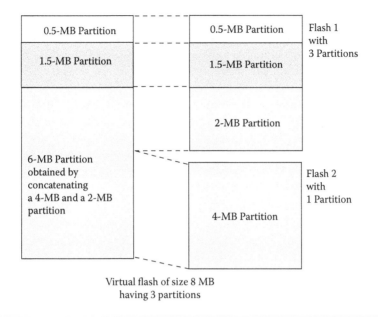

Virtual flash of size 8 MB
having 3 partitions

Figure 4.5   Two flash devices concatenated into one virtual device.

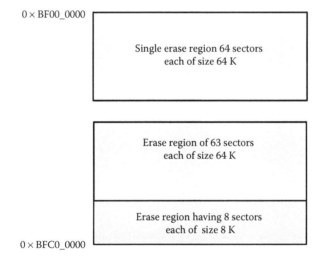

Figure 4.6   Flash memory map.

This can be prevented by concatenating the two flash chips into a single virtual device as shown in Figure 4.5. Then only one instance of the file system needs to be mounted on the system.

4.5.4 Sample Mapping Driver for NOR Flash

Let's take an example of a MIPS-based board having two flash chips placed at addresses as shown in Figure 4.6.

The following are the usage details of these flash chips.

- The first flash chip is mapped at address 0xBFC00000 and is of size 4 MB. The first flash is the boot flash and it has two erase regions. The first erase region has eight sectors each of size 8 K; this 64-K area is used for storing boot loader and boot-up configuration parameters. The second erase region has sectors of size 64 K and is totally used for storing a JFFS2 file system.
- The second flash chip is mapped at address 0xBF000000 and is again of size 4 MB. The second flash contains only one erase region with all sectors of size 64 K. This flash is totally used for storing the JFFS2 file system.

The requirement from our flash-mapping driver is to partition the first flash starting at address 0xBFC00000 into two. The first partition of size 64 K will be the boot partition. The second partition will be concatenated with the flash starting at address 0xBF000000 to store the JFFS2 file system.

First let us start with the header files and the definitions.

```
/* mtd-bsp.c */
#include <linux/config.h>
#include <linux/module.h>
#include <linux/types.h>
#include <linux/kernel.h>
#include <asm/io.h>
#include <linux/mtd/mtd.h>
#include <linux/mtd/map.h>
#include <linux/mtd/cfi.h>
#include <linux/mtd/partitions.h>
#include <linux/mtd/concat.h>

#define WINDOW_ADDR_0    0xBFC00000
#define WINDOW_SIZE_0    0x00400000
#define WINDOW_ADDR_1    0xBF000000
#define WINDOW_SIZE_1    0x00400000
```

The map_info contains the details of the starting address (physical) of each chip, size, and bus width. These are used by the chip probe routines.

```
static struct map_info dummy_mips_map[2] = {
  {
   .name      = "DUMMY boot flash",
   .phys      = WINDOW_ADDR_0,
   .size      = WINDOW_SIZE_0,
   .bankwidth = 4,
  },
  {
   .name      = "Dummy non boot flash",
   .phys      = WINDOW_ADDR_1,
   .size      = WINDOW_SIZE_1,
   .bankwidth = 4,
  }
};
```

The following structure is used to set up the partitions on the boot flash.

```
static struct mtd_partition boot_flash_partitions [] = {
 {
  .name    = "BOOT",
  .offset  = 0,
  .size    = 0x00010000,
 },
 {
  .name    = "JFFS2",
  .offset  = 0x00010000,
  .size    = 0x003f0000,
 },
};

/*
 * Following structure holds the mtd_info pointers for the
 * partitions we will be concatenating
 */
static struct mtd_info *concat_partitions[2];

/*
 * Following structure holds the mtd_info structure pointers for
 * each of the flash devices
 */
static struct mtd_info * mymtd[2], *concat_mtd;
```

The function `init_dummy_mips_mtd_bsp()` is the main function. Refer to Listing 4.6 for its implementation. The function does the following.

- Probes for the flash at the address 0xBFC00000 and populates the MTD structure for this flash in `mymtd[0]`
- Probes for the flash at the address 0xBF000000 and populates the MTD structure for this flash in `mymtd[1]`
- Creates two partitions for the flash with starting address 0xBFC00000
- Concatenates the second partition with the flash whose starting address is 0xBF000000 and then creates a new device by calling the function `add_mtd_device()`

Finally the cleanup function is as follows.

```
static void __exit cleanup_dummy_mips_mtd_bsp(void)
{
 mtd_concat_destroy(concat_mtd);
 del_mtd_partitions(mymtd[0]);
 map_destroy(mymtd[0]);
 map_destroy(mymtd[1]);
}

module_init (init_dummy_mips_mtd_bsp);
module_exit (cleanup_dummy_mips_mtd_bsp);
MODULE_LICENSE ("GPL");
MODULE_AUTHOR ("Embedded Linux book");
MODULE_DESCRIPTION ("Sample Mapping driver");
```

Listing 4.6 `init_dummy_mips_mtd_bsp` **Function**

```
int __init init_dummy_mips_mtd_bsp (void)
{

  /* First probe for the boot flash */
  dummy_mips_map[0].virt =
    (unsigned long)ioremap(
                  dummy_mips_map[0].phys,dummy_mips_map[0].size);
  simple_map_init(&dummy_mips_map[0]);
  mymtd[0] = do_map_probe("cfi_probe", &dummy_mips_map[0]);
  if(mymtd[0])
    mymtd[0]->owner = THIS_MODULE;

    /* Repeat for the second flash */
  dummy_mips_map[1].virt =
    (unsigned long)ioremap(dummy_mips_map[1].phys,
                          dummy_mips_map[1].size);
  simple_map_init(&dummy_mips_map[1]);
  mymtd[1] = do_map_probe("cfi_probe", &dummy_mips_map[1]);
  if(mymtd[1])
    mymtd[1]->owner = THIS_MODULE;
  if (!mymtd[0] || !mymtd[1])
    return -ENXIO;

 /*
  * Now we will partition the boot flash. We are interested in the
  * new mtd object for the second partition since we will be
  * concatenating it with the other flash.
  */
  boot_flash_partitions[1].mtdp = &concat_partitions[0];
  add_mtd_partitions(mymtd[0], boot_flash_partitions, 2);

  /*
   * concat_partitions[1] should contain the mtd_info pointer for the
   * 2nd partition. Do the concatenation
   */
  concat_partitions[1] = mymtd[1];
  concat_mtd = mtd_concat_create(concat_partitions, 2,
                              "JFFS2 flash concatenate");
  if(concat_mtd)
    add_mtd_device(concat_mtd);
  return 0;
}
```

4.6 MTD Block and Character Devices

As mentioned earlier, the MTD devices are exported in two modes to the user
space: as character and as block devices. The character devices are represented
using the following device names.

```
/dev/mtd0
/dev/mtdr0
/dev/mtd1
```

```
/dev/mtdr1
...
/dev/mtd15
/dev/mtdr15
```

All the character devices have a major number of 90. The character devices are exported as either read-write character devices or read-only character devices. This usage is obtained using minor numbers. All MTD devices having odd minor numbers (1, 3, 5, . . .) are exported as read-only devices. So both /dev/mtd1 and /dev/mtdr1 point to the same device (the device holding the second slot in the mtd_table[]); the former can be opened in read-write mode whereas the latter can be opened only in the read-only mode. The following is the list of ioctls that are supported by the MTD character devices.

- MEMGETREGIONCOUNT: Ioctl to pass the number of erase regions back to the user
- MEMGETREGIONINFO: Ioctl to get erase region information
- MEMERASE: Ioctl to erase specific sector of flash
- MEMWRITEOOB/MEMREADOOB: Ioctls used for accessing out-of-band data
- MEMLOCK/MEMUNLOCK: Ioctls used for locking specified sectors provided there is support from hardware

Block devices have a major number of 31. Up to 16 minor devices are supported. The block devices are used to mount file systems on top of the flash devices (see Figure 4.7).

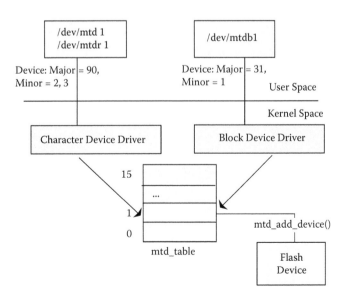

Figure 4.7   MTD device exported as character and block device.

4.7 Mtdutils Package

The mtdutils package is a set of useful programs such as for creating file systems and testing flash device integrity. Note that some of the utilities are host based (such as tools to create a JFFS2 file image) and some can be used on the target (such as utilities to erase a flash device). The target-based programs need to be cross-compiled for usage on the target. The following is a description of the individual utilities in this package.

- `erase`: This utility is used to erase a specified number of blocks at a given offset.
- `eraseall`: This utility is used to erase an entire device (because partitions are represented by devices, an entire partition can be erased using this program).
- `nftl_fromat`: This utility is used to create a NFTL (NAND Flash Translation Layer) partition on an MTD device. This gets used for the disk-on-chip systems to format the disk on a chip.
- `nftldump`: This utility is used to dump the NFTL partition.
- `doc_loadbios`: This disk-on-chip utility is used to reprogram the disk-on-chip with a new firmware (such as GRUB).
- `doc_loadip1`: This utility is used to load an IPL (initialization code) into the DOC flash.
- `ftl_fromat`: This utility is used to create an FTL partition on a flash device.
- `nanddump`: This utility dumps the contents of NAND chips (either raw or those contained in the DOC).
- `nandtest`: This utility tests NAND devices (such as writing and reading back to a NAND flash and checking if the write succeeds).
- `nandwrite`: This utility is used to write a binary image into a NAND flash.
- `mkfs.jffs`: Given a directory tree, this utility creates a JFFS image, which can be burnt into the flash.
- `mkfs.jffs2`: Given a directory tree, this utility creates a JFFS2 image, which can be burnt into the flash.
- `lock`: This utility locks one or more sectors of the flash.
- `unlock`: This utility unlocks all sectors of a flash device.
- `mtd_debug`: This is a very useful utility that can be used to get information about a flash device, read, write, and erase to flash devices.
- `fcp`: This is a flash copy utility used to copy a file into a flash device.

4.8 Embedded File Systems

This section talks about the popular embedded file systems. Most of them are flash-based whereas the rest are memory-based file systems. Memory-based file systems can be used at boot-up time to hold a root file system and also for storing volatile data that need not be saved across reboots; these are discussed first.

4.8.1 Ramdisk

Ramdisk, as the name suggests, is a way by which Linux emulates a hard disk using memory. You would need a ramdisk when you do not have a traditional storage device such as a hard disk or a flash for storing a root file system. Note that ramdisk is not a file system but a mechanism by which you can load an actual file system into memory and use it as the root file system.

Initrd provides a mechanism by which a boot loader loads the kernel image along with a root file system into memory. Using initrd would require the following effort.

- Creating the initrd image and packing it with the kernel image. You need to create the ramdisk image on the development (host) machine. Then you need to pack the ramdisk image with the kernel. On certain platforms this option is available when building the kernel. Normally there is an ELF section called the `.initrd` that holds the ramdisk image, which can be directly used by the boot loader.
- Changes to the boot loader to load the initrd.

Initrd also gives a mechanism by which you can switch to a new root file system at a later point of time during system execution. Thus you can use initrd for system recovery and upgrade procedures too for your production releases. Chapter 8 discusses the steps necessary for building an initrd image.

4.8.2 RAMFS

Often an embedded system has files that are not useful across reboots and these would be normally stored in the `/tmp` directory. Storing these files in memory would be a better option than storing them in flash because flash writes are expensive. Instead you could use a RAMFS (RAM File System); these do not have a fixed size and they shrink and grow with the files stored.

4.8.3 CRAMFS (Compressed RAM File System)

This is a very useful file system for flash storage and was introduced in the 2.4 kernel. It is a high-compression "read-only" file system. CRAMFS is a regular file system; that is, it goes via the buffer cache to talk to a block device holding the actual data. Hence you need to enable the MTD block device driver mode you want to use CRAMFS. CRAMFS uses the zlib routines for compression and it does compression for every 4-KB (page size) block. The CRAMFS image that needs to be burned in flash can be created using a program called `mkcramfs`.

4.8.4 Journaling Flash File Systems — JFFS and JFFS2

The traditional file systems were not designed for embedded systems and not for flash types of storage mechanisms. Let us do a quick recap of what we want out of the flash file systems:

- Wear leveling
- No data corruption on sudden power outage
- Directly use the MTD-level APIs instead of going through the flash translation layers

In 1999, Axis Communications released the JFFS for the Linux 2.0 kernel with all the above features. It was quickly ported to the 2.2 and 2.3 kernel series. But then it lacked support for compression and hence the JFFS2 project was started. JFFS2 was released to the 2.4 kernel series and quickly overtook JFFS because of its advanced features. Both JFFS and JFFS2 are log-structured file systems; any change to a file gets recorded as a log, which gets directly stored on the flash (logs are also called nodes).

The contents of this log will be:

- Identification of the file to which the log belongs
- Version that is unique per log belonging to a particular file
- Metadata such as timestamp
- Data and data size
- Offset of the data in the file

A write to a file creates a log that records the offset in the file to where the data is written and the size of the data written along with the actual data. When a file needs to be read, the logs are played back and using the data size and the offset, the file gets re-created. As time proceeds, certain logs become obsolete partially or totally; they need to be cleaned. This process is called garbage collection. The output of garbage collection is to identify clean erase blocks. Garbage collection should also provide wear leveling to make sure that all erase blocks have a chance to appear in the free list.

The main features of the JFFS2 file system are as follows.

- *Management of erase blocks:* In JFFS2, the erase blocks are placed in three lists: clean, dirty, and free. The clean list contains only valid logs (i.e., logs not invalidated by newer ones). The dirty list contains one or many logs that are obsolete and hence can be purged when garbage collection is called. The free list contains no logs and hence can be used for storing new logs.
- *Garbage collection:* JFFS2 garbage collection happens in the context of a separate thread, which gets started when you mount a JFFS2 file system. For every 99 out of 100 times, this thread will pick up a block from the dirty list and for the other one out of 100 will pick up a block from the clean list to ensure wear leveling. JFFS2 reserves five blocks for doing garbage collection (this number seems to have been decided by heuristics).
- *Compression:* The distinguishing factor between JFFS and JFFS2 is that JFFS2 gives a host of compression including zlib and rubin.

The JFFS/JFFS2 file system image can be created on the target using the mkfs.jffs and mkfs.jffs2 commands. Both of these commands take a directory tree as an argument and create an image on the host development machine. These images need to be downloaded onto the target and burnt on the corresponding flash partition; this support is provided by most of the Linux boot loaders.

4.8.5 NFS — Network File System

The network file system can be used to mount a file system over the network. The popular desktop file systems EXT2 and EXT3 are exportable via NFS; hence the developer can use a standard Linux desktop for storing an EXT2 or EXT3 file system and access it as a root file system on the embedded system. During the debugging stage, often the developer would like to make changes to the root file system. In such a case writing to flash can be costly (because flash has limited write cycles) and time consuming. NFS can be a good choice provided the network driver is ready. Also with NFS you do not have any size restrictions because all the storage is done on the remote server.

The Linux kernel provides a mechanism for automatically mounting a file system using NFS at boot time using the following steps.

- The config options `CONFIG_NFS_FS`, which allow you to mount a file system from a remote server and `CONFIG_ROOT_NFS`, which allows you to use NFS as root file system needs to be turned on at build time. Also if you are mounting an EXT2 or EXT3 root file system from the remote desktop, the support for that file system needs to be included in the kernel.
- Because an IP address becomes necessary to connect to a NFS server at boot time, you might want to turn on the network auto configuration using BOOTP, RARP, or DHCP.
- Kernel command-line parameters to specify the NFS server have to be specified.

For more details on the syntax of the command-line arguments refer to `Documentation/nfsroot.txt` in the kernel source tree.

4.8.6 PROC File System

The proc file system is a logical file system used by the kernel to export its information to the external world. The proc file system can be used for system monitoring, debugging, and tuning. The proc files are created on the fly when they get opened. The files can be read-only or read-write depending on the information exported by the files. The read-only proc files can be used to get some kernel status that cannot be modified at runtime. Examples of read-only proc files are the process status information. The read-write proc files contain information that can be changed at runtime; the kernel uses the changed value on the fly. An example of this is the tcp keep-alive time. The proc file system gets mounted by the startup scripts at the standard mount point /proc.

This file system makes use of the system RAM. Although system RAM is expensive, still the advantages of having the proc file system outweigh the disadvantages. The proc file system gets used by standard Linux programs such as ps and mount. Hence readers are advised not to remove the proc file system unless they are very sure.

4.9 Optimizing Storage Space

This section deals with a major problem often encountered on embedded systems, which is how to use the storage space effectively. This is because flash chips are costly. Though their prices have seen sharp declines in the last few years, they are still a major component of the hardware BOM (Bill Of Materials). The problem gets more acute when you pick up an open source from the Web for running on your system; unless the program has been written keeping in mind the embedded system, there is a very small chance that the program has been optimized for space. Such a program might have lots of unwanted code, which may add to unwanted storage space. We divide this section into three main parts:

- Optimizing the Linux kernel for effective storage
- Space optimizing the applications
- Using compressed file systems for storing kernel and applications. Because the file systems such as CRAMFS and JFFS2 that provide compression have already been discussed, this section ignores this topic.

4.9.1 Kernel Space Optimization

The main way to reduce the size of the kernel is to remove unwanted code from the kernel. Other than this, the compiler optimization technique (using the -Os option) can be used to make smaller kernel images. (This holds true for applications too.) The 2.6 kernel has a separate build option for embedded systems; the CONFIG_EMBEDDED option is used to build a sleeker kernel. Also some kernel submodules such as the swap subsystem can be disabled at build time. Irrespective of the kernel version, it is imperative to make sure that while you are configuring the kernel for choosing the various subsystems only the necessary options are selected lest you should bloat the kernel size unnecessarily.

The 2.6 kernel has an open source community project that is aimed at making it run on embedded systems. This is the "Linux tiny kernel project" started by Matt Mackall. The aim of this project is to maintain a kernel source tree that includes patches aimed at making the kernel size smaller and making the kernel use memory optimally. Some of the interesting patches that are aimed at making a smaller kernel include:

- Option to remove printk and all the strings passed to printk
- Compilation checks that complains too much usage of inline functions because they bloat code size

The tiny kernel tree can be referenced at www.selenic.com.

Because kernel memory tuning shares many tricks with kernel space optimization, the last section of this chapter discusses techniques for tuning kernel memory.

4.9.2 Application Space Optimization

The application space optimization can be effectively done using the following steps.

- Pruning individual applications with respect to unwanted code
- Using tools such as the library optimizer
- Using smaller and sleeker programs/distributions aimed at embedded systems
- Using a smaller C library such as uClibc

Library Optimizer

This tool is intended to remove unwanted code from shared libraries. Remember from the discussion of shared libraries in Chapter 2 that the shared libraries may contain unwanted code that may never get referenced but still may waste valuable storage space. The library optimizer is an open source tool that is used at the end of the build to scan shared libraries and rebuild them so that they contain only the necessary object files necessary for the system. The Web site for the development of the library optimizer is http://libraryopt.sourceforge.net.

However, the library optimizer cannot be used on systems on which applications need to be downloaded and executed dynamically (it may happen very rarely for embedded systems) because the C library may not contain the functions necessary for the new applications to execute.

Smaller C Libraries

The C library is a crucial component of the user space; all applications need to link against the C library for commonly used functions. The standard C library libc.so and libc.a, which is available from the GNU Web site, is often known as the glibc. However, the glibc is aimed more towards desktop and server environments. It contains redundant code that does not find much use on embedded systems thus using expensive storage space. To quote the maintainer of glibc, Ulrich Drepper,

> Normally, something like glib or the gnu utilities would not be for embedded systems. ... The ports are not really meant for embedded environments, but the systems which Linux runs on (i.e. [S]VGA, Hard drive, mouse, 64mb ram, etc).

There are two popular alternatives to using glibc on embedded systems: the dietlibc and the uclibc. Both are discussed below.

- *Dietlibc:* dietlibc is a small libc, which can be downloaded from http://www.dietlibc.org/
- *Uclibc:* uclibc is a very popular embedded libc. This project was started and is maintained by Erik Andersen at the following Web site: www.uclibc.org. One important feature of uclibc is that it can be used on both MMU and MMU-less processors. The list of processors that are supported by uclibc are:
  - x86
  - ARM
  - MIPS
  - PPC
  - M68K
  - SH
  - V850
  - CRIS
  - Microblaze™

4.9.3 Applications for Embedded Linux

We now discuss some popular distributions and applications used for embedded linux systems.

Busybox

The Busybox program is a multicall program. This means that a single small executable implements some commonly used programs in an embedded system. Busybox is aimed at embedded systems. It also has a configure mechanism wherein only the required programs for the system can be chosen at build time. The Busybox can be downloaded from http://busybox.net. The Busybox contains the following main programs known as applets in Busybox terminology.

- Shells such as the `ash`, `lash`, `hush`, and so on
- Core utilities such as `cat`, `chmod`, `cp`, `dd`, `mv`, `ls`, `pwd`, `rm`, and so on
- Process control and monitoring utilities such as `ps`, `kill`, and so on
- Module-loading utilities such as `lsmod`, `rmmod`, `modprobe`, `insmod`, and `depmod`
- System tools such `reboot`, `init`, and so on
- Networking utilities such as `ifconfig`, `route`, `ping`, `tftp`, `httpd`, `telnet`, `wget`, `udhcpc` (dhcp client), and so on
- Log-in and password management utilities such as `login`, `passwd`, `adduser`, `deluser`, and so on
- Archival utilities such as `ar`, `cpio`, `gzip`, `tar`, and so on
- System logging utilities such as `syslogd`

Building Busybox is divided into two steps:

- *Configure:* Run `make menuconfig` to select applets you want to build.
- *Building busybox:* Run `make` to build `busybox` executable.

The next step is installing Busybox in your target. This is achieved by calling Busybox with the `--install` option in the system startup script (for example, `rc` script).

```
busybox mount -n -t proc /proc /proc
busybox --install -s
```

The Busybox `install` command creates soft links of all the applets selected during configuration process. For example, after installation `ls -l` in the `/bin` directory gives output as below.

```
-rwxr-xr-x   1 0        0      1065308 busybox
lrwxrwxrwx   1 0        0            7 init -> busybox
lrwxrwxrwx   1 0        0           12 ash -> /bin/busybox
lrwxrwxrwx   1 0        0           12 cat -> /bin/busybox
lrwxrwxrwx   1 0        0           12 chmod -> /bin/busybox
lrwxrwxrwx   1 0        0           12 cp -> /bin/busybox
lrwxrwxrwx   1 0        0           12 dd -> /bin/busybox
lrwxrwxrwx   1 0        0           12 echo -> /bin/busybox
```

As you can see, for each selected applet, Busybox `install` has created a soft link by the name of that applet to itself. When any program is invoked (say `chmod`), Busybox fetches the program name from its first command-line argument and calls the associated function.

Tinylogin

Tinylogin is a multicall program similar to Busybox and is used for implementing UNIX log-in and access applications. The following is the list of functionalities implemented by Tinylogin.

- Adding and deleting users
- `login` and `getty` applications
- Changing password `passwd` application

Tinylogin can be downloaded from www.tinylogin.org.

Ftp Server

An ftp server is useful to copy files to and from an embedded system. There are two ftp servers available, the standard wu-ftpd server and the more popular proftpd server, which is highly configurable. They can be downloaded from www.wu-ftpd.org and www.proftpd.org, respectively.

Web Server

Web servers are needed for remote management of an embedded device. There are many Web servers aimed at embedded Linux, of which the most popular are discussed below.

- *BOA:* An embedded single-tasking http server available from http://www. boa.org/
- *mini_httpd:* A small Web server meant for low and medium Web traffic. It can be downloaded from http://www.acme.com/
- *GoAhead:* It is a popular open source Web server meant for embedded systems and can be downloaded from http://www.goahead.com

4.10 Tuning Kernel Memory

This section explains techniques to reduce memory usage by the kernel. The Linux kernel does not participate in paging and hence the entire kernel (code, data, and stack) always resides in main memory. Before going into the optimization techniques, let us understand how to estimate the memory utilized by the kernel. You can find the static memory that will be used by the kernel by using the `size` command; this utility lists the various section sizes and total size for an object file. The following is the output on a kernel compiled for the MIPS processor.

```
bash >mips-linux-size vmlinux
text        data      bss      dec      hex     filename
 621244    44128    128848   794220   c1e6c     vmlinux
```

The above output shows that 621 K of memory is used by kernel text, 44 K by the data, and 128 K by the BSS. Note that the BSS is not part of the kernel storage image; the start-up code allocates memory for the BSS and fills it with 0, thus effectively creating it during runtime.

The next piece of useful information is displayed during Linux start-up:

```
Memory: 61204k/65536k available (1347k kernel code, 4008k
reserved, 999k data, 132k init, 0k highmem)
```

The above message indicates that out of the 65,536 K memory present on the system, around 4 M has been used for storing the kernel text, code, and init sections and for setting up the data structures for memory management. The rest of the 61 M is available to the kernel for dynamic memory allocation.

The `/proc/meminfo` records the runtime memory on the system. Sample output for the 2.4 kernel is:

```
# cat /proc/meminfo

           total:      used:      free:   shared: buffers:   cached:
Mem:    62894080  47947776  14946304         0  4964352  23674880
Swap:          0         0         0
MemTotal:       61420 Kb
MemFree:        14596 Kb
MemShared:          0 Kb
Buffers:         4848 Kb
Cached:         23120 Kb
SwapCached:         0 Kb
```

```
Active:           32340 Kb
ActiveAnon:       10760 Kb
ActiveCache:      21580 Kb
Inact_dirty:       6336 Kb
Inact_clean:        236 Kb
Inact_target:      7780 Kb
HighTotal:            0 Kb
HighFree:             0 Kb
LowTotal:         61420 Kb
LowFree:          14596 Kb
SwapTotal:            0 Kb
SwapFree:             0 Kb
```

The important fields are the used and free fields. The rest of the information is about how the various caches on the system (buffer, page, etc.) have locked up memory. In case the reader is interested in knowing these details, she can refer to the documentation available along with the Linux kernel. The Documentation/proc.txt file has a section that explains each field displayed by /proc/meminfo.

Now let us look at techniques to optimize kernel memory usage.

- *Cutting down on statically allocated data structures:* Statically allocated data structures reside either in the .data or in the .bss section. Many of the data structures that get pulled in do not have a configurable option (this would make the build process very complicated) and hence rest on a default size, which would be of limited option to an embedded system. Some of them are listed below.
  - Number of default TTY consoles (MAX_NR_CONSOLES and MAX_NR_USER_CONSOLES) defined in include/linux/tty.h as 63.
  - Size of the console log buffer LOG_BUF_LEN defined in kernel/printk.c as 16 K.
  - Number of character and block devices (MAX_CHRDEV and MAX_BLKDEV) defined in include/linux/major.h
- *System.map file:* The System.map file generated by the kernel build can be a useful source of information in this regard. This file contains the symbol addresses of each symbol; the difference between consecutive symbol addresses will give the size of a symbol, which is either text or data. All large-size data structures are targets of investigation. You can also use the nm command with the --size option to get sizes of various symbols in the kernel image.
- *Cutting down unused code within the kernel:* The kernel code can be scanned to remove unused modules and functions. Note that the techniques discussed for a smaller kernel in the section on kernel space optimization holds good here.
- *Improper usage of* kmalloc: kmalloc is the generic kernel memory allocator. Device drivers normally make use of kmalloc() for allocating memory dynamically. kmalloc() operates on cache objects that are multiples of 32 bytes; so any allocation of memory that lies between two consecutive multiples of 32 bytes causes internal fragmentation. Assume that a submodule does kmalloc of size 80 bytes; it gets allocated from

an object of 128 bytes and hence 48 bytes get wasted per allocation. If your submodule or driver does lots of such allocations, then much memory gets wasted. The remedy for this problem is to create private caches from which you can allocate objects exactly of the size that is required. This is done using the following two steps.

-   Creating the cache associated with the slab object using the `kmem_cache_create()`. (To destroy the cache call `kmem_cache_destroy().`)
-   Creating an object associated with the cache using the `kmem_cache_alloc()`. (The free function is `kmem_cache_free().`)

■ *Using the* `__init` *directive:* The `.init` section holds all the functions that can be thrown away once the kernel is initialized. Usually all the initialization functions are placed under the `.init` section. If you are including your own driver or module within the kernel, identify sections that need to be used only once during system start-up and place them under the `.init` section using the `__init` directive. This will ensure that some free kernel is released back to the system once all the functions in the `.init` section are run.

■ *Cutting down on holes in physical memory:* Holes in physical memory are common phenomena with embedded systems. Sometimes board design or processor design does not allow all the physical memory to be contiguous thus causing holes. However large holes in physical memory can waste space. This is because every 4 K of physical memory (page) requires a 60-byte `page_struct` data structure for maintenance. If there is a huge hole, then these structures are unnecessarily allocated and the pages that lie within the hold are marked unused. To prevent this, the `CONFIG_DISCONTIGMEM` support provided by the Linux kernel can be used.

■ *XIP:* XIP or "eXecute In Place" is a technology by which a program executes directly from flash; there is no need to copy the program to flash to get it executing. Other than decreasing the memory requirements, it also decreases the start-up time because the kernel need not be uncompressed or copied to the RAM. The flip side is that compression cannot be used on the file system where the kernel image is stored and hence you need to have lots of flash. However, using XIP in file systems is of limited use for applications because the code pages are loaded on demand (demand paging). XIP is more popular in uClinux because of the lack of virtual memory on uClinux systems. XIP is discussed at length in Chapter 10.

Chapter 5

Embedded Drivers

Porting device drivers from other RTOSs (Real-Time Operating System) to embedded Linux is a challenging job. Device drivers are part of the Linux IO subsystem. The IO subsystem provides access to low-level hardware to applications using a well-defined system call interface. Figure 5.1 gives a high-level overview of how the applications make use of device drivers.

Device drivers in Linux are classified into three types:

- *Character device drivers:* These are used for driving sequential access devices. The amount of data accessed is not of fixed size. The character device drivers are accessed by the application using the standard calls such as open, read, write. For example, a serial driver is a character device driver.
- *Block device drivers:* These are used for driving random access devices. The data exchange happens in terms of blocks. The block device drivers are used for storing file systems. Unlike character drivers, the applications cannot directly access block device drivers; they can be accessed only through a file system. A file system is mounted on a block device thus making the block device driver a mediator between the storage media and the file system. For example, a disk driver is a block device driver.
- *Network device drivers:* Network device drivers are treated as a separate class of device drivers because they interact with the network protocol stack. Applications do not access them directly; only the networking subsystem interacts with them.

This chapter explains some of the commonly used device driver subsystems on embedded platforms. We discuss serial, Ethernet, I2C, USB gadgets, and watchdog drivers.

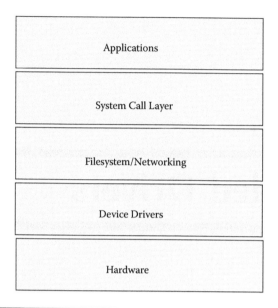

Figure 5.1   Linux device driver architecture overview.

5.1 Linux Serial Driver

The Linux serial driver is tightly coupled with the TTY subsystem. The TTY layer is a separate class of character driver. On embedded systems having a serial port, the TTY layer is used for providing access to the low-level serial port. Often an embedded board may have more than one serial port; typically the other ports may be used for dial-up access using protocols such as PPP or SLIP. The question often asked is whether in such a case, different serial drivers should be provided. The answer is no as TTY shields the serial driver from the application so that a single serial driver can be provided irrespective of how it gets used.

A user process does not talk to the serial driver directly. TTY presents a stack of software over the driver and exports the entire functionality via TTY devices. The TTY subsystem is split into three layers as shown in Figure 5.2. As Figure 5.2 suggests, every device associated with the TTY subsystem is bound to a line discipline that enforces how the transmitted or received data is processed by the low-level driver. Linux offers a default line discipline N_TTY that can be used for using a serial port as a standard terminal. But line disciplines can also be used for implementing more complex protocols such as X.25 or the PPP/SLIP protocol.

In Linux, user processes normally have a controlling terminal. The controlling terminal is where the process takes its input from and to where its standard output and error is redirected. The TTY and process management automatically take care of assigning and managing controlling terminals.[1]

There is another set of TTY devices that are used in embedded systems. These are the virtual or pseudo TTY devices (PTYs). PTYs are a powerful

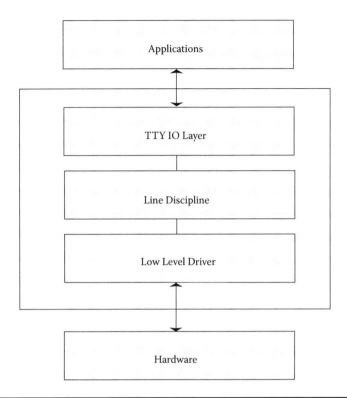

Figure 5.2   TTY subsystem.

means of IPC. Processes using pseudo TTYs get all the benefits of both IPC and the TTY subsystem. For example, the Telnet subsystem on Linux makes use of a pseudo terminal for communication between the `telnetd` (master Telnet daemon) and the process that is spawned by `telnetd`. By default the number of pseudo TTYs is set to 256; this can be tweaked into a smaller number because of its restricted usage in embedded systems.

Now we discuss an implementation of a serial driver in Linux. In the 2.4 kernel, the data structure used for hooking up a serial driver to the TTY subsystem is `tty_driver`. The serial driver fills this structure with information such as name of the device, major/minor numbers, and all the APIs needed by the TTY IO and the line discipline layer to access the serial driver. In 2.4, the file `drivers/char/generic_serial.c` contains functions exported to the TTY layer from a serial driver; it can be used for hooking your low-level serial driver to the TTY layer.

In the 2.6 kernel, the serial driver layer was cleaned up so that porting a new serial driver to Linux becomes easier. The serial driver need not bother about the TTY hookups; rather an abstraction layer handles it. This makes the job of writing the serial driver easier. This section explains how a serial driver can be written in the new framework.

We assume a fictitious UART hardware MY_UART with the following functionalities:

- Simple transmission and reception logic; one register for sending data out and one register for getting data
- Allows speed settings of either 9600 or 19200 bauds
- Uses interrupt to intimate either end of transmission or on reception of data
- The hardware has only one UART port (i.e., it's single ported)

We assume that the macros shown in Listing 5.1 are already available for accessing the hardware. Again these macros assume that the registers and the buffers are mapped starting from the base address MY_UART_BASE. We also assume that the BSP for this particular board has done this mapping so that we can start using the address MY_UART_BASE effectively. However, we do not discuss modem support by the driver; it is beyond the scope of this section.

First we discuss the device configuration. In the drivers/serial/Kconfig file add the following lines.

```
config MY_UART
  select SERIAL_CORE
  help
  Test UART driver
```

Then add the following lines in the drivers/serial/Makefile.

```
obj-$(CONFIG_MY_UART)+= my_uart.o
```

The configuration option selects the file my_uart.c to be compiled along with drivers/serial/serial_core.c. The file serial_core.c contains the generic UART routines that interface with TTY and the line discipline modules. Henceforth the generic UART layer implemented in serial_core.c is referred to as the *UART core*.

5.1.1 Driver Initialization and Start-Up

Now let us discuss the initialization function for the driver. The initialization function registers a TTY device and then sets the path between the UART core and the driver. The main data structures involved in this process and declared in file include/linux/serial_core.h are as follows.

- struct uart_driver: This data structure contains information about the name, major and minor numbers, and number of ports of this driver.
- struct uart_port: This data structure contains all the configuration data of the low-level hardware.
- struct uart_ops: This data structure contains the pointers to functions that operate on the hardware.

These three data structures are linked together as shown in Figure 5.3 for a UART device having two hardware ports. We are using a dual-ported hardware as an example for now; however, our sample hardware is single-ported.

Listing 5.1 MY_UART Hardware Access Macros

```
/* my_uart.h */

/*
 * Indicate to hardware to setup the registers necessary for
 * sending out data
 */
#define START_TX()

/*
 * Indicate to hardware that we are no longer sending out any
 * data.
 */
#define STOP_TX()

/* Hardware macro to transmit a character */
#define SEND_CHAR()

/*
 * Macro that indicates that there is data in the UART receive
 * register
 */
#define CHAR_READY()

/* Macro that reads a character from the UART hardware */
#define READ_CHAR()

/* Macro to read the receive status register */
#define READ_RX_STATUS
/* Macros that show the error bits */
#define PARITY_ERROR
#define FRAME_ERROR
#define OVERRUN_ERROR
#define IGNORE_ERROR_NUM

/*
 * Macro that indicates the hardware to stop receiving
 * characters
 */
#define STOP_RX()

/*
 * Macros for interrupt processing; read interrupt mask and check
 * the interrupt type
 */
#define READ_INTERRUPT_STATUS
#define TX_INT_MASK
#define RX_INT_MASK

/*
 * Macro that indicates that the transmit buffer is empty
 */
#define TX_EMPTY()

/* Macros to set speed, stop bits, parity and number of bits */
#define SET_SPEED()
#define SET_STOP_BITS
#define SET_PARITY
#define SET_BITS
```

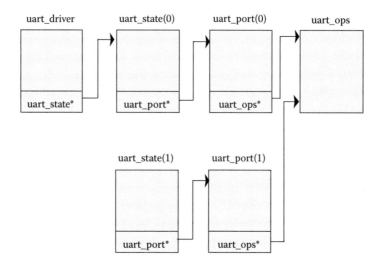

Figure 5.3   UART data structure linkage.

There is one private structure held by the kernel — uart_state. The number of uart_state is equivalent to the number of hardware ports that are accessed via the driver. Each state contains a pointer to the per-port settings uart_port, which in turn contains the structure uart_ops holding the routines for accessing the hardware.

Data structures for MY_UART are defined as shown in Listing 5.2.

First we have the initialization routine.

```
int __init my_uart_init(void)
{
  /*
   * uart_register_driver binds the low level driver with
   * the serial CORE which in turn registers with the TTY
   * layer using the tty_register_driver() function. Also
   * the uart_state structures are created (the number of
   * these structures are equivalent to number of hardware
   * ports) and pointer to this array is stored in
   * my_uart_driver.
   */
  uart_register_driver (&my_uart_driver);

  /*
   * As indicated in the Figure 5.3 this function
   * connects the uart_state to the uart_port. Also this
   * function lets the TTY layer know that a device has
   * been added using the function tty_register_device().
   */
  uart_add_one_port (&my_uart_driver, &my_uart_port);

  return 0;
}
```

Listing 5.2   MY_UART Data Structures

```
static struct uart_ops my_uart_ops= {
  .tx_empty      = my_uart_tx_empty,
  .get_mctrl     = my_uart_get_mctrl,
  .set_mctrl     = my_uart_set_mctrl,
  .stop_tx       = my_uart_stop_tx,
  .start_tx      = my_uart_start_tx,
  .stop_rx       = my_uart_stop_rx,
  .enable_ms     = my_uart_enable_ms,
  .break_ctl     = my_uart_break_ctl,
  .startup       = my_uart_startup,
  .shutdown      = my_uart_shutdown,
  .set_termios   = my_uart_set_termios,
  .type          =  my_uart_type,
  .release_port  = my_uart_release_port,
  .request_port  = my_uart_request_port,
  .config_port   = my_uart_config_port,
  .verify_port   = my_uart_verify_port,
};

static struct uart_driver my_uart_driver = {
  .owner        = THIS_MODULE,
  .driver_name  = "serial",
  .dev_name     = "ttyS%d",
  .major        = TTY_MAJOR,
  .minor        = MY_UART_MINOR,
  .nr           = 1
};

static struct uart_port my_uart_port = {
  .membase   = MY_UART_MEMBASE,
  .iotype    = SERIAL_IO_MEM,
  .irq       = MY_UART_IRQ,
  .fifosize = 1,
  .line      = 0,
  .ops       = &my_uart_ops
}
```

We now discuss the functions in the my_uart_ops structure. The functions request_port() and release_port() are typically used to request IO and memory regions used by the port. Start-up and shutdown functions my_uart_startup() and my_uart_shutdown() do the interrupt setup and teardown, respectively.

```
static int my_uart_startup(struct uart_port *port)
{
  return(request_irq(MY_UART_IRQ, my_uart_irq_handler, 0,
                     "my uart", port));
}

static void my_uart_shutdown(struct uart_port *port)
{
  free_irq(MY_UART_IRQ, port);
}
```

5.1.2 Data Transmission

The functions involved in transmission of data are shown in Listing 5.3. Transmission starts with the `my_uart_start_tx()` function; this function is invoked by the line discipline to start transmission. After the first character is transmitted, the rest of the transmission is done from the interrupt handler until all the characters queued up by the line discipline layer are transmitted. It is implemented by the generic transmission function `my_uart_char_tx()`. The serial core provides a circular buffer mechanism for storing the characters that need to be transmitted. The serial core provides macros to operate on this buffer of which the following are used in this driver.

- `uart_circ_empty()` is used to find if the buffer is empty.
- `uart_circ_clear()` is used to empty the buffer.
- `uart_circ_chars_pending()` is used to find the number of characters that are yet to be sent out.

5.1.3 Data Reception

Data reception happens in the context of an interrupt handler. The data receive path is explained using a flowchart as shown in Figure 5.4.

The basis of the receive operation is the TTY flip buffer. This is a pair of buffers that is provided by the TTY layer. While one buffer is consumed by the line discipline for processing the characters received, the other buffer is available for writing. The TTY layer provides standard APIs for accessing the flip buffers. We are interested only in the functions for inserting the received character inside the available flip buffer and then flushing the received characters to the line discipline from the flip buffer. These are done using the functions `tty_insert_flip_char` and `tty_flip_buffer_push`, respectively. The functions `my_uart_char_rx` and `my_uart_stop_rx` are shown in Listing 5.4.

5.1.4 Interrupt Handler

Now we list the interrupt handler that makes use of transmit and receive functions.

```
static irqreturn_t
my_uart_irq_handler(int irq, void *dev_id,
                    struct pt_regs *regs)
{
  unsigned int st= READ_INT_STATUS;

  if(st & TX_INT_MASK) my_uart_char_tx(my_uart_port); &
  if(st & RX_INT_MASK) my_uart_char_rx(my_uart_port);

  return IRQ_HANDLED;
}
```

Listing 5.3   Transmit Functions

```
static void my_uart_char_tx(struct uart_port *port)
{
  struct circ_buf *xmit = &port->info->xmit;

  /*
   * If a XON/XOFF character needs to be transmitted out, the
   * x_char field of the port is set by the serial core
   */
  if(port->x_char)
  {
    SEND_CHAR(port->x_char);
    port->x_char = 0; /* Reset the field */
    return;
  }

  if(uart_tx_stopped(port) || uart_circ_empty(xmit))
  {
    my_uart_stop_tx(port, 0);
    return;
  }

  SEND_CHAR(xmit->buf[xmit->tail]);

  /*
   * UART_XMIT_SIZE is defined in include/linux/serial_core.h
   */
  xmit->tail = (xmit->tail + 1) & (UART_XMIT_SIZE - 1);

  /*
   * Now check if there are more characters that need to be sent
   * and we have enough space in the transmission buffer which is
   * defined by the macro WAKEUP_CHARS set to 256 in the file
   * include/linux/serial_core.h. The function uart_write_wakeup
   * provided by the serial core ultimately ends up calling the
   * TTY wakeup handler function which in turn informs the line
   * discipline that the low level driver is ready to receive
   * more data.
   */
  if(uart_circ_chars_pending(xmit) < WAKEUP_CHARS)
    uart_write_wakeup(port);

  if(uart_circ_empty(xmit))
    my_uart_stop_tx(port, 0);
}


static void
my_uart_stop_tx(struct uart_port *port, unsigned int c)
{
  STOP_TX();
}
```

Listing 5.3   Transmit Functions (continued)

```
static void
my_uart_start_tx(struct uart_port *port, unsigned int start)
{
  START_TX();
  my_uart_char_tx(port);
}


/* Return 0 if not empty */
static unsigned int my_uart_tx_empty(struct uart_port *port)
{
  return (TX_EMPTY()? TIOCSER_TEMT : 0);
}
```

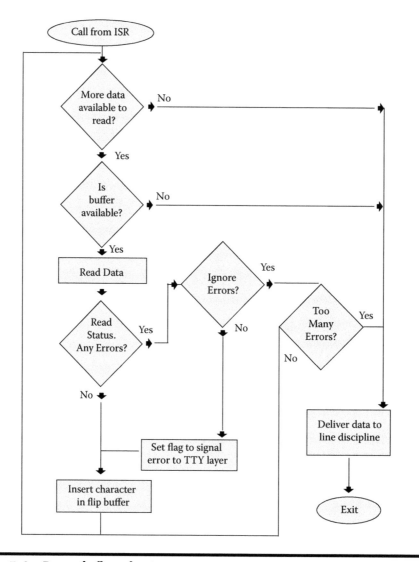

Figure 5.4   Rx path flowchart.

Listing 5.4 Receive Functions

```
void my_uart_char_rx(struct uart_port *port)
{
  struct tty_struct *tty = port->info->tty;
  struct uart_count *icount = &port->icount;
  unsigned int i=0;

  while(CHAR_READY())
  {
    unsigned char c;
    unsigned char flag = TTY_NORMAL;
    unsigned char st = READ_RX_STATUS();

    if(tty->flip.count >= TTY_FLIPBUF_SIZE)
      break;

    c = READ_CHAR();

    icount->rx++;

    if(st & (PARITY_ERROR | FRAME_ERROR | OVERRUN _ERROR) )
    {
      if(st & PARITY_ERROR)
        icount->parity ++;
      if(st & FRAME_ERROR)
        icount->frame ++;
      if(st & OVERRUN_ERROR)
        icount->overrun ++;

      /*
       * If we have been asked to ignore errors then do the
       * following
       */
      if(st & port->ignore_status_mask)
      {
        if(++i > IGNORE_ERROR_NUM)
          break;
        goto ignore;
      }

      /*
       * Report the errors that we have not been asked to ignore
       */
      st &= port->read_status_mask;
      if(st & PARITY_ERROR) flag = TTY_PARITY;
      if(st & FRAME_ERROR) flag = TTY_FRAME;
      /*
       * Overrun is a special case; it does not affect the
       * character read
       */
      if(st & OVERRUN_ERROR)
      {
        tty_insert_flip_char(tty, c, flag);
        c = 0;
        flag = TTY_OVERRUN;
      }
    }
```

Listing 5.4   Receive Functions (continued)

```
    tty_insert_flip_char(tty,c,flag);

ignore:
  }
  tty_flip_buffer_push(tty);
}


static void my_uart_stop_rx(struct uart_port *port)
{
  STOP_RX();
}
```

5.1.5 Termios Settings

Finally we discuss the function that does the termios settings. Termios settings are the set of terminal settings that include a variety of options; these are roughly classified into:

- Control options such the baud rate, number of data bits, parity, and stop bits
- Line options, input options, and output options

Implementing the termios settings is done across various TTY layers; the low-level driver has to bother only about the control options. These options are set using the `c_cflag` field of the terminos structure. The function `my_uart_set_terminos` that sets these options is shown in Listing 5.5.

5.2 Ethernet Driver

In Linux, the network device driver is treated as a separate class of drivers. The network drivers are not bound to the file system but are rather bound to a subsystem interface (such as an Ethernet interface). The application program does not talk to the network device driver directly but rather makes use of sockets and IP addresses. The network layer forwards the requests done over a socket to the network driver. This section explains the process of writing an Ethernet driver for the 2.4 Linux kernel.

This section makes use of a fictitious Ethernet hardware to explain the architecture of the Ethernet driver. The Ethernet card is plugged directly to the processor's address space and hence its registers and internal memory are mapped directly to the processor's address space. We assume two banks of memory: one for transmission and one for receiving. For the sake of simplicity we assume the absence of DMA; the driver has to invoke a `memcpy` procedure for transferring data from the system RAM to the Ethernet card and vice versa.

Again we assume the following functions/macros are available.

Listing 5.5 Setting Termios

```
static void
my_uart_set_termios(struct uart_port *port,
                    struct termios *termios, struct termios *old)
{
  unsigned int c_cflag = termios->c_cflag;
  unsigned int baud=9600, stop_bits=1, parity=0, data_bits=8;
  unsigned long flags;

  /* Calculate the number of data bits */
  switch (c_cflag & CSIZE) {
    case CS5: data_bits = 5; break;
    case CS6: data_bits = 6; break;
    case CS7: data_bits = 7; break;
    case CS8: data_bits = 8; break;
    default: data_bits = 8;
  }

  if(c_cflag & CSTOPB) stop_bits = 2;

  if(c_cflag & PARENB) parity = 1;
  if(c_cflag & PARODD) parity = 2;

  /*
   * We support only 2 speeds of 9600 and 19200. Translate the
   * termios settings into any one of these
   */
  baud = uart_get_baud_rate(port, termios, old_termios, 9600,
                                                        19200)

  spin_lock_irqsave(&port->lock, flags);
  SET_SPEED(baud);
  SET_STOP_BITS(stop_bits);
  SET_PARITY(parity);
  SET_BITS(data_bits);

  port->read_status_mask = OVERRUN_ERROR;

  if(termios->c_iflag & INPCK)
    port->read_status_mask |= PARITY_ERROR | FRAME_ERROR;
  port->ignore_status_mask = 0;

  if(termios->c_iflag & IGNPAR)
    port->ignore_status_mask |= PARITY_ERROR | FRAME_ERROR;

  spin_lock_irqrestore(&port->lock, flags);
}
```

- NW_IOADDR: This is the base address for accessing the IO on the card. We assume that system initialization has given a valid base address.
- NW_IRQ: The interrupt line used for the network card.
- FILL_ETHER_ADDRESS: A macro that programs the hardware with an Ethernet address.
- INIT_NW: A routine that initializes the network card.
- RESET_NW: A routine that resets the network card.

- READ_INTERRUPT_CONDITION: This macro specifies what has caused the interrupt to happen. In our case, there are two reasons: one is receipt of incoming data and the other is end of transmission.
- FILL_TX_NW: A routine to copy data from the network buffers to the hardware memory. It is used on the transmit path.
- READ_RX_NW: A routine that copies the data from hardware memory to network buffers. It is used on the receive path.

5.2.1 Device Initialization and Clean-Up

Linux maintains a struct net_device declared in include/linux/ netdevice.h. This control structure encompasses all the information required by the device, from the high-level details such as driver settings and pointers to functions supplied by the driver to the low-level details such as the queue discipline and protocol pointers used internally by the kernel. The usage of this structure by the driver is explained in this section.

During kernel build, enable CONFIG_NET, CONFIG_NETDEVICES, and CONFIG_NET_ETHERNET config options. There are two methods of doing the registration; one method is used when the network driver is loaded as a module and the other method is used when the network driver is linked as a part of the kernel. Both methods are explained below.

When the device driver is linked directly to the kernel address space then the struct net_device structure is allocated by the kernel. The driver has to supply a probe routine, which is called by the kernel at start-up time. The file drivers/net/space.c contains the probe routines for various hardware devices; so you need to add support for your Ethernet device here. Each Ethernet device is associated with its unique probe list, which associates the machine with its architecture and bus. Once a probe list has been identified, then the probe function is added in that list as

```
#ifdef TEST_HARDWARE
  {lxNWProbe, 0},
#endif
```

During device initialization the kernel calls the probe functions. In our case, the function lxNWProbe is called; the argument to the function includes a struct net_device, which is initialized with default values including device name.[2] It is the responsibility of the probe function to fill in the rest of the details in the net_device structure. We are assuming that this is the only Ethernet card on the system and hence there is no necessity for doing any hardware probing. lxNWprobe is shown in Listing 5.6.

In the case where the driver is written as a kernel module, the net_device structure is allocated by the module and registered explicitly using the register_netdev function. This function assigns a name to the device, calls the initialization function (in this case it is lxNWprobe), adds it to the chain of the network devices, and notifies the upper-layer protocols that a new device has appeared.

Listing 5.6   Probe Function

```
int __init lxNWprobe(struct net_device *dev)
{
  /*
   * This function is used only in case the driver is used as
   * module in which case this function initializes the owner of
   * the device
   */
  SET_MODULE_OWNER(dev);

  /*
   * Set the starting address for the IO access; this will be
   * used by the inb()/outb() family of commands
   */
  dev->base_addr = NW_IOADDR;

  dev->irq = NW_IRQ;

  /*
   * Fill up the ethernet address; this is normally obtained from
   * a some initial boot settings
   */
  FILL_ETHER_ADDRESS(dev->dev_addr);

  /* request IRQ */
  request_irq(dev->irq, &LXNWIsr, 0, "NW", dev);

  /* do the chip initialization */
  RESET_NW();

  /* Fill in the important functions in the device structure */
  dev->open = lxNW_open;
  dev->hard_start_xmit = lxNW_send_packet;
  dev->stop = lxNW_close;
  dev->get_stats = lxNW_get_stats;
  dev->set_multicast_list = lxNW_set_multicast_list;
  dev->watchdog_timeo = HZ;
  dev->set_mac_address = lxNW_set_mac_address;

 /*
  * ether_setup is provided to fill in the default ethernet
  * fields. One important field here is the transmit queue length
  * maintained per device. The default is 100. Also the
  * dev->flags set are IFF_BROADCAST and IFF_MULTICAST which
  * means that the device supports broadcasting and has multicast
  * support. In case your device does not support multicasting,
  * it needs to be explicitly cleared.
  */

  ether_setup(dev);

  return 0;
}
```

```
#ifdef MODULE

static struct net_device lxNW_dev;

static int init_module(void)
{
  dev->init = lxNWprobe;

  register_netdev(dev);
  return 0;
}

static void cleanup_module(void)
{
  unregister_netdev(dev);
}

module_init(init_module);
module_exit(cleanup_module);

#endif
```

The open function is called whenever the device is taken from the DOWN to the UP state.

```
static int LXHWopen(struct net_device *dev)
{

  RESET_NW(); INIT_NW();

  /* Start the device's transmit queue */
  netif_start_queue(dev);
}
```

The close function is called to move the interface from the UP to the DOWN state.

```
static int LXHWclose(struct net_device *dev)
{
  RESET_NW();

  /* Stop the device's transmit queue */
  netif_stop_queue(dev);
}
```

5.2.2 Data Transmission and Reception

Transmitting the packets from the driver to the hardware is complicated because it involves data flow control between the kernel (layer 3 stack), the driver's transmission routine, the interrupt handler, and the hardware. The implementation is dependent on the hardware transmit capabilities. Our example device has only one onboard transmit buffer. So the software has to make sure that the transmit buffer on the hardware is protected from overwrites when the buffer is still being transmitted out by the hardware onto the network. The buffers used by Linux for transmission and reception are called `skbuff`.

The kernel maintains a transmit queue for every device with a default size of 100. There are two operations on this queue.[3]

1. Adding packets to the queue. This is done by the protocol stacks.
2. Removing packets from the queue. The output of the operation is a buffer that is passed to the device driver's transmit API.

In the second step the transmission API copies the buffer to the hardware. In case the hardware has limited space this function should not be invoked when the hardware is processing the buffer. Only after interrupts have signaled that transmission is done and that the hardware is safe to use, should this function be called. The Linux kernel provides this control using three functions.

- `netif_start_queue`: This is used by the driver to signal to the upper layers that it is safe to call the driver transmission API for sending more data.
- `netif_stop_queue`: This is used by the driver to signal to the upper layers that the transmission buffers are full and hence the driver transmission API should not be invoked.
- `netif_wake_queue`: Linux provides a softirq to automatically drain packets when the *end of transmit* interrupt has occurred and the upper stack is disabled to send packets to the device driver. The softirq calls the device driver's transmission API to flush out the next packet in the queue. The softirq is triggered by calling the function `netif_wake_queue` from the interrupt handler.

So depending on the hardware, you need to call the above functions to do flow control. Following is the thumb rule.

- If the transmission API of your driver stops the dequeueing from qdisc because of limited buffer size, then the interrupt handler should arrange for the softirq to drain the packets from qdisc using the `netif_wake_queue()`.
- However, if there is more space in the hardware when the transmission API is called so that it can be called again by the upper layer, the function `netif_stop_queue` need not be called.

For our sample driver we need to stop the device driver's transmit function being called until the end of transmit interrupt has occurred. Thus during the time when the packet is being transmitted out, the higher-level stack can only queue to the qdisc; the packets cannot be drained from the qdisc.

Reception is comparatively simpler; it allocates a `skbuff` and calls the function `netif_rx`, which schedules a softirq to process the packet (see Listing 5.7).

Listing 5.7   Transmit and Receive Functions

```
void LXNWIsr(int irq, void *id, struct pt_regs *regs)
{
  struct net_device *dev = id;

  switch (READ_INTERRUPT_CONDITION())
  {
    case TX_EVENT:
      netif_wake_queue(dev);
      break;

    case RX_Event:
      LXHWReceive(nCS);
      break;
  }

}

int LXNWSendPacket(struct sk_buff *skb, struct net_device *dev)
{

  /* disable the irq since that can trigger a softirq */
  disable_irq(dev->irq);
  netif_stop_queue(dev);
  FILL_TX_NW(skb);
  enable_irq(dev->irq);
  dev_kfree_skb(skb);

  return 0;

}

void LXHWReceive(struct net_device *dev)
{
  struct sk_buff *skb;

  /*
   * Allocate the skb after getting the length of the frame from
   *
   */
  skb = dev_alloc_skb(READ_RX_LEN + 2);

  /* This is done for alignment to 16 bytes */
  skb_reserve(skb,2);

  skb->dev = dev;
  READ_RX_NW(skb);
  skb->protocol = eth_type_trans(skb,dev);
  netif_rx(skb);
}
```

5.3 I2C Subsystem on Linux

The I2C (inter IC) bus is a two-wire serial bus developed by Philips Semiconductor in the early 1980s. When originally invented its main intention was to

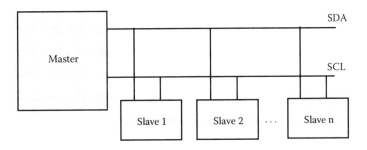

Figure 5.5   I2C bus.

connect various ICs onboard to the TV. However its ease of use and the lower overhead in board design has made it a universal standard and it's now used to connect a variety of peripherals in a wide diversity of configurations. Initially it was a slow-speed bus; it has evolved to offer a variety of speeds from 100 KB/sec to 3.4 MB/sec. The I2C bus offers various advantages such as saving board space, saving the overall cost of the hardware, and offering easier debugging facilities.

Today the I2C bus is heavily used in embedded systems and it is very uncommon to find boards without a I2C bus. This section explains the I2C subsystem in Linux. Before going into the details we have an overview of how the I2C bus works.

5.3.1 I2C Bus

The I2C bus has two lines: the SDA (data) line and the SCL (clock) line. The SDA line carries information such as address, data, and acknowledgment one bit at a time. The receiver and the sender synchronize themselves via the clock line. Many I2C devices can reside on a single I2C bus; devices are classified as master or slave. A master is a device that starts and stops the transfer and generates signals on the clock line. A slave is a device that is addressed by the master. A master can be either a transmitter or receiver; the same applies for slave devices too. Each device on the I2C bus has a unique 7-bit or 10-bit address that is used to identify that particular device. Figure 5.5 gives a sample implementation.

The I2C data transfer is divided into the following phases.

- *Idle phase:* When the I2C bus is not in use, both the SDA and SCL lines are kept in the HIGH state.
- *Start phase:* When the SDA line changes from HIGH to LOW and when the SCL is kept in the HIGH state, it indicates the start of the data phase. This is initiated by the master.
- *Address phase:* During this phase, the master sends the address of the target slave device and the transfer mode (read or write). The slave device needs to reply with an acknowledgment so that the data transfer phase can be initiated.

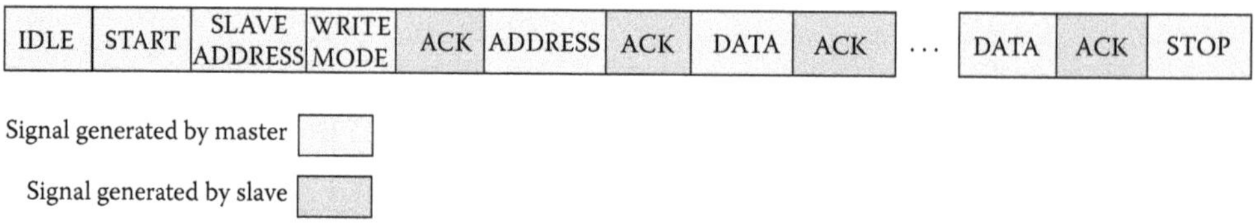

IDLE	START	SLAVE ADDRESS	WRITE MODE	ACK	ADDRESS	ACK	DATA	ACK	...	DATA	ACK	STOP

Signal generated by master [ ]

Signal generated by slave [ ]

Figure 5.6   I2C data write.

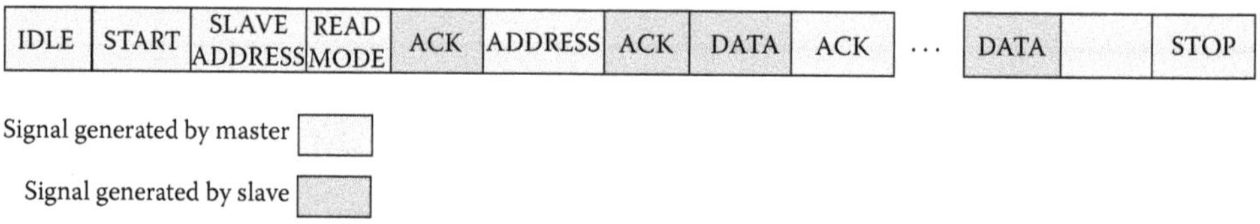

IDLE	START	SLAVE ADDRESS	READ MODE	ACK	ADDRESS	ACK	DATA	ACK	...	DATA		STOP

Signal generated by master [ ]

Signal generated by slave [ ]

Figure 5.7   I2C data read.

- *Data transfer phase:* The data is transmitted bitwise on the I2C bus. At the end of each byte transfer, one bit acknowledgment is sent by the receiver to the transmitter.
- *Stop phase:* The master indicates this by pulling the SDA line from LOW to HIGH and when the SCL line is kept HIGH.

The following steps are performed when the master needs to send data to a slave device on the I2C bus as shown in Figure 5.6.

1. Master signals a START condition.
2. Master sends the address of the slave it wishes to send data to and sends write mode of transfer.
3. Slave sends an acknowledgment to the master.
4. Master sends the address where the data has to be written on the slave device.
5. Slave sends an acknowledgment to the master.
6. Master sends data to be written on the SDA bus.
7. At the end of the byte transfer, the slave sends an acknowledgment bit.
8. The above two steps are again performed until all the required bytes are written. The write address is automatically incremented.
9. Master signals a STOP condition.

The following steps are performed when the master needs to read data from a slave device on the I2C bus as shown in Figure 5.7.

1. Master signals a START condition.
2. Master sends the address of the slave it wishes to send data to and sends the mode of transfer to read.
3. Slave sends an acknowledgment to the master.
4. Master sends the address from where the data has to be read on the slave device.

5. Slave sends an acknowledgment to the master.
6. Slave sends the data to be read on the SDA bus.
7. At the end of the byte transfer, the master sends an acknowledgment bit.
8. The above two steps are again performed until all the required bytes are written. The read address is automatically incremented. However, for the last byte the master does not send an acknowledgment. This prevents the slave from sending any more data on the bus.
9. Master signals a STOP condition.

5.3.2 I2C Software Architecture

The I2C subsystem has seen a major overhaul with the 2.6 kernel release. In this section we discuss the I2C architecture in the 2.6 kernel. Though the bus by itself is very simple, the I2C subsystem architecture in Linux is quite complex and is best understood using an example.

Assume your board is using I2C as shown in Figure 5.8, which shows two I2C buses on a board; each I2C bus is controlled by a PCF8584-style I2C bus adapter, which acts as the I2C master for that particular bus and additionally acts as the interface between the CPU bus and the I2C bus. Thus the CPU can access any of the I2C devices on the I2C buses by programming these adapters. On the first I2C bus two EEPROMs are connected and on the other I2C bus an RTC is connected.

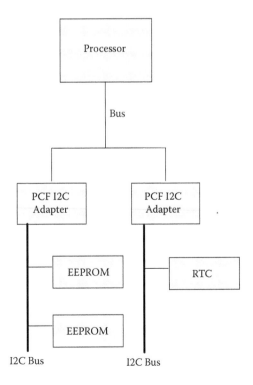

Figure 5.8 Sample I2C bus topology.

The following are the logical software components as defined by the Linux I2C subsystem.

- *The I2C algorithm driver:* Each I2C bus adapter has its own way of interfacing with the processor and the I2C bus. In the above example both bus adapters use the PCF style of interfacing, which defines the registers that need to be implemented by the bus adapter and the implementation of the algorithms for transmitting and receiving data. The algorithm driver implements the basic data handshake routines (transmit and receive). For example, in Figure 5.8 we provide just one algorithm driver, the PCF8584 algorithm driver.
- *The I2C adapter driver:* This can be considered as a BSP layer for the I2C subsystem. The I2C adapter driver and the algorithm driver together drive the I2C buses on the system. In the above example we define two I2C adapter drivers for each of the two buses on the system. Both these adapter drivers are bound to the PCF8584 algorithm driver.
- *The I2C slave driver:* The slave driver contains the routines to access a particular kind of slave device on the I2C bus. In our example we provide two slave drivers: one for accessing the EEPROMs on the first I2C bus and the other for accessing the RTC chip on the second I2C bus.
- *The I2C client driver:* One client driver is instantiated for hardware that needs to be accessed via the I2C bus. The slave and client drivers are bound together. In our example we need to define three client drivers: two EEPROM client drivers and one RTC client driver.

Why is the subsystem divided so? This is done to reuse software as much as possible and to allow portability. This is done at the cost of complexity. The I2C subsystem is located in the `drivers/i2c` directory of the kernel source tree. In that directory the `buses` subdirectory contains the various bus adapter drivers, `algos` contains the various algorithm drivers, and the `chips` directory contains the various slave and client drivers. The generic portion of the entire I2C subsystem is referred to as the I2C core and is implemented in the file `drivers/ic2/i2c-core.c`.

Algorithm and Bus Adapter Driver

To understand more about how to write these drivers, we look at the implementation of the PCF8584 algorithm driver in Linux and a bus adapter that uses this algorithm. Before we dig into the source code let's have a very high-level overview of the PCF8584 I2C interfacing. The PCF8584 is an interface device between standard high-speed parallel buses and the I2C bus. It carries out the transfer between the I2C bus and the parallel bus microcontroller on a wide basis using either an interrupt or polled handshake. The PCF8584 defines the following registers on the I2C bus adapter.

- S0: Data buffer/shift register that performs the parallel-to-serial conversion between the processor and the I2C bus.

- S0': This is the internal address register and is filled during the initialization time.
- S1: Control register and the status register used for bus access and control.
- S2: Clock register.
- S3: Interrupt vector register.

The PCF8584 data sheet contains more information on how to program the registers for initialization, transmission, and reception. The data sheet can be downloaded from the Philips Semiconductor Web site.

Each algorithm driver is associated with a data structure `i2c_algorithm` declared in the file `include/linux/i2c.h`. This data structure has a function pointer `master_xfer`, which points to the function that implements the actual I2C transmit and receive algorithm. Other important fields of this structure are:

- name: Name of the algorithm.
- id: Each algorithm is identified using a unique number. The different types of algorithms are defined in the header file `include/linux/i2c-id.h`.
- algo_control: This is a pointer to an ioctl-like function.
- functionality: This is a pointer to a function that returns those features supported by the adapter such as what message types are supported by the I2C driver.

```
static struct i2c_algorithm pcf_algo = {
  .name           = "PCF8584 algorithm",
  .id             = I2C_ALGO_PCF,
  .master_xfer    = pcf_xfer,
  .functionality  = pcf_func,
};
```

The algorithm driver by itself does not make sense unless it is bound by the I2C bus adapter driver. The PCF algorithm driver provides a binding function for this purpose: `i2c_pcf_add_bus()`. Each adapter driver is associated with a data structure `i2c_adapter` (declared in the file `include/linux/i2c.h`) that is instantiated by the adapter driver. The adapter driver calls the function `i2c_pcf_add_bus` with a pointer to the `i2c_adapter` structure. The important fields of the `i2c_adapter` structure that are set up by the adapter driver are:

- name: Name for the adapter.
- class: This indicates the type of I2C class devices that this driver supports.
- algo: The pointer to the `i2c_algorithm` data structure. The `i2c_pcf_add_bus()` sets algo point to `pcf_algo`.
- algo_data: This is a pointer to the algorithm-specific private data structure. For example, the PCF algorithm driver defines a data structure `i2c_algo_pcf_data` private pointer set to this field. This data structure contains the pointer to routines to access the various registers of the adapter. Thus the algorithm driver is shielded from the board-level details; the adapter driver exports the board-level details using this data structure. The adapter driver defines the various routines that are defined in the `i2c_algo_pcf_data` data structure as follows.

```
static struct i2c_algo_pcf_data pcf_data = {
  .setpcf      = pcf_setbyte,
  .getpcf      = pcf_getbyte,
  .getown      = pcf_getown,
  .getclock    = pcf_getclock,
  .waitforpin  = pcf_waitforpin,
  .udelay      = 10,
  .mdelay      = 10,
  .timeout     = 100,
};
```

The bus adapter driver needs to do the following to associate itself with the algorithm driver.

- Define a structure of type `i2c_adapter` as follows.

```
static struct i2c_adapter pcf_ops = {
  .owner        = THIS_MODULE,
  .id           = I2C_HW_P_ID,
  .algo_data    = &pcf_data,
  .name         = "PCF8584 type adapter",
};
```

- Define the initialization function that does the following.
  - Request the various resources needed for the adapter driver such as the interrupt line.
  - Call the function `i2c_pcf_add_bus` to bind the PCF algorithm with this adapter driver. The `i2c_pcf_add_bus` function internally calls the I2C core function `i2c_add_adapter`, which registers a new adapter driver to the core. Thereafter the adapter is available for clients to register.

I2C Slave and Client Drivers

To understand the I2C client driver model we assume a fictional device connected on an I2C bus that implements one 32-bit register. The functionality of the driver is to provide routines to perform register read and write. We also assume the presence of an algorithm and an adapter driver software. This involves creating a slave and client driver. The slave driver makes use of the data structure `i2c_driver` declared in the header file `include/linux/i2c.h`. The important fields of this data structure are:

- name: Name of the client.
- id: Unique id of this device. The list of all IDs can be found from the file `include/linux/i2c-id.h`.
- flags: This is set to `I2C_DF_NOTIFY`, which allows for notification on bus detection so that the driver can detect new devices.
- attach_adapter: It points to the function that detects the presence of I2C devices on an I2C bus. If a device is found then it calls the function for instantiating a new client and attaching the client to the I2C core.

- `detach_client:` It points to the function that deletes the client instance and notifies the I2C core about its removal.
- `command:` This is an ioctl-like command that can be used to do private functions within the device.

For our sample driver we define the `i2c_driver` structure as follows.

```
static struct i2c_driver i2c_test_driver = {
  .owner          = THIS_MODULE,
  .name           = "TEST",
  .id             = I2C_DRIVERID_TEST,
  .flags          = I2C_DF_NOTIFY,
  .attach_adapter = i2c_test_scan_bus
  .detach_client  = i2c_test_detach,
  .command        = i2c_test_command
};
```

We first look at the `i2c_test_scan_bus` function, which is called when a new adapter or a new device is added. The argument to this function is the pointer to the `i2c_adapter` structure for the bus on which the slave device is detected and added.

```
static int i2c_test_scan_bus(struct i2c_adapter *d)
{
  return i2c_probe(d, &addr_data, i2c_test_attach);
}
```

The `i2c_probe` function is provided by the I2C core; this function uses the information in the data structure `addr_data` to call the function `i2c_test_attach`; the latter instantiates a new client and registers it to the subsystem. The `addr_data` structure is declared in the file `include/linux/i2c.h`. The `addr_data` function is used to do the following.

- Force an I2C device at a given address to be registered as a client without detection
- Ignore an I2C device at a given address
- Probe an I2C device at a given address using the adapter and detect its presence
- Function in a normal mode that just picks up an I2C device at a given address and detects its presence

The function `i2c_test_attach` creates the `i2c_client` data structure for the client and populates it. The `i2c_client` data structure is again declared in the file `include/linux/i2c.h` and its important fields are:

- `id:` identification
- `addr:` The I2C address where the slave was detected
- `adapter:` Pointer to the `i2c_adapter` structure for the bus on which the client was detected
- `driver:` Pointer to the `i2c_driver` structure

```
static int
i2c_test_attach(struct i2c_adapter *adap, int addr,
                int type)
{
  struct i2c_client *client =
      kmalloc(sizeof(struct i2c_client), GFP_KERNEL);

  client->id = TEST_CLIENT_ID:
  client->addr = addr;
  client->adapter = adapter;
  client->driver = &i2c_test_driver;

  return(i2c_attach_client(client));
}
```

Finally the command function that implements the functionality of reading and writing the single register on the chip is as follows.

```
static int
i2c_test_command(struct i2c_client *client,
                 unsigned int cmd, void *arg)
{
  if(cmd == READ)
    return i2c_test_read(client, arg);
  else if(cmd == WRITE)
    return i2c_test_write(client, arg); return -EINVAL;
}

static int
i2c_test_read(struct i2c_client *client, void *arg)
{
  i2c_master_recv(client,arg,4);
}

static int
i2c_test_write(struct i2c_client *client, void *arg)
{
  i2c_master_send(client, arg ,4);
}
```

The i2c_master_recv and i2c_master_send functions read and write bytes from a given client. They internally call the master_xfer function of the driver. Another function i2c_transfer is also available; it sends a series of messages that can be a mix of reads and writes causing combined transactions.

5.4 USB Gadgets

The universal serial bus (USB) is a master–slave communication bus for connecting a PC to a set of peripherals. The bus topology is like a tree, with the USB *host* at the root. The USB host/root runs a USB *controller driver* responsible for controlling *devices* connected to the bus. New devices can be attached or detached to or from the bus on the fly. The host is responsible for identifying these events and configuring the bus as required. Also devices attached to the bus use a unique id to transfer data to or from the host. All data transfer is host triggered. This means that even if a device has some data, it cannot be transferred unless asked by the host to do so. The system also allows for configuring bus bandwidth allocations on a device basis. This allows the host to reserve bandwidth for a particular device. For example, a video or audio device may request a specific bandwidth requirement when compared to that of a human interface device such as a keyboard or mouse. The latest standards allow high-speed USB connections with a theoretical transfer rate of 480 Mbps.

The Linux USB driver framework provides support for both the host and slave devices. The host part is generally employed when devices need to connect to a Linux system. For example, a PDA running Linux may detect a USB storage class device attached to its bus. The slave part is used for embedded devices that run Linux and get plugged into the bus of another host. For example, consider a portable MP3 player running Linux with a USB interface for transferring songs from the host.

This chapter explains the infrastructure/driver framework provided by the Linux kernel on the slave (or device) side. This driver framework is called the *USB gadget device drivers*. Before going into details of these drivers, we have a high-level overview of the USB device architecture.

5.4.1 USB Basics

As stated earlier, USB is a high-speed serial bus capable of a maximum transfer rate of 480 Mbps. Devices are attached to a root node, the host. The host device is the USB bus controller attached via PCI to the system bus. Devices are classified to fall under various standard device classes such as

- *Storage Class:* Hard disk, flash drives, and so on
- *Human Interface Class:* Mouse, keyboard, touchpad, and so on
- *Extender /Hub:* Hubs (used for providing additional connection points on the bus)
- *Communication Class:* Modem, network cards, and so on

Figure 5.9 represents a typical bus topology.

Communication to a USB device happens over unidirectional pipes called *endpoints*. Every logical USB device is a collection of endpoints. Each logical device on the bus is assigned a unique number by the host when the device is attached to the bus. Each endpoint on a device is associated with a device-specified endpoint number. The combination of device and endpoint number allows each endpoint to be identified uniquely.

USB defines four transfer types.

- *Control transfers:* They are setup/configuration transfers that usually happen over a configuration endpoint. Every device must have at least one endpoint required for configuring the device on detection. This is called *endpoint 0.*

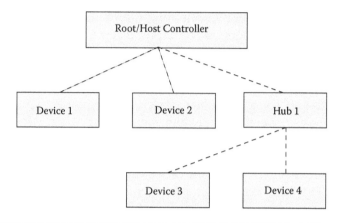

Figure 5.9   USB bus topology.

- *Interrupt transfers:* They are used to transfer low-frequency, interrupt driver data. HID devices use interrupt transfers.
- *Bulk transfers:* They are used to transfer large chunks of data that are not bandwidth restricted. Printers and communication devices use bulk transfers.
- *Isochronous transfers:* They are used for periodic, continuous data transfers. Video, audio, and other streaming devices use isochronous transfers.

An endpoint is usually implemented over some memory registers or buffer area exported by the hardware. The USB device driver writes data to these registers to program the endpoint. High-speed transfer devices might provide DMA transfers for their endpoints. One or more endpoints are grouped together to form a *device interface.* An interface represents a logical device such as a mouse or keyboard. Each logical device must have the corresponding USB driver interface available on the host. Figure 5.10 shows an integrated keyboard and mouse device and their corresponding drivers on the host.

Interfaces are grouped to form *configurations.* Each configuration sets the device in a specific mode. For example, a modem might be configured with two 64-KBps lines or in another configuration as a single 128-KBps line. The host driver accesses the host controller to control the bus whereas the driver on the device exposes the device to the bus. The USB gadget driver framework provides the necessary APIs and data structures for implementing a USB device function or interface. The framework consists of two layers.

- *Controller driver:* This layer provides hardware abstraction for the USB device and implements the *gadget APIs.* The driver implements the hardware-specific portion and provides the hardware-independent gadget API layer to be used by the higher-level drivers.
- *Gadget driver:* This layer is the actual device implementation of the USB device function using the gadget API. Each USB device function requires a separate gadget driver to be written. The USB device functions supported depend on the capability of the hardware underneath.

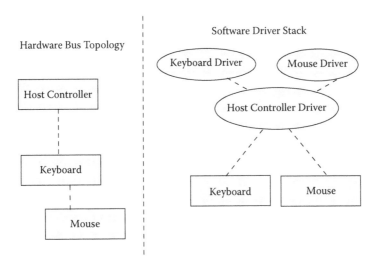

Figure 5.10 USB driver stack.

The controller driver handles only a limited set of standard USB control requests related to device and endpoint state. All the other control requests, including those pertaining to device configuration, are handled by the gadget driver. The controller driver also manages the endpoint's I/O queue and data transfer between the hardware and the gadget driver's buffers using DMA wherever possible.

As discussed earlier, a gadget driver implements a particular device function. For example, the Ethernet gadget driver implements functionalities such as transmitting and receiving network packets. For this purpose the gadget driver needs to bind itself to the Linux kernel and fit in the corresponding driver stack. The driver on the higher end calls functions like `netif_rx` and `netdev_register` and on the lower end it calls the controller driver via the gadget API layer to perform the required hardware-specific action. Figure 5.11 shows the layers of the gadget USB drivers and how they interact with the rest of the Linux system.

Generally, the controller attaches itself to the kernel as a regular PCI device using the `pci_driver.probe` method. The controller driver provides `usb_gadget_register_driver` API for device registration. The logical steps involved in the controller probe function are as follows.

1. Register and allocate PCI resources using `pci_enable_device()` and `request_mem_region()`.
2. Initialize USB endpoint controller hardware such as resetting endpoints and endpoint data structures.
3. Register for the controller's interrupt handling using `request_irq()`.
4. Initialize DMA registers of the controller and allocate DMA memory.
5. Register controller device to kernel using `device_register()`.

The most important data structure is the `usb_gadget_driver` that hooks a gadget device to the controller. Another important aspect of the controller

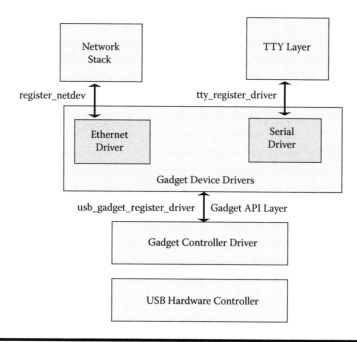

Figure 5.11   USB gadget driver architecture.

driver is that it takes care of various endpoint interactions. To implement this the gadget layer provides a structure `struct usb_ep_ops`. Both data structures are shown in Listing 5.8.

Most function pointers in `usb_ep_ops` are wrapped by gadget API calls that are used by gadget drivers. For example, the gadget driver API `usb_ep_enable` enables operations on an endpoint.

```
static inline int
usb_ep_enable (struct usb_ep *ep,
               const struct usb_endpoint_descriptor *desc)
{
  return ep->ops->enable (ep, desc);
}
```

Similarly the gadget driver uses the `usb_ep_queue` function to submit any USB to the device.

```
static inline int
usb_ep_queue (struct usb_ep *ep, struct usb_request *req,
              int gfp_flags)
{
  return ep->ops->queue (ep, req, gfp_flags);
}
```

The `ops->queue` is a controller-specific queue function. For a complete list of gadget APIs refer to `include/linux/usb_gadget.h`.

Listing 5.8   USB Gadget Driver Data Structures

```
struct usb_gadget_driver {

  /* String describing the gadget's device function */
  char *function;

  /*
   * Highest speed the driver handles. (One of USB_SPEED_HIGH,
   * USB_SPEED_FULL, USB_SPEED_LOW)
   */
  enum usb_device_speed speed;

  /*
   * Device attach called from gadget driver during registration
   */
  int (*bind)(struct usb_gadget *);

  /*
   * setup is called for handling ep0 control requests that are
   * not handled by the controller driver
   */
  int (*setup)(struct usb_gadget *,
               const struct usb_ctrlrequest *);

  /* Host disconnection of device indicated using this call */
  void (*disconnect)(struct usb_gadget *);

  /* Called after device disconnect */
  void (*unbind)(struct usb_gadget *);

  /* Indicates USB suspend */
  void (*suspend)(struct usb_gadget *);

  /* Indicates USB resume */
  void (*resume)(struct usb_gadget *);
}

struct usb_ep_ops {

  /* Enable or Disable the endpoint */
  int (*enable) (struct usb_ep *ep,
               const struct usb_endpoint_descriptor *desc);
  int (*disable) (struct usb_ep *ep);

  /* URB Alloc and free routines */
  struct usb_request * (*alloc_request) (struct usb_ep *ep,
                                         int gfp_flags);
  void (*free_request) (struct usb_ep *ep,
                        struct usb_request *req);
  void *(*alloc_buffer)(struct usb_ep *ep, unsigned bytes,
                        dma_addr_t *dma, int gfp_flags);
  void (*free_buffer)   (struct usb_ep *ep, void *buf,
                        dma_addr_t dma, unsigned bytes);

  /* Endpoint Queue management functions */
```

Listing 5.8   USB Gadget Driver Data Structures (continued)

```
   int (*queue) (struct usb_ep *ep, struct usb_request *req,
                 int gfp_flags);
   int (*dequeue) (struct usb_ep *ep, struct usb_request *req);

   int (*set_halt) (struct usb_ep *ep, int value);
   int (*fifo_status) (struct usb_ep *ep);
   void (*fifo_flush) (struct usb_ep *ep);
};
```

5.4.2 Ethernet Gadget Driver

We take the Ethernet device as an example to explain the gadget device driver model. It is implemented in the file `drivers/usb/gadget/ether.c`.

The driver init of any gadget device driver needs to call the `usb_gadget_register_driver` API.

```
static int __init init (void)
{
  return usb_gadget_register_driver (&eth_driver);
}
module_init (init);
```

`eth_driver` is the `usb_gadget_driver` structure filled with the respective handlers.

```
static struct usb_gadget_driver eth_driver = {

#ifdef CONFIG_USB_GADGET_DUALSPEED
  .speed        = USB_SPEED_HIGH,
#else
  .speed        = USB_SPEED_FULL,
#endif

  .function     = (char *) driver_desc,
  .bind         = eth_bind,
  .unbind       = eth_unbind,
  .setup        = eth_setup,
  .disconnect   = eth_disconnect,
};
```

`usb_gadget_driver.bind` is called from the controller driver during the registration call. The `bind()` of a gadget driver is expected to do the following.

- Initialize device-specific data structures.
- Attach to the necessary kernel driver subsystem (such as serial driver, network, storage, etc.).
- Initialize the endpoint 0 request block.

`eth_bind` is the bind function.

```
static int
eth_bind (struct usb_gadget *gadget)
{
      ...

      ...
  net = alloc_etherdev (sizeof *dev);

      ...
  net->hard_start_xmit = eth_start_xmit;
  net->open = eth_open;
  net->stop = eth_stop;
  net->do_ioctl = eth_ioctl;

  /* EP0 allocation*/
  dev->req = usb_ep_alloc_request (gadget->ep0,
                                  GFP_KERNEL);
      ...
  dev->req->complete = eth_setup_complete;
  dev->req->buf = usb_ep_alloc_buffer (gadget->ep0,
                USB_BUFSIZ, &dev->req->dma, GFP_KERNEL);
      ...
  status = register_netdev (dev->net);
      ...
}
```

Once the setup is complete the device is fully configured and functional as a normal device on the kernel driver stack. In the example the USB Ethernet driver has attached itself to the network driver stack using `register_netdev()`. This enables applications to use this interface as a standard network interface.

> *Each USB request block (URB) requires the block to be allocated and has to be associated with a completion routine. All endpoint requests are queued, because they wait for the host/root controller of the bus to poll for data. Once the request has been processed by the hardware, the controller driver calls the associated completion routine.*

The data transmission function in any driver essentially does the following.

- Creates a new URB or gets one from a preallocated pool
- Points the URB's data and length to the data and length provided by the upper layer driver
- Queues the URB into the corresponding endpoint for data transmission

`eth_start_xmit` is the transmit function of the Ethernet gadget driver.

```
static int eth_start_xmit (struct sk_buff *skb,
                           struct net_device *net)
{
  struct eth_dev*dev = (struct eth_dev *) net->priv;
  int length = skb->len;
      ...
  req->buf = skb->data;
  req->context = skb;
```

```
    req->complete = tx_complete;
    req->length = length;
        ...
    retval = usb_ep_queue (dev->in_ep, req, GFP_ATOMIC);
        ...
}
```

Data reception also requires the usage of URBs and is done as follows.

- Create a list of empty URBs.
- Initialize each of them with a proper completion routine. The completion routine for receive indicates upper layers of the network stack of the arrival of data.
- Queue them up in the corresponding endpoint.

The Ethernet gadget driver fills up the endpoint queue with URBs at the start-up using the rx_submit function.

```
static int
rx_submit (struct eth_dev *dev, struct usb_request *req,
            int gfp_flags)
{
  struct sk_buff *skb;
  size_t size;

  size = (sizeof (struct ethhdr) + dev->net->mtu +
                          RX_EXTRA);

  skb = alloc_skb (size, gfp_flags);
      ...
  req->buf = skb->data;
  req->length = size;
  req->complete = rx_complete;
  req->context = skb;
  retval = usb_ep_queue (dev->out_ep, req, gfp_flags);
      ...
}
```

The indication of data reception to the network layer happens in the completion routine.

```
static void rx_complete (struct usb_ep *ep,
                          struct usb_request *req)
{
  struct sk_buff *skb = req->context;
  struct eth_dev *dev = ep->driver_da
      ...
  skb_put (skb, req->actual);
  skb->dev = dev->net;
  skb->protocol = eth_type_trans (skb, dev->net);
      ...
  netif_rx (skb);
}
```

5.5 Watchdog Timer

Watchdog timers are hardware components that are used to help the system recover from software anomalies by resetting the processor. A watchdog timer needs to be primed with a counter and the watchdog starts counting down from the primed value to zero. If the counter reaches zero before the software reprimes it, then it is presumed that the system is malfunctioning and system reset is required. Some watchdog timers have advanced support built in them such as monitoring temperature and power over voltage.

Typically watchdog timers provide four sets of operations.

- Starting the watchdog
- Setting watchdog timeout
- Stopping the watchdog
- Repriming the watchdog

In Linux, the watchdog is exported as a character device to the applications. The watchdog devices are registered as minor devices to a special character device called *miscellaneous device*. The watchdog driver makes use of the minor number 130.

The watchdog character device can be used by a daemon to reprime the watchdog after a fixed interval. Many distributions provide a daemon called the watchdog daemon[4] that does this job. This approach can be used in the 2.6 kernel because of improved real-time features of the kernel. In the 2.4 kernel or if the watchdog timer has a very small reprime interval, it is better to use a kernel timer to reprime the watchdog.[5]

A typical watchdog driver needs to implement the following functions.

- *Initialization function:* It includes
  - Registering the watchdog driver as a miscellaneous character driver (using the function `misc_register`)
  - Registering a function that disables the watchdog to the system reboot notifier (using the `register_boot_notifier` function). The registered function is called before the system is rebooted. This makes sure that after the system is rebooted the watchdog is not running lest it should reset the system again.
- *Open function:* It is called when the `/dev/watchdog` device is opened. This function should fire the watchdog.
- *Release function:* Closing the driver should cause the watchdog to be stopped. However, in Linux when a task exits, all the file descriptors are automatically closed, irrespective of whether it exited safely or it crashed. So if the watchdog daemon does not exit safely, then there is a chance that the watchdog is disabled. To prevent such a condition in 2.6 kernel before the safe exit of the watchdog daemon, it needs to signal to the driver that it intends to do a clean disable of the watchdog. Normally the magic character "V" is written to the watchdog driver and then this function is invoked. Alternatively you can choose not to implement watchdog disabling totally in your driver. Existent watchdog drivers on Linux provide this option if config option `CONFIG_WATCHDOG_NOWAYOUT` is chosen.

- *Write function:* This function is invoked by the application to reprime the watchdog.
- *Ioctl:* However, you can also use ioctl to reprime the watchdog. WDIOC_KEEPALIVE does this. Also you can set a timeout using WDIOC_SETTIMEOUT.

Linux provides a software watchdog in case there is no watchdog support from the hardware. The software watchdog makes use of timers internally, however, software watchdogs do not always work; their working depends on the system state and interrupt state.

5.6 Kernel Modules

Finally we discuss kernel modules in brief. Kernel modules are added dynamically in a running kernel. This reduces the size of the kernel by making sure that the kernel modules get loaded only when they are used. There are three components to the kernel module interface.

- *Module interface/APIs:* How do you write a module?
- *Module building:* How do you build a module?
- *Module loading and unloading:* How can you load and unload modules?

All three components have undergone significant changes across the 2.4 and the 2.6 kernels. Module building is explained in detail in Chapter 8. This section explains the other two components.

5.6.1 Module APIs

Listing 5.9 shows an example of a kernel module on the 2.4 and 2.6 kernels. The module prints a string Hello world every time it is loaded and Bye world every time it is unloaded. The number of times the first string gets printed depends on a module parameter defined here as excount.
Some points to be noted are as follows.

- *Entry and exit functions:* A module must have an entry and an exit function that is automatically invoked by the kernel when the module is loaded and unloaded, respectively. In the 2.4 kernel, functions init_module() and cleanup_module() are entry and exit functions. However, in the 2.6 kernel, they are specifically registered using the module_init() and module_exit() macros.
- *Parameter passing:* Every module can be passed parameters; these are passed as command-line arguments when the module is loaded. In the 2.4 kernel, the macro MODULE_PARM is used to supply the arguments to the module. In the 2.6 kernel, parameters are declared with the module_param()[6] macro as shown in Listing 5.1.

Listing 5.9   Kernel Modules

```
/* 2.4 kernel based module */

static int excount = 1;
MODULE_PARM(excount,"i");
static int init_module(void)
{
  int i;
  if(excount <= 0) return -EINVAL;
  for(i=0; i<excount;i++)
    printk("Hello world\n");
  return 0;
}

static void cleanup_module(void)
{
  printk("Bye world\n");
}

/* 2.6 kernel based module code */

MODULE_LICENSE("GPL");
module_param(excount, int, 0);
static int init_module(void)
{
  int i;
  if(excount <= 0) return -EINVAL;
  for(i=0; i<excount;i++)
    printk("Hello world\n");
  return 0;
}

static void cleanup_module(void)
{
printk("Bye world\n");
}

module_init(init_module);
module_exit(cleanup_module);
```

■ *Maintaining module usage count:* Every module has a usage count that indicates the number of references to this module. Reference count 0 means that the module can be safely unloaded. In the 2.4 kernel, the module count was maintained by the individual modules. This approach was defective with module unloading code on SMP systems. Hence on 2.6 systems, the module need not maintain the usage count but instead the kernel maintains it. However, this leads to a problem if a module function is being referenced after the module is unloaded. If you are calling through a function pointer into a different module, you must hold a reference to that module. Otherwise you risk sleeping in the module while it is unloaded. To solve this the kernel provides APIs to access the module; reference to the module is obtained using the try_module_get() API and its reference is released using the module_put() API.

- *Declaring the license:* Every module needs to declare if it is a proprietary or a nonproprietary module. This is done using the MODULE_LICENSE macro. If the argument passed is GPL, it means that it is released under GPL.

5.6.2 Module Loading and Unloading

The kernel provides system calls for loading, unloading, and accessing the kernel modules. However, standard programs are available that do the job of loading and unloading a module. The insmod program installs a loadable module in the running kernel. insmod tries to link a module into the running kernel by resolving all symbols from the kernel's exported symbol table. Sometimes the loading of a module is dependent on loading of other modules. This dependence is stored in the file modules.dep. modprobe parses the file and loads all the required modules before loading a given module. Finally rmmod unlinks the module from the kernel. This step is successful of there are no users of the module in the kernel and its reference count is zero.

Notes

1. Processes can prefer to run without a controlling terminal. Such processes are called daemons. Daemons are used for running tasks in the background after detaching from the controlling terminal so that they are not affected when the terminal gets closed.
2. Ethernet devices are initialized by default with names from "eth0" to "eth7".
3. This queue is known more popularly as qdisc (because every queue can have a discipline associated with it that determines the mechanism by which packets are enqueued and dequeued).
4. Busybox has a simple watchdog implementation too.
5. Some drivers use this approach; look at the AMD Elan SC520 processor watchdog driver code.
6. MODULE_PARAM is deprecated on the 2.6 kernel.

Chapter 6

Porting Applications

A developer faces a challenging task when porting applications from a traditional RTOS such as VxWorks, pSoS, Nucleus, and so on, to embedded Linux. The difficulty arises because of the entirely different programming model of Linux as compared to other RTOSs. This chapter discusses a roadmap for porting applications from a traditional RTOS to embedded Linux. It also discusses various techniques that are generally employed to facilitate porting.

6.1 Architectural Comparison

In this section we compare the architecture of a traditional RTOS with embedded Linux. A traditional RTOS is generally based on a flat memory model. All the applications along with the kernel are part of a single image that is then loaded into the target. Kernel services such as schedulers, memory management, timers, and the like, run in the same physical address space as user applications. Applications request any kernel service using a simple function call interface. User applications also share common address space among themselves. Figure 6.1 shows a flat memory model of a traditional RTOS.

The major drawback of such an RTOS is that it is based on a flat memory model. MMU is not utilized for memory protection. Consequently any user application can corrupt kernel code or data. It can also corrupt data structures of some other application.

Linux on the other hand utilizes MMU to provide separate virtual address space to each process. The virtual address space is protected; that is, a process cannot access any data structure belonging to some other process. Kernel code and data structures are also protected. Access to kernel services by user applications is provided through a well-defined system call an interface. Figure 6.2 shows an MMU-based memory model of Linux.

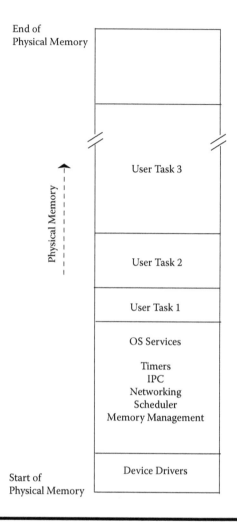

Figure 6.1   RTOS flat memory model.

From now on any reference to RTOS refers to a traditional RTOS with a flat memory model and no memory protection unless specified.

The porting issues that are evident from the above comparison are

- Applications that "share" single address space in an RTOS should be ported to the protected virtual address space model of Linux.
- An RTOS generally provides its own native set of APIs for various services such as task creation, IPC, timers, and so on. Thus a mapping of each such native API to an equivalent Linux API must be defined.
- A kernel interface in Linux is not a simple function call interface. So user applications cannot make any direct driver or kernel calls.

End of Virtual Memory

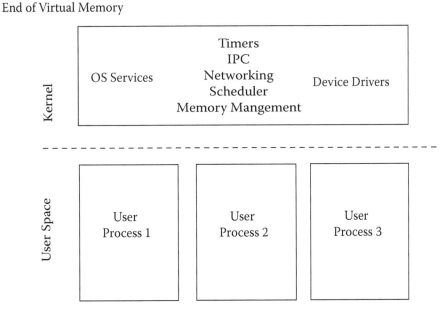

Figure 6.2   Linux memory model.

6.2 Application Porting Roadmap

In this section we discuss a generic application porting roadmap from an RTOS to embedded Linux. The following sections cover the porting roadmap in detail.

6.2.1 Decide Porting Strategy

Divide all your RTOS tasks into two broad categories: user-space tasks and kernel tasks. For example, any UI task is a user-space task and any hardware initialization task is a kernel task. You should also identify a list of user-space and kernel functions. For example, any function that manipulates device registers is a kernel function and any function that reads some data from a file is a user-space function.

Two porting strategies could be adopted. Note that in both approaches kernel tasks migrate as Linux kernel threads. The following discussion applies to user space tasks only.

One-Process Model

In this approach user-space RTOS tasks migrate as separate threads in a single Linux process as shown in Figure 6.3. The advantage of this approach is the reduced porting effort as it requires fewer modifications in the existing code

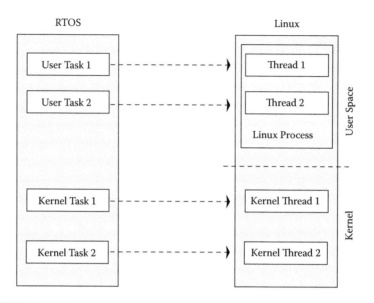

Figure 6.3   Migration in one-process model.

base. The biggest disadvantage is no memory protection between threads inside the process. However kernel services, drivers, and so on are fully protected.

Multiprocess Model

Categorize tasks as unrelated, related, and key tasks.

- *Unrelated tasks:* Loosely coupled tasks that use IPC mechanisms offered by the RTOS to communicate with other tasks or stand-alone tasks[1] that are not related to other tasks could be migrated as separate Linux processes.
- *Related tasks:* Tasks that share global variables and function callbacks fall under this category. They could be migrated as separate threads in one Linux process.
- *Key tasks:* Tasks that perform key activities such as system watchdog tasks should be migrated as separate Linux processes. This ensures that key tasks are protected from memory corruption of other tasks.

Figure 6.4 shows this approach. The advantages of this model are

- Per-process memory protection is achieved. A task cannot corrupt address space belonging to some other process.
- It's extensible. New features can be added keeping this model in mind.
- Applications can fully exploit the benefits of the Linux programming model.

The biggest disadvantage of this approach is that migration to Linux using this model is a time-consuming process. You may need to redesign most of the applications. One such time-consuming activity is porting user-space

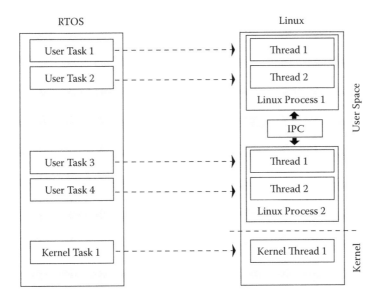

Figure 6.4   Migration in multiprocess model.

libraries. The trouble comes when the library maintains some global variables that are manipulated by multiple tasks. Assume you decide to port a library as a shared library in Linux. Thus you get the advantage of text sharing across multiple processes. Now what about the global data in the library? In a shared library only text is shared and data is per-process private. Thus all the global variables in the library now become per-process globals. You cannot modify them in one process and expect changes to become visible in another. Thus to support this, you need to redesign applications using the library to use proper IPC mechanisms among themselves. You may also be tempted to put such tasks under the related tasks category but you lose the benefits of the multiprocess model in that case.

6.2.2 Write an Operating System Porting Layer (OSPL)

This layer emulates RTOS APIs using Linux APIs as shown in Figure 6.5. A well-written OSPL minimizes changes to your existing code base. To achieve this, mapping between RTOS APIs and Linux APIs must be defined. The mapping falls under the following two categories.

- *One-to-one mapping:* Every RTOS API can be emulated using a single Linux API. The arguments or return value of the equivalent Linux API may differ but the expected function behavior is the same.
- *One-to-many mapping:* More than one Linux API is necessary to emulate an RTOS API.

For many RTOS APIs you also need to define the mapping with Linux kernel APIs as these APIs may be used by kernel tasks. You can either have

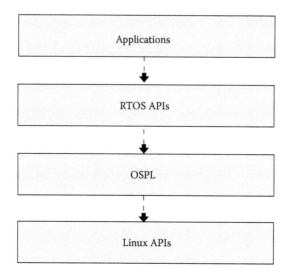

Figure 6.5   Operating system porting layer.

a separate kernel and user OSPL or have a single library that links in both user and kernel. An OSPL API for the latter case looks like the following.

```
void rtosAPI(void){
  #ifndef __KERNEL__
      /* Equivalent user space Linux API */
  #else
      /* Equivalent Linux kernel API */
  #endif
}
```

Note that when defining mapping of RTOS APIs to Linux APIs you may come across some RTOS APIs that cannot be emulated using Linux APIs without avoiding any changes to the existing code base. In such cases you may need to rewrite some portion of your existing code.

6.2.3 Write a Kernel API Driver

Sometimes you face a difficulty when making a decision of porting a task to user or kernel space as it calls both user and kernel functions. The same problem occurs with the function that calls both user-space and kernel functions. For example, consider function `func` calling function `func1` and `func2`. `func1` is a user-space function and `func2` is a kernel function.

```
void func(){
  func1();  <-- User-space function
  func2();  <-- Kernel function
}
```

Now where should the function `func` be ported? In user space or kernel space? You need to write a kernel API driver to support such cases. In the

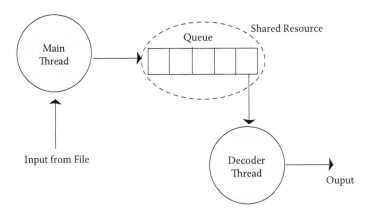

Figure 6.6   Simple audio player.

kernel API driver model, function `func` is ported in user space by providing an interface for function `func2` in user space. The kernel API driver is discussed in detail in Section 6.5.

In this section we discussed an application porting roadmap from an RTOS to Linux. The rest of the chapter is divided into three parts.

- In the first part we discuss pthreads (POSIX threads) in brief. Pthreads is a Linux threading model. The section covers all the pthreads operations that one should understand before starting the porting process.
- In the second part we write a small OSPL supporting only task creation, task destruction, and mutex APIs.
- Finally we discuss the kernel API driver.

6.3 Programming with Pthreads

To discuss various pthreads operations we have taken a very simple MP3 player located in file `player.c`. There are two main components of the player.

- *Initialization:* This includes audio subsystem initialization in a separate thread. It's used for demonstrating thread creation and exit routines.
- *Decoding:* This is the core of the application. Two threads of execution are involved. The main thread reads MP3 data from a file and adds it in a queue. The decoder thread dequeues the data, decodes it, and plays it out. The queue is a shared data structure between the main and decoder threads. Figure 6.6 shows the various entities that are involved during the decoding phase. The idea here is to demonstrate various pthread synchronization primitives in a greater detail.

Please note that this section is not a complete pthreads reference manual. Our aim is give you sufficient details to kickstart your development with pthreads. Also in our player example we have intentionally omitted player-specific details regarding decoding and playback. This is done to give more emphasis to pthreads operations in the player.

6.3.1 Thread Creation and Exit

A new thread of execution is created by calling the `pthread_create` function. The prototype of the function is

```
int pthread_create (pthread_t * thread_id,
                    pthread_attr_t *thread_attributes,
                    void * (*start_routine)(void *),
                    void * arg);
```

The function returns zero on success and the identifier of the created thread is stored in the first argument `thread_id`. The new thread starts its execution from the `start_routine` function. `arg` is an argument to `start_routine`. `thread_attributes` represents various thread attributes such as scheduling policy, priority, stacksize, and the like. The function returns a nonzero value on failure.

Let's take our MP3 player in `player.c`. The player start-up calls `system_init` function for various subsystem initializations. `system_init` function runs in the context of the main thread.

```
int system_init(){
  pthread_t audio_tid;
  int sample = 1;
  void * audio_init_status;

  /* Initialize audio subsystem in a separate thread */
  if (pthread_create(&audio_tid, NULL, audio_init,
                     (void *)sample) != 0){
    printf("Audio thread creation failed.\n");
    return FAIL;
  }

  /*
   * Initialize rest of application, data structures etc
   */

  . . . .
  . . . .
}
```

`system_init` calls `pthread_create` to perform audio subsystem initialization in a new thread. On success, the thread id of the created thread is stored in `audio_tid`. The new thread executes the `audio_init` function. `audio_init` takes an integer argument sample. As the second argument to `pthread_create` is `NULL`, the `audio_tid` thread starts with a default set of attributes. (For example, scheduling policy and priority of the thread is inherited from the caller.)

The new thread initializes the decoder and audio output subsystem. If requested it also plays a sample sound for two seconds to verify if the initialization is successful.

```
void* audio_init(void *sample){
  int init_status = SUCCESS;
  printf("Audio init thread created with ID %d\n",
                              pthread_self());

  /*
   * Initialize MP3 decoder subsystem.
   * set init_status = FAIL for failure.
   */

  /*
   * Initialize Audio output subsystem.
   * set init_status = FAIL for failure.
   */

 if ((int)sample){

   /*
    * Play sample output for 2 seconds.
    * Set init_status = FAIL if play fails
    */

  }
  printf("Audio subsystem initialized\n");

  pthread_exit((void *)init_status);
}
```

Two questions arise.

■ How can the audio_init thread send its exit status to the main thread?
■ Is it possible for the system_init function to wait for termination of the audio_init thread before quitting? How can it fetch the exit status of audio_init thread?

A thread sets its exit status using the pthread_exit function. This function also terminates execution of the calling thread.

```
void pthread_exit(void *return_val);
```

audio_init calls pthread_exit to terminate its execution and also to set its exit status. pthread_exit is analogous to the exit system call. From the application developer's point of view there is only one difference: exit terminates the complete process and pthread_exit terminates the calling thread only.

A thread can get the exit status of another thread by calling the pthread_join function.

```
int pthread_join(pthread_t tid, void **thread_return_val);
```

pthread_join suspends execution of the calling thread until thread tid exits. When pthread_join returns, the exit status of thread tid is stored in the thread_return_val argument. pthread_join is analogous to the wait4 system call. wait4 suspends the execution of a parent process until the child specified in its argument terminates. Similarly pthread_join also suspends the execution of the calling thread until the thread specified in its argument exits. As you can see, system_init calls pthread_join to wait for the audio_init thread to exit before returning. It also prints an error message if audio_init fails.

```
int system_init(){
   ...
  void * audio_init_status;
   ...
   ...
  /* Wait for audio_init thread to complete */
  pthread_join(audio_tid, &audio_init_status);

  /* If audio init failed then return error */
  if ((int)audio_init_status == FAIL){
    printf("Audio init failed.\n");
    return FAIL;
  }

  return SUCCESS;
}
```

Note that a thread created using pthread_create with a default set of attributes (the second argument to pthread_create is NULL) is a joinable thread. Resources allocated to a joinable thread are not released until some other thread calls pthread_join on the thread. It becomes a zombie.

6.3.2 Thread Synchronization

Pthreads provides thread synchronization in the form of mutex and condition variables.

A mutex is a binary semaphore that provides exclusive access to a shared data structure. It supports two basic operations: lock and unlock. A thread should lock the mutex before entering the critical section and unlock it when it is done. A thread blocks if it tries to lock an already locked mutex. It is awakened when the mutex is unlocked. Mutex lock operation is atomic. If two threads try to acquire the mutex at the same time, it's assured that one operation will complete or block before the other starts. A nonblocking version of the lock operation, trylock, is also supported. Trylock returns success if the mutex is acquired; it returns failure if the mutex is already locked.

A general sequence to protect a shared data structure using mutex is

```
lock the mutex
operate on shared data
unlock the mutex
```

A condition variable is a synchronization mechanism that is more useful for waiting for events than for resource locking. A condition variable is associated with a predicate (a logical expression that evaluates to either TRUE or FALSE) based on some shared data. Functions are provided to sleep on the condition variable and to wake up single or all threads when the result of the predicate changes.

In our player example the shared data structure between the main thread and decoder thread is a queue. The main thread reads the data from a file and enqueues it. The decoder thread dequeues the data and processes it. If the queue is empty, the decoder thread sleeps until the data arrives in the queue. The main thread after enqueueing the data awakens the decoder thread. The whole synchronization logic is implemented by associating a condition variable with the queue. The shared data is the queue and the predicate is "queue is not empty." The decoder thread sleeps on the condition variable if the predicate is FALSE (i.e., the queue is empty). It is awakened when the main thread "changes" the predicate by adding data in the queue.

Let's now discuss in detail the pthreads implementation of mutex and condition variable.

Pthreads Mutex

A mutex is initialized at the definition time as

```
pthread_mutex_t lock = PTHREAD_MUTEX_INITIALIZER;
```

It can also be initialized at runtime by calling the pthread_mutex_init function.

```
int pthread_mutex_init(pthread_mutex_t *mutex,
              const pthread_mutexattr_t *mutexattr);
```

The first argument is a pointer to mutex that is being initialized and the second argument is the mutex attributes. Default attributes are set if mutexattr is NULL (more about mutex attributes later).

A mutex is acquired by calling the pthread_mutex_lock function. It is released by calling the pthread_mutex_unlock function. pthread_mutex_lock either acquires the mutex or suspends the execution of the calling thread until the owner of the mutex (i.e., a thread that has acquired the mutex by calling the pthread_mutex_lock function earlier) releases it by calling pthread_mutex_unlock.

```
int pthread_mutex_lock(pthread_mutex_t *mutex);
int pthread_mutex_unlock(pthread_mutex_t *mutex);
```

Shared data can be protected by using the mutex lock and unlock functions as

```
pthread_mutex_lock(&lock);
/* operate on shared data */
pthread_mutex_unlock(&lock);
```

There are three types of mutex.

- Fast mutex
- Recursive mutex
- Error-check mutex

The behavior of these three types of mutex is similar; they only differ when the owner of the mutex again calls `pthread_mutex_lock` to reacquire it.

- For fast mutex, a deadlock condition occurs as the thread is now waiting for itself to unlock the mutex
- For recursive mutex, the function returns immediately and the mutex acquire count is incremented. The mutex is unlocked only if the count reaches zero; that is, a thread has to call `pthread_mutex_unlock` for every call to `pthread_mutex_lock`.
- For error-check mutex, `pthread_mutex_lock` returns the error with error code `EDEADLK`.

Fast, recursive, and error-check mutex are initialized at definition time as

```
/* Fast Mutex */
pthread_mutex_t lock = PTHREAD_MUTEX_INITIALIZER;

/* Recursive mutex */
pthread_mutex_t lock =
    PTHREAD_RECURSIVE_MUTEX_INITIALIZER_NP;

/* Error-check mutex */
pthread_mutex_t lock =
    PTHREAD_ERRORCHECK_MUTEX_INITIALIZER_NP;
```

They can also be initialized at runtime by calling the `pthread_mutex_init` function. Recall that passing NULL as the second argument of `pthread_mutex_init` sets default attributes for the mutex. By default a mutex is initialized as a fast mutex.

```
/* Fast Mutex */
pthread_mutex_t lock;
pthread_mutex_init(&lock, NULL);
```

A recursive mutex is initialized at runtime as

```
pthread_mutex_t lock;
pthread_mutexattr_t mutex_attr;
pthread_mutexattr_init(&mutex_attr);
pthread_mutexattr_settype(&mutex_attr,
    PTHREAD_RECURSIVE_MUTEX_INITIALIZER_NP);
pthread_mutex_init(&lock, &mutex_attr);
```

Error-check mutex is initialized at runtime similarly to the above; only change the mutex type to PTHREAD_ERRORCHECK_MUTEX_INITIALIZER_NP in the call to pthread_mutexattr_settype.

Pthreads Condition Variable

Like mutex, a condition variable is initialized either at definition time or at runtime by calling the pthread_cond_init function.

```
pthread_cond_t cond_var = PTHREAD_COND_INITIALIZER;
```

or

```
pthread_cond_t cond_var;
pthread_cond_init(&cond_var, NULL);
```

Let's come back to our MP3 player to understand the various pthreads condition variable operations. Three entities are involved as shown in Figure 6.6.

- *Main thread:* It spawns the audio decoder thread. It's also the producer of data for the decoder thread.
- *Decoder thread:* It decodes and plays back the data provided by the main thread.
- *Queue:* This is a shared data structure between the main and decoder threads. The main thread reads the data from the file and enqueues it and the decoder thread dequeues the data and consumes it.

The main thread spawns the decoder thread at application start-up.

```
int main(){

  pthread_t decoder_tid;
    ...

  /* Create audio decoder thread */
  if (pthread_create(&decoder_tid, NULL, audio_decoder,
                  NULL ) != 0){
    printf("Audio decoder thread creation failed.\n");
    return FAIL;
  }
    ...
    ...
}
```

Three questions arise.

- How does the decoder thread know that there is data available in the queue? Should it poll? Is there some better mechanism?

- Is there any way for the main thread to inform the decoder thread of data availability in the queue?
- How can the queue be protected from simultaneous access by the main and decoder threads?

To answer these questions let's first see the details of the audio decoder thread.

```
void* audio_decoder(void *unused){

  char *buffer;
  printf("Audio Decoder thread started\n");

  for(;;){
    pthread_mutex_lock(&lock);
    while(is_empty_queue())
      pthread_cond_wait(&cond, &lock);

    buffer = get_queue();

    pthread_mutex_unlock(&lock);

    /* decode data in buffer */
    /* send decoded data to ouput for playback */

    free(buffer);
  }
}
```

Please pay attention to the following piece of code in the `audio_decoder` function.

```
while(is_empty_queue())
  pthread_cond_wait(&cond, &lock);
```

Here we have introduced a condition variable `cond`. The predicate for this condition variable is "queue is not empty." Thus if the predicate is false (i.e., queue is empty), the thread sleeps on the condition variable by calling the `pthread_cond_wait` function. The thread would remain in wait state until some other thread signals the condition (i.e., changes the predicate by adding data in the queue, which makes it nonempty). The prototype of the function is

```
int pthread_cond_wait(pthread_cond_t *cond,
                      pthread_mutex_t *mutex);
```

You can see in the above declaration that a mutex is also associated with a condition variable. The mutex is required to *protect* the predicate when a thread is checking its status. It avoids the race condition where a thread prepares to wait on a condition variable and another thread signals the condition just before the first thread actually waits on it.

```
while(is_empty_queue())
    <--- Other thread signals the condition --->
  pthread_cond_wait(...);
```

In our example, without mutex the decoder thread would wait on the condition variable even if data is available in the queue. So the rule is: *checking the predicate and sleeping on the condition variable should be an atomic operation*. This atomicity is achieved by introducing a mutex along with a condition variable. Thus the steps are

```
pthread_mutex_lock(&lock);    <-- Get the mutex
while(is_empty_queue())       <-- check the predicate
    pthread_cond_wait(&cond,&lock);<-- sleep on condition var
```

To make this work it is necessary that all the participating threads should acquire the mutex, change/check the condition, and then release the mutex.

Now what happens to the mutex when a thread goes to sleep in `pthread_cond_wait`? If the mutex remains in the lock state then no other thread can signal the condition as that thread too would try to acquire the same mutex before changing the predicate. We have a deadlock: one thread holding the lock and sleeping on the condition variable, and the other thread waiting for the lock to change the condition. To avoid deadlock the associated mutex should be unlocked after a thread slept on a condition variable. This is done in the function `pthread_cond_wait`. The function puts the thread in the sleep state and releases the mutex automatically.

The thread sleeping on a condition variable is awakened and the function `pthread_cond_wait` returns when some other thread signals the condition (by calling the `pthread_cond_signal` or `pthread_cond_broadcast` function as discussed later in the section). `pthread_cond_wait` also reacquires the mutex before returning. The thread can now operate on the condition and release the mutex.

```
pthread_mutex_lock(&lock); <-- Get the mutex
while(is_empty_queue()) <-- Check the condition
    pthread_cond_wait(&cond,&lock); <-- wait on condition var

<-- Mutex is reacquired internally by pthread_cond_wait-->

buffer = get_queue(); <-- Operate on the condition
pthread_mutex_unlock(&lock);<-- Release the mutex when done
```

Let's see how a thread can signal a condition. The steps are

- Get the mutex.
- Change the condition.
- Release the mutex.
- Wake up single or all threads that are sleeping on the condition variable.

The main thread of our player awakens the audio decoder thread after adding data in the queue.

```
fp = fopen("song.mp3", "r");
while (!feof(fp)){
  char *buffer = (char *)malloc(MAX_SIZE);
  fread(buffer, MAX_SIZE, 1, fp);

  pthread_mutex_lock(&lock); <-- Get the mutex
  add_queue(buffer); <-- change the condition. Adding
                            buffer in queue makes it non
                            empty

  pthread_mutex_unlock(&lock); <-- Release the mutex
  pthread_cond_signal(&cond); <-- Wakeup decoder thread

  usleep(300*1000);
}
```

The `pthread_cond_signal` awakens a single thread sleeping on the condition variable. A function `pthread_cond_broadcast` is also available to wake up all the threads that are sleeping on a condition variable.

```
int pthread_cond_signal(pthread_cond_t *cond);
int pthread_cond_broadcast(pthread_cond_t *cond);
```

6.3.3 Thread Cancellation

How can a thread terminate execution of another thread? In our player example, after playback is done, the main thread should terminate the decoder thread before the application quits. This is achieved by the `pthread_cancel` function.

```
int pthread_cancel(pthread_t thread_id);
```

`pthread_cancel` sends a termination request to thread `thread_id`. In our player the main thread calls the `pthread_cancel` function to send the cancellation request to the decoder thread and waits to terminate before exiting.

```
int main(){
   ...
   ...
  pthread_cancel(decoder_tid); <-- send cancellation
                                      request
  pthread_join(decoder_tid, NULL);
}
```

The thread that receives the cancellation request can ignore it, honor it immediately, or defer the request. Two functions are provided that determine the action taken whenever a cancellation request is received by a thread.

```
int pthread_setcancelstate(int state, int *oldstate);
int pthread_setcanceltype(int type, int *oldtype);
```

pthread_setcancelstate is called to ignore or accept the cancellation request. The request is ignored if the state argument is PTHREAD_CANCEL_DISABLE. Cancellation is enabled if the state is PTHREAD_CANCEL_ENABLE. If cancellation is enabled, pthread_setcanceltype is called to set either the immediate or deferred cancellation type. Cancellation is immediately executed if the type argument is PTHREAD_CANCEL_ASYNCHRONOUS. If the type is PTHREAD_CANCEL_DEFERRED, the cancellation request is deferred until the next cancellation point.

By default a thread always starts with the cancellation enabled with the deferred cancellation type. In the player example, the decoder thread calls the function pthread_setcanceltype to set the immediate cancellation type.

```
void* audio_decoder(void *unused){
    . . .
    . . .
    pthread_setcanceltype(PTHREAD_CANCEL_ASYNCHRONOUS, NULL);
    . . .
}
```

As mentioned earlier, execution of a cancellation request can be deferred until the next cancellation point. So what are these cancellation points? Cancellation points are those functions where the test for a pending cancellation request is performed. Cancellation is immediately executed if the request is pending. In general any function that suspends the execution of a current thread for a long time should be a cancellation point. The pthread functions pthread_join, pthread_cond_wait, pthread_cond_timedwait, and pthread_testcancel serve as cancellation points. Please note that executing a cancellation request at any given point is equivalent to calling pthread_exit(PTHREAD_CANCELED) at that point.

A thread can check whether a cancellation request is pending by calling the pthread_testcancel function.

```
void pthread_testcancel(void);
```

Cancellation is immediately executed if a cancellation request is pending when the function is called.

6.3.4 Detached Threads

As discussed earlier, a thread created using pthread_create with a default set of attributes is a joinable thread. It is necessary to call pthread_join on joinable threads to release resources allocated to them. Sometimes we want to create "independent" threads. They should exit whenever they want without any need for some other thread to join them. To achieve this we need to put them in a detached state. It could be done in two ways.

■ Setting the DETACH attribute at thread creation time

```
pthread_attr_t attr;
pthread_attr_init(&attr);
pthread_attr_setdetachstate(&attr, PTHREAD_CREATE_DETACHED);
pthread_create(&tid, &attr, routine, arg);
```

■ pthread_detach function

```
int pthread_detach(pthread_t tid);
```

■ Any thread can put thread `tid` in the detached state by calling the
pthread_detach function. A thread can also put itself in the detached
state by calling

```
pthread_detach(pthread_self());
```

6.4 Operating System Porting Layer (OSPL)

An OSPL emulates your RTOS APIs using Linux APIs. A well-written OSPL
should minimize changes in your existing code base. In this section we discuss
the structure of an OSPL. For this purpose we have defined our own RTOS
APIs. These APIs are similar to APIs found in a traditional RTOS. We discuss
task creation, task destruction, and mutex APIs. Our OSPL is a single library
that links in both kernel and user space. The definitions are present in the
file ospl.c. The ospl.h header file emulates RTOS datatypes using Linux
datatypes. We discuss RTOS mutex APIs first as they have one-to-one mapping
with Linux mutex APIs in our implementation. RTOS task APIs have one-to-
many mapping with equivalent Linux APIs.

> *In this section we discuss OSPL for tasks that are implemented as threads
> in a Linux process. In Section 6.4.3 we show the mapping of timers and
> IPC APIs that can be used across Linux processes.*

6.4.1 RTOS Mutex APIs Emulation

The prototypes of our RTOS mutex APIs are

■ rtosError_t rtosMutexInit(rtosMutex_t *mutex): Initialize a
mutex for lock, unlock, and trylock mutex operations.
■ rtosError_t rtosMutexLock(rtosMutex_t *mutex): Acquire
mutex if it is unlocked; sleep if the mutex is already locked.
■ rtosError_t rtosMutexUnlock(rtosMutex_t *mutex): Unlock
mutex that was acquired previously by calling rtosMutexLock.
■ rtosError_t rtosMutexTrylock(rtosMutex_t *mutex): Acquire
mutex if it is unlocked. Return RTOS_AGAIN if the mutex is already locked.

Note that all the above APIs return one of the values in enum `rtosError_t` in file `rtosTypes.h`. This RTOS file is included in `ospl.h`.

```
typedef enum {
  RTOS_OK,
  RTOS_AGAIN,
  RTOS_UNSUPPORTED,
    ...
  RTOS_ERROR,
}rtosError_t;
```

The functions take the pointer to `rtosMutex_t` object as an argument. `rtosMutex_t` is emulated in file `ospl.h` as

```
#ifndef __KERNEL__
  typedef pthread_mutex_t rtosMutex_t; <-- user space
                                            definition
#else
  typedef struct semaphore rtosMutex_t; <-- kernel
                                             definition
#endif
```

In user space, RTOS mutex APIs are emulated using pthreads mutex operations. In the kernel they are emulated using kernel semaphores. Let's discuss the implementation of these APIs in our OSPL.

The function `rtosMutexInit` is emulated in user space using the `pthread_mutex_init` function. In the kernel the `init_MUTEX` function is used. `init_MUTEX` initializes a semaphore with value 1.

```
rtosError_t rtosMutexInit(rtosMutex_t *mutex){
#ifndef __KERNEL__
  pthread_mutex_init(mutex, NULL);
#else
  init_MUTEX(mutex);
#endif
  return RTOS_OK;
}
```

The user-space version of `rtosMutexLock` uses the `pthread_mutex_lock` function. In the kernel the `down` function is used.

```
rtosError_t rtosMutexLock(rtosMutex_t *mutex){
  int err;
#ifndef __KERNEL__
  err = pthread_mutex_lock(mutex);
#else
  down(mutex);
  err = 0;
#endif
  return (err == 0) ? RTOS_OK : RTOS_ERROR;
}
```

down automatically decreases the semaphore count. The semaphore is acquired if the count becomes zero after decrement; if the count becomes negative then the current task is put to uninterruptible sleep on the semaphore's wait queue. The task only wakes up when the owner of the semaphore releases it by calling up function. The disadvantage of using down is its uninterruptible sleep nature. You can by no means terminate the execution of a task that is sleeping in down. To fully control execution of a task the down_interruptible function should be used instead. The function is similar to down except it returns -EINTR if the sleep is interrupted. Thus the new rtosMutexLock implementation is

```
rtosError_t rtosMutexLock(rtosMutex_t *mutex){
  int err;
#ifndef __KERNEL__
  err = pthread_mutex_lock(mutex);
#else
  err = down_interruptible(mutex);
#endif
  return (err == 0) ? RTOS_OK : RTOS_ERROR;
}
```

The function rtosMutexUnlock is implemented in user space using the pthread_mutex_unlock function. In the kernel the function up is used. up atomically increments the semaphore count and awakens the tasks sleeping (interruptible or uninterruptible) on the semaphore's wait queue.

```
rtosError_t rtosMutexUnlock(rtosMutex_t *mutex){
  int err;
#ifndef __KERNEL__
  err = pthread_mutex_unlock(mutex);
#else
  up(mutex);
  err = 0;
#endif
  return (err == 0) ? RTOS_OK : RTOS_ERROR;
}
```

Finally rtosMutexTryLock uses pthread_mutex_trylock in user space and the function down_trylock in the kernel. down_trylock does not block and returns immediately if the semaphore is already acquired.

```
rtosError_t rtosMutexTrylock(rtosMutex_t *mutex){
  int err;
#ifndef __KERNEL__
  err = pthread_mutex_trylock(mutex);
  if (err == 0)
    return RTOS_OK;
  if (errno == EBUSY)
    return RTOS_AGAIN;
  return RTOS_ERROR;
```

Table 6.1   RTOS and Linux Mutex APIs

	Linux	
RTOS	*User Space*	*Kernel Space*
Mutex init	`pthread_mutex_init`	`init_MUTEX`
Mutex lock	`pthread_mutex_lock`	`down, down_interruptible`
Mutex unlock	`pthread_mutex_unlock`	`up`
Mutex trylock	`pthread_mutex_trylock`	`down_trylock`

```
#else
  err = down_trylock(mutex);
  if (err == 0)
    return RTOS_OK;
  return RTOS_AGAIN;
#endif
}
```

To summarize, one-to-one mapping between RTOS mutex APIs and Linux mutex APIs are listed in Table 6.1.

6.4.2 RTOS Task APIs Emulation

Let's look into a slightly complex part of an OSPL, one-to-many mapping of RTOS APIs with Linux APIs. We take task creation and termination RTOS APIs as an example. The prototypes of our RTOS task creation and termination APIs are

```
rtosError_t rtosCreateTask
                (char *name, <-- name of the task
                 rtosEntry_t routine, <-- entry point
                 char * arg1, <-- Argument to entry point
                 int arg, <-- Argument to entry point
                 void * arg3, <-- Argument to entry point
                 int priority, <-- Priority of new task
                 int stackSize, <-- Stacksize
                 rtosTask_t *tHandle); <-- task handle
```

The function `rtosCreateTask` spawns a new task that starts its execution from the function `routine`. Priority of the new task is set using argument `priority`. The function returns RTOS_OK on success and stores the task handle of the created task in the `tHandle` argument.

```
void rtosDeleteTask(rtosTask_t tHandle <-- task handle
                );
```

The function `rtosDeleteTask` terminates the execution of task `tHandle` and waits for its termination. When the function `rtosDeleteTask` returns, it is guaranteed that task `tHandle` is dead. We first discuss the user-space implementation of these APIs followed by the kernel implementation.

User-Space Task APIs Emulation

Before moving to implementation details of `rtosCreateTask` and `rtos-DeleteTask` let's discuss two datatypes involved: `rtosEntry_t` and `rtosTask_t`. `rtosEntry_t` is defined in `ospl.h` and it should be used without redefining as in our implementation. Changing this type would mean changing declarations of all the functions based on this type, which we want to avoid. `rtosEntry_t` is defined as

```
typedef void (*rtosEntry_t) (char *arg1, int arg2,
                             void *arg3);
```

The internals of `rtosTask_t` are understood only by the task APIs. For other APIs it's just an opaque data type. As we are implementing RTOS task APIs using Linux APIs, we have the liberty to redefine this type as per our needs. The new definition is in file `ospl.h`.

```
typedef struct {
  char name[100]; <-- name of the task
  pthread_t thread_id; <-- thread id
}rtosTask_t;
```

First we discuss `rtosCreateTask`.

```
rtosError_t
rtosCreateTask(char *name, rtosEntry_t routine,
               char * arg1, int arg2, void *arg3,
               int priority, int stackSize,
               rtosTask_t *tHandle){
#ifndef __KERNEL__

int     err;
uarg_t uarg;
strcpy(tHandle->name, name);
uarg.entry_routine = routine;
uarg.priority = priority;
uarg.arg1 = arg1;
uarg.arg2 = arg2;
uarg.arg3 = arg3;
err = pthread_create (&tHandle->thread_id, NULL,
                      wrapper_routine, (void *)&uarg);
return (err) ? RTOS_ERROR : RTOS_OK;

#else
   ...
}
```

We define a new structure `uarg_t` that holds all the RTOS task entry routine arguments, the pointer to the entry routine, and the priority of the task.

```
typedef struct _uarg_t {
  rtosEntry_t entry_routine;
  int priority;
  char *arg1;
  int  arg2;
  void *arg3;
}uarg_t;
```

For every call to `rtosCreateTask` a new thread of execution is created by calling the `pthread_create` function. The identifier of the created thread is stored in the `tHandle->thread_id` argument. The new thread executes the `wrapper_routine` function.

```
void wrapper_routine(void *arg){
  uarg_t *uarg = (uarg_t *)arg;
  nice(rtos_to_nice(uarg->priority));
  uarg->entry_routine(uarg->arg1, uarg->arg2,
                      uarg->arg3);
}
```

In `wrapper_routine`, the priority of the thread is adjusted using the `nice` system call. The `rtos_to_nice` function does priority scale conversion from RTOS to Linux. You need to rewrite this function depending on your RTOS. Finally it transfers control to the actual entry routine with proper arguments.

You may be surprised to see that we have ignored the `stackSize` argument in the implementation. In Linux, it's not necessary to specify the stack size of a thread or a task. The kernel takes care of stack allocation. It grows the stack dynamically when needed. If for any reason you want to specify stack size, call `pthread_attr_setstacksize` before calling `pthread_create`.

Now we discuss `rtosDeleteTask`.

```
void rtosDeleteTask(rtosTask_t tHandle){
#ifndef __KERNEL__
  pthread_cancel(tHandle.thread_id);
  pthread_join(tHandle.thread_id, NULL);
#else
  ...
}
```

The function calls `pthread_cancel` to send a cancellation request to the thread `tHandle`. It then calls `pthread_join` to wait for its termination.

Note from our earlier discussion of thread cancellation that `pthread_cancel` does not terminate the execution of a given thread. It just sends a cancellation request. The thread that receives the request has the option of either accepting it or ignoring it. Thus to successfully emulate `rtosTaskdelete` all threads should accept the cancellation request. They can do this by adding explicit cancellation points in the code such as the following.

```
static void rtosTask (char * arg1, int arg2, void * arg3){
  while(1){
    /*
     * Thread body
     */
    pthread_testcancel(); <-- Add explicit cancellation
                                point
  }
}
```

In fact a thread can use any method discussed earlier to accept a cancellation request. But you should be careful when using the immediate thread cancellation type (PTHREAD_CANCEL_ASYNCHRONOUS). A thread using immediate cancellation could be terminated when it is holding some lock and is in a critical section. On termination the lock is not released and this could lead to deadlock if some other thread tries to get the lock.

Kernel Task APIs Emulation

Let's discuss implementation of rtosCreateTask and rtosDeleteTask task APIs in the kernel. Before moving to implementation details we first discuss two kernel functions: wait_for_completion and complete. These two functions are used in the kernel for synchronizing code execution. They are also used for event notification. A kernel thread can wait for an event to occur by calling wait_for_completion on a completion variable. It is awakened by another thread by calling complete on that completion variable when the event occurs.

Where do we need wait_for_completion and complete kernel functions? In our OSPL a RTOS task is implemented using a kernel thread. A kernel thread is created using the kernel_thread function. It can be terminated by sending a signal to it. Our rtosDeleteTask implementation sends a signal to the kernel thread and calls wait_for_completion to wait for the termination. The kernel thread, on reception of the signal, calls complete to wake up the caller of rtosDeleteTask before exiting.

First is rtosCreateTask.

```
rtosError_t
rtosCreateTask(char *name, rtosEntry_t routine, void * arg,
               int priority, int stackSize,
               rtosTask_t *tHandle){
#ifndef __KERNEL__
    ...
#else

struct completion *complete_ptr =
    (struct completion *)kmalloc(sizeof(structcompletion),
                          GFP_KERNEL);
```

```
karg_t *karg = (karg_t *)kmalloc(sizeof(karg_t),
                                 GFP_KERNEL);
strcpy(tHandle->name, name);
init_completion(complete_ptr); <-- Initialize a completion
                                   variable
tHandle->exit = complete_ptr;
karg->entry_routine = routine;
karg->priority = priority;
karg->arg1 = arg1;
karg->arg2 = arg2;
karg->arg3 = arg3;
karg->exit = complete_ptr;
tHandle->karg = karg;
tHandle->thread_pid =
  kernel_thread(wrapper_routine, (void *)karg, CLONE_KERNEL);
return RTOS_OK;

#endif


}
```

Every kernel RTOS task is associated with a completion variable `complete_ptr` to facilitate its termination. It is initialized by calling the `init_completion` kernel function. `complete_ptr` is wrapped along with entry routine arguments `arg` and priority `priority` in a structure `karg` of type `karg_t`. Finally the `kernel_thread` function is called to create a kernel thread that starts its execution from the `wrapper_routine` function. The argument to `wrapper_routine` is `karg`. `kernel_thread` returns the thread identifer of the created thread that is stored in `tHandle->thread_pid`. Note that the `tHandle` structure also holds `complete_ptr` and `karg` for later use in the `rtosDeleteTask` function.

The `wrapper_routine` sets the priority using `sys_nice` and calls the actual entry routine.

```
void wrapper_routine(void *arg){
    karg_t *karg = (karg_t *)arg;
    sys_nice(rtos_to_nice(karg->priority));
    karg->entry_routine(karg->arg1, karg->arg2,
                        karg->arg3,karg->exit);
}
```

Note that we made changes to the prototype of the entry routine function to accommodate one more argument, the completion variable pointer.

```
typedef void (*rtosEntry_t) (char *arg1, int arg2,
             void *arg3, struct completion * exit);
```

The change is necessary to facilitate kernel thread termination in `rtosDeleteTask` as discussed next.

Finally we discuss `rtosDeleteTask`.

```
void rtosDeleteTask(rtosTask_t tHandle){
#ifndef __KERNEL__
   ...
#else
  kill_proc(tHandle.thread_pid, SIGTERM, 1);
  wait_for_completion(tHandle.exit);
  kfree(tHandle.exit);
  kfree(tHandle.karg);
#endif
}
```

The implementation calls the `kill_proc` kernel function to send the signal SIGTERM to the thread `tHandle.thread_pid`. The caller of `rtosDeleteTask` then waits for the thread to exit by calling `wait_for_completion` on the `tHandle.exit` completion variable. On wake-up it frees the resources allocated in `rtosCreateTask` and returns.

Sending a signal to a kernel thread is not enough for its termination. The thread that received the signal should check for pending signals in its execution path. If the termination signal (in our case SIGTERM) is pending then it should call `complete` on the completion variable before exiting. A kernel thread in this implementation would look like

```
static int
my_kernel_thread (char *arg1, int arg2, void *arg3,
                  struct completion * exit)
{
   daemonize("%s", "my_thread");
   allow_signal(SIGTERM);

   while (1) {

     /*
      * Thread body
      */

     /* Check for termination */
     if (signal_pending (current)) {
       flush_signals(current);
       break;
     }

   }

   /* signal and complete */
   complete_and_exit (exit, 0);
}
```

To summarize, mappings between RTOS mutex APIs and Linux mutex APIs are listed in Table 6.2.

Table 6.2 RTOS and Linux Task APIs

RTOS	Linux	
	User Space	Kernel Space
Task create	`pthread_create`	`kernel_thread`
Task delete	`pthread_cancel`	`kill_proc`

Table 6.3 RTOS, Linux Timers, and IPC APIs

RTOS	Linux	
	User Space	Kernel Space
Timers	POSIX.1b timers, BSD timers	Kernel timer APIs — `add_timer`, `mod_timer`, and `del_timer`
Shared memory	SVR4 shared memory, POSIX.1b shared memory	Custom implementation
Message queues and mailboxes	SVR4 message queues, POSIX.1b message queues	Custom implementation
Semaphores	SVR4 semaphores, POSIX.1b semaphores	Kernel semaphore functions: `down`, `up`, and friends
Events and signals	POSIX.1b Real-time signals	Kernel signal functions: `kill_proc`, `send_signal`, and friends

6.4.3 IPC and Timer APIs Emulation

The next major set of APIs after successfully emulating task APIs are the IPC and timers. The mapping of IPC and timer APIs with equivalent Linux APIs is shown in Table 6.3. As you can see, the majority of timers and IPC functions can be implemented using POSIX.1b real-time extensions. We discuss more about POSIX.1b support in Linux in Chapter 7.

6.5 Kernel API Driver

One of the major challenges a developer faces when porting applications to embedded Linux is the kernel-space/user-space mode of programming in Linux. In Linux, because of the protected kernel address space, an application cannot directly call any kernel function or access any kernel data structure. All the kernel facilities must be accessed using well-defined interfaces called system calls. The protected kernel address space significantly increases the application porting effort from a traditional RTOS that has a flat memory model to embedded Linux.

Let's take an example to understand the difficulty a developer faces when porting applications from an RTOS to Linux.

A target running an RTOS has an RTC. A function `rtc_set` is available to set the RTC. `rtc_set` modifies RTC registers to configure the new value.

```
rtc_set(new_time){
  Get year, month, day, hour, min & sec from new_time;
  program RTC registers with new values;
}
```

A function `rtc_get_from_user` is also available that takes the new RTC value from the user and calls the function `rtc_set`.

```
rtc_get_from_user(){
  read time value entered by user in new_time;
  call rtc_set(new_time);
}
```

The developer faces a dilemma when porting the above application to Linux. The function `rtc_set` directly modifies RTC registers so it should go in the kernel. On the other hand, the function `rtc_get_from_user` reads the user input so it should go in the user space. In Linux, the function `rtc_get_from_user` cannot call the function `rtc_set` as the latter is a kernel function.

The following solutions are available when porting such applications to Linux.

- *Port everything in the kernel:* This solution may work but this defeats the advantage of moving to Linux, memory protection.
- *Write new system calls:* In this approach, for every function ported in the kernel a system call interface could be provided to call that function in user space. The drawbacks of this approach are
  - All the system calls are registered in a kernel system call table. This table would be difficult to maintain if the number of functions ported in the kernel is large.
  - Upgrading to a new kernel version requires revisiting the system call table to verify whether the kernel has not allocated a system call table entry of your function for some other kernel function.

In this section we discuss an efficient technique for porting such applications to Linux. We call it the *kernel API driver (kapi)*. In this approach, a user-space stub is written for every kernel function that should be exported to user space. The stub when called traps into the kernel API driver that then calls the actual function in the kernel. The kernel API driver (or kapi driver) is implemented as a character driver `/dev/kapi`. It provides an `ioctl`

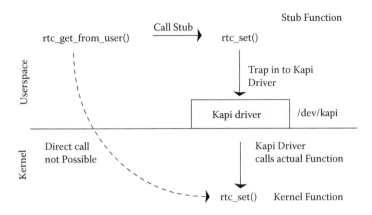

Figure 6.7   Exporting kernel functions using kapi.

interface for all the functions that should be exported to user space. Figure 6.7 explains the case of our above RTC example.

Thus to port the above RTC application to Linux a developer has to

- *Provide an ioctl* `RTC_SET` *in kapi driver:* The implementation of this ioctl in the driver calls the `rtc_set` kernel function with necessary arguments.
- *Write a user-space stub* `rtc_set`: The stub calls `RTC_SET` ioctl on `/dev/kapi`. It also passes the necessary parameters to the ioctl.

Thus using kapi driver, user-space function `rtc_get_from_user` calls stub function `rtc_set` as if it's calling the actual kernel function.

In this section we discuss

- Steps for writing user-space stubs
- Implementation of the kapi driver
- How to add the custom function ioctl in the kapi driver

A sample kapi driver is a kernel module written for the 2.6 kernel. The sources are divided into the following files.

- `kapi-user.c`: Contains a sample user-space stub
- `kapi-kernel.c`: Contains source code of kapi driver
- `kapi.h`: A header file that should be included by both `kapi-user.c` and `kapi-kernel.c`

In this example we export the `my_kernel_func` kernel function in user space. The prototype of the function is

```
int my_kernel_func(int val, char* in_str, char *out_str);
```

This function takes three arguments, one integer and two character pointers. The first character pointer is input to the function (copy-in) and the second pointer is populated by the function (copy-out). The return value of the function is an integer.

Listing 6.1   Kapi Header File

```
/* kapi.h */

#ifndef _KAPI_H
#define _KAPI_H

#define MAX_ARGS 7

typedef enum _dir_t {
  DIR_IN = 1,
  DIR_OUT,
}dir_t;

typedef struct _arg_struct {
  void *val;
  unsigned int size;
  dir_t dir;
}arg_t;

typedef struct _kfunc_struct {
  int num;
  arg_t arg[MAX_ARGS];
  arg_t ret;
}kfunc_t;

enum _function_id {
  MY_KERNEL_FUNC = 1,
  MAX_FUNC
};

#endif /* _KAPI_H */
```

6.5.1 Writing User-Space Stubs

Listing 6.1 shows the data structures involved in writing stubs and they are located in file `kapi.h`.

The stub must fill appropriate data structures before calling the appropriate kapi driver ioctl. The data structures are

- `dir_t`: Every argument passed to the function has a *direction* associated with it. An argument with `DIR_IN` direction is an input to the function. An argument with `DIR_OUT` direction is populated by the function.
- `arg_t`: This is a placeholder for a single argument to the function. The actual argument is cast as a `void *` pointer and its size and direction of copy are stored in `size` and `dir` fields, respectively.
- `kfunc_t`: This is the main data structure. A pointer to an object of type `kfunc_t` is passed as an argument to the ioctl. The kapi driver also uses this structure to send back the return value of the kernel function to the stub.
  - `num`: Number of arguments
  - `args`: Objects of type `arg_t` filled for each argument
  - `ret`: Return value of the function
- `function_id`: The enum contains ioctl commands for every function that should be exported to user space.

So the stub `my_kernel_func` that represents the actual `my_kernel_func` in the kernel is in file `kapi-user.c` and listed in Listing 6.2.

Before calling stub functions you should ensure that you have successfully opened kapi driver as it is done in function main in `kapi-user.c`.

```
char out[MAX_SIZE];
int ret;

dev_fd = open("/dev/kapi", O_RDONLY, 0666);

if (dev_fd < 0){
  perror("open failed");
  return 0;
}

/* call the stub */
ret = my_kernel_func(10, "Hello Kernel World", out);

printf("result = %d, out_str = %s\n", ret, out);
```

6.5.2 Kapi Driver Implementation

Kapi driver is a character driver implemented as a kernel module. This section discusses the implementation details of the driver for the 2.6 kernel.

There are two main data structures.

- `struct file_operations kapi_fops`: This table contains file operation routines such as `open`, `close`, `ioctl`, and so on for the driver.

  ```
  static struct file_operations kapi_fops = {
    .owner      = THIS_MODULE,
    .llseek     = NULL,
    .read       = NULL,
    .write      = NULL,
    .ioctl      = kapi_ioctl,
    .open       = kapi_open,
    .release    = kapi_release,
  };
  ```

- Note that `read`, `write`, and `lseek` file operations are set to `NULL`. These operations are not valid for the kapi driver as all the operations are performed through the `ioctl` interface.
- `struct miscdevice kapi_dev`: kapi driver is registered as a *miscellaneous* character driver. The minor number is `KAPI_MINOR (111)`. The major number of any miscellaneous character driver is 10.

  ```
  static struct miscdevice kapi_dev = {
    KAPI_MINOR,
    "kapi",
    &kapi_fops,
  };
  ```

Listing 6.2 Sample User Stub

```
/* kapi-user.c */

#include <fcntl.h>
#include "kapi.h"

/* File handler for "/dev/kapi" */
int dev_fd;

#define MAX_SIZE 50

int my_kernel_func(int val, char* in_str, char *out_str){

  kfunc_t data;
  int ret_val;

  /* Total number of arguments are three */
  data.num = 3;

  /*
   * Argument 1.
   * Even non pointer arguments should be passed as pointers. The
   * direction for such arguments is DIR_IN
   */
  data.arg[0].val = (void *)&val;
  data.arg[0].size = sizeof(int);
  data.arg[0].dir = DIR_IN;

  /* Argument 2 */
  data.arg[1].val = (void *)in_str;
  data.arg[1].size = strlen(in_str) + 1;
  data.arg[1].dir = DIR_IN;

  /*
   * Argument 3. As this is copy-out argument, we need to specify
   * the receive buffer size
   */
  data.arg[2].val = (void *)out_str;
  data.arg[2].size = MAX_SIZE;
  data.arg[2].dir = DIR_OUT;

  /*
   * kernel function return value. Setting direction field is not
   * needed as it is always copy-out
   */
  data.ret.val = (void *)&ret_val;
  data.ret.size = sizeof(int);

  /*
   * Finally call ioctl on /dev/kapi. Kapi driver then calls
   * my_kernel_func kernel function. It also populates
   * data.ret.val with the return value of the kernel function
   */
  if (ioctl(dev_fd, MY_KERNEL_FUNC, (void *)&data) < 0){
    perror("ioctl failed");
    return -1;
  }
```

Listing 6.2   Sample User Stub (continued)

```
/* return value of the function */
  return ret_val;
}
```

- Every kernel module has a module init function and a module clean-up function. The kapi driver provides `kapi_init` and `kapi_cleanup_module` as its init and clean-up functions, respectively.

The `kapi_init` function registers kapi driver as a miscellaneous character driver with minor number `KAPI_MINOR`. The function is called when the module is loaded.

```
static int __init
kapi_init(void)
{
 int ret;

 ret = misc_register(&kapi_dev);
 if (ret)
   printk(KERN_ERR "kapi: can't misc_register on
                    minor=%d\n", KAPI_MINOR);
 return ret;
}
```

The `kapi_cleanup_module` is called when the module is unloaded. The function unregisters as a miscellaneous character driver.

```
static void __exit
kapi_cleanup_module(void)
{
  misc_deregister(&kapi_dev);
}
```

The open and `close` routines just keep track of a number of simultaneous users of this driver. They are mainly for debugging purposes.

```
static int
kapi_open(struct inode *inode, struct file *file)
{
  kapi_open_cnt++;
  return 0;
}

static int
kapi_release(struct inode *inode, struct file *file)
{

  kapi_open_cnt--;
  return 0;
}
```

Let's now discuss the core of kapi driver, the `kapi_ioctl` function. `kapi_ioctl` is registered as an `ioctl` operation for this driver in the `fops` table.

The `kapi_ioctl` function performs the following operations.

1. Copy-in the user-passed `kfunc_t` object in a kernel `kfunc_t` object.
2. Allocate memory for the `DIR_IN` and `DIR_OUT` arguments.
3. Copy-in all the arguments that have the `DIR_IN` direction flag in kernel buffers from user buffers.
4. Call the requested kernel function.
5. Copy-out all the arguments with the `DIR_OUT` direction flag from kernel buffers to user buffers.
6. Finally, copy-out the return value of the kernel function to user space and free all the kernel buffers allocated.

The argument to `kapi_ioctl` is the pointer to an object of type `kfunc_t`. The first step is to copy the `kfunc_t` object in the kernel memory.

```
static int
kapi_ioctl(struct inode *inode, struct file *file,
           unsigned int cmd, unsigned long arg)
{
  int i,err;
  kfunc_t kdata,udata;

  if(copy_from_user(&udata, (kfunc_t *)arg,
                  sizeof(kfunc_t)))
    return -EFAULT;
```

Allocate kernel buffers for all the arguments and return value. Perform copy-in operation if any argument has `DIR_IN` direction.

```
for (i = 0 ; i < udata.num ; i++){
  kdata.arg[i].val = kmalloc(udata.arg[i].size,
                        GFP_KERNEL);
  if (udata.arg[i].dir == DIR_IN){
    if (copy_from_user(kdata.arg[i].val, udata.arg[i].val,
                  udata.arg[i].size))
    goto error;
  }
}
kdata.ret.val = kmalloc(udata.ret.size, GFP_KERNEL);
```

Call the requested kernel function. In this example we have provided ioctl for the `my_kernel_func` kernel function. You need to add your functions similarly in the switch statement. The function id should also be added in the `function_id` enum in `kapi.h`. The return value of the called function should be stored in `kdata.ret.val`.

```
switch (cmd) {

  case MY_KERNEL_FUNC:
```

```
      *(int *)(kdata.ret.val) =
          my_kernel_func(*(int *)kdata.arg[0].val,
                         (char *)kdata.arg[1].val,
                         (char *)kdata.arg[2].val);
      break;

  default:
    return -EINVAL;
}
```

Now it's time to send the result of the called kernel function back to the user-space stub. Copy-out all the DIR_OUT arguments and function return value to the user space. Also free the allocated kernel buffers.

```
err = 0;
for (i = 0 ; i < udata.num ; i++){
  if (udata.arg[i].dir == DIR_OUT){
    if (copy_to_user(udata.arg[i].val, kdata.arg[i].val,
                     udata.arg[i].size))
      err = -EFAULT;
  }
  kfree(kdata.arg[i].val);
}

/* copy-out the return value */
if (copy_to_user(udata.ret.val, kdata.ret.val,
                 udata.ret.size))
  err = -EFAULT;

kfree(kdata.ret.val);
return err;
}
```

Finally, the my_kernel_func just prints out the user input and returns an integer value 2. For the sake of simplicity we have put this function in kapi-kernel.c. You should not add your functions in this file. Also remember to export the function using EXPORT_SYMBOL as kapi driver is loaded as a kernel module.

```
int my_kernel_func(int val, char *in_str, char *out_str){
  printk(KERN_DEBUG"val = %d, str = %s\n", val, in_str);
  strcpy(out_str, "Hello User Space");
  return 2;
}

EXPORT_SYMBOL(my_kernel_func);
```

6.5.3 Using the Kapi Driver

- Build kapi driver as a kernel module. Refer to Chapter 8, Building and Debugging, for instructions.
- Compile kapi-user.c.

  ```
  # gcc -o kapi-user kapi-user.c
  ```

- Load the kernel module.

  ```
  # insmod kapi-kernel.ko
  ```

- Create /dev/kapi character device.

  ```
  # mknod /dev/kapi c 10 111
  ```

- Finally, run the application.

  ```
  # ./kapi-user

  result = 2, out_str = Hello User Space
  ```

- See the kapi driver output.

  ```
  # dmesg
    ...
  val = 10, str = Hello Kernel World
  ```

Note

1. For example, DHCP client is a stand-alone task. It can easily migrate as a separate Linux process.

Chapter 7

Real-Time Linux

Real-time systems are those in which the correctness of the system depends not only on its functional correctness but also on the time at which the results are produced. For example, if the MPEG decoder inside your DVD player is not capable of decoding frames at a specified rate (say 25 or 30 frames per second) then you will experience video glitches. Thus although the MPEG decoder is functionally correct because it is able to decode the input video stream, it is not able to produce the result at the required time. Depending on how critical the timing requirement is, a real-time system can be classified either as a hard real-time or a soft real-time system.

- *Hard real-time systems:* A hard real-time system needs a guaranteed worst case response time. The entire system including OS, applications, HW, and so on must be designed to guarantee that response requirements are met. It doesn't matter what the timings requirements are to be hard real-time (microseconds, milliseconds, etc.), just that they must be met every time. Failure to do so can lead to drastic consequences such as loss of life. Some examples of hard real-time systems include defense systems, flight and vehicle control systems, satellite systems, data acquisition systems, medical instrumentation, controlling space shuttles or nuclear reactors, gaming systems, and so on.
- *Soft real-time systems:* In soft real-time systems it is not necessary for system success that *every* time constraint be met. In the above DVD player example, if the decoder is not able to meet the timing requirement once in an hour, it's ok. But frequent deadline misses by the decoder in a short period of time can leave an impression that the system has failed. Some examples are multimedia applications, VoIP, CE devices, audio or video streaming, and so on.

7.1 Real-Time Operating System

POSIX 1003.1b defines real-time for operating systems as the ability of the operating system to provide a required level of service in a bounded response time.

The following set of features can be ascribed to an RTOS.

- *Multitasking/multithreading:* An RTOS should support multitasking and multithreading.
- *Priorities:* The tasks should have priorities. Critical and time-bound functionalities should be processed by tasks having higher priorities.
- *Priority inheritance:* An RTOS should have a mechanism to support priority inheritance.
- *Preemption:* An RTOS should be preemptive; that is, when a task of higher priority is ready to run, it should preempt a lower-priority task.
- *Interrupt latency:* Interrupt latency is the time taken between a hardware interrupt being raised and the interrupt handler being called. An RTOS should have predictable interrupt latencies and preferably be as small as possible.
- *Scheduler latency:* This is the time difference when a task becomes runnable and actually starts running. An RTOS should have deterministic scheduler latencies.
- *Interprocess communication and synchronization:* The most popular form of communication between tasks in an embedded system is message passing. An RTOS should offer a constant time message-passing mechanism. Also it should provide semaphores and mutexes for synchronization purposes.
- *Dynamic memory allocation:* An RTOS should provide fixed-time memory allocation routines for applications.

7.2 Linux and Real-Time

Linux evolved as a general-purpose operating system. As Linux started making inroads into embedded devices, the necessity for making it real-time was felt. The main reasons stated for the non–real-time nature of Linux were:

- High interrupt latency
- High scheduler latency due to nonpreemptive nature of the kernel
- Various OS services such as IPC mechanisms, memory allocation, and the like do not have deterministic timing behavior.
- Other features such as virtual memory and system calls also make Linux undeterministic in its response.

The key difference between any general-purpose operating system like Linux and a hard real-time OS is the deterministic timing behavior of all the OS services in an RTOS. By deterministic timing we mean that any latency involved or time taken by any OS service should be well bounded. In mathematical terms you should be able express these timings using an algebraic formula with no variable component. The variable component introduces nondeterminism, a scenario unacceptable for hard real-time systems.

As Linux has its roots as a general-purpose OS, it requires major changes to get a well-bounded response time for all the OS services. Hence a fork was done: hard real-time variants of Linux, RTLinux, and RTAI are done to use Linux in a hard real-time system. On the other hand, support was added in the kernel to reduce latencies and improve response times of various OS services to make it suitable for soft real-time needs.

This section discusses the kernel framework that supports the usage of Linux as a soft real-time OS. The best way to understand this is to trace the flow of an interrupt in the system and note the various latencies involved. Let's take an example where a task is waiting for an I/O from a disk to complete and the I/O finishes. The following steps are performed.

- The I/O is complete. The device raises an interrupt. This causes the block device driver's ISR to run.
- The ISR checks the driver wait queue and finds a task waiting for I/O. It then calls one of the wake-up family of functions. The function removes the task from the wait queue and adds it to the scheduler run queue.
- The kernel then calls the function `schedule` when it gets to a point where scheduling is allowed.
- Finally `schedule()` finds the next suitable candidate for running. The kernel context switches to our task if it has sufficient high priority to get scheduled.

Thus *kernel response time* is the amount of time that elapses from when the interrupt is raised to when the task that was waiting for I/O to complete runs. As you can see from the example there are four components to the kernel response time.

- *Interrupt latency:* Interrupt latency is the time difference between a device raising an interrupt and the corresponding handler being called.
- *ISR duration:* the time needed by an interrupt handler to execute.
- *Scheduler latency:* Scheduler latency is the amount of time that elapses between the interrupt service routine completing and the scheduling function being run.
- *Scheduler duration:* This is the time taken by the scheduler function to select the next task to run and context switch to it.

Now we discuss various causes of the above latencies and the ways that are incorporated to reduce them.

7.2.1 Interrupt Latency

As already mentioned, interrupt latency is one of the major factors contributing to nondeterministic system response times. In this section we discuss some of the common causes for high-interrupt latency.

- *Disabling all interrupts for a long time:* Whenever a driver or other piece of kernel code needs to protect some data from the interrupt handler, it generally disables all the interrupts using macros `local_irq_disable` or `local_irq_save`. Holding a spinlock using functions `spin_lock_irqsave` or `spin_lock_irq` before entering the critical section also disables all the interrupts. All this increases the interrupt latency of the system.
- *Registering a fast interrupt handler by improperly written device drivers:* A device driver can register its interrupt handler with the kernel either as a fast interrupt or a slow interrupt. All the interrupts are disabled whenever a fast interrupt handler is executing and interrupts are enabled for slow interrupt handlers. Interrupt latency is increased if a low-priority device registers its interrupt handler as a fast interrupt and a high-priority device registers its interrupt as a slow interrupt.

As a kernel programmer or a driver writer you need to ensure that your module or driver does not contribute to the interrupt latency. Interrupt latency could be measured using a tool `intlat` written by Andrew Morton. It was last modified during the 2.3 and 2.4 kernel series, and was also x86 architecture specific. You may need to port it for your architecture. It can be downloaded from http://www.zipworld.com. You can also write a custom driver for measuring interrupt latency For example, in ARM, this could be achieved by causing an interrupt to fire from the timer at a known point in time and then comparing that to the actual time when your interrupt handler is executed.

7.2.2 ISR Duration

ISR duration is the time taken by an interrupt handler to execute and it is under the control of the ISR writer. However nondeterminism could arise if an ISR has a softirq component also. What exactly is a softirq? We all know that in order to have less interrupt latency, an interrupt handler needs to do minimal work (such as copying some IO buffers to the system RAM) and the rest of the work (such as processing of the IO data, waking up tasks) should be done outside the interrupt handler. So an interrupt handler has been split into two portions: the top half that does the minimal job and the softirq that does the rest of the processing. The latency involved in softirq processing is unbounded. The following latencies are involved during softirq processing.

- A softirq runs with interrupts enabled and can be interrupted by a hard IRQ (except at some critical sections).
- A softirq can also be executed in the context of a kernel daemon `ksoftirqd`, which is a non–real-time thread.

Thus you should make sure that the ISR of your real-time device does not have any softirq component and all the work should be performed in the top half only.

7.2.3 Scheduler Latency

Among all the latencies discussed, scheduler latency is the major contributor to the increased kernel response time. Some of the reasons for large scheduler latencies in the earlier Linux 2.4 kernel are as follows.

■ *Nonpreemptive nature of the kernel:* Scheduling decisions are made by the kernel in the places such as return from interrupt or return from system call, and so on. However, if the current process is running in kernel mode (i.e., executing a system call), the decision is postponed until the process comes back to user mode. This means that a high-priority process cannot preempt a low-priority process if the latter is executing a system call. Thus, because of the nonpreemptive nature of kernel mode execution, scheduling latencies may vary from tens to hundreds of milliseconds depending on the duration of a system call.

■ *Interrupt disable times:* A scheduling decision is made as early as the return from the next timer interrupt. If the global interrupts are disabled for a long time, the timer interrupt is delayed thus increasing scheduling latency.

Much effort is being made to reduce the scheduling latency in Linux. Two major efforts are kernel preemption and low-latency patches.

Kernel Preemption

As support for SMP in Linux grew, its locking infrastructure also began to improve. More and more critical sections were identified and they were protected using spinlocks. It was observed that it's safe to preempt a process executing in the kernel mode if it is not in any critical section protected using spinlock. This property was exploited by embedded Linux vendor MontaVista and they introduced the kernel preemption patch. The patch was incorporated in the mainstream kernel during the 2.5 kernel development and is now maintained by Robert Love.

Kernel preemption support introduced a new member `preempt_count` in the process task structure. If the `preemp_count` is zero, the kernel can be safely preempted. Kernel preemption is disabled for nonzero `preempt_count`. `preemp_count` is operated on by the following main macros.

■ `preempt_disable`: Disable preemption by incrementing `preemp_count`.

■ `preempt_enable`: Decrement `preemp_count`. Preemption is only enabled if the count reaches zero.

All the spinlock routines were modified to call `preempt_disable` and `preempt_enable` macros appropriately. Spinlock routines call `preempt_disable` on entry and unlock routines call `preempt_enable` on exit. The architecture-specific files that contain assembly code for return from interrupts and the system call were also modified to check `preempt_count` before making scheduling decisions. If the count is zero then the scheduler is called irrespective of whether the process is in kernel or user mode.

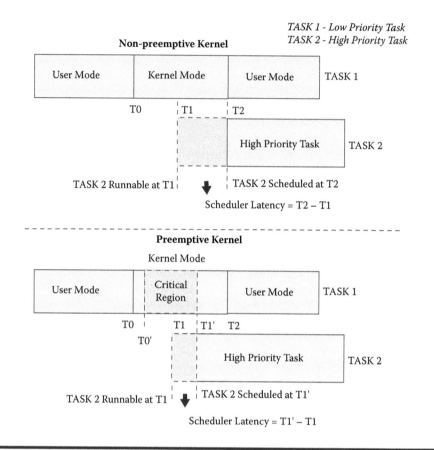

Figure 7.1   Scheduler latency in preemptible and nonpreemptible kernels.

Please see files `include/linux/preempt.h`, `kernel/sched.c`, and `arch/<your-arch>/entry.S` in kernel sources for more details. Figure 7.1 shows how scheduler latency decreases when the kernel is made preemptible.

Low-Latency Patches

Low-latency patches by Ingo Molnar and Andrew Morton focus on reducing the scheduling latency by adding explicit schedule points in the blocks of kernel code that execute for longer duration. Such areas in the code (such as iterating a lengthy list of some data structure) were identified. That piece of code was rewritten to safely introduce a schedule point. Sometimes this involved dropping a spinlock, doing a rescheduling, and then reacquiring the spinlock. This is called lock breaking.

Using the low-latency patches, the maximum scheduling latency decreases to the maximum time between two rescheduling points. Because these patches have been tuned for quite a long time, they perform surprisingly well. Scheduling latency can be measured using the tool `schedstat`. You can download the patch from http://eaglet.rain.com/.

The measurements show that using both kernel preemption and low-latency patches gives the best result.

7.2.4 Scheduler Duration

As discussed earlier the scheduler duration is the time taken by the scheduler to select the next task for execution and context switch to it. The Linux scheduler like the rest of the system was written originally for the desktop and it remained almost unchanged except for the addition of the POSIX real-time capabilities. The major drawback of the scheduler was its nondeterministic behavior: The scheduler duration increased linearly with the number of tasks in the system, the reason being that all the tasks including real-time tasks are maintained in a single run queue and every time the scheduler was called it went through the entire run queue to find the highest-priority task. This loop is called the *goodness loop*. Also when the time quantum of all runnable processes expires, it recalculates their new timeslices all over again. This loop is famous as the *recalculation loop*. The greater the number of tasks (irrespective of whether they are real- or non–real-time), the greater was the time spent by the scheduler in both these loops.

Making the Scheduler Real-Time: The O(1) Scheduler

In the 2.4.20 kernel the O(1) scheduler was introduced, which brought in determinism. The O(1) scheduler by Ingo Molnar is a beautiful piece of code that tries to fix scheduling problems on big servers trying to do load balancing all the way to embedded systems that require deterministic scheduling time. As the name suggests, the scheduler does an O(1) calculation instead of the previous O(n) (where n stands for the number of processes in the run queue) for recalculating the timeslices of the processes and rescheduling them. It does this by implementing two arrays: the active array and the expired array. Both arrays are priority ordered and they maintain a separate run queue for each priority. The array indices are maintained in a bitmap, so searching for the highest-priority task becomes an O(1) search operation. When a task exhausts its time quantum, it is moved to the expired array and its new time quantum is refilled. When the active array becomes empty the scheduler switches both arrays so that the expired array becomes the new active array and starts scheduling from the new array. The active and the expired queue are accessed using pointers, so switching between the two arrays involves just switching pointers.

Thus having the ordered arrays solves the goodness loop problem and switching between pointers solves the recalculation loop problem. Along with these the O(1) scheduler offers giving higher priority to interactive tasks. Although this is more useful for desktop environments, real-time systems running a mix of real-time and ordinary processes too can benefit from this feature. Figure 7.2 shows the O(1) scheduler in a simplified manner.

Context Switch Time

Linux context switching time measurements have been a favorite pastime for Linux real-time enthusiasts. How does Linux scale against a commercial RTOS

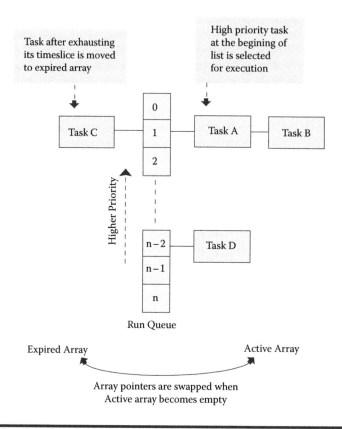

Figure 7.2 Simplified O(1) scheduler.

context switching time? Because the context switch is done by the scheduler it affects the scheduler duration and hence the kernel response time. The schedulable items on Linux are:

- *Kernel threads:* They spend their lifetimes in the kernel mode only. They do not have memory mappings in the user space.
- *User processes and user threads:* The user-space threads share a common text, data, and heap space. They have separate stacks. Other resources such as open files and signal handlers are also shared across the threads.

While making scheduling decisions, the scheduler does not distinguish among any of these entities. The context switch time varies when the scheduler tries to switch processes against threads. The context switching basically involves the following.

- *Switching to new register set and kernel stack:* The context switch time is common across threads and processes.
- *Switching from one virtual memory area to other:* This is required for context switching across processes. It either explicitly or implicitly causes the TLB (or page tables) to be reloaded with new values, which is an expensive operation.

The context switching numbers vary across architectures. Measurement of the context switching is done using the lmbench program. Please visit www.bit-mover.com/lmbench/ for more information on LMBench™.

7.2.5 User-Space Real-Time

Until now we have discussed various enhancements made in the kernel to improve its responsiveness. The O(1) scheduler along with kernel preemption and low-latency patches make Linux a soft real-time operating system. Now what about user-space applications? Can't something be done to make sure that they too have some guidelines to behave in a deterministic manner?

To support real-time applications, IEEE came out with a standard POSIX.1b. The IEEE 1003.1b (or POSIX.1b) standard defines interfaces to support portability of applications with real-time requirements. Apart from 1003.1b, POSIX also defines 1003.1d, .1j, .21, and .2h standards for real-time systems but extensions defined in .1b are commonly implemented. The various real-time extensions defined in POSIX.1b are:

- Fixed-priority scheduling with real-time scheduling classes
- Memory locking
- POSIX message queues
- POSIX shared memory
- Real-time signals
- POSIX semaphores
- POSIX clocks and timers
- Asynchronous I/O (AIO)

The real-time scheduling classes, memory locking, shared memory, and real-time signals have been supported in Linux since the very early days. POSIX message queues, clocks, and timers are supported in the 2.6 kernel. Asynchronous I/O has also been supported since the early days but that implementation was completely done in the user-space C library. Linux 2.6 has a kernel support for AIO. Note that along with the kernel, GNU C library and glibc also underwent changes to support these real-time extensions. Both the kernel and glibc work together to provide better POSIX.1b support in Linux.

In this section we discussed soft real-time support in Linux. We also briefly discussed various POSIX.1b real-time extensions. As an application developer it's your responsibility to write applications in a manner such that the soft real-time benefits provided by Linux are not nullified. The end user needs to understand each of these techniques so that the applications can be written to support the real-time framework provided in Linux. The rest of this chapter explains each of these techniques with suitable examples.

7.3 Real-Time Programming in Linux

In this section we discuss various POSIX 1003.1b real-time extensions supported in Linux and their effective usage. We discuss in detail scheduling,

clocks and timers, real-time message queues, real-time signals, memory locking, Async I/O, POSIX shared memory, and POSIX semaphores. Most of the
real-time extensions are implemented and distributed in the glibc package but
are located in a separate library librt. Therefore, to compile a program that
makes use of POSIX.1b real-time features in Linux, the program must also
link with librt along with glibc. This section covers the various POSIX.1b
real-time extensions supported in the Linux 2.6 kernel.

7.3.1 Process Scheduling

In the previous section we discussed the details of the Linux scheduler. Now
we understand how the real-time tasks are managed by the scheduler. In this
section we discuss the scheduler for the 2.6 kernel as reference. There are
three basic parameters to define a real-time task on Linux:

- Scheduling class
- Process priority
- Timeslice

These are further explained below.

Scheduling Class

The Linux scheduler offers three scheduling classes, two for real-time applications and one for non–real-time applications. The three classes are:

- SCHED_FIFO: First-in first-out real-time scheduling policy. The scheduling
  algorithm does not use any timeslicing. A SCHED_FIFO process runs to
  completion unless it is blocked by an I/O request, preempted by a higher-
  priority process, or it voluntarily relinquishes the CPU. The following points
  should be noted.
  - A SCHED_FIFO process that has been preempted by another process of
    higher priority stays at the head of the list for its priority and will resume
    execution as soon as all processes of higher priority are blocked again.
  - When a SCHED_FIFO process is ready to run (e.g., after waking from
    a blocking operation), it will be inserted at the end of the list of its
    priority.
  - A call to sched_setscheduler or sched_setparam will put the
    SCHED_FIFO process at the start of the list. As a consequence, it may
    preempt the currently running process if its priority is the same as that
    of the running process.
- SCHED_RR: Round-robin real-time scheduling policy. It's similar to
  SCHED_FIFO with the only difference being that the SCHED_RR process
  is allowed to run for a maximum time quantum. If a SCHED_RR process
  exhausts its time quantum, it is put at the end of the list of its priority. A
  SCHED_RR process that has been preempted by a higher-priority process
  will complete the unexpired portion of its time quantum after resuming
  execution.

- SCHED_OTHER: Standard Linux time-sharing scheduler for non–real-time processes.

Functions sched_setscheduler and sched_getscheduler are used to set and get the scheduling policy of a process, respectively.

Priority

Priority ranges for various scheduling policies are listed in Table 7.1. Functions sched_get_priority_max and sched_get_priority_min return the maximum and minimum priority allowed for a scheduling policy, respectively. The higher the number, the higher is the priority. Thus the SCHED_FIFO or SCHED_RR process always has higher priority than SCHED_OTHER processes. For SCHED_FIFO and SCHED_RR processes, functions sched_setparam and sched_getparam are used to set and get the priority, respectively. The nice system call (or command) is used to change the priority of SCHED_OTHER processes.

The kernel allows the nice value to be set for SCHED_RR or SCHED_FIFO process but it won't have any effect on scheduling until the task is made SCHED_OTHER.

The kernel view of process priorities is different from the process view. Figure 7.3 shows the mapping between user-space and kernel-space priorities for real-time tasks in 2.6.3 kernel.

Table 7.1 User-Space Priority Range

Scheduling Class	Priority Range
SCHED_OTHER	0
SCHED_FIFO	1–99
SCHED_RR	1–99

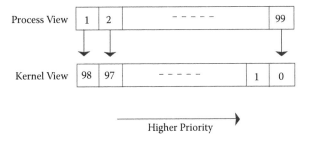

Figure 7.3 Real-time task priority mapping.

For the kernel, a low value implies high priority. Real-time priorities in the kernel range from 0 to 98. The kernel maps SCHED_FIFO and SCHED_RR user priorities to kernel priorities using the following macros.

```
#define MAX_USER_RT_PRIO 100
kernel priority = MAX_USER_RT_PRIO -1 - (user priority);
```

Thus user priority 1 maps to kernel priority 98, priority 2 to 97, and so on.

Timeslice

As discussed earlier, timeslice is valid only for SCHED_RR processes. SCHED_FIFO processes can be thought of as having an infinite timeslice. So this discussion applies only to SCHED_RR processes.

Linux sets a minimum timeslice for a process to 10 msec, default timeslice to 100 msec, and maximum timeslice to 200 msec. Timeslices get refilled after they expire. In 2.6.3, the timeslice of a process is calculated as

```
#define MIN_TIMESLICE (10)
#define MAX_TIMESLICE (200)
#define MAX_PRIO (139)    // MAX internal kernel priority
#define MAX_USER_PRIO 39 // MAX nice when converted to
                            positive scale

/* 'p' is task structure of a process */
#define BASE_TIMESLICE(p) \
    (MIN_TIMESLICE + ((MAX_TIMESLICE - MIN_TIMESLICE) *
    (MAX_PRIO-1 - (p)->static_prio) / (MAX_USER_PRIO-1)))
```

static_prio holds the nice value of a process. The kernel converts the −20 to +19 nice range to an internal kernel nice range of 100 to 139. The nice of the process is converted to this scale and stored in static_prio. Thus −20 nice corresponds to static_prio 100 and +19 nice is static_prio 139. Finally the task_timeslice function returns the timeslice of a process.

```
static inline unsigned int task_timeslice(task_t *p) {
  return BASE_TIMESLICE(p);
}
```

Please note that the static_prio is the only variable in calculating the timeslice. Thus we can draw some important conclusions.

- All SCHED_RR processes run at the default timeslice of 100 msec as they normally have nice 0.
- A nice −20 SCHED_RR process will get a timeslice of 200 msec and a nice +19 SCHED_RR process will get a timeslice of 10 msec. Thus the nice value can be used to control timeslice allocation for SCHED_RR processes.
- The lower the nice value (i.e., higher priority), the higher the timeslice is.

Table 7.2 POSIX.1b Scheduling Functions

Method	Description
sched_getscheduler	Get the scheduling class of a process.
sched_setscheduler	Set the scheduling class of a process.
sched_getparam	Get the priority of a process.
sched_setparam	Set the priority of a process.
sched_get_priority_max	Get the max allowed priority for a scheduling class.
sched_get_priority_min	Get the min allowed priority for a scheduling class.
sched_rr_get_interval	Get the current timeslice of the SCHED_RR process.
sched_yield	Yield execution to another process.

Scheduling Functions

Scheduling functions provided for supporting real-time applications under Linux are listed in Table 7.2.

> *Functions* sched_setscheduler *and* sched_setparam *should be called with superuser privileges.*

Listing 7.1 illustrates the usage of these functions. The example creates a SCHED_FIFO process with priority, which is the average of minimum and maximum priority for the SCHED_FIFO scheduling class. It also dynamically changes the priority of the SCHED_FIFO process. Listing 7.2 shows how nice can be used to control the SCHED_RR timeslice allocation.

> *The effect of* nice *on the* SCHED_RR *timeslice allocation is not mandated by POSIX. It's the scheduler implementation in Linux that makes this happen. You should not use this feature in portable programs. This behavior of* nice *on* SCHED_RR *is derived from 2.6.3 kernel and may change in the future.*

7.3.2 Memory Locking

One of the latencies that real-time applications needs to deal with is demand paging. Real-time application requires deterministic response timing and paging is one major cause of unexpected program execution delays. Latency due to paging could be avoided by using memory locking. Functions are provided either to lock complete program address space or selective memory area.

Memory Locking Functions

Memory locking functions are listed in Table 7.3. mlock disables paging for the specified range of memory and mlockall disables paging for all the pages that map into process address space. This includes the pages of code, data,

Listing 7.1   Process Scheduling Operations

```
/* sched.c */

#include <sched.h>
int main(){
  struct sched_param param, new_param;

  /*
   * A process starts with the default policy SCHED_OTHER unless
   * spawned by a SCHED_RR or SCHED_FIFO process.
   */

  printf("start policy = %d\n", sched_getscheduler(0));
  /*
   * output -> start policy = 0 .
   * (For SCHED_FIFO or SCHED_RR policies, sched_getscheduler
   * returns 1 and 2 respectively
   */

  /*
   * Create a SCHED_FIFO process running with average priority
   */
  param.sched_priority = (sched_get_priority_min(SCHED_FIFO) +
                      sched_get_priority_max(SCHED_FIFO))/2;

  printf("max priority = %d, min priority = %d,
        my priority = %d\n",sched_get_priority_max(SCHED_FIFO),
                          sched_get_priority_min(SCHED_FIFO),
                          param.sched_priority);
  /*
   * output -> max priority = 99, min priority = 1,
   * my priority = 50
   */

  /* Make the process SCHED_FIFO */
  if (sched_setscheduler(0, SCHED_FIFO, &param) != 0){
    perror("sched_setscheduler failed\n");
    return;
  }

  /*
   * perform time critical operation
   */

  /*
   * Give some other RT thread / process a chance to run.
   * Note that call to sched_yield will put the current process
   * at the end of its priority queue. If there are no other
   * process in the queue then the call will have no effect
   */
  sched_yield();

  /* You can also change the priority at run time */
  param.sched_priority = sched_get_priority_max(SCHED_FIFO);
  if (sched_setparam(0, &param) != 0){
    perror("sched_setparam failed\n");
    return;
  }
```

Listing 7.1   Process Scheduling Operations (continued)

```
sched_getparam(0, &new_param);
  printf("I am running at priority %d\n",
                new_param.sched_priority);
  /* output -> I am running at priority 99 */

  return ;
}
```

Listing 7.2   Controlling Timeslice of SCHED_RR Process

```
/* sched_rr.c */

#include <sched.h>
int main(){
  struct sched_param param;
  struct timespec ts;
  param.sched_priority = sched_get_priority_max(SCHED_RR);

  /* Need maximum timeslice */
  nice(-20);
  sched_setscheduler(0, SCHED_RR, &param);
  sched_rr_get_interval(0, &ts);
  printf ("max timeslice = %d msec\n", ts.tv_nsec/1000000);
  /* output -> max timeslice = 199 msec */

  /* Need minimum timeslice. Also note the argument to nice
   * is 'increment' and not absolute value. Thus we are
   * doing nice(39) to make it running at nice priority +19
   */
  nice(39);
  sched_setscheduler(0, SCHED_RR, &param);
  sched_rr_get_interval(0, &ts);
  printf ("min timeslice = %d", ts.tv_nsec/1000000);
  /* output -> min timeslice = 9 msec */

  return ;
}
```

Table 7.3   POSIX.1b Memory Locking Functions

Method	Description
mlock	Lock specified region of process address space
mlockall	Lock complete process address space
munlock	Unlock region locked using mlock
munlockall	Unlock complete process address

Listing 7.3 Memory Locking Operations

```
/* mlock.c */

#include <sys/mman.h>
#include <unistd.h>

#define RT_BUFSIZE 1024
int main(){

  /* rt_buffer should be locked in memory */
  char *rt_buffer = (char *)malloc(RT_BUFSIZE);
  unsigned long pagesize, offset;

  /*
   * In Linux, you need not page align the address before
   * mlocking, kernel does that for you. But POSIX mandates page
   * alignment of memory address before calling mlock to
   * increase portability. So page align rt_buffer.
   */
  pagesize = sysconf(_SC_PAGESIZE);
  offset = (unsigned long) rt_buffer % pagesize;
  /* Lock rt_buffer in memory */
  if (mlock(rt_buffer - offset, RT_BUFSIZE + offset) != 0){
    perror("cannot mlock");
    return 0;
  }

  /*
   * After mlock is successful the page that contains rt_buffer
   * is in memory and locked. It will never get paged out. So
   * rt_buffer can safely be used without worrying about
   * latencies due to paging.
   */

  /* After use, unlock rt_buffer */
  if (munlock(rt_buffer - offset, RT_BUFSIZE + offset) != 0){
    perror("cannot mulock");
    return 0;
  }

  /*
   * Depending on the application, you can choose to lock
   * complete process address space in memory.
   */

  /* Lock current process memory as well as all the future
   * memory allocations.
   *     MCL_CURRENT - Lock all the pages that are currently
   *                   mapped in process address space
   *     MCL_FUTURE  - Lock all the future mappings as well.
   */
  if (mlockall(MCL_CURRENT | MCL_FUTURE) != 0){
    perror("cannot mlockall");
    return 0;
  }
}
```

Listing 7.3   Memory Locking Operations (continued)

```
/*
   * if mlockall above is successful, all new memory allocations
   * will be locked. Thus page containing rt_buffer will get
   * locked in memory
   */
  rt_buffer = (char *)realloc(rt_buffer , 2*RT_BUFSIZE);

  /*
   * Finally unlock any memory that was locked either by mlock
   * or by mlockall by calling munlockall function
   */
  if (munlockall() != 0){
    perror("cannot munlock");
    return 0;
  }
  return 0;
}
```

stack, shared libraries, shared memory, and memory-mapped files. Listing 7.3 illustrates the usage of these functions. These functions should be called with superuser privilege.

An application with a real-time requirement is generally multithreaded with some real-time threads and some non–real-time threads. For such applications `mlockall` should not be used as this also locks the memory of non–real-time threads. In the next two sections we discuss two linker approaches to perform selective memory locking in such applications.

Effective Locking Using Linker Script

The idea is to place object files containing real-time code and data in a separate linker section using linker script. `mlocking` that section at program start-up would do the trick of locking only the real-time code and data. We take a sample application to illustrate this. In Listing 7.4 we assume that `hello_rt_world` is a real-time function that operates on `rt_data` with `rt_bss` as uninitialized data.

The following steps should be performed for achieving selective locking.

1. Divide the application at file level into real-time and non–real-time files. Do not include any non–real-time function in real-time files and vice versa. In this example we have
   a. `hello_world.c`: Contains non–real-time function
   b. `hello_rt_world.c`: Contains real-time function
   c. `hello_rt_data.c`: Contains real-time data
   d. `hello_rt_bss.c`: Contains real-time bss
   e. `hello_main.c`: Final application
2. Generate object code but do not link.

```
# gcc -c hello_world.c hello_rt_world.c hello_rt_data.c \
      hello_rt_bss.c hello_main.c
```

Listing 7.4 Effective Locking—1

```c
/*  hello_world.c */

#include <stdio.h>
/* Non-real time function */
void hello_world(void) {
  printf("hello world");
  return;
}


/* hello_rt_world.c */

#include <stdio.h>
/* This is a real-time function */
void hello_rt_world(void){
  extern char rt_data[],rt_bss[];
  /* operating on rt_data */
  printf("%s", rt_data);
  /* operating on rt_bss */
  memset(rt_bss, 0xff, sizeof(rt_bss));
  return ;
}


/* hello_rt_data.c */

/* Real-time data */
char rt_data[] = "Hello Real-time World";


/* hello_rt_bss.c */

/* real-time bss */
char rt_bss[100];


/* hello_main.c */

#include <stdio.h>
extern void hello_world(void);
extern void hello_rt_world(void);

/*
 * We are defining these symbols in linker script. It shall get
 * clear in coming steps
 */
extern unsigned long __start_rt_text, __end_rt_text;
extern unsigned long __start_rt_data, __end_rt_data;
extern unsigned long __start_rt_bss, __end_rt_bss;

/*
 * This function locks all the real-time function and data in
 * memory
 */
```

Listing 7.4   Effective Locking—1 (continued)

```
void rt_lockall(void){
  /* lock real-time text segment */
  mlock(&__start_rt_text, &__end_rt_text - &__start_rt_text);
  /* lock real-time data */
  mlock(&__start_rt_data, &__end_rt_data - &__start_rt_data);
  /* lock real-time bss */
  mlock(&__start_rt_bss, &__end_rt_bss - &__start_rt_bss);
}

int main(){
  /* First step is to do memory locking */
  rt_lockall();
  hello_world();
  /* This is our rt function */
  hello_rt_world();
  return 0;
}
```

3. Get the default linker script and make a copy.

   ```
   # ld -verbose > default
   # cp default rt_script
   ```

4. Edit `rt_script` and remove linker details. (Remove everything before the `OUTPUT_FORMAT` command and also `====` .. at the end of the file.)

5. Locate `.text`, `.data`, and `.bss` sections in `rt_script` and add entries `rt_text`, `rt_data`, and `rt_bss` before them, respectively, as shown in Listing 7.5. Thus all the functions defined in `hello_rt_world.c` go in the `rt_text` section. Data defined in `hello_rt_data.c` goes in the `rt_data` section and all uninitialized data in `hello_rt_bss.c` goes in the `rt_bss` section. Variables `__start_rt_text`, `__start_rt_data`, and `__start_rt_bss` mark the beginning of sections `rt_text`, `rt_data`, and `rt_bss`, respectively. Similarly `__end_rt_text`, `__end_rt_data`, and `__end_rt_bss` mark the end address of the respective sections.

6. Finally link the application.

   ```
   # gcc -o hello hello_main.o hello_rt_bss.o \
         hello_rt_data.o hello_rt_world.o hello_world.o \
         -T rt_script
   ```

You can verify that all the real-time functions and data are in proper sections using the `objdump` command as below.

```
# objdump -t hello
  .....
08049720  g     .rt_bss  00000000  __start_rt_bss
08049760  g  O  .rt_bss  00000064  rt_bss
080497c4  g     .rt_bss  00000000  __end_rt_bss.....
```

Listing 7.5 Modified Linker Script

```
    .....
    .....
.plt      : { *(.plt) }
.rt_text  :
{
  PROVIDE (__start_rt_text = .);
  hello_rt_world.o
  PROVIDE (__end_rt_text = .);
} =0x90909090
.text     :
    ....
    ....
.got.plt  : { . = DATA_SEGMENT_RELRO_END (. + 12); *(.got.plt) }
.rt_data  :
{
  PROVIDE (__start_rt_data = .);
  hello_rt_data.o
  PROVIDE (__end_rt_data = .);
}
.data     :
    ....
    ....
__bss_start = .;
.rt_bss   :
{
  PROVIDE (__start_rt_bss = .);
  hello_rt_bss.o
  . = ALIGN(32 / 8);
  PROVIDE (__end_rt_bss = .);
}
.bss      :
    ......
    ......
```

```
080482f4  g       .rt_text  00000000  __start_rt_text
080482f4  g   F   .rt_text  0000001d  hello_rt_world
0804834a  g       .rt_text  00000000  __end_rt_text
                     ......
080496c0  g       .rt_data  00000000  __start_rt_data
080496c0  g   O   .rt_data  00000011  rt_data
08049707  g       .rt_data  00000000  __end_rt_data
```

Effective Locking Using GCC Section Attribute

If it is difficult to put real-time and non–real-time code in separate files, this approach could be used. In this approach we use the GCC section attribute to place our real-time code and data in appropriate sections. Finally locking those sections alone achieves our goal. This approach is very flexible and easy to use. Listing 7.6 shows Listing 7.4 rewritten to fall in this category.

You can verify that all the real-time functions and data are in proper sections using the objdump command as below.

Listing 7.6   Effective Locking—2

```c
/* hello.c */

#include <stdio.h>

/*
 * Define macros for using GCC section attribute. We define three
 * sections, real_text, read_data & real_bss to hold our realtime
 * code, data and bss
 */
#define __rt_text __attribute__ ((__section__ ("real_text")))
#define __rt_data __attribute__ ((__section__ ("real_data")))
#define __rt_bss  __attribute__ ((__section__ ("real_bss")))

/*
 * Linker is very kind. It generally defines symbols holding
 * start and end address of sections. Following symbols are
 * defined by linker
 */
extern unsigned long __start_real_text, __stop_real_text;
extern unsigned long __start_real_data, __stop_real_data;
extern unsigned long __start_real_bss, __stop_real_bss;

/* Initialized data for real_bss section */
char rt_bss[100] __rt_bss;

/* Uninitialized data for real_data section */
char rt_data[] __rt_data = "Hello Real-time World";

/* Function that goes in real_text section */
void __rt_text hello_rt_world(void){
  printf("%s", rt_data);
  memset(rt_bss, 0xff, sizeof(rt_bss));
  return ;
}

/* Finally lock our 'real-time' sections in memory */
void rt_lockall(void){
  mlock(&__start_real_text,
        &__stop_real_text - &__start_real_text);
  mlock(&__start_real_data,
        &__stop_real_data - &__start_real_data);
  mlock(&__start_real_bss,
        &__stop_real_bss - &__start_real_bss);
}

/* Non real-time function */
void hello_world(void) {
  printf("hello world");
  return;
}

int main(){
  rt_lockall();
  hello_world();
  hello_rt_world();
  return 0;
}
```

```
# gcc -o hello hello.c
# objdump -t hello
   .....
   .....
08049724 g      *ABS*        00000000    __stop_real_bss
08048560 g      *ABS*        00000000    __stop_real_text
080496a0 g      *ABS*        00000000    __start_real_data
080496b1 g      *ABS*        00000000    __stop_real_data
080496c0 g      *ABS*        00000000    __start_real_bss
0804852c g      *ABS*        00000000    __start_real_text
080496c0 g   O  real_bss     00000064    rt_bss
080496a0 g   O  real_data    00000011    rt_data
0804852c g   F  real_text    00000034    hello_rt_world
   ......
   ......
```

Note the linker-defined symbols __start_real_text, __stop_real_ text, and so on.

Points to Remember

- Single call to munlock or munlockall will unlock the region of memory even if it's being locked multiple times by a process.
- Pages mapped to several locations or by several processes stay locked into RAM as long as they are locked by at least one process or at one location.
- Child processes do not inherit page locks across a fork.
- Pages locked by mlock or mlockall are guaranteed to stay in RAM until the pages are unlocked by munlock or munlockall, the pages are unmapped via munmap, or until the process terminates or starts another program with exec.
- It is better to do memory locking at program initialization. All the dynamic memory allocations, shared memory creation, and file mapping should be done at initialization followed by mlocking them.
- In case you want to make sure that stack allocations also remain deterministic, then you also need to lock some pages of stack. To avoid paging for the stack segment, you can write a small function lock_stack and call it at init time.

```
void lock_stack(void){
   char dummy[MAX_APPROX_STACK_SIZE];
   /* This is done to page in the stack pages */
   memset(dummy, 0, MAX_APPROX_STACK_SIZE);
   mlock(dummy, MAX_APPROX_STACK_SIZE);
   return;
}
```

MAX_APPROX_STACK_SIZE is an estimate of stack usage of your real-time thread. Once this is done, the kernel ensures that this space for the stack always remains in memory.

- Be generous to other processes running in your system. Aggressive locking may take resources from other processes.

Table 7.4 POSIX.1b Shared Memory Functions

Method	Description
shm_open	Open a shared memory object
shm_unlink	Remove the shared memory object

7.3.3 POSIX Shared Memory

Real-time applications often require fast, high-bandwidth interprocess communication mechanisms. In this section we discuss POSIX shared memory, which is the fastest and lightest weight IPC mechanism. Shared memory is the fastest IPC mechanism for two reasons:

- There is no system call overhead while reading or writing data.
- Data is directly copied to the shared memory region. No kernel buffers or other intermediate buffers are involved.

Functions used to create and remove shared memory are listed in Table 7.4. shm_open creates a new POSIX shared memory object or opens an existing one. The function returns a handle that can be used by other functions such as ftruncate and mmap. shm_open creates a shared memory segment of size 0. ftruncate sets the desired shared memory segment size and mmap then maps the segment in process address space. The shared memory segment is deleted by shm_unlink. Listing 7.7 illustrates the usage.

Linux Implementation

The POSIX shared memory support in Linux makes use of the tmpfs file system mounted under /dev/shm.

```
# cat /etc/fstab
none   /dev/shm   tmpfs   defaults   0 0
```

The shared memory object created using shm_open is represented as a file in tmpfs. In Listing 7.7 remove the call to shm_unlink and run the program again. You should see file my_shm in /dev/shm

```
# ls -l /dev/shm
-rw-r--r--  1 root root 1024 Aug 19 18:57 my_shm
```

This shows a file my_shm with size 1024 bytes, which is our shared memory size. Thus we can use all the file operations on shared memory. For example, we can get the contents of shared memory by cat'ing the file. We can also use the rm command directly from the shell to remove the shared memory.

Points to Remember

- Remember mlocking the shared memory region.
- Use POSIX semaphores to synchronize access to the shared memory region.

Listing 7.7   POSIX Shared Memory Operations

```
/* shm.c */

#include <sys/types.h>
#include <sys/mman.h>
#include <fcntl.h>

/* Size of our shared memory segment */
#define SHM_SIZE 1024

int main(){
  int shm_fd;
  void *vaddr;

  /* Get shared memory handle */
  if ((shm_fd = shm_open("my_shm", O_CREAT | O_RDWR, 0666)) ==
                                                         -1){
    perror("cannot open");
    return -1;
  }

  /* set the shared memory size to SHM_SIZE */
  if (ftruncate(shm_fd, SHM_SIZE) != 0){
    perror("cannot set size");
    return -1;
  }

  /*
   * Map shared memory in address space. MAP_SHARED flag tells
   * that this is a shared mapping
   */
  if ((vaddr = mmap(0, SHM_SIZE, PROT_WRITE, MAP_SHARED,
              shm_fd, 0)) == MAP_FAILED){
    perror("cannot mmap");
    return -1;
  }

  /* lock the shared memory. Do not forget this step */
  if (mlock(vaddr, SHM_SIZE) != 0){
    perror("cannot mlock");
    return -1;
  }

  /*
   * Shared memory is ready for use
   */

  /*
   * Finally unmap shared memory segment from address space. This
   * will unlock the segment also
   */
  munmap(vaddr, SHM_SIZE);
  close(shm_fd);
  /* remove shared memory segment */
  shm_unlink("my_shm");
  return 0;
}
```

Table 7.5 POSIX.1b Message Queue Functions

Method	Description
mq_open	Open/create a message queue.
mq_close	Close the message queue.
mq_getattr	Get the message queue attributes.
mq_setattr	Set the message queue attributes.
mq_send	Send a message to queue.
mq_receive	Receive a message from queue.
mq_timedsend	Send a message to queue. Block until timeout.
mq_timedreceive	Receive a message from queue. Block until timeout.
mq_notify	Register for notification whenever a message is received on an empty message queue.
mq_unlink	Delete the message queue.

- Size of shared memory region can be queried using the `fstat` function.
- If multiple processes open the same shared memory region, the region is deleted only after the final call to `shm_unlink`.
- Don't call `shm_unlink` if you want to keep the shared memory region even after the process exits.

7.3.4 POSIX Message Queues

The POSIX 1003.1b message queue provides deterministic and efficient means of IPC. It offers the following advantages for real-time applications.

- Message buffers in the message queue are preallocated ensuring availability of resources when they are needed.
- Messages can be assigned priority. A high-priority message is always received first, irrespective of the number of messages in the queue.
- It offers asynchronous notification when the message arrives if receiver doesn't want to wait to receive a message.
- Message send and receive functions by default are blocking calls. Applications can specify a wait timeout while sending or receiving messages to avoid nondeterministic blocking.

The interfaces are listed in Table 7.5. Listing 7.8 illustrates the usage of some basic message queue functions. In this example two processes are created: one sending a message on the message queue and the other receiving the message from the queue.

Compiling and running the above two programs gives the following output.

Listing 7.8   POSIX Message Queue Operations

```
/* mqueue-1.c */

/* This program sends a message to the queue */
#include <stdio.h>
#include <string.h>
#include <mqueue.h>

#define QUEUE_NAME   "/my_queue"
#define PRIORITY     1
#define SIZE         256

int main(){

  mqd_t ds;
  char text[] = "Hello Posix World";
  struct mq_attr queue_attr;

  /*
   * Attributes for our queue. They can be set only during
   * creating.
   */
  queue_attr.mq_maxmsg = 32;   /* max. number of messages in queue
                                  at the same time */
  queue_attr.mq_msgsize = SIZE;   /* max. message size */

  /*
   * Create a new queue named "/my_queue" and open it for sending
   * and receiving. The queue file permissions are set rw for
   * owner and nothing for group/others. Queue limits set to
   * values provided above.
   */
  if ((ds = mq_open(QUEUE_NAME, O_CREAT | O_RDWR , 0600,
                    &queue_attr)) == (mqd_t)-1){
    perror("Creating queue error");
    return -1;
  }

  /*
   * Send a message to the queue with priority 1. Higher the
   * number, higher is the priority. A high priority message is
   * inserted before a low priority message. First-in First-out
   * for equal priority messages.
   */
  if (mq_send(ds, text, strlen(text), PRIORITY) == -1){
    perror("Sending message error");
    return -1;
  }

  /* Close queue... */
  if (mq_close(ds) == -1)
    perror("Closing queue error");

  return 0;
}
```

Listing 7.8 POSIX Message Queue Operations (continued)

```c
/* mqueue-2.c */

/* This program receives the message from the Queue */
#include <stdio.h>
#include <mqueue.h>

#define QUEUE_NAME   "/my_queue"
#define PRIORITY     1
#define SIZE         256

int main(){

  mqd_t ds;
  char new_text[SIZE];
  struct mq_attr attr, old_attr;
  int prio;

  /*
   * Open "/my_queue" for sending and receiving. No blocking when
   * receiving a message(O_NONBLOCK). The queue file permissions
   * are set rw for owner and nothing for group/others.
   */
  if ((ds = mq_open(QUEUE_NAME,  O_RDWR | O_NONBLOCK, 0600,
                    NULL)) == (mqd_t)-1){
    perror("Creating queue error");
    return -1;
  }


  /*
   * Change to blocking receive. (This is done to demonstrate
   * usage of mq_setattr and mq_getattr functions. To put the
   * queue in blocking mode you can also call mq_open above
   * without O_NONBLOCK). Remember that mq_setattr cannot be used
   * to changes values of message queue parameters mq_maxmsg,
   * mq_msgsize etc. It can only be used to change
   * mq_flags field of mq_attr struct. mq_flags is one of
   * O_NONBLOCK, O_RDWR etc.
   */
  attr.mq_flags = 0; /* set !O_NONBLOCK */
  if (mq_setattr(ds, &attr, NULL)){
    perror("mq_setattr");
    return -1;
  }

  /*
   * Here we will convince ourself that O_NONBLOCK is not
   * set. Infact this function also populates message queue
   * parameters in structure old_addr
   */
  if (mq_getattr(ds, &old_attr)) {
    perror("mq_getattr");
    return -1;
  }
```

Listing 7.8   POSIX Message Queue Operations (continued)

```
if (!(old_attr.mq_flags & O_NONBLOCK))
  printf("O_NONBLOCK not set\n");

/*
 * Now receive the message from queue. This is a blocking call.
 * Priority of message received is stored in prio.The function
 * receives the oldest of the highest priority message(s) from
 * the message queue. If the size of the buffer, specified by
 * the msg_len argument, is less than the  mq_msgsize
 * attribute of the message queue the function shall fail and
 * return an error
 */
if (mq_receive(ds, new_text, SIZE, &prio) == -1){
  perror("cannot receive");
  return -1;
}

printf("Message: %s, prio = %d\n", new_text, prio);

/* Close queue... */
if (mq_close(ds) == -1)
  perror("Closing queue error");

/*
 * ...and finally unlink it. After unlink message queue is
 * removed from system.
 */
if (mq_unlink(QUEUE_NAME) == -1)
  perror("Removing queue error");

return 0;
}
```

```
# gcc –o mqueue-1 mqueue-1.c –lrt
# gcc –o mqueue-2 mqueue-2.c –lrt
# ./mqueue-1
# ./mqueue-2
O_NONBLOCK not set
Message: Hello Posix World, prio = 1
```

The blocking time of an application for sending or receiving messages can be controlled by using the mq_timedsend and mq_timedreceive functions. If the message queue is full and O_NONBLOCK is not set, the mq_timedsend function terminates at a specified timeout (it may happen if the queue is full and the send function blocks until it gets a free buffer). Similarly, mq_timedreceive terminates at a specified timeout if there are no messages in the queue. The following code fragment illustrates the usage of the mq_timedsend and mq_timedreceive functions. Both wait for a maximum of 10 seconds for sending or receiving a message.

```
/* sending message */
struct timespec ts;
```

```
/* Specify timeout as 10 seconds from now */
ts.tv_sec = time(NULL) + 10;
ts.tv_nsec = 0;
if (mq_timedsend(ds, text, SIZE,PRIOTITY, &ts) == -1){
  if (errno == ETIMEDOUT){
    printf("Timeout when waiting for message.");
    return 0;
  }
  return -1;
}

/* receiving message */
if (mq_timedreceive(ds, new_text, SIZE, &prio, &ts) == -1){
  if (errno == ETIMEDOUT){
    printf("Timeout when waiting for message.");
    return 0;
  }
  return -1;
}
```

Asynchronous Notification

The mq_notify function provides an asynchronous mechanism for processes to receive notification that messages are available in a message queue rather than synchronously blocking in mq_receive or mq_timedreceive. This interface is very useful for real-time applications. A process can call the mq_notify function to register for asynchronous notification and then it can proceed to do some other work. A notification is sent to the process when a message arrives in the queue. After notification, the process can call mq_receive to receive the message. The prototype of mq_notify is

```
int mq_notify(mqd_t mqdes,
              const struct sigevent *notification);
```

An application can register for two types of notification.

- SIGEV_SIGNAL: Send signal specified in notification->sigev_signo to the process when a message arrives in the queue. Listing 7.9 illustrates the usage.
- SIGEV_THREAD: Call notification->sigev_notify_function in a separate thread when a message arrives in the queue. Listing 7.10 illustrates the usage.

Linux Implementation

Like POSIX shared memory, Linux implements POSIX message queues as an mqueue file system. The mqueue file system provides the necessary kernel support for the user-space library that implements the POSIX message queue APIs. By default, the kernel mounts the file system internally and it is not visible in user space. However, you can mount mqueue fs.

Listing 7.9   Asynchronous Notification Using SIGEV_SIGNAL

```
struct sigevent notif;
sigset_t sig_set;
siginfo_t info;
        ....

/* SIGUSR1 is notification signal.*/
sigemptyset(&sig_set);
sigaddset(&sig_set, SIGUSR1);

/*
 * Block SIGUSR1 as we shall wait for it in sigwaitinfo call
 */
sigprocmask(SIG_BLOCK, &sig_set, NULL);

/* Now set notification */
notif.sigev_notify = SIGEV_SIGNAL;
notif.sigev_signo = SIGUSR1;

if (mq_notify(ds, &notif)){
  perror("mq_notify");
  return -1;
}

/*
 * SIGUSR1 will get delivered if a message
 * arrives in the queue
 */
do {
  sigwaitinfo(&sig_set, &info);
} while(info.si_signo != SIGUSR1);

/* Now we can receive the message. */
if (mq_receive(ds, new_text, SIZE, &prio) == -1)
  perror("Receiving message error");

        ....
```

```
# mkdir /dev/mqueue
# mount -t mqueue none /dev/mqueue
```

This command mounts the mqueue file system under /dev/mqueue. A message queue is represented as a file under /dev/mqueue. But you can't send or receive a message from the queue by "writing" or "reading" from the message queue "file." Reading the file gives the queue size and notification information that isn't accessible through standard routines. Remove mq_unlink from Listing 7.8 and then compile and execute it.

```
# gcc mqueue-1.c -lrt
# ./a.out
# cat /dev/mqueue/my_queue
QSIZE:17         NOTIFY:0      SIGNO:0      NOTIFY_PID:0
```

In the above output

Listing 7.10 Asynchronous Notification Using SIGEV_THREAD

```
struct sigevent notif;
sigset_t sig_set;
siginfo_t info;
        ....

/*
 * Set SIGEV_THREAD notification. Note that notification
 * function, when invoked, runs in a separate thread
 */
notif.sigev_notify = SIGEV_THREAD;
/* notification routine to be called */
notif.sigev_notify_function = notify_routine;

/*
 * Pass message queue id as argument to the notification function
 * when it is called
 */
notif.sigev_value.sival_int = ds;
/* Notification thread should be in DETACHED state */
notif.sigev_notify_attributes = NULL;

/* Finally set the notification */
if (mq_notify(ds, &notif)){
  perror("mq_notify");
  return -1;
}
         ....

/*
 * .. and this is the notification routine. This will be called
 * whenever there is a message in the queue
 */
void notify_routine(sigval_t value){
        ...
  /* now of course we can receive this message. */
  if ((len = mq_receive(value.sival_int, new_text, SIZE,
                        &prio)) == -1)
    perror("Receiving message error");
        ...
}
```

- QSIZE: Message queue size
- NOTIFY: Either 0, SIGEV_SIGNAL, or SIGEV_THREAD
- SIGNAL: Signal number used for notification
- NOTIFY_PID: PID of process waiting for notification

The mqueue file system also provides sysctls in folder /proc/sys/fs/ mqueue for tuning the amount of resources used by the file system. The sysctls are:

- queues_max: read/write file for getting/setting the maximum number of message queues allowed in the system. For example, echo 128 > queues_max allows creation of a maximum of 128 message queues in the system.

- msg_max: read/write file for getting/setting the maximum number of messages in a queue. The maximum number of messages specified during mq_open should be less than or equal to msg_max.
- msgsize_max: read/write file for getting/setting the maximum message size value. It is the default if the maximum message size is not specified during mq_open.

Points to Remember

- When a process receives a message from a queue, the message is removed from the queue.
- If O_NONBLOCK is not specified, mq_send blocks until space becomes available in the queue to enqueue the message. If more than one thread or process is waiting to send a message and space becomes available in the queue, then the thread/process of the highest priority that has been waiting the longest is unblocked to send its message. The same applies for mq_receive.
- At any time only one process may be registered for notification on a message queue. If the calling process or any other process has already registered for notification of message arrival, subsequent attempts to register for that message queue by the same or a different process will fail.
- Call mq_notify with NULL notification to cancel the existing registration.
- After sending notification to the registered process, its registration is removed and the message queue is available for further registration.
- If some thread of a process is blocked in mq_receive and the process has also registered a notification, the arriving message satisfies the mq_receive and no notification is sent.

7.3.5 POSIX Semaphores

Semaphores are counters for resources shared between threads or processes. The basic operations on semaphores are:

- Increment the counter atomically.
- Wait until the counter is not zero and then decrement it atomically.

Binary semaphores can be also be used for interprocess or interthread synchronization. They are mostly used in synchronizing access to shared resources such as shared memory, global data structures, and so on. There are two types of POSIX semaphores.

- *Named semaphores:* They can be used between multiple unrelated processes.
- *Unnamed semaphores:* They can be used by threads inside a process or between related processes (such as the parent and child processes).

Table 7.6   POSIX.1b Semaphore Functions

Method	Description
sem_open	Open/create a named semaphore.
sem_close	Close a named semaphore.
sem_unlink	Remove a named semaphore.
sem_init	Initialize unnamed semaphore.
sem_destroy	Delete unnamed semaphore.
sem_getvalue	Get current semaphore count.
sem_wait	Perform semaphore lock operation.
sem_trywait	Perform semaphore timed lock operation.
sem_post	Release the semaphore.

The pthread library, which is part of the glibc package, implements POSIX 1003.1b semaphores in Linux. Glibc 2.3 with NPTL has full support for semaphores, including named and process-shared semaphores. Earlier glibc versions supported only unnamed semaphores. Semaphore operations are listed in Table 7.6. Listing 7.11 illustrates the usage of a named semaphore.

Points to Remember

- Semaphore protection works only between cooperating processes; that is, a process should wait for a semaphore if it is not available and should release the semaphore after use.
- Semaphore descriptor is inherited across the fork. Child processes need not open the semaphore again. They can call sem_close after usage.
- sem_post function is async-signal safe and can be called from signal handlers.
- Priority inversion can happen if a low-priority process locks a semaphore needed by a high-priority process.

7.3.6 Real-Time Signals

POSIX 1003.1b signal extensions play a very important role in real-time applications. They are used to notify processes of the occurrence of asynchronous events such as high-resolution timer expiration, asynchronous I/O completion, message reception in an empty POSIX message queue, and so on. Some of the advantages that real-time signals have over native signals are listed in Table 7.7. These advantages make them suitable for real-time applications. POSIX.1b real-time signal interfaces are listed in Table 7.8.

We explain the above interfaces with an example. In this example, the parent process sends real-time signals to the child process and later handles them. The example is divided into two parts as shown in Figure 7.4.

Listing 7.11   POSIX Semaphore Operations

```c
/* sem.c */

#include <stdio.h>
#include <semaphore.h>
#include <sys/types.h>
#include <sys/mman.h>
#include <sys/stat.h>
#include <sys/fcntl.h>
#include <errno.h>

#define SEM_NAME "/mysem"
/*
 * Named semaphore interfaces are called in following order
 *     sem_open()
 *       ...
 *     sem_close()
 *     sem_unlink()
 * Unnamned semaphore interfaces are called in following order
 *     sem_init()
 *        ...
 *     sem_destroy()
 */

int main(){
  /* Our named semaphore */
  sem_t *sema_n;
  int ret,val;

  /*
   * Create a named semaphore (O_CREAT) with initial value 1
   * (i.e. unlocked)(If you want to create unnamed semaphore then
   * replace call to sem_open with sem_init)
   */
  if ((sema_n = sem_open(SEM_NAME, O_CREAT , 0600, 1)) ==
                                           SEM_FAILED){
    perror("sem_open");
    return -1;
  }

  /* Get the current semaphore value */
  sem_getvalue(sema_n, &val);
  printf("semaphore value = %d\n", val);

  /*
   * Try to get the semaphore. If it fails then use the blocking
   * version. This is only done to give sematics of both
   * sem_trywait and sem_wait. You need not call them like this
   * in real code
   */
  if ((ret = sem_trywait(sema_n)) != 0 && errno == EAGAIN)
    /* permanent wait */
    sem_wait(sema_n);
  else if (ret != 0){
    perror("sem_trywait");
    return -1;
  }
```

Listing 7.11   POSIX Semaphore Operations (continued)

```
/*
 * Semaphore is acquired. Operate on shared data
 */

/*
 * release the semaphore after shared data has been manipulated
 */
if (sem_post(sema_n) != 0)
  perror("post error");

/*
 * close and remove the semaphore. (For unnamed semaphores,
 * replace following two calls with sem_destroy. sem_unlink is
 * not valid for unnamed semaphore)
 */
sem_close(sema_n);
sem_unlink(SEM_NAME);
return 0;
}
```

Table 7.7   Real-Time Signals versus Native Signals

Real-Time Signals	Native Signals
Range of application-specific signals from `SIGRTMIN` to `SIGRTMAX`. All real-time signals are defined in this range such as `SIGRTMIN + 1`, `SIGRTMIN + 2`, `SIGRTMAX - 2`, etc.	Only two application-specific signals, `SIGUSR1` and `SIGUSR2`.
Delivery of signals can be prioritized. The lower the signal number the higher the priority. For example, if `SIGRTMIN` and `SIGRTMIN + 1` are pending, then `SIGRTMIN` will be delivered first.	No priority for signal delivery.
Sender can deliver extra information along with the real-time signal to the receiving process.	Cannot send extra information with signal.
Signals are queued (i.e., if a signal is delivered multiple times to a process, the receiver will process all the signal instances). Real-time signals are not lost.	Signals can get lost. If a signal is delivered multiple times to a process, the receiver will process only one instance.

Main Application

```
#include <signal.h>
#include <sys/types.h>
#include <unistd.h>
#include <errno.h>

int child(void);
int parent(pid_t);
/* Signal handler */
```

Table 7.8   POSIX.1b Real-Time Signal Functions

Method	Description
sigaction	Register signal handler and notification mechanism.
sigqueue	Send a signal and extra information to a process.
sigwaitinfo	Wait for signal delivery.
sigtimedwait	Wait for signal delivery and timeout if signal doesn't arrive.
sigsuspend	Suspend a process until signal is delivered.
sigprocmask	Operate on process's current block mask.
sigaddset	Add a signal to the signal set.
sigdelset	Remove a signal from the signal set.
sigemptyset	Clear all the signals in the signal set.
sigfillset	Set all the signals in the signal set.
sigismember	Test whether a signal is a member of a signal set.

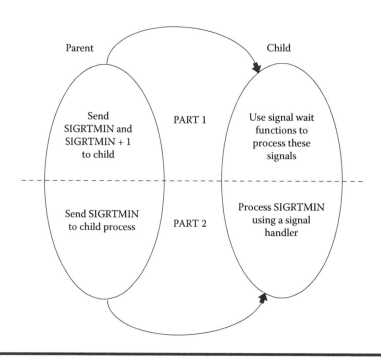

Figure 7.4   Real-time signals: sample application.

```
void rt_handler(int signum, siginfo_t *siginfo,
                void * extra);

int main(){
  pid_t cpid;
  if ((cpid = fork()) == 0)
    child();
```

```
    else
      parent(cpid);
}
```

Parent Process

The parent uses the `sigqueue` function to send `SIGRTMIN` and `SIGRTMIN` + 1 to the child process. The last argument of the function is used to send extra information with the signal.

```
int parent(pid_t cpid){
  union sigval value;

  /* ------- PART 1 STARTS -------------- */

  /* Sleep a while for child to get start */
  sleep(3);
  /* Extra information for SIGRTMIN */
  value.sival_int = 1;
  /* send SIGRTMIN to child */
  sigqueue(cpid, SIGRTMIN, value);

  /* send SIGRTMIN+1 to child */
  sleep(3);
  value.sival_int = 2;
  sigqueue(cpid, SIGRTMIN+1, value);

  /* ------- PART 2 STARTS -------------- */

  /* Finally send SIGRTMIN once more */
  sleep(3);
  value.sival_int = 3;
  sigqueue(cpid, SIGRTMIN, value);

  /* ------- PART 2 ENDS -------------- */
}
```

Child Process

```
int child(void){
  sigset_t mask, oldmask;
  siginfo_t siginfo;
  struct sigaction action;
  struct timespec tv;
  int count = 0, recv_sig;
```

We define `mask` of type `sigset_t` to hold the signals that we need to block. Before proceeding, clear the mask by calling `sigemptyset`. This function initializes the mask to exclude all the signals. Then call `sigaddset` to add the signals `SIGRTMIN` and `SIGRTMIN` + 1 to the blocked set. Finally call `sigprocmask` to block the signal delivery. (We are blocking these signals to process their delivery using signal wait functions instead of using a signal handler.)

```
/* ------- PART 1 STARTS -------------- */

/* clear mask */
sigemptyset(&mask);
/* add SIGRTMIN to mask */
sigaddset(&mask, SIGRTMIN);
/* add SIGRTMIN+1 to mask */
sigaddset(&mask, SIGRTMIN+1);

/*
 * Block SIGRTMIN, SIGRTMIN+1 signal delivery. After
 * return, previous value of blocked signal mask is stored
 * in oldmask
 */
sigprocmask(SIG_BLOCK, &mask, &oldmask);
```

The child now waits for the delivery of SIGRTMIN and SIGRTMIN + 1. Functions sigwaitinfo or sigtimedwait are used to wait for blocked signals. The set of signals to wait for is the first argument. The second argument is populated with any extra information received along with the signal (more about siginfo_t later). For sigtimedwait, the last argument is the wait time.

```
/* specify 1 sec timeout */
tv.tv_sec = 1;
tv.tv_nsec = 0;

/*
 * wait for signal delivery. We wait for two signals,
 * SIGRTMIN and SIGRTMIN+1. Loop will terminate when
 * both of them are received
 */
while(count < 2){
  if ((recv_sig = sigtimedwait(&mask, &siginfo, &tv)) ==
                          -1){
    if (errno == EAGAIN){
      printf("Timed out\n");
      continue;
    }else{
      perror("sigtimedwait");
      return -1;
    }
  }else{
    printf("signal %d received\n", recv_sig);
    count++;
  }
}
/* ------- PART 1 ENDS -------------- */
```

The other method to handle signals is to register a signal handler. In this case, the process should not block the signal. The registered signal handler is called when the signal is delivered to the process. The sigaction function registers a signal handler. Its second argument struct sigaction is defined as

```
struct sigaction {
  void (*sa_handler)(int);
  void (*sa_sigaction)(int, siginfo_t *, void *);
  sigset_t sa_mask;
  int sa_flags;
}
```

Fields of this structure are:

- `sa_handler`: Signal handler registration function for non–real-time signals.
- `sa_sigaction`: Signal handler registration function for real-time signals.
- `sa_mask`: Mask of signals that should be blocked when signal handler is executing.
- `sa_flags`: `SA_SIGINFO` is used for real-time signals. On reception of a signal that has `SA_SIGINFO` set, the `sa_sigaction` function is called instead of `sa_handler`.

The child now registers a signal handler `rt_handler` for handling the `SIGRTMIN` real-time signal. This function will be called when `SIGRTMIN` is delivered to the child.

```
/* ------- PART 2 STARTS -------------- */

/* Set SA_SIGINFO */
action.sa_flags = SA_SIGINFO;
/* Clear the mask */
sigemptyset(&action.sa_mask);

/*
 * Register signal handler for SIGRTMIN. Note that we are
 * using action.sa_sigaction interface to register the
 * handler
 */
action.sa_sigaction = rt_handler;
if (sigaction(SIGRTMIN, &action, NULL) == -1){
  perror("sigaction");
  return 0;
}
```

The child then waits for the signal to be delivered. `sigsuspend` temporarily replaces the current signal mask with the mask specified in its argument. It then waits for delivery of an unblocked signal. On signal delivery, `sigsuspend` restores the original mask and returns after the signal handler is executed. If the signal handler causes process termination, `sigsuspend` does not return.

```
/* Wait from SIGRTMIN */
sigsuspend(&oldmask);

/* ------- PART 2 ENDS -------------- */
}
```

Thus the child has successfully handled signals using both signal wait functions and using a signal handler.

Finally the signal handler is:

```
/* Signal handler for SIGRTMIN */
void rt_handler(int signum, siginfo_t *siginfo,
                void * extra){
  printf("signal %d received. code = %d, value = %d\n",
         siginfo->si_signo, siginfo->si_code,
         siginfo->si_int);
}
```

The second argument of the signal handler is of type `siginfo_t` and it contains all the information of the received signal. The structure is defined as:

```
siginfo_t {
  int   si_signo;   // Signal number
  int   si_errno;   // Signal error
  int   si_code;    // Signal code
  union {
    ...
    // POSIX .1b signals
    struct {
      pid_t pid;
      uid_t uid;
      sigval_t sigval;
    }_rt;
    ...
  }_sifields
}
```

Please refer to `/usr/include/bits/siginfo.h` for all the fields of the structure. Apart from `si_signo`, `si_errno`, and `si_code` all the rest of the fields are union. So one should only read the fields that are meaningful in the given context. For example, the fields shown above are valid only for POSIX.1b signals.

- `si_signo` is the signal number of the received signal. This is the same as the first argument of the signal handler.
- `si_code` gives the source of the signal. Important `si_code` values for real-time signals are listed in Table 7.9.
- `si_value` is extra information given by the sender.
- `pid` and `uid` are the process ID and user ID of the sender, respectively.

The above fields should be accessed using the following macros, which are defined in `siginfo.h`.

```
#define si_value    _sifields._rt._sigval
#define si_int      _sifields._rt._sigval.sival_int
#define si_ptr      _sifields._rt._sigval.sival_ptr
#define si_pid      _sifields._kill._pid
#define si_uid      _sifields._kill._uid
```

Table 7.9   Signal Codes

SignalCode	Value	Origin
SI_USER	0	`kill`, `sigsend`, or `raise`
SI_KERNEL	0x80	Kernel
SI_QUEUE	-1	`sigqueue` function
SI_TIMER	-2	POSIX timer expiration
SI_MESGQ	-3	POSIX message queue state change from nonempty to empty
SI_ASYNCIO	-4	Async IO completed

Thus you can use `siginfo->si_int` and `siginfo->si_ptr` to access the extra information given by the sender.

7.3.7 POSIX.1b Clock and Timers

Traditional BSD timers in Linux, `setitimer` and `getitimer` functions, are inadequate for most of the real-time applications. POSIX.1b timers offer the following advantages over BSD timers.

■ A process can have multiple timers.
■ Better timer precision. Timers can be specified in nanosecond resolution.
■ Timeout notification can be done either using any arbitrary (real-time) signal or using threads. There are only limited signals for timeout notification in BSD timers.
■ POSIX.1b timers provide support for various clocks such as CLOCK_REALTIME, CLOCK_MONOTONIC, and so on that can have different sources with different resolutions. The BSD timer on the other hand is tied to the system clock.

The core of POSIX.1b timers is a set of clocks that are used as a timing reference. Linux provides support for the following clocks.

■ CLOCK_REALTIME: The systemwide real-time clock, visible to all processes running in the system. The clock measures the amount of time in seconds and nanoseconds since Epoch (i.e., 00:00:00 Jan 1, 1970, GMT). The resolution of the clock is `1/HZ` seconds. Thus if `HZ` is 100 then the clock resolution is 10 msec. If `HZ` is 1000 then the clock resolution is 1 msec. Please see file `<kernel-source>/include/asm/param.h` for the value of `HZ` in your system. As this clock is based on wall time, it can be changed.
■ CLOCK_MONOTONIC: The system uptime clock visible to all processes on the system. In Linux, it measures the amount of time in seconds and nanoseconds since system boot. Its resolution is `1/HZ` sec. Its support is available since kernel 2.5 and glibc 2.3.3. This clock cannot be changed by any process.

Table 7.10   POSIX.1b Clock and Timer Functions

Method	Description
clock_settime	Set specified clock to a value.
clock_gettime	Get clock value.
clock_getres	Get clock resolution.
clock_nanosleep	Suspend calling process execution for specified time.
timer_create	Create a timer based on specified clock.
timer_delete	Delete a timer.
timer_settime	Arm the timer.
timer_gettime	Return current timer value.
timer_getoverrun	Return number of times timer expired between signal generation and delivery.

- CLOCK_PROCESS_CPUTIME_ID: The clock measuring process up-time. The time the current process has spent executing on the system is measured in seconds and nanoseconds. The resolution is 1/HZ. The clock can be changed.
- CLOCK_THREAD_CPUTIME_ID: The same as CLOCK_PROCESS_CPUTIME_ID but for the current thread.

Generally CLOCK_REALTIME is used for specifying absolute timeouts. CLOCK_MONOTONIC is used for relative timeouts and periodic tasks. Because this clock cannot be changed, periodic tasks need not bother about premature or delayed wake-up that could occur with CLOCK_REALTIME. The other two clocks can be used for accounting purposes. The POSIX.1b clock and timer interfaces are listed in Table 7.10.

We explain usage of the above interfaces with an example. In this example we create a POSIX timer based on CLOCK_MONOTONIC. It's a periodic timer with a period of four seconds. Timer expiration is notified to the process using the SIGRTMIN real-time signal. The process has registered a signal handler for SIGRTMIN that keeps count of timer expiration. When the counter reaches a specified value referred to as MAX_EXPIRE in the example, the timer is disarmed and the process exits.

```
#include <unistd.h>
#include <time.h>
#include <signal.h>

#define MAX_EXPIRE 10
int expire;

void timer_handler(int signo, siginfo_t *info,
                   void *context);

int main(){
```

```
struct timespec ts, tm, sleep;
sigset_t mask;
siginfo_t info;
struct sigevent sigev;
struct sigaction sa;
struct itimerspec ival;
timer_t tid;
```

First print some statistics of CLOCK_MONOTONIC. clock_getres gives the resolution of the clock and clock_gettime gives system up-time. Please note that the resolution of CLOCK_MONOTONIC is 1/HZ.

```
clock_getres(CLOCK_MONOTONIC, &ts);
clock_gettime(CLOCK_MONOTONIC, &tm);
printf("CLOCK_MONOTONIC res: [%d]sec [%d]nsec/n",
                      ts.tv_sec, ts.tv_nsec);
printf("system up time: [%d]sec [%d]nsec\n",
                      tm.tv_sec, tm.tv_nsec);
```

Set up a signal handler for SIGRTMIN. As mentioned earlier, the process will receive a SIGRTMIN real-time signal at timer expiration.

```
/* We don't want any blocked signals */
sigemptyset(&mask);
sigprocmask(SIG_SETMASK, &mask, NULL);

/* Register handler for SIGRTMIN */
sa.sa_flags = SA_SIGINFO;
sigemptyset(&sa.sa_mask);
sa.sa_sigaction = timer_handler;
if (sigaction(SIGRTMIN, &sa, NULL) == -1) {
  perror("sigaction failed");
  return -1;
}
```

Create the timer. The second argument of timer_create is the type of notification desired on timer expiration. Please recall from our discussion on POSIX message queues that the notifications are of two types, SIGEV_SIGNAL and SIGEV_THREAD. With POSIX timers, either could be used as a notification mechanism. In this example we are using the SIGEV_SIGNAL notification mechanism.

```
/*
 * Timer expiration should send SIGRTMIN signal with some
 * dummy value 1
 */
sigev.sigev_notify = SIGEV_SIGNAL;
sigev.sigev_signo = SIGRTMIN;
sigev.sigev_value.sival_int = 1;

/*
 * Create timer. Note that if the call is successful,
 * timer-id is returned in the third argument.
```

```
 */
if (timer_create(CLOCK_MONOTONIC, &sigev, &tid) == -1){
  perror("timer_create");
  return -1;
}
printf("timer-id = %d\n", tid);
```

Arm the timer. The time will expire after five seconds and after every four seconds subsequently.

```
ival.it_value.tv_sec = 5;
ival.it_value.tv_nsec = 0;
ival.it_interval.tv_sec = 4;
ival.it_interval.tv_nsec = 0;
if (timer_settime(tid, 0, &ival, NULL) == -1){
  perror("timer_settime");
  return -1;
}
```

Finally wait for timer to expire. If timer expiration count `expire` reaches `MAX_EXPIRE` then disarm the timer and quit.

```
/* Sleep and wait for signal */
for(;;){
  sleep.tv_sec = 3;
  sleep.tv_nsec = 0;
  clock_nanosleep(CLOCK_MONOTONIC, 0, &sleep, NULL);
  printf("woken up\n");
  if (expire >= MAX_EXPIRE){
    printf("Program quitting.\n");
    /*
     * If it_value == 0 then call to timer_settime
     * disarms the the timer
     */
    memset(&ival, 0, sizeof (ival));
      timer_settime(tid, 0, &ival, NULL);
      return 0;
  }
}
return 0;
}
```

Finally we have `timer_handler:` Recall our discussion on signal handlers from Section 7.3.6. The second argument of the handler is of type `siginfo_t`, which contains information regarding the received signal. In this case `info->si_code` is `SI_TIMER`.

```
void timer_handler(int signo, siginfo_t *info,
                   void *context)
{
  int overrun;
  printf("signal details: signal (%d), code (%d)\n",
                   info->si_signo, info->si_code);
```

```
if (info->si_code == SI_TIMER){
  printf("timer-id = %d \n", info->si_timerid);
  expire++;

  /*
   * Specification says that only a single signal
   * instance is queued to the process for a given
   * timer at any point in time. When a timer for which a
   * signal is still pending expires, no signal is
   * queued and a timer overrun condition occurs.
   * timer_getoverrun returns the number of extra timer
   * expirations that occurred between the time the
   * signal was generated (queued) and when it was
   * delivered or accepted
   */
  if ((overrun = timer_getoverrun(info->si_timerid)) !=
                            -1 && overrun != 0){
    printf("timer overrun %d\n", overrun);
    expire += overrun;
  }
 }
}
```

High-Resolution Timers

For the clocks discussed above, Linux provides the best resolution of 1 msec (HZ = 1000). This resolution is not enough for most real-time applications as they require resolution on the order of microseconds and nanoseconds. To support such applications, the High-Resolution Timers (HRT) project was started by engineers at MontaVista. HRT are POSIX timers with microsecond resolution. Two additional POSIX clocks are introduced, CLOCK_REALTIME_ HR and CLOCK_MONOTONIC_HR. They are the same as their non-HR counterpart; the only difference is the clock resolution that is on the order of microseconds or nanoseconds depending on the hardware clock source. At the time of this writing the HRT support is not included in the main source tree and is available as a patch. More details about the project are available at www.sourceforge.net/projects/high-res-timers.

Points to Remember

- Resolution of the clock is fixed and cannot be changed at runtime by the application.
- To disarm a timer, call timer_settime with it_value member of itimespec set to zero.
- A timer can be periodic or one-shot. If the it_interval member of itimerspec during call to timer_setime is zero then the timer is one-shot; otherwise it is periodic.
- POSIX.1b also provides a nanosleep function. This is the same as clock_nanosleep with CLOCK_REALTIME as its first argument.
- Per-process timers are not inherited by a child process.

7.3.8 Asynchronous I/O

Traditional read and write system calls are blocking calls. Most real-time applications may need to overlap their compute and I/O processing to improve determinism. For example, an application may prefer Asynchronous I/O (AIO) if it requires high-volume data collection from some source and if data processing is computation intensive. POSIX.1b defines asynchronous I/O interfaces to fulfill demands of such applications.

The mechanism is very simple. An application can queue a request for AIO and then continue normal processing. The application is notified when the I/O completes. It can then query the status of I/O for success or failure. An application can do the following operations using AIO interfaces.

- Issue multiple nonblocking I/O requests from different sources with a single call. (Thus an application can have many I/O operations in progress while it is executing other code.)
- Cancel any outstanding I/O request.
- Wait for I/O completion.
- Track the status of I/O: in-progress, error, or completed.

AIO Control Block

The AIO control block, `struct aiocb`, is the core of POSIX.1b AIO. The structure contains the details that are necessary for submitting an AIO. The structure is defined as follows.

```
struct aiocb
{
  int aio_fildes;              /* File desriptor. */
  int aio_lio_opcode;          /* Operation to be performed,
                                  read or write. Used while
                                  submitting multiple AIOs in a
                                  single request */
  int aio_reqprio;             /* Request priority offset. */
  volatile void *aio_buf;      /* Location of buffer for read
                                  or write */
  size_t aio_nbytes;           /* Length of transfer. */
  struct sigevent aio_sigevent; /* Notification info. */
  off_t aio_offset             /* File offset to start read or
                                  write from */
}
```

Note that unlike traditional read or write operations, you need to specify the file offset from where to start the AIO. After performing the I/O, the kernel won't increment the file offset field in the file descriptor. You need to keep track of file offsets manually.

Table 7.11   AIO Functions

Method	Description
`aio_read`	Start async read.
`aio_write`	Start async write.
`aio_error`	Return completion status of last aio_read or aio_write.
`aio_return`	Return number of bytes transferred in aio_read or aio_write.
`aio_cancel`	Cancel any pending AIO operations.
`aio_suspend`	Call process until any of specified requests complete.
`lio_listio`	Submit multiple async read or write operation.

AIO Functions

The AIO functions are listed in Table 7.11. Listing 7.12 illustrates the usage of POSIX.1b AIO interfaces. The example simply copies one file to another using AIO. For the sake of simplicity we assume that the AIO functions don't return an error.

List-Directed I/O

The `lio_listio` function could be used to submit an arbitrary number of read or write requests in one call.

```
int lio_listio(int mode, struct aiocb *list[], int nent,
                            struct sigevent *sig);
```

- mode: This argument could be `LIO_WAIT` or `LIO_NOWAIT`. If the argument is `LIO_WAIT`, the function waits until all I/O is complete and `sig` is ignored. If the argument is `LIO_NOWAIT`, the function returns immediately and async notification will occur as specified in `sig` after I/O completes.
- `aiocb list`: This argument contains the list of aiocbs.
- nent: Number of aiocbs in second argument.
- `sig`: Desired notification mechanism. No notification is generated if this argument is `NULL`.

Listing 7.12 could be modified to use the `lio_listio` function.

```
while(1){
  memcpy(write_buf, read_buf, read_n);
  a_write.aio_nbytes = read_n;
  a_read.aio_nbytes = XFER_SIZE;

  /* Prepare aiocb list for lio_listio */
  cblist_lio[0] = &a_read;
```

Listing 7.12   File Copy Using AIO

```c
/* aio_cp.c */

#include <unistd.h>
#include <aio.h>
#include <sys/types.h>
#include <errno.h>

#define INPUT_FILE "./input"
#define OUTPUT_FILE "./output"
/* Transfer size of one read or write operation */
#define XFER_SIZE   1024
#define MAX 3

/* Function to fill the aiocb values */
void populate_aiocb(struct aiocb *aio, int fd, off_t offset,
                    int bytes, char *buf){
  aio->aio_fildes = fd;
  aio->aio_offset = offset;

  /*
   * We are not using any notification mechanism here to put more
   * emphasis on AIO interfaces. We can use SIGEV_SIGNAL or
   * SIGEV_THREAD notification mechanisms to get notification
   * after AIO is complete.
   */
  aio->aio_sigevent.sigev_notify = SIGEV_NONE;
  aio->aio_nbytes = bytes;
  aio->aio_buf = buf;
}


/*
 * The application copies one file to the other
 */
int main(){

  /* read/write file descriptors */
  int fd_r , fd_w;
  /* AIO control blocks for reading and writing */
  struct aiocb a_write, a_read;

  /*
   * This list is used to hold control blocks of outstanding
   * read or write requests
   */
  struct aiocb *cblist[MAX];
  /* Status of read or write operation */
  int err_r, err_w;
  /* no. of bytes actually read */
  int read_n = 0;
  /* Marks end of stream for source file */
  int quit = 0;
  /* Used for xfer from source to destination file */
  char read_buf[XFER_SIZE];
  char write_buf[XFER_SIZE];
```

Listing 7.12   File Copy Using AIO (continued)

```c
/*
 * Open the source and destination files. Call populate_aiocb
 * function to initialize AIO control blocks for read and write
 * operation. Its good practice to clear the aiocbs before
 * using them
 */
fd_r = open(INPUT_FILE, O_RDONLY, 0444);
fd_w = open(OUTPUT_FILE, O_CREAT | O_WRONLY, 0644);

memset(&a_write, 0 , sizeof(struct aiocb));
memset(&a_read, 0 , sizeof(struct aiocb));

/* populate aiocbs to defaults */
populate_aiocb(&a_read, fd_r, 0, XFER_SIZE, read_buf);
populate_aiocb(&a_write, fd_w, 0, XFER_SIZE, write_buf);

/*
 * Start async read from the source file using aio_read
 * function. The function reads a_read.aio_nbytes bytes from
 * file a_read.aio_fildes starting from offset
 * a_read.aio_offset into buffer a_read.aio_buf. On success 0
 * is returned. This function returns immediately after
 * queuing the request
 */
aio_read(&a_read);

/*
 * Wait for read to complete. After starting any async
 * operation (read or write), you can get its status using
 * aio_error function. The function returns EINPROGRESS if the
 * request has not been completed, it returns 0 if the request
 * completed successfully, otherwise an error value is
 * returned. If aio_read return EINPROGRESS, then call
 * aio_suspend to wait for operation to complete.
 */
while((err_r = aio_error(&a_read)) == EINPROGRESS){
  /*
   * The  aio_suspend  function  suspends the calling process
   * until at least one of the asynchronous I/O requests in the
   * list cblist have completed or a signal is delivered, Here
   * we arc waiting for aio_read completion on a_read.
   */
  cblist[0] = &a_read;
  aio_suspend(cblist, 1, NULL);
}

/*
 * If the return value of aio_error function is 0 then the read
 * operation was successful. Call aio_return to find of number
 * of bytes read. The function should be called only once after
 * aio_error returns something other than EINPROGRESS.
 */
if (err_r == 0){
  read_n  = aio_return(&a_read);
  if (read_n == XFER_SIZE)
```

Listing 7.12   File Copy Using AIO (continued)

```
        /* We need to manage the offsets */
        a_read.aio_offset += XFER_SIZE;
      else {
        /*
         * For the sake of simplicity we assume source file size is
         * greater than XFER_SIZE
         */
        printf("Source file size < %d\n", XFER_SIZE);
        exit(1);
      }
    }

  /*
   * In this loop we copy data read above into the write buffer
   * and start async write operation. We also go ahead and queue
   * read request for the next cycle.
   */
  while(1){
    memcpy(write_buf, read_buf, read_n);

    /*
     * Setup write control block. Call aio_write to queue write
     * request. The function will write a_write.aio_nbytes bytes
     * from buffer a_write.aio_buf to file a_write.aio_fildes at
     * offset a_write.aio_offset. Returns 0 on success
     */
    a_write.aio_nbytes = read_n;
    aio_write(&a_write);

    /* Queue next read request */
    a_read.aio_nbytes = XFER_SIZE;
    aio_read(&a_read);

    /*
     * Wait for both read and write to get complete before
     * proceeding
     */
    while((err_r = aio_error(&a_read)) == EINPROGRESS ||
                 (err_w = aio_error(&a_write)) == EINPROGRESS){
      cblist[0] = &a_read;
      cblist[1] = &a_write;
      aio_suspend(cblist, 2, NULL);
    }

    /* Is this the end ? */
    if (quit)
      break;

    /* Increment the write pointer */
    a_write.aio_offset += aio_return(&a_write);
    /* Increment the read pointer */
    read_n = aio_return(&a_read);
    if (read_n == XFER_SIZE)
      a_read.aio_offset += XFER_SIZE;
    else
```

Listing 7.12   File Copy Using AIO (continued)

```
      /* This is the last block */
      quit = 1;
    }
  }

  /* cleanup */
  close(fd_r);
  close(fd_w);
}
```

Table 7.12   Kernel AIO Interfaces

Method	Description
io_setup	Create a new request context for an AIO.
io_submit	Submit an AIO request (aka aio_read, aio_write, lio_listio).
io_getevents	Reap completed I/O operations (aka aio_error, aio_return).
io_wait	Wait for I/O to complete (aka aio_suspend).
io_cancel	Cancel I/O (aka aio_cancel).
io_destroy	Destroy the AIO context. Happens by default on process exit.

```
    cblist_lio[1] = &a_write;

    /*
     * Call lio_listio to submit read and write AIO requests
     */
    lio_listio(LIO_NOWAIT, cblist_lio, 2, NULL);
              ..............
}
```

Linux Implementation

Initially AIO in Linux was completely implemented in the user space using threads. There was one user thread created per request. This resulted in poor scalability and poor performance. Since 2.5, kernel support for AIO has been added. However, the interfaces the kernel provides for AIO are different from POSIX interfaces. The interfaces are based on a new set of system calls. They are listed in Table 7.12. The interfaces are provided in user space by the libaio library.

Points to Remember

■ The control block should not change while the read or write operation is in progress. Also the buffer pointer in aiocb should be valid until the request is completed.

■ Return value of `lio_listio` does not indicate the status of individual I/O requests. Failure of a request does not prevent completion of other requests.

7.4 Hard Real-Time Linux

Recall that standard Linux does not provide hard real-time deadline guarantees. Several extensions are added to support hard real-time applications under Linux. The most popular is the dual-kernel approach in which Linux is treated as a lowest-priority task of a real-time executive. Figure 7.5 shows the basic architecture of a dual-kernel approach.

In the dual-kernel approach, Linux executes only when there are no real-time tasks to run. It can never disable interrupts or prevent itself from preemption. The interrupt hardware is controlled by the real-time executive and interrupts are only dispatched to Linux if there are no takers for it in the real-time executive. Even if Linux disables an interrupt (using `cli`), the hardware interrupt is not disabled. The real-time executive just won't send an interrupt to Linux if the latter has disabled it. Thus the real-time executive behaves like an "interrupt controller" for Linux. Linux never adds any latency to the interrupt response time of the real-time executive. In this design, Linux handles all the non–real-time activities such as logging, system initialization, managing hardware not involved in real-time processing, and so on.

There are two primary variants of hard real-time Linux: RTLinux and RTAI. RTLinux was developed at the New Mexico Institute of Technology by Michael Barabanov under the direction of Professor Victor Yodaiken. RTAI was developed at the Dipartimento di Ingeneria Aerospaziale, Politecnico di Milano by

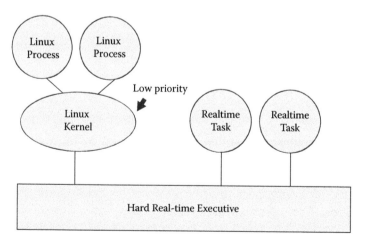

Figure 7.5　Dual-kernel architecture.

Professor Paolo Mantegazza. Both these variants are implemented as Linux kernel modules. They are similar in nature in that all the interrupts are initially handled by the real-time kernel and then passed to Linux if there are no active real-time tasks.

In this section we discuss the RTAI solution for providing hard real-time support in Linux. In the end we also discuss very briefly ADEOS, which is a framework for supporting the real-time kernel and general-purpose OS (such as Linux) on the same platform.

7.4.1 Real-Time Application Interface (RTAI)

RTAI is an open source real-time extension to Linux. The core of RTAI is the hardware abstraction layer on the top of which Linux and hard real-time core can run. The HAL provides a mechanism to trap the peripheral interrupts and route them to Linux only if it is not required for any hard real-time processing. A hard real-time task can be created and scheduled under RTAI using RTAI APIs. RTAI uses its own scheduler to schedule real-time tasks. This scheduler is different from the native Linux scheduler. The real-time task can use IPC mechanisms provided by RTAI to communicate with other real-time tasks or normal Linux processes.

> *We use the term real-time task for the task scheduled under RTAI unless specified.*

Figure 7.6 shows the architecture of an RTAI-based Linux system. (For the sake of simplicity we have omitted LXRT tasks from the diagram.) The details in the diagram become clear in the coming paragraphs.

RTAI supports several architectures such as x86, ARM, MIPS, PowerPC, CRIS, and so on. RTAI modules such as the scheduler, IPC, and so on do not run in separate address space. They are implemented as Linux kernel modules; thus they run in the address space of Linux. Not all the kernel modules need to be present always; `rtai` is the core module and should always be present and other modules can be loaded dynamically when required. For example, `rtai_fifo` implements RTAI FIFO functionality and should be loaded only if this feature is required.

HAL

The HAL intercepts all hardware interrupts and routes them to either standard Linux or to real-time tasks depending on the requirements of the RTAI schedulers. Interrupts meant for a scheduled real-time task are sent directly to that task, whereas interrupts not required by any scheduled real-time task are sent to Linux. In this manner, the HAL provides a framework onto which RTAI is mounted with the ability to fully control peripheral interrupts and preempt Linux. There are two implementations of HAL in RTAI.

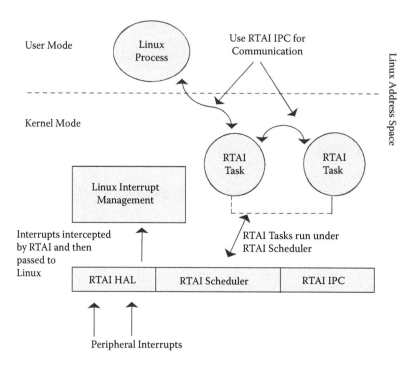

Figure 7.6   RTAI architecture.

- *RTHAL (Real-Time Hardware Abstraction Layer):* It replaces Linux interrupt descriptor tables with its own table to intercept peripheral interrupts.
- *ADEOS:* In this model, RTAI is a higher-priority domain than Linux.

Schedulers

The RTAI distribution includes four different priority-based, preemptive real-time schedulers.

- *UP:* The scheduler is intended for uniprocessor platforms.
- SMP: Intended for SMP machines.
- MUP: Intended for multiprocessor non-SMP machines.
- *NEWLXRT:* It unifies the above three schedulers and can schedule Linux tasks and kernel threads along with RTAI kernel tasks thus extending hard real-time application interface to Linux tasks and kernel threads.

   UP, MUP, and SMP schedulers can schedule only RTAI kernel tasks.

LXRT

All the real-time tasks scheduled under RTAI run in the kernel address space. RTAI applications are loaded as kernel modules. The first function they call is `rt_task_init`. `rt_task_init` creates an RTAI real-time task that is scheduled under the RTAI scheduler. The task can now use all the RTAI real-time services.

Table 7.13   RTAI IPC Mechanisms

IPC	Description	Kernel Module
Event flags	They are used to synchronize a task with the occurrence of multiple events. Their usage is similar to semaphores except that the signal and wait operation does not depend on a counter but on the set of events that can occur.	`rtai_bits.o`
FIFO	They allow communication between Linux user-space applications and kernel-space RTAI tasks.	`rtai_fifos.o`
Shared memory	Module allows sharing memory between RTAI tasks and Linux processes.	`rtai_shm.o`
Semaphores	RTAI semaphores support priority inheritance.	`rtai_sem.o`

Mailbox	Very flexible IPC mechanism. It can be used for sending variable-size messages between Linux and RTAI. RTAI also supports typed mailboxes for message broadcasting and urgent message delivery.	`rtai_mbx.o,`
		`rtai_tmbx.o`
		(typed mailbox)

NetRPC	Intertask message-passing mechanism that extends RTAI in distributed environment.	`rtai_netrpc.o`
Pqueues	RTAI pqueues implement POSIX 1003.1b message queue APIs.	`rtai_mq.o`

LXRT extends the RTAI real-time services in user space. Thus any normal Linux process can call RTAI APIs. This is a very powerful mechanism that bridges the gap between RTAI real-time tasks and normal user-space Linux processes. When a Linux process calls `rt_task_init`, LXRT creates an RTAI kernel task that acts as a proxy for the Linux process. The proxy executes RTAI services on behalf of the Linux process. For example, if a Linux process calls `rt_sleep`, the proxy will execute the function under the RTAI scheduler. Control returns to the Linux process when the proxy returns from `rt_sleep`.

IPC

RTAI supports a number of IPC mechanisms that can be used for communication between RTAI–RTAI tasks and RTAI–Linux processes. They are listed in Table 7.13.

Miscellaneous Modules

RTAI also provides the following.

- *Real-time malloc* (`rtai_malloc`): RTAI provides a real-time implementation of `malloc()`. An RTAI task can safely allocate or free memory without any blocking. This is achieved by satisfying real-time memory allocation from the preallocated global heap.

- *Tasklets* (`rtai_tasklets`): Sometimes applications need to execute a function periodically or when some event occurs. Using RTAI scheduler services for this purpose could be expensive in terms of resources used. RTAI provides tasklets to address such application needs. They are of two types.
  - *Normal tasklets:* They are simple functions executed in kernel space. They are called either from a real-time task or an interrupt handler.
  - *Timed tasklets:* They are simple timer functions that are executed by an RTAI server task in one shot or periodic mode.

- *Pthreads* (`rtai_pthread`): Supports POSIX.1c threads (including mutexes and condition variables).

- *Watchdog* (`rtai_wd`): This module protects RTAI and Linux from programming errors in RTAI applications.

- *Xenomai*: This subsystem facilitates smooth movement from proprietary OS (such as VxWorks, pSOS, and VRTX™) to RTAI.

- *Real-time drivers:* RTAI provides real-time serial line and parallel port drivers. It also supports the comedi device driver interface. The comedi project develops open source drivers, tools, and libraries for data acquisition cards (http://www.comedi.org/).

Writing RTAI Applications

A real-time task under RTAI could either be a kernel module or an LXRT user-space task. In this section we explain both approaches using simple examples.

An RTAI task running as a kernel module consists of three parts.

- `module_init` *function:* This function is called whenever a module is loaded (using `insmod` or `modprobe`). It should allocate necessary resources, create a real-time task, and schedule it for execution.

- *Real-time task specific code:* It consists of various routines that implement the functionality of the real-time task.

- `module_cleanup` *function:* This function is called whenever a kernel module is unloaded. It should destroy all the resources allocated, stop and delete the real-time task, and so on.

Listing 7.13 shows the structure of an RTAI task as a kernel module. In this example we create a periodic task that prints "Hello Real-Time World."

As already mentioned, LXRT exports RTAI APIs in user space. To support this, LXRT requires user-space tasks to use the `SCHED_FIFO` scheduling policy with all its memory locked (by calling `mlockall` system call). LXRT offers the following advantages over an RTAI task running as a kernel module.

- User-space debugging tools can be used to debug the LXRT real-time task.

Listing 7.13   RTAI Task as a Kernel Module

```
/* rtai-kernel.c */

/* Kernel module header file */
#include <linux/module.h>

/* RTAI APIs that we are using are in these headers */
#include <rtai.h>
#include <rtai_sched.h>

/* Timer tick rate in nanosecond */
#define TIMER_TICK500000    /* 0.5 msec */

/* Task structure for our real-time task */
static RT_TASK hello_task;

/* This will be called when the module is loaded */
int init_module(void)
{
  /* 'period' of our periodic task*/
  RTIME period;
  RTIME curr;  /* current time */

  /*
   * rt_task_init creates a real-time task in suspended state
   */
  rt_task_init(&hello_task,      /* task structure */
               hello_thread,     /* task function  */
               0,                /* argument to task function */
               1024,             /* stack size */
               0,                /* Priority.
                                     Highest priority ->0,
                                     Lowest ->RT_LOWEST_PRIORITY
                                  */
               0,                /* task does not use FPU */
               0                 /* no signal handler */
              );

  /*
   * The following two timer functions are meant to be called
   * just once at the start of the whole real-time activity. The
   * timer started is actually 'real-time system clock'. The
   * timer is used by scheduler as a timing reference
   */

  /* Timers can be set in periodic or oneshot mode */
  rt_set_oneshot_mode();

  /*
   * Timer tick in nanoseconds is converted into internal
   * countunits
   */
  period = start_rt_timer(nano2count(TICKS));

  /* Get the current time */
  curr = rt_get_time();
```

Listing 7.13   RTAI Task as a Kernel Module (continued)

```
   /* Finally make the task periodic */
   rt_task_make_periodic(&hello_task,  // pointer to task
                                           structure
                          curr + 5*period, /* start time of the
                                              task */

                          period      // period of the task
                          );
   return 0;
}

void cleanup_module(void)
{
  /*
   * Stop the timer, busy wait for some time and finally delete
   * the task
   */
  stop_rt_timer();
  rt_busy_sleep(10000000);
  rt_task_delete(&hello_task);
}

/* Our main real-time thread */
static void hello_thread(int dummy)
{
  while(1){
    rt_printk("Hello Real-time world\n");

    /* Wait for next period */
    rt_task_wait_period();
  }
}
```

- LXRT real-time tasks are subject to the Linux memory protection mechanism. Thus a bug in the task does not crash the whole system.
- As there is no kernel dependency, a binary-only task can be shipped without giving out source code.
- You need not be the root to run the task (this support is provided via an API rt_allow_nonroot_hrt).

We again write our "Hello Real-Time World" example to illustrate the structure of the user-space LXRT real-time task. Please refer to Listing 7.14.

7.4.2 ADEOS

ADEOS (Adaptive Domain Environment for Operating Systems) provides an environment that enables sharing of hardware resources among multiple operating systems or among multiple instances of the same operating system. Every OS in ADEOS is represented as a domain. Interrupt handling is the key in an ADEOS environment. To handle interrupts it uses an interrupt pipeline.

Listing 7.14   LXRT Process

```c
/* lxrt.c */

/* Headers that define scheduling and memory locking functions */
#include <sys/mman.h>
#include <sched.h>

/* RTAI headers */
#include <rtai.h>
#include <rtai_sched.h>
#include "rtai_lxrt.h"

#define TICK_TIME 500000

int main(){

  RT_TASK *task;
  RTIME period;
  struct sched_param sched;

  /* Create a SCHED_FIFO task with max priority */
  sched.sched_priority = sched_get_priority_max(SCHED_FIFO);
  if (sched_setscheduler(0, SCHED_FIFO, &sched) != 0){
    perror("sched_setscheduler failed\n");
    exit(1);
  }

  /* Lock all the current and future memory allocations */
  mlockall(MCL_CURRENT | MCL_FUTURE);

  /* ---- module_init ---- */

  /* rt_task_init creates a real-time proxy in kernel for this
   * task. All the RTAI APIs will be executed by the proxy under
   * RTAI scheduler on the behalf of this task. Please note that
   * the first argument is a unsigned long. A string can be
   * converted to unsigned long using nam2num function.
   */
  if (!(task = rt_task_init(nam2num("hello"), 0, 0, 0))) {
    printf("LXRT task creation failed\n");
    exit(2);
  }

  rt_set_oneshot_mode();
  period = start_rt_timer(nano2count(TICK_TIME));
  /* Finally make the task periodic */
  rt_task_make_periodic(task, rt_get_time() + 5*period, period);

  /* ---- Main job of our real-time task ---- */

  count = 100;
  while(count--) {
    rt_printk("Hello Real-time World\n");
    rt_task_wait_period();
  }
```

Listing 7.14   LXRT Process (continued)

```
/* ---- cleanup_module ---- */

stop_rt_timer();
rt_busy_sleep(10000000);
rt_task_delete(task);
}
```

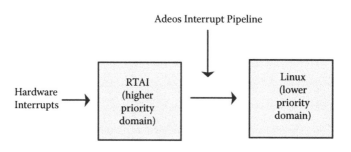

Figure 7.7   ADEOS interrupt pipeline.

Each domain is represented as a pipeline stage. Interrupts are propagated from a higher-priority domain to a lower-priority domain in the pipeline. A domain can choose to accept, discard, or terminate an interrupt. If a domain accepts the interrupt, ADEOS calls its interrupt handler and then passes the interrupt to the lower-priority domain next in the pipeline. If a domain discards an interrupt, the interrupt is simply passed to the next pipeline stage. If a domain terminates an interrupt, the interrupt is passed no further in the pipeline.

ADEOS and Linux

ADEOS can provide hard real-time support in Linux. Two domains could be implemented under ADEOS: one domain encompassing normal Linux and the other a real-time executive that provides hard real-time guarantees. RTAI is already using ADEOS as its HAL. Figure 7.7 shows the ADEOS interrupt pipeline in RTAI.

ADEOS also provides an environment for implementing kernel debuggers and profilers in Linux. In the ADEOS framework, kernel debuggers and profilers can be represented as a high-priority domain and Linux as a low-priority domain. They can then easily control the behavior of Linux by trapping various interrupts.

Chapter 8

Building and Debugging

This chapter is divided into two parts. The first half deals with the Linux build environment. This includes:

- Building the Linux kernel
- Building user-space applications
- Building the root file system
- Discussion of popular Integrated Development Environments (IDEs)

The second half of the chapter deals with debugging and profiling techniques in embedded Linux. This includes:

- Memory profiling
- Kernel and application debugging
- Application and kernel profiling

Generally a traditional RTOS builds the kernel and applications together into a single image. It has no delineation between kernel and applications. Linux offers a completely different build paradigm. Recall that in Linux, each application has its own address space, which is in no way related to the kernel address space. As long as the proper header files and C library are used, any application can be built independently of the kernel. The result is that the kernel build and application build are totally disjoint.

Having a separate kernel and application build has its advantages and disadvantages. The main advantage is that it is easy to use. If you want to introduce a new application, you need to just build that application and download it to the board. The procedure is simple and fast. This is unlike most real-time executives where the entire image has to be rebuilt and the system has to be rebooted. However, the main disadvantage of the disjoint build procedure is that there is no automatic correlation between the kernel features and applications. Most of the embedded developers would like to have a system build mechanism where once the configuration is chosen for the system, the individual components (kernel, applications, and root file system) get automatically built with all dependencies in place. However, in Linux this is not the case. Added to the build complexity is the boot loader building and the process of packing the root file system into a single downloadable image.

In order to elaborate this problem let us consider the case of an OEM who is shipping two products: an Ethernet bridge and a router on a single hardware design. Though much of the software remains the same (such as the boot loader, the BSP, etc.), the basic differentiating capabilities between the two products lie in the software. As a result the OEM would like to maintain a single code base for both the products but the software for the system gets built depending on the system choice (bridge versus router). This in effect boils down to something as follows: a `make bridge` from a top-level directory needs to choose the software needed for the bridge product and a similar `make router` would build the software for a router. There is a lot of work that needs to be done to achieve this:

- The kernel needs to be configured accordingly and the corresponding protocols (such as the spanning bridge for the bridge or IP forwarding for the router), drivers, and so on should be selected.
- The user-space applications should be built accordingly (such as the `routed` daemon needs to be built).
- The corresponding start-up files should be configured accordingly (such as the network interface initialization).
- The corresponding configuration files (such as HTML files and CGI scripts) need to be selected and packed into the root file system.

The user would be tempted to ask: why not push the software needed for both the bridge and router into the root file system and then exercise the drivers and applications depending on the runtime usage? Unfortunately such an exercise would require waste storage space, which is not a luxury with embedded systems; hence component selection at build time is advisable. The desktops and servers can do this; hence this is rarely a concern for desktop and server distributors.

The component selection during the build process needs some intelligence so that a framework for a systemwide build can be developed. This can be done by developing in-house scripts and integrating the various build procedures. Alternatively the user can evaluate some IDEs available in the marketplace for his or her requirements. The IDE market for Linux is still in the infant phase and there is more concentration on the kernel build mechanisms simply because application building varies across applications (there are no standards followed by application builds). Adding your own applications or exporting the dependencies across applications simply may not be offered by many IDEs; even if they do offer it, it may require a learning curve. IDEs are discussed in a separate section. If you have decided to use an IDE then skip the build section and go directly to the debugging section. But in case you plan to tweak the build procedures stay on and read ahead.

8.1 Building the Kernel

The kernel build system (a more popular term for it is kbuild) is bundled along with the kernel sources. The kbuild system is based on the GNU make; hence all the commands are given to make. The kbuild mechanism gives a highly simplified build procedure to build the kernel; in a few steps one can configure and build the kernel and modules. Also it is very extensible in the sense that adding your own hooks in the build procedure or customizing the configuration process is very easy.

The kbuild procedure has seen some major changes in the 2.6 kernel release. Hence this chapter explains both the 2.4 and 2.6 kernel build procedures. Building the kernel is divided into four steps.

1. *Setting up the cross-development environment:* Because Linux has support for many architectures, the kbuild procedure should be configured for the architecture for which the kernel image and modules are being built. By default the kernel build environment builds the host-based images (on which the build is being done).

2. *Configuration process:* This is the component selection procedure. The list of what software needs to go into the kernel and what can be compiled as modules can be specified using this step. At the end of this step, kbuild records this information in a set of known files so that the rest of kbuild is aware of the selected components. Component selection objects are normally:

   a. Processor selection
   b. Board selection
   c. Driver selection
   d. Some generic kernel options

   There are many front ends to the configuration procedure; the following are the ones that can be used on both the 2.4 and 2.6 kernels.

   a. make config: This is a complicated way of configuring because this would throw the component selection on your terminal.
   b. make menuconfig: This is a curses-based front end to the kbuild procedure as shown in Figure 8.1. This is useful on hosts that do not have access to a graphic display; however, you need to install the ncurses development library for running this.
   c. make xconfig: This is a graphical front end to the configuration process as shown in Figure 8.2. The 2.4 version made use of X whereas the 2.6 version uses QT. The 2.6 has another version that makes use of GTK and is invoked by running make gconfig.
   d. make oldconfig: Often you would want to do minimal changes to an existing configuration. This option allows the build to retain defaults from an existing configuration and prompt only for the new changes. This option is very useful when you want to automate the build procedure using scripts.

3. *Building the object files and linking them to make the kernel image:* Once the component selection is done, the following steps are necessary to build the kernel.

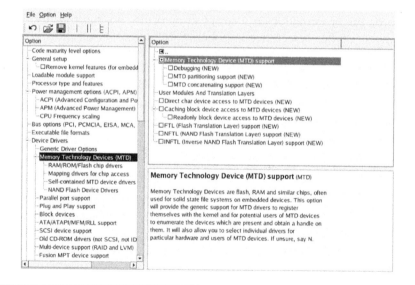

```
┌─────────────────── Linux Kernel Configuration ───────────────────┐
│ Arrow keys navigate the menu.  <Enter> selects submenus --->.  Highlighted │
│ letters are hotkeys.  Pressing <Y> includes, <N> excludes, <M> modularizes │
│ features.  Press <Esc><Esc> to exit, <?> for Help.  Legend: [*] built-in   │
│ [ ] excluded  <M> module  < > module capable                               │
│ ┌─────────────────────────────────────────────────────────────────────┐ │
│ │ █  Code maturity level options  --->                                 │ │
│ │      eneral setup  --->                                              │ │
│ │      oadable module support  --->                                   │ │
│ │      rocessor type and features  --->                               │ │
│ │      ower management options (ACPI, APM)  --->                      │ │
│ │      us options (PCI, PCMCIA, EISA, MCA, ISA)  --->                 │ │
│ │      xecutable file formats  --->                                   │ │
│ │      evice Drivers  --->                                            │ │
│ │      ile systems  --->                                              │ │
│ │      rofiling support  --->                                         │ │
│ │      ernel hacking  --->                                            │ │
│ │      ecurity options  --->                                          │ │
│ │      ryptographic options  --->                                     │ │
│ │      ibrary routines  --->                                          │ │
│ │      ---                                                            │ │
│ │      oad an Alternate Configuration File                            │ │
│ │      ave Configuration to an Alternate File                         │ │
│ └─────────────────────────────────────────────────────────────────────┘ │
│              <Select>      < Exit >     < Help >                          │
└───────────────────────────────────────────────────────────────────────────┘
```

Figure 8.1   Curses-based kernel configuration.

Figure 8.2   X-based kernel configuration.

a. On the 2.4 kernel, the header file dependency information (which .c file depends on which .h files) needs to be generated using a command make dep. This is not necessary on the 2.6 kernel.

b. However, the clean-up step is common to both the 2.4 and 2.6 kernel; the make clean command cleans up all object files, kernel image, and all intermediate files but the configuration information is maintained. There is one more command that does whatever make clean does along with cleaning the configuration information: this is the make mrpoper command.

c. The final step is to create the kernel image. The name of the kernel image is `vmlinux` and is the output if you just type `make`. However, the kernel build does not stop here; there is usually some postprocessing that needs to be done such as compressing it, adding bootstrapping code, and so on. The postprocessing actually creates the image that can be used in the target (the postprocessing is not standardized because it varies across platforms and boot loaders used).

4. *Building dynamically loadable modules:* The command `make modules` will do the job of creating modules.

The above commands are sufficient for an end user to use the kbuild for building the kernel. On embedded systems, however, you would want to customize the build process further; some reasons are quoted below.

■ You may want to add your BSP in a separate directory and alter the configuration so that the kbuild builds the software components necessary for your board.
■ You may want to add your own linker, compiler, and assembler flags to the build process.
■ You may want to customize postprocessing of the kernel image once it is built.
■ You may want to build intelligence in the kbuild for doing a systemwide build.

Taking into account these reasons, the next section will go into finer details of the build process.

8.1.1 Understanding Build Procedure

The salient features of the kbuild procedure for both the 2.4 and 2.6 kernels are described below.

■ The top-level `Makefile` in the kernel sources is responsible for building both the kernel image and the modules. It does so by recursively descending into the subdirectories of the kernel source tree. The list of the subdirectories that need to be entered into depends on the component selection, that is, the kernel configuration procedure. How exactly this is done is explained later. The subdirectory Makefiles inherits the rules for building objects; in 2.4 they do so by including a rules file called `Rules.make`, which needs to be explicitly included in every subdirectory `Makefile`. However, this requirement was dropped in the 2.6 kbuild procedure.
■ Every architecture (the processor port) needs to export a list of components for selection during the configuration process; this includes:
 – Any processor flavor. For example, if your architecture is defined as ARM, then you will be prompted as to which ARM flavor needs to be chosen.
 – The hardware board
 – Any board-specific hardware configuration

- The kernel subsystem components, which more or less remain uniform across all architectures such as the networking stack

Each architecture maintains a component, database in a file; this can be found in the `arch/$ARCH` subdirectory. In the 2.4 kernel, the name of this file is `config.in`, whereas on the 2.6 kernel it is the `Kconfig` file. During the kernel configuration, this file is parsed and the user is prompted with a component list for selection. You may need to add your hardware-specific configuration in this file.

- Every architecture needs to export an architecture-specific Makefile; the following list of build information is unique to every architecture.
  - The flags that need to be passed to the various tools
  - The subdirectories that need to be visited for building the kernel
  - The postprocessing steps once the image is built

These are supplied in the architecture-specific `Makefile` in the `arch/$(ARCH)` subdirectory. The top-level `Makefile` imports the architecture-specific `Makefile`. The reader is advised to go through some architecture-specific file in the kernel source tree (such as `arch/mips/Makefile`) to understand the architecture-specific build definitions.

The following are some of the major differences between the 2.4 and 2.6 kernel build procedures.

- The 2.6 configuration and build mechanism has a different framework. The 2.6 kbuild is much simpler. For example, in the 2.4 kernel the architecture-specific Makefile does not have any standard; hence it varies across various architectures. In 2.6 the framework has been fixed to maintain uniformity.
- In 2.4, just typing a `make` would end up in different results depending on the state of the build procedure. For example, if the user has not done configuration and types `make`, kbuild would invoke `make config` throwing questions on the terminal to the confused user. In 2.6, however, it would result in an error with the proper help to guide the user.
- In 2.4, the object files get created in the same source directory. However, 2.6 allows the source tree and the output object tree (including configuration output) to be in totally different files; this is done by an option to `make O=dir` where `dir` is the object tree.
- In 2.4, the source files are touched (i.e., their timestamps are modified) when doing a `make dep`. It causes problems with some source management systems. On the other hand, in the 2.6 kernel the source files are not touched during kernel build. This ensures that you can have a read-only source tree. It saves disk space if many users want to share a single source tree but have their individual object trees.

8.1.2 The Configuration Process

Though the configuration process is invoked using the `make` command, a separate configuration grammar has been defined. This again differs across the 2.4 and 2.6 kernels. Note that this grammar is simple and close to spoken

English; so just a glance at the configuration files (`Kconfig` for 2.6 kernel and the `Config.in` files for the 2.4 kernel) can help you understand it. This section does not go into the details of the grammar; rather it focuses on the techniques used.[1]

- Every kernel subsection defines the rules for configuration in a separate file. For example, the networking configuration is maintained in a `Config.in` (for the 2.4 kernel) or `Kconfig` file (for 2.6 kernel) in the kernel source directory `net/`. This file is imported by the architecture-defined configuration file. For example, in 2.4, the MIPS architecture configuration file `arch/mips/config-shared.in` has the line for importing the configuration rules for the VFS source (`fs/config.in`).
- A configuration item is stored as a `name=value` pair. The name of the configuration item starts with a `CONFIG_` prefix. The rest of the name is the component name as defined in the configuration file. The following are the values that a configuration variable can have:
  - `bool`: The configuration variable can have value y or n.
  - `tristate`: Here the variable can have the values y, n, or m (for module).
  - `string`: Any ASCII string can be given here. For example, in case you need to pass the address of the NFS server from where you want to mount the initial root file system, it can be given at build time using a variable that holds a string value.
  - `integer`: Any decimal number can be assigned to the variable.
  - `hexadecimal`: Any hexadecimal can be assigned to the variable.
- While defining the configuration variable, it can be specified if the user should be prompted for assigning a value to this variable. If not, a default value is assigned to this variable.
- Dependencies can be created while defining a variable. Dependencies are used to determine the visibility of an entry.
- Each configuration variable can have a help text associated with it. It is displayed at the time of configuration. In the 2.4 kernel, all the help text is stored in a single file `Documentation/Configure.help`; the help text associated with a particular variable is stored following the name of the variable. However, on the 2.6 kernel, the individual `Kconfig` files hold it.

Now we come to the last but the most important part. This is to understand how the configuration process exports the list of selected components to the rest of the kbuild. To achieve this it creates a `.config` file that contains the list of selected components in `name = value` format. The `.config` file is stored in the kernel base directory and is included in the top-level `Makefile`. While evaluating a source file as a build candidate, the component value field is used to find out if the component should be built (as a module or directly linked to kernel). The kbuild uses a clever technique for this. Let's assume there is a driver `sample.c` in directory `drivers/net` that is exported to the configuration process under the name `CONFIG_SAMPLE`. At the time of configuration using the command `make config` the user will be prompted:

```
Build sample network driver (CONFIG_SAMPLE) [y/N]?
```

If he chooses y then `CONFIG_SAMPLE=y` will be added in the `.config` file. In the `drivers/net/Makefile` there will be a line

```
obj-$(CONFIG_SAMPLE)+= sample.o
```

When this Makefile is encountered while recursing into the `drivers/net` subdirectory, the kbuild will translate this line to

```
obj-y+= sample.o
```

This is because the `.config` file that is included has defined `CONFIG_SAMPLE=y`. The kernel build has a rule to build `obj-y`; hence this source file is chosen to be built. Likewise if this variable is selected as a module then at the time of building modules this line would appear as

```
obj-m+= sample.o
```

Again the rule to build `obj-m` is defined by the kbuild. The kernel source code too needs to be made aware of the list of components that are selected. For example, in the 2.4 kernel `init/main.c` code there is a line as follows:

```
#ifdef CONFIG_PCI
 pci_init();
#endif
```

The macro `CONFIG_PCI` must be defined if the user has chosen PCI at the time of configuration. In order to do this, the kbuild translates the `name=value` pair as macro definitions in a file `include/linux/autoconf.h`. This file gets split into a set of header files under the `include/config` directory. For example, in the above example, there would be a file `include/config/pci.h` having the line

```
#define CONFIG_PCI
```

Thus the kbuild mechanism ensures that the source files too can be component aware.

8.1.3 Kernel Makefile Framework

We take a sample driver Makefile to understand the kernel Makefile framework. For this we take `drivers/net/Makefile`. We look at the 2.4 Makefile followed by the 2.6 version of it.

Listing 8.1 shows the Linux 2.4 `drivers/net/Makefile` simplified for reading purposes. The initial four variables have special meaning. The `obj-y` stands for the list of objects that are built into the kernel directly. The `obj-m` stands for the list of object files that are built as modules. The other two variables are just ignored by the build process.

Listing 8.1   2.4 Kernel Sample Makefile

```
obj-y      :=
obj-m      :=
obj-n      :=
obj-       :=

mod-subdirs     := appletalk arcnet fc irda … wan

O_TARGET        := net.o

export-objs     := 8390.o arlan.o … mii.o

list-multi      := rcpci.o
rcpci-objs      := rcpci45.o rclanmtl.o

ifeq ($(CONFIG_TULIP),y)
obj-y+=    tulip/tulip.o
endif

subdir-$(CONFIG_NET_PCMCIA)+= pcmcia
…
subdir-$(CONFIG_E1000)      += e1000

obj-$(CONFIG_PLIP)          += plip.o
…
obj-$(CONFIG_NETCONSOLE)    += netconsole.o

include $(TOPDIR)/Rules.make

clean:
    rm -f core *.o *.a *.s

rcpci.o : $(rcpci-objs)
    $(LD) -r -o $@ $(rcpci-objs)
```

The O_TARGET is the target (i.e., output) for this Makefile; the final kernel image is created by pulling all the O_TARGET files from various subdirectories. The rule for packing all the object files into the file specified by O_TARGET is defined by $TOPDIR/Rules.make[2], which is included explicitly by the Makefile. The file net.o gets pulled into the final kernel image by the top-level Makefile.

A special object file called multipart objects is given a special rule by the make process. A multipart object is generated using multiple object files. A single-part object does not require a special rule; the build mechanism chooses the source file for building by replacing the .o part of the target object with .c. On the other hand while building the multipart object, the list of objects that make up the multipart object needs to be specified. The list of multipart objects is defined in the variable list-multi. For each name that appears in this list, the variable got by appending the string -objs to the name gets the list of objects needed to build the multipart module.

Along with the obj-$(…), the 2.4 kernel needs to specify the list of subdirectories to traverse using subdir-$(…). Again the same rule that applies

Listing 8.2   2.6 Kernel Sample Makefile

```
rcpci-objs:= rcpci45.o rclanmtl.o

ifeq ($(CONFIG_ISDN_PPP),y)
  obj-$(CONFIG_ISDN) += slhc.o
endif

obj-$(CONFIG_E100) += e100/
...
obj-$(CONFIG_PLIP) += plip.o
...
obj-$(CONFIG_IRDA) +=irda
```

for `obj-*` holds for subdirs also (i.e., `subdir-y` is used to traverse the list of directories while building a kernel image, whereas `subdir-m` is used to traverse while building modules). Finally we come to the `export-objs` variable. This is the list of files that can export symbols.

The 2.6 kernel Makefile is much simpler as shown in Listing 8.2.

The major differences in the 2.6 build procedure as compared to the 2.4 build procedure are:

- There is no need to pull in `Rules.make`; the rules for building get exported implicitly.
- The Makefile does not specify the target name because there is a build-identified target `built-in.o`. The `built-in.o` from the various subdi-rectories is linked to build the kernel image.
- The list of subdirectories that need to be visited uses the same variable `obj-*` (unlike 2.4 where the `subdirs-*` variable is used).
- Objects that export symbols need not be specifically mentioned (the build process uses the `EXPORT_SYMBOL` macro encountered in the source to deduce this information).

8.2 Building Applications

Now that we have understood the procedure to build the kernel, we proceed to building user-space programs. This domain is very diverse; there may be umpteen build mechanisms employed by individual packages. However, most of the open source programs follow a common method for configuration and building. Considering the richness of the open source software that can be deployed for embedded systems, understanding this topic can ease the porting of the commonly available open source programs to your target board. Also you would want to tweak the build procedure to make sure that unwanted components are not chosen for building the program; this ensures that your valuable storage space is not wasted in storing unnecessary software.

Like the kernel, the applications also have to be built using the cross-development tools. Most of the open source programs follow the GNU build standard. The GNU build system addresses the following portability issues.

- Hardware differences such as endianness, data type sizes, and so on
- OS differences such as device file naming conventions, and so on
- Library differences such as version number, API arguments, and so on
- Compiler differences such as compiler name, arguments, and so on

GNU build tools are a collection of several tools, the most important of which are listed below.

- *autoconf:* It provides a general portability framework, based on testing the features of the host system at build time. It does this by performing tests to discover the host features.
- *automake:* It is a system for describing how to build a program, permitting the developer to write a simplified Makefile.
- *libtool:* It is a standardized approach to building shared libraries.

Note that understanding these tools is a primary concern only if a developer of an application intends to create an application to be used on multiple platforms including various hardware architectures as well as various UNIX platforms such as Linux, FreeBSD, and Solaris. On the other hand if the reader is interested in only cross-compiling the application, then all that she needs to do is to type the following commands on the command line.

```
# ./configure
# make
```

In this chapter we discuss in brief the various pieces that help the configure script to generate the Makefiles necessary for compilation of the program. Also we provide tips on troubleshooting and working around some common problems that arise when using configure for cross-compilation. However, how to write the configure script for a program is not discussed and is beyond the scope of this book. If the reader is interested in writing the configure script then please refer to www.gnu.org on the GNU configure system.

All programs that employ the GNU configure build system, ship a shell script called configure and a couple of support files, along with the program sources. Any Linux project that uses the GNU configure build system requires this set of support files for the build process. Along with the set of files that accompanies the distribution statically, there are files generated dynamically during the build process. Both these sets of files are described below.

Files that are part of the distribution include configure, Makefile.in, and config.in. configure is a shell script. Use ./configure --help to see the various options that it takes. The configure script in essence contains a series of programs or test cases to be executed on the host system based on which the build inputs change. For the reader to understand the type of tests done by configure, some commonly performed checks are listed below.

- Checking for the existence of a header files such as stdlib.h, unistd.h, and so on

- Checking for the presence of library APIs such as `strcpy`, `memcpy`, and so on
- Obtaining the size of a data type such as `sizeof(int)`, `sizeof(float)`, and so on
- Checking/locating the presence of other external libraries required by the program. For example, `libjpeg` for JPEG support, or `libpng` for PNG support
- Checking if the library version number matches

These are generally the dependencies that make a program system-dependent. Making the `configure` script aware of these dependencies will ensure that the program becomes portable across UNIX platforms. For performing the above tasks `configure` uses two main techniques.

- *Trial build of a test program:* This is used where `configure` has to find the presence of a header or an API or library. `configure` just uses a simple program like the one listed below to look for the presence of `stdlib.h`.

```
#include <stdlib.h>
main() {
  return 0;
}
```

  If the above program compiles successfully, that indicates the presence of a usable `stdlib.h`. Similar tests are done for API and library presence detection.
- *Execute a test program and capture the output:* In situations where `configure` has to obtain the size of a data type, the only method available is to compile, execute, and obtain output of the program. For instance, to find the size of an integer on a platform, the program given below is employed.

```
main() {
  return sizeof(int)
};
```

The result of the tests/programs executed by `configure` are generally stored in `config.h` as configuration (preprocessor) macros and if this completes successfully, `configure` starts the creation of Makefiles. These configuration macros can then be used in code to select portions of code required for a particular UNIX platform. The `configure` script takes many input arguments; they can be found out by running `configure` with the `–help` option.

The `configure` script works on `Makefile.in` to create `Makefile` at build time. There will be one such file in each subdirectory of the program. The configure script also converts `config.in` to `config.h`, which alters `CFLAGS` defined for compilation. The `CFLAGS` definition gets changed based on the host system on which the build process is run. Most of the portability issues are addressed using the preprocessor macros that get defined in this file.

Files that are generated during the application build include:

- `Makefile`: This is the file that `make` will use to build the program. The configure script transforms `Makefile.in` to `Makefile`.
- `config.status`: The `configure` script creates a file `config.status`, which is a shell script. It contains the rules to regenerate the generated files and is invoked automatically when any of the input file changes. For example, let us take the case when you have an already preconfigured build directory (i.e., one in which the configure script has been run at least once). Now if you change `Makefile.in`, then Makefiles will get generated automatically when you just invoke the `make` command. The regeneration happens using this script without having to invoke the `configure` script.
- `config.h`: This file defines the config preprocessor macros that C code can use to adjust its behavior on different systems.
- `config.cache`: `configure` caches results between the script runs in this file. The output results for various configure steps are saved to this file. Each line is a `variable = value` assignment. The variable is a script-generated name that is used by `configure` at build time. The configure script reads the values of the variables in this file into memory before proceeding with the actual checks on the host.
- `config.log`: It stores the output when the configure script is run. Experienced users of configure can use this script to discover problems with the configuration process.

8.2.1 Cross-Compiling Using Configure

The most generic form of using configure for cross-compilation is:

```
# export CC=<target>-linux-gcc
# export NM=<target>-linux-nm
# export AR=<target>-linux-ar
# ./configure --host=<target> --build=<build_system>
```

The `<build_system>` is the system on which the build is done to create programs that run on `<target>`. For example, for a Linux/i686 desktop and ARM-based target, `<build_system>` is `i686-linux` and the `<target>` is `arm-linux`.

```
# export CC=arm-linux-gcc
# export NM=arm-linux-nm
# export AR=arm-linux-ar
# ./configure --host=arm-linux --build=i686-linux
```

The `--build` flag need not always be supplied. In most cases the configure script makes a decent guess of the build system.

Note that it's not always necessary that running `configure` for cross-compilation be successful in the first attempt. The most common error during cross-compilation is:

```
configure: error: cannot run test program while
                  cross compiling
```

This error occurs because `configure` is trying to run some test program and obtain its output. If you are cross-compiling, in that case the test program compiled is an executable for the target and cannot run on the build system.

To fix this problem, study the output of the `configure` script to identify the test that is failing. Open the `config.log` file to get more details about the error. For example, assume you run `configure` and get an error.

```
# export CC=arm-linux-gcc
# ./configure --host=arm-linux


    ...
checking for fcntl.h... yes
checking for unistd.h... yes
checking for working const... yes
checking size of int...
configure: error: cannot run test program while
                  cross compiling
```

In the above run `configure` is trying to find the size of `int`. To achieve this it compiles a program of form `main() { return (sizeof(int))}` to find the size of an integer on the target system. The program execution will fail as the build system does not match the target system.

To fix such problems you need to edit the `config.cache` file. Recall that `configure` reads in values from the `config.cache` file before starting the checks. All you need to do is look for the test variable in the `configure` script and add its entry as desired in the `config.cache` file. In the above example, assume the `ac_sizeof_int_set` variable defines the size of an integer in the `configure` script. Then add the following line in `config.cache`.

```
ac_sizeof_int_set=4
```

After this change the output of `configure` is:

```
    ...
checking for fcntl.h... yes
checking for unistd.h... yes
checking for working const... yes
checking size of int...(cached) yes
    ...
```

8.2.2 Troubleshooting Configure Script

Now that we have the idea of what the configure script does, we try to see what can go wrong. There are two failure triggers. One is when the configure script is correct, and your system really does lack a prerequisite. Most often, this will be correctly diagnosed by the configure script. A more disturbing case is when the configure script is incorrect. This can result either in failing to produce a configuration, or producing an incorrect configuration. In the first case when the configure script detects that a prerequisite is missing, usually most configure scripts are good enough to spit out a decent error message describing the required version of the missing component. All that we have to do is install this required missing component and rerun the configure script. Following are some tips to troubleshoot problems related to configure script.

- *Read the* README *and go through the options in* ./configure --help: There might be some special option to specify the path to a dependent library, which when not specified might default to some wrong path information.
- *Plot the dependency tree*: Take care when reading the project documentation and note down the dependent libraries and the version number requirements. This will save a lot of your time. For example, the GTK library depends on GLIB library, which depends on ATK and PANGO libraries. PANGO library in turn depends on FREETYPE library. It is better to have a dependency chart handy, so that you compile and install the independent nodes (libraries) in the tree and then compile the parent (library).
- *Trial run on* i386: Sometimes before cross-compiling, running a configure script on i386 might be helpful in understanding the flow of the script and its dependencies.
- *Learn to read* config.log: When the configure script runs, it creates a file called the config.log. This file has the complete log of the execution path of the script. Each line has the exact shell command that is being executed. Reading the log file carefully will reveal the test being made and will help you understand the reason for the failure.
- *Fixing poor configure scripts*: Poorly written configure scripts are always a nightmare to handle. They might be doing incorrect test programs or have hard codings for library paths and the like. All you need is a little patience and time to fix the script.

8.3 Building the Root File System

Now that we have learned the process of building the kernel and applications, the next logical step is to understand the process of making a root file system. As explained in Chapters 2 and 4, there are three techniques that can be used for this purpose.

- *Using the initrd/initramfs:* The initrd was discussed in detail in Chapters 2 and 4. In this section we discuss initramfs. The scripts at the end of this section can be used to create these images.
- *Mounting the root file system over the network using NFS:* This makes sense during the development stages; all changes can be done on the development (host) machine and the root file system can be mounted across the network from the host. The details of how to mount the root file system using NFS can be obtained from the documentation that is part of the kernel source tree under Documentation/nfsroot.

Listing 8.3   mkinitrd

```
#!/bin/sh

# create ramdisk image file
/bin/rm -f /tmp/ramdisk.img
dd if=/dev/zero of=/tmp/ramdisk.img bs=1k count=$2

# Setup loop device
/sbin/losetup -d /dev/loop0 > /dev/null 2>&1
/sbin/losetup /dev/loop0 /tmp/ramdisk.img || exit $!

# First, unmount /tmp/ramdisk0 just in case it's already mounted
if [ -e /tmp/ramdisk0 ]; then
  umount /tmp/ramdisk0 > /dev/null 2>&1
fi

# Create filesystem
/sbin/mkfs -t ext2 /dev/loop0 || exit $!

# Create mount-point
if [ -e /tmp/ramdisk0 ]; then
  rm -rf /tmp/ramdisk0
fi
mkdir /tmp/ramdisk0


# Mount filesystem
mount /dev/loop0 /tmp/ramdisk0 || exit $!

# Copy filesystem data
echo "Copying files and directories from $1"
(cd $1; tar -cf - * ) | (cd /tmp/ramdisk0; tar xf -)
chown -R root /tmp/ramdisk0/*
chgrp -R root /tmp/ramdisk0/*

ls -lR /tmp/ramdisk0

# unmount
umount /tmp/ramdisk0
rm -rf /tmp/ramdisk0

# unhook loop device
/sbin/losetup -d /dev/loop0
```

- *Burning the root file system into flash:* This is done during the production stage. The image of the root file system to be run on the target (such as JFFS2 or CRAMFS) is created on the host and is then burned to flash. The various tools that are available for making the images are explained in Chapter 4.

Listing 8.3 shows a generic initrd script. Its usage is:

```
mkinitrd <rfs-folder> <ramdisk-size>
```

where

- `<rfs-folder>` is the absolute path of the parent directory containing the root file system.
- `<ramdisk-size>` is the size of initrd.

The script creates an initrd image `/tmp/ramdisk.img` that could be mounted as an ext2 file system on the target. It uses a loopback device `/dev/loop0` to copy files from the root file system folder `<rfs-folder>` to the target image `/tmp/ramdisk.img`.

Initramfs was introduced in the 2.6 kernel to provide early user space. The idea was to move a lot of initialization stuff from kernel to user space. It was observed that initializations such as finding the root device, mounting the root file system either locally or over NFS, and so on that were part of the kernel boot-up sequence can easily be handled in user space. It makes the kernel clean. Thus initramfs was devised to achieve this purpose.

As you can mount the initrd image as the root file system, you can also similarly mount the initramfs image as the root file system. Initramfs is based on the RAMFS file system and initrd is based on ramdisk. The differences between RAMFS and ramdisk are shown in Table 8.1. The initramfs image can be created using `mkinitramfs` script. Its usage is:

```
mkinitramfs <rfs-folder>
```

Table 8.1   RAMFS versus RAMDISK

RAMDISK	*RAMFS*
Ramdisk is implemented as a block device in RAM and one needs to create a file system on top of it to use it.	RAMFS on the other hand is a file system implemented directly in RAM. For every file created in the RAMFS, the kernel maintains the file data and metadata in the kernel caches.
Ramdisk needs to be preallocated in RAM before use.	No preallocation necessary, dynamic growth based on requirement.
Two copies of program pages are maintained: one in the ramdisk and the other in the kernel page cache when any program is executed out of ramdisk.	Whenever a program is executed from a RAMFS, only one copy that is in the kernel cache is used. No duplication.
Ramdisk is slower because any data access needs to go through the file system and block device driver.	RAMFS is relatively faster as actual file data and metadata are in kernel cache and no file system and block device driver overheads are involved.

where `<rfs-folder>` is the absolute path of the parent directory containing the root file system. To create an initramfs image you need to create a `cpio` archive of the `<rfs-folder>` followed by gziping the archive.

```
#!/bin/sh

#mkinitramfs

(cd $1 ; find . | cpio --quiet -o -H newc | gzip -9
                               >/tmp/img.cpio.gz)
```

8.4 Integrated Development Environment

As a programming project grows in size so do its building and management needs. The components that are involved during program development are:

- *Text editor*: It is needed to write the source code files. It's an advantage having text editors that understand your programming language. Syntax highlighting, symbol completion, and code navigation are some of the other desired features.
- *Compiler*: To generate the object code.
- *Libraries:* To localize the reusable code.
- *Linker:* To link the object code and produce the final binary.
- *Debugger:* A source-level debugger to find programming errors.
- *Make system*: To manage the build process effectively.

A lot of time can be saved if the tools needed to accomplish the above tasks work together under a single development environment, that is, under an IDE. An IDE integrates all the tools that are needed in the development process into one single environment.

An IDE used for an embedded Linux development should have the following features.

- *Building applications*: Generating Makefiles for imported source code, importing existing Makefiles, and checking source code dependencies are some of the desired features.
- *Managing applications*: It should integrate with source code management tools such as CVS, ClearCase®, Perforce®, and so on.
- *Configuring and building the kernel*: It should provide an interface to configure and build the kernel.
- *Building the root file system*: The root file system may be flash-based, memory-based, or network-based depending on the system. An IDE should provide a mechanism to add or remove applications, utilities, and so on in the root file system.
- *Debugging applications*: It should provide a source code–level debugging of applications running on the target.
- *Debugging kernel*: This is an added advantage if an IDE provides support for debugging the kernel and kernel modules.

In this section we discuss both open source and commercial IDEs that can be used as a development environment.

8.4.1 Eclipse

Eclipse is an open source software development project (www.eclipse.org) dedicated to providing a robust, full-featured platform for the development of IDEs. Eclipse provides a basic framework and various features of the IDEs are implemented as separate modules called plug-ins. It is actually this plug-in framework that makes Eclipse very powerful. When the Eclipse is launched, the user is presented with an IDE composed of the set of available plug-ins. Most of the commercial IDEs such as TimeStorm are built using the Eclipse framework.

8.4.2 KDevelop

KDevelop is an open source IDE for KDE™ (www.kdevelop.org). Some of the features of KDevelop are:

- It manages all development tools such as compiler, linker, and debugger in one environment.
- It provides an easy-to-use front end for most needed functions of source code management systems such as CVS.
- It supports *Automake Projects* for automatic Makefile generation and managing the build process. It also supports *Custom Projects* to let the user manage the Makefiles and build processes.
- Cross-compilation support.
- Integrated text editor based on KDE's Kwrite, Trolltec's Qeditor, and so on with features such as syntax highlighting, auto symbol completion, and so on.
- Doxygen integration to generate API documentation.
- Application wizard to generate sample applications.
- Support for Qt/embedded projects.
- GUI-based front end for GDB.

8.4.3 TimeStorm

The TimeStorm Linux Development Suite (LDS) is a commercial embedded Linux development environment provided by TimeSys (www.timesys.com). It is based on the Eclipse IDE framework. Some of the features are:

- Runs on Linux and Windows systems.
- Integrated with source code management tools such as CVS, ClearCase, Perforce, and so on.
- Tools for developing and debugging embedded applications.
- Works with non-TimeSys Linux distributions.

- Interface for configuring and compiling the Linux kernel for the specified target.
- GUI-based interface for creating root file system for the target.
- It gives an ability to download and execute the programs on the target.
- GUI front end for remote debugging of applications using GDB.

8.4.4 CodeWarrior

Metrowerks CodeWarrior Development Studio is a complete commercial IDE that facilitates development from hardware bring-up to debugging applications (www.metrowerks.com). Some of the features are:

- Integrated text editor with features such as syntax coloring, auto-indenting, and so on.
- Includes a search engine for fast source code navigation.
- Integrated instruction set simulator for kickstarting application development.
- It provides a high-performance, windowed, source-level debugger. The debugger includes a flash programmer and a hardware diagnostic tool.
- Integrated version control system such as CVS, Perforce, and so on.

8.5 Debugging Virtual Memory Problems

When running applications on Linux, often the user runs into memory management problems. They can be roughly classified into three categories:

- *Memory leaks:* Memory leaks are caused when a memory chunk that has been allocated is not freed. Repeated memory leaks can prove fatal to an embedded system because the system may run short of memory.
- *Overflow:* Overflow is the condition wherein addresses beyond the end of an allocated area are accessed. Overflow is a very grave security hazard and is used by intruders to hack into a system.
- *Corruption:* Memory corruption happens when the memory pointers hold wrong or invalid values. Usage of these pointers may lead to haywire program execution and usually lead to program termination.

Memory management problems are very trying in the sense that they are very difficult to find by code inspection or may happen inconsistently or after many hours of system usage. Fortunately there are a number of open source tools to trace problems related to memory management. The following subsections talk about them in detail with adequate examples. Chapter 10 discusses how dynamic memory gets allocated on Linux.

Memory leaks are due primarily to two reasons:

- *Carelessness by the coder:* The developer of a program does not pay much attention to freeing the allocated memory when it is no longer used.
- *Pointer corruption:* This happens when a pointer holding a reference to a memory chunk gets corrupted hence losing reference to the memory chunk.

Repeated memory leaks on an embedded system without swap makes the system go low on memory. How does the system behave in such a case? When the system goes low on memory, it goes into a prune mode and tries to squeeze the system caches (such as page cache, buffer cache, and file system caches as well as the slab caches) and in this process flushes process image files. Even at the end of this exercise if the system is low on memory, the infamous *out of memory* or OOM killer is invoked. When OOM is invoked you see the following message on the console.

```
Out of Memory: Killed process 10(iisd)
```

In this case OOM killer killed a process `iisd` (with pid 10). Rik Van Reil introduced the OOM killer in the 2.2.15 kernel. The underlying philosophy behind the OOM killer is that when the memory is very low on the system, instead of allowing the kernel to panic or the system to be locked out, kill a process or set of processes so that the memory is released back to the system. So instead of allowing the system to crash, let it run with one or some applications killed. Obviously the key to the OOM implementation is the choice of process to be killed; killing systemwide important processes can be as harmful as a system crash. Hence the OOM killer has been a highly debated topic especially because it is very difficult to give a generic solution as Linux runs on a wide variety of systems. The OOM design has seen evolution in this regard. In the 2.6 kernel, the OOM killer goes through the list of all processes and comes up with a memory badness value. The process that has the maximum badness value is killed.

The OOM is a last-ditch effort by the system to recover from low-memory problems. It is the responsibility of the developer to make sure that the condition does not happen in the first place. Following are two techniques that can make the system more robust to memory leaks:

- *Setting a memory water mark for every process:* The first step in this direction is to identify bad programs that cause memory leaks. This can be done by setting an RSS limit for every process running on the system using the `setrlimit()` system call. There are two system calls provided by the Linux kernel in this regard: `setrlimit()` and `getrlimit()` for setting and getting resource limits, respectively. Each resource has a hard and soft limit as defined by an `rlimit` structure (see header file `sys/resource.h`). The soft limit is the value that the kernel enforces for the corresponding resource. The hard limit acts as a ceiling for the soft limit. Various kinds of resource limitations can be placed; the most significant one related to memory is the `RLIMIT_RSS`, which limits the number of pages belonging to a process resident in RAM. (Refer to the main page of `setrlimit` for its usage.)
- *Disabling over-commit on the system:* Over-commit is a memory mortgage scheme wherein the kernel commits more dynamic memory to an application even though it may not have adequate memory resources. The idea behind over-commit is that normally desktop-based applications allocate lots of memory but seldom use most of it. Hence the kernel passes the

memory allocation without caring to check if it has the resources. (Anyway because of demand paging the actual memory does not get allocated unless it is used.) On an embedded system, it is not advisable to turn on this feature for two reasons:

- You should not have any application wanting to allocate a huge amount and then use it only partially. Such applications are careless with memory usage and are not optimized for embedded systems. (If an application is careless about memory allocations, it may be careless about freeing memory too.)
- It is better to fail when an application requests memory and memory is scarce rather than allowing the memory allocation to pass and then trigger an out-of-memory condition later when the memory is accessed. The former is easy to debug and it can be rectified more easily. Linux offers the user to turn off over-commit using a proc file `/proc/sys/vm/overcommit`. Writing a 0 to this file turns off over-commit.

However, in case you hit the OOM condition and you are sure that some application is leaking memory, then the best solution is to use memory debuggers that are aimed towards detecting leaks.

8.5.1 Debugging Memory Leaks

In this section we discuss mtrace and dmalloc tools to debug memory leaks.

mtrace

mtrace is a glibc tool for fighting memory leaks. As the name suggests, it is used to trace memory allocations and freeing. There are two glibc calls that are provided for this purpose:

- `mtrace(void)`: This starts the tracing. When the `mtrace` function is called it looks for an environment variable named MALLOC_TRACE. This variable is supposed to contain a valid file name for which the user needs to have write access. Nothing is done if the environment variable is not set or if the file cannot be opened for writing. However, if the named file is successfully opened, `mtrace` installs special handlers for the allocator functions, which writes the trace logs into the file.
- `muntrace(void)`: This stops the tracing by deinstalling the trace handlers.

Listing 8.4 shows a simple program that causes a memory leak. We show how the leak can be detected using mtrace. Compile the program and execute the following steps.

```
# gcc -g leak.c -o leak
# export MALLOC_TRACE=./log
# ./a.out
# cat log
```

Listing 8.4   Mtrace Usage

```
/* leak.c */

#include <mcheck.h>
func()
{
  char *str[2];
  mtrace();
  str[0] = (char *)malloc(sizeof("memory leak start\n"));
  str[1] = (char *)malloc(sizeof("memory leak end\n"));
  strcpy(str[0] ,"memory leak start\n");
  strcpy(str[1] ,"memory leak end\n");
  printf("%s",str[0]);
  printf("%s",str[1]);
  free(str[1]);
  muntrace();
  return;
}

main()
{
  func();
}
```

```
= Start
@ ./a.out:(mtrace+0xf5)[0x8048445] + 0x8049a40 0x13
@ ./a.out:(mtrace+0x105)[0x8048455] + 0x8049a58 0x11
@ ./a.out:(mtrace+0x162)[0x80484b2] - 0x8049a58
= End
```

As you see, the log file that has been generated by mtrace is rather cryptic. Glibc provides a program with the name as mtrace again (which is derived from a Perl script `mtrace.pl`). This program parses the contents of the log file and shows the actual leak in a human-friendly manner.

```
# mtrace ./a.out log
Memory not freed:
-----------------
Address      Size      Caller
0x8048445    0x13   at  ./leak.c:6
```

Thus the user is informed that while tracing was turned on, a memory leak was detected. A chunk of memory of size 19 bytes (0×13) that was allocated in the file `leak.c` at line number 6 was not freed.

dmalloc

dmalloc is a more advanced tool that provides memory leak detection along with a host of other features such as fencepost checking and heap verification. This section focuses on usage of dmalloc primarily for memory leak detection. The official Web site for dmalloc is http://dmalloc.com.

Listing 8.5   Dmalloc Usage

```
/* dmalloc_test.c */

#include <stdio.h>
#include <stdlib.h>

#ifdef USE_DMALLOC
#include <dmalloc.h>
#endif

int main()
{
  char *test[5];
  unsigned int i;

  for (i=0; i < 5; i++)
  {
    unsigned int size = rand()%1024;
    test[i] = (char *)malloc(size);
    printf ("Allocated memory of size %d\n",size);
  }
  for (i=0; i<2; i++)
    free(test[i*2]);
}
```

dmalloc is implemented using a library that provides a wrapper around memory allocation APIs such as `malloc`, `free`, and so on. Hence the application needs to be linked against this library to make use of dmalloc. We illustrate this further using an example shown in Listing 8.5. Compile and link `dmalloc_test.c` with `libdmalloc.a`.[3]

```
# ls -l libdmalloc.a
-rw-rw-r-- 1 raghav raghav  255408 Sep 4 10:48 libdmalloc.a
# gcc dmalloc_test.c -o dmalloc_test ./libdmalloc.a
```

Now that we have linked our application, it is time to run it. But before we run the program we need to set an environment variable that will inform the library that runtime debugging needs to be turned on and where logging has to be done among a host of other things. We discuss the environment variable in detail later.

```
# export DMALLOC_OPTIONS=debug=0x3,log=dlog
# ./dmalloc_test
```

The output is shown in Listing 8.6. The lines marked bold indicate the number of memory leaks. Note that the debugging information such as file number and line number is absent. We can get this information by using tools such as `gdb` or `addr2line`. However, dmalloc provides a mechanism to include more debugging information in the log file using the `dmalloc.h` file. This file comes with the dmalloc package. All the C files that are linked to form the application to be debugged need to include this header file. This header file declares the memory allocator functions such as `malloc()` and

Listing 8.6   Dmalloc Output

```
calling dmalloc malloc
Allocated memory of size 359
calling dmalloc malloc
Allocated memory of size 966
calling dmalloc malloc
Allocated memory of size 105
calling dmalloc malloc
Allocated memory of size 115
calling dmalloc malloc
Allocated memory of size 81
bash>cat dlog
1094293908: 8: Dmalloc version '5.3.0' from 'http://dmalloc.com/'
1094293908: 8: flags = 0x3, logfile 'dlog'
1094293908: 8: interval = 0, addr = 0, seen # = 0, limit = 0
1094293908: 8: starting time = 1094293908
1094293908: 8: process pid = 4709
1094293908: 8: Dumping Chunk Statistics:
1094293908: 8: basic-block 4096 bytes, alignment 8 bytes, heap
               grows up
1094293908: 8: heap address range: 0x80c3000 to 0x80ca000, 28672
               bytes
1094293908: 8:    user blocks: 3 blocks, 12217 bytes (42%)
1094293908: 8:    admin blocks: 4 blocks, 16384 bytes (57%)
1094293908: 8: external blocks: 0 blocks, 0 bytes (0%)
1094293908: 8:    total blocks: 7 blocks, 28672 bytes
1094293908: 8: heap checked 0
1094293908: 8: alloc calls: malloc 5, calloc 0, realloc 0, free 3
1094293908: 8: alloc calls: recalloc 0, memalign 0, valloc 0
1094293908: 8: alloc calls: new 0, delete 0
1094293908: 8:   current memory in use: 1081 bytes (2 pnts)
1094293908: 8:   total memory allocated: 1626 bytes (5 pnts)
1094293908: 8:   max in use at one time: 1626 bytes (5 pnts)
1094293908: 8: max alloced with 1 call: 966 bytes
1094293908: 8: max unused memory space: 294 bytes (15%)
1094293908: 8: top 10 allocations:
1094293908: 8:   total-size  count in-use-size   count   source
1094293908: 8:        1626       5         1081    2   ra=0x8048a46
1094293908: 8:        1626       5         1081    2   Total of 1
1094293908: 8: Dumping Not-Freed Pointers Changed Since Start:
1094293908: 8:   not freed: '0x80c6c00|s1' (966 bytes) from
                 'ra=0x8048a46'
1094293908: 8:   not freed: '0x80c8f00|s1' (115 bytes) from
                 'ra=0x8048a46'
1094293908: 8:   total-size   count   source
1094293908: 8:        1081       2   ra=0x8048a46
1094293908: 8:        1081       2   Total of 1
1094293908: 8: ending time = 1094293908, elapsed since start =
               0:00:00
```

free() with the preprocessor macros such as __FILE__ and __LINE__. For example, the definition of malloc from dmalloc.h goes as follows.

```
  #undef malloc
  #define malloc(size) \
   dmalloc_malloc(__FILE__, __LINE__, (size), DMALLOC_FUNC_MALLOC,
 0, 0)
```

The first line is to undefine any `malloc` declarations that come in from previously included header files (`stdlib.h`). Needless to say, the `dmalloc.h` should be the last file to be included.

The `DMALLOC_OPTIONS` as shown in the above example controls the debugging at runtime. This environment variable can be set manually or by using a utility program called `dmalloc`. For an embedded environment you may prefer setting this option manually. To get more information on the `dmalloc` utility, run it on the command line with the argument `--usage`. The `DMALLOC_OPTIONS` is a list of the following (important) tokens separated by commas:

- `debug`: This token takes a hexadecimal value derived by adding all functionality tokens. A functionality token turns on a debugging feature at runtime. For example, the functionality token 0x1 turns on logging general statistics and 0x2 turns on logging memory leaks. So adding them yields 0x3 and turns on logging of general statistics and memory leaks. The list of all functionality tokens can be obtained by running the dmalloc program with the argument `--DV`.
- `log`: This is used to set a filename for logging statistics, leaks, and other errors.
- `addr`: When this is set, dmalloc will abort when it operates on that address.
- `inter`: This is used if the heap checking functionality is turned on. For example, if this value is set to 10, then the heap is checked for errors every 10 times.

8.5.2 Debugging Memory Overflows

Though easy to use, the C language is an insecure language because it does not prevent buffer overflows. Many functions in the C library are documented as unsafe to use (such as the infamous `gets()` function) but that does not prevent a careless programmer from using such functions and causing security breaches in the system. The following are some of the exploits that are encountered due to such careless programming.

- *Changing code execution:* The buffer overflow can modify the return address in the stack or an arbitrary function pointer in memory.
- *Overwriting a data variable:* The variable that holds some secret information such as a database connect string.

If you have downloaded an application source from the Net and would like to scan it for overflows, there are ready tools available for helping you. The tool that was primarily written to hunt buffer overflows is the *Electric Fence*. Note that dmalloc is also capable of doing fencepost checking. But the method provided by dmalloc is not exactly foolproof because it is implemented totally in software. There are two drawbacks to the dmalloc scheme:

- dmalloc implements fencepost checking by padding the allocated area with a magic number and making sure that the magic number does not get overwritten. The frequency of the checks is controlled using the debug token `inter`. This scheme can be effective in finding if there was an overflow but it may not be effective in pointing to the offending instruction.

- dmalloc can detect only writes beyond buffer boundaries; however, reads beyond buffer boundaries still go undetected.

Electric Fence makes use of the hardware to catch the exact offending instruction that tries to read and write beyond buffer boundaries. Additionally, it can be used to detect any conditions of software accessing memory that has already been freed. Electric Fence manages this by allocating a page (or set of pages) for every memory request and then rendering the pages beyond the buffer inaccessible for reading or writing. Thus if the software tries to access memory beyond the boundaries, it results in a segmentation fault. Similarly if memory released by the `free()` call is made inaccessible by virtual memory protection, any code that touches the freed memory will get a segmentation fault.

Electric Fence is available as a library `libefence.a`; this needs to be linked against the application that needs to be debugged for buffer overruns. Listing 8.7 illustrates the usage of Electric Fence. As you see in Listing 8.7, the recommended way of running Electric Fence is to run it from gdb so that the offending instruction can be caught with full debugging information. This example shows the case of buffer overflow. Underflows can also be caught by Electric Fence but in order to do this an environment variable `EF_PROTECT_BELOW` needs to be exported before running the application. This is necessary because by default Electric Fence catches only buffer overflows by placing inaccessible memory after the end of every allocation. Setting this variable makes sure that the inaccessible memory is placed before the start of the allocation. Thus in order to make sure that the application has neither overflows nor underruns the application should be invoked twice: once without setting the `EF_PROTECT_BELOW` variable and the second time after setting it.

Because Electric Fence requires that at least one memory page be allocated for every allocation, it can be quite a memory hog. The recommended use of Electric Fence is only for debugging systems; for production systems it should be turned off.

8.5.3 Debugging Memory Corruption

Memory corruption happens when a memory location gets written with a wrong value leading to wrong program behavior. Memory overflow discussed in the previous section is a type of memory corruption. Some common examples of memory corruption are:

- Memory pointers holding uninitialized values are dereferenced.
- Memory pointers are overwritten with wrong values and then dereferenced.
- Dereferencing memory pointers after the original memory has been freed.

Listing 8.7   Electric Fence Usage

```
/* efence-test.c */

#include <stdio.h>

main()
{
  int i,j;
  char * c = (char *)malloc(20);
  printf("start of efence test\n");
  for(i=0; i < 24; i++)
    c[i] = 'c';
    free(c);
    printf("end of efence test\n");
  }

# ls -l libefence.a
-rw-rw-r-- 1 raghav    raghav   76650 Sep  4 20:38 libefence.a

# gcc -g efence-test.c  -L. -lefence -lpthread -o efence-test
# gdb ./efence-test

...
(gdb) run
Starting program: /home/raghav/BK/tmp/memory-debugging/src/efence/
efence-test
[New Thread 1073838752 (LWP 6413)]

Electric Fence 2.4.10
Copyright (C) 1987-1999 Bruce Perens <bruce@perens.com>
Copyright (C) 2002-
2004 Hayati Ayguen <hayati.ayguen@epost.de>, Procitec GmbH
start of efence test:4004dfec

Program received signal SIGSEGV, Segmentation fault.
[Switching to Thread 1073838752 (LWP 6413)]
0x08048a20 in main () at efence-test.c:9
9                    c[i] = 'c';
(gdb) print i
$1 = 20
(gdb)
```

Such bugs are extremely difficult to catch. Finding the bug manually may prove to be a Herculean task as it would mean scanning the entire code base. We inspect a programming tool to deal with memory corruptions, *Valgrind*. Valgrind can be downloaded from the Web site http://valgrind.kde.org.

The following are some of the important features of Valgrind.

- Valgrind works only for Linux on the x86 platform. This may appear as a major deterrent from using it considering that many embedded platforms are not based on x86 architecture. However, many embedded development projects initially run their applications on the x86-based platform before porting them to their target; this is because the target may not be available when the applications are being developed. In such cases the developers

Listing 8.8   Valgrind Example

```
shell> valgrind ps
==4187== Memcheck, a.k.a. Valgrind, a memory error detector for
        x86-linux.
==4187== Copyright (C) 2002-2003, and GNU GPL'd, by Julian
        Seward.
==4187== Using valgrind-2.0.0, a program supervision framework
        for x86-linux.
==4187== Copyright (C) 2000-2003, and GNU GPL'd, by Julian
        Seward.
==4187== Estimated CPU clock rate is 2194 MHz
==4187== For more details, rerun with: -v
==4187==
  PID TTY           TIME CMD
 3753 pts/3    00:00:00 bash
 4187 pts/3    00:00:00 ps
==4187== discard syms in /lib/libnss_files-2.3.2.so due to
        munmap()
==4187==
==4187== ERROR SUMMARY: 0 errors from 0 contexts (suppressed: 2
        from 1)
==4187== malloc/free: in use at exit: 125277 bytes in 117 blocks.
==4187== malloc/free: 353 allocs, 236 frees, 252784 bytes
        allocated.
==4187== For a detailed leak analysis,  rerun with: --leak-
        check=yes
==4187== For counts of detected errors, rerun with: -v
```

can test their applications completely on the x86 platform for memory
corruption before transferring them to the target.

■ Valgrind is very much tied to the OS and the libraries; at the time of this
writing, the 2.2.0 distribution of Valgrind is supposed to run on the 2.4 or
2.6 kernel and glibc version 2.2.x or 2.3.x.

■ The application can run as it is with Valgrind without any rebuilding. For
example, if you want to run Valgrind with the ps executable you would
run it as shown in Listing 8.8.

■ Valgrind works by simulating a x86 CPU for running your program. The
side effect of this is that the program runs slower because Valgrind traps
the appropriate calls (system calls, memory calls) for bookkeeping. Also
the application tends to consume more memory when used with Valgrind.
Valgrind is an advanced tool that can do much more than fight memory
corruption such as cache profiling and finding race conditions for multithreaded programs. However, the present section studies the usage of
Valgrind in fighting memory corruption. The following is the list of the
memory checks that can be done using Valgrind.

 – Using uninitialized memory
 – Memory leaks
 – Memory overflows
 – Stack corruption
 – Using memory pointers after the original memory has been freed
 – Nonmatching malloc/free pointers

The Valgrind architecture can be decomposed into two layers: the core and the skins. The core is the x86 simulator that translates all the executable code into its own opcode. The translated opcode is then instrumented and executed on the real CPU. The instrumentation depends on the skin type chosen. The architecture of Valgrind is very modular allowing a new skin to be plugged easily with the core.

We focus our attention on the memory checker skin, *memcheck*. This is the default skin used by Valgrind (any other skin has to be specifically invoked using the command line argument --skin). Memcheck works by associating every byte of working memory with two values: the V (valid value) bit and the A (valid address) bit. The V bit defines whether the byte has been defined a value by the program. For example, the initialized byte of memory has the V bit set; thus uninitialized variables can be tracked using the A bit. The A bit tracks whether the memory location can be accessed. Similarly when a call to memory allocation using malloc() is done, all the memory bytes allocated have their V bit set. Another skin, *addrcheck*, provides all the features of memcheck other than the undefined value check. It does this by making use of the A bit only. The addrcheck skin can be used as a lightweight memory checker; it is faster and lighter than memcheck.

Now let us look at some practical demonstrations of Valgrind. The first example shows how Valgrind detects using an uninitialized variable. Valgrind detects the wrong usage of an uninitialized variable in a conditional branch or when it is used to generate memory address as shown below.

```
#include <stdlib.h>
main()
{
  int *p;
  int c = *p;
  if(c == 0)
    ...
  return;
}
```

When running this program with Valgrind it will generate the following output.

```
==4409== Use of uninitialized value of size 4
==4409==    at 0x804833B: main (in /tmp/x)
==4409==    by 0x40258A46: __libc_start_main
            (in /lib/libc-2.3.2.so)
==4409==    by 0x8048298: ??? (start.S:81)
==4409==
==4409== ERROR SUMMARY: 1 errors from 1 contexts
            (suppressed: 0 from 0)
==4409== malloc/free: in use at exit: 0 bytes in 0 blocks.
==4409== malloc/free: 0 allocs, 0 frees, 0 bytes allocated.
```

The second example shows how Valgrind can be used to detect a memory pointer dereferencing after the memory has been freed.

```
#include <stdlib.h>
main()
{
  int *i = (int *)malloc(sizeof(int));
  *i = 10;
  free(i);
  printf("%d\n",*i);
}
```

When running this program with Valgrind it will generate the following output.

```
==4437== 1 errors in context 1 of 1:
==4437== Invalid read of size 4
==4437==    at 0x80483CD: main (x.c:6)
==4437==    by 0x40258A46: __libc_start_main
                          (in /lib/libc-2.3.2.so)
==4437==    by 0x8048300: ??? (start.S:81)
==4437==    Address 0x411C7024 is 0 bytes inside a block of
            size 4 free'd
```

8.6 Kernel Debuggers

Unlike a conventional RTOS where there is a single debugger to debug the software, a Linux-based system requires two debuggers: a kernel debugger and an application debugger. This is because the kernel and applications make use of different address spaces. This section talks about using two popular kernel debuggers: KDB and KGDB.

The Linux kernel does not have any inbuilt debugger; the kernel debuggers are maintained as separate projects.[4] KDB and KGDB have different operating environments and provide varied functionalities. Whereas KDB is a part of the Linux kernel and provides a runtime mechanism to view the various components such as memory and kernel data structures, KGDB works in tandem with GDB and requires a host machine to communicate with a KGDB stub running on the target. Table 8.2 compares KGDB and KDB.

The usage of KDB can be divided into two steps.

■ *Building the kernel with the KDB patch:* Download the patches from the Web site given in Table 8.2 and apply to the kernel source tree. Build the kernel after configuring the kernel with the KDB option turned on.
■ *Running the kernel with KDB enabled:* The build configuration KDB_OFF decides if KDB is turned on or off when the kernel is booted; when this option is selected KDB is not activated. In such a case, KDB has to be explicitly activated; this is done by two methods. One method is to pass a boot line argument to the kernel kdb=on. The other method is to activate it using the file /proc/sys/kernel/kdb by the following command.

```
echo "1" > /proc/sys/kernel/kdb
```

Table 8.2 KDB versus KGDB

	KDB	*KGDB*
Debugger environment	It is a debugger that needs to be built inside the kernel. All it requires is a console using which commands can be entered and output displayed on the console.	It requires a development machine to run the debugger as a normal process that communicates with the target using the GDB protocol over a serial cable. Recent versions of KGDB support the Ethernet interface.
Kernel support/ patches required	KDB requires two patches: a common kernel patch that implements the architecture-independent functionality and an architecture-dependent patch.	KGDB makes use of a single patch that has three components: ■ GDB stub that implements the GDB protocol on the target side, ■ Changes to the serial (or Ethernet) driver for sending and receiving the messages between the target and the development machine, ■ The changes to the exception handlers for giving control to the debugger when an exception happens.
Support for source-level debugging	No support for source-level debugging	Support for source-level debugging provided the kernel is compiled with the -g flag on the development machine and the kernel source tree is available. On the development machine where the debugger application runs, -g option tells gcc to generate debugging information while compiling, which in conjunction with source files provides source-level debugging.

The list of KDB commands can be found from the files in the `Documentation/kdb` directory under the patched kernel source tree.

The usage of KGDB can be divided into three steps:

■ *Building the kernel with the KGDB patch:* This requires getting the KGDB kernel patch, patching the kernel, building the kernel with the KGDB support enabled, and building the kernel.
■ *Making the connection between the target and host using the GDB protocol:* When the kernel boots up, it waits for a connection establishment from the host using the KGDB protocol and indicates this to the user by throwing the following output.

```
Waiting for connection from remote gdb...
```

Table 8.2 KDB versus KGDB (continued)

	KDB	KGDB
Debugging features offered	The most commonly used debugging features of KDB are: ■ displaying and modifying memory and registers ■ applying breakpoints ■ stack backtrace Along with the user-applied breakpoints, KDB is invoked when the kernel hits an irrecoverable error condition such as panic or OOPS. The user can use the output of KDB to diagnose the problem.	Supports GDB execution control commands, stack trace, and KGDB-specific watchpoints among a host of other features such as thread analysis.
Kernel module debugging	KDB provides support for kernel module debugging.	Debugging modules using KGDB is tricky because the module is loaded on the target machine and the debugger (GDB) runs on a different machine; so the KGDB debugger needs to be informed of the module load address. KGDB 1.9 is accompanied by a special GDB that can automatically detect module loading and unloading. For KGDB versions equal to or less than 1.8, the developer has to make use of an explicit GDB command `add-symbol-file` to load the module object into GDB's memory along with the module load address.
Web sites for download	http://oss.sgi.com/projects/kdb/	http://kgdb.linsyssoft.com/

On the host machine, the user is expected to launch the debugger and connect to the target, which will indicate to the kernel to continue booting.

■ *Using the debugger to debug the kernel:* After this the kernel can be remotely debugged using the standard GDB commands.

8.7 Profiling

Profiling is a way to find bottlenecks during program execution so that the results can be used to increase its performance. There are some important questions that need to be answered.

- *Why profile?* Most embedded systems have very limited resources in terms of total memory and CPU frequency. Therefore it is very important to ensure that these resources are used optimally. By profiling, various bottlenecks in the program are identified. Fixing those bottlenecks will result in increased system performance and optimal resource utilization.
- *What is measured during profiling?* This includes the quantities such as percentage of execution time in each part of the program and memory utilization by the various modules of the program. For drivers, it could be the total interrupt disable time, and so on.
- *How are the profiling results used?* The profiling results are used to optimize the programs; problematic portions of the code can be written using a better algorithm.
- *What are profiling tools?* The role of the profiling tool is to associate bottlenecks that are identified during execution with the underlying source code. Profiling tools also present to the user of the profiling data in the form of a graph, histogram, or some other human-readable format.
- *What should the profiling environment be?* Realistic inputs should be given to the program during profiling. All the debugging information should be disabled to get more accurate profiling results. Finally the impact of the profiling tool itself on the results should be known a priori.

In this section, we discuss three profilers: eProf, OProfile, and Kernel Function Instrumentation (KFI). First we discuss *eProf*, an embedded profiler that could be used during program development. Next we discuss *OProfile*, which is a very powerful profiling tool. Finally we discuss KFI to profile kernel functions. These profilers mainly concentrate on the execution time of various parts of the program.

8.7.1 eProf—An Embedded Profiler

At the time of program development you often want to find the time a function takes to execute or the time taken to reach from one point of the program to another. At this stage, you do not need a full-blown profiler. You can write your own profiler (which the authors call eProf) to assist you with your small profiling needs. eProf is a function-based profiler. The interfaces provided can be embedded into the program to measure the execution delays between any two points in the program. eProf provides multiple profiler instances with each instance capable of timing different program areas at the same time. The interfaces provided are listed in Table 8.3.

Let us first discuss the usage of these interfaces followed by their implementation. In Listing 8.9 we profile two functions that are executing concurrently. Run the program in Listing 8.9 to get the profiling results.

```
# gcc -o prof prof.c eprof.c -lpthread
# ./prof

eProf Result:
```

Table 8.3   eProf Functions

Interface	Description
`eprof_init`	Initialize the profiler subsystem.
`eprof_alloc`	Allocate a profiler instance.
`eprof_start`	Start profiling.
`eprof_stop`	Stop profiling.
`eprof_free`	Free profiler instance.
`eprof_print`	Print profiler results.

```
ID name                        calls        usec/call
-------------------------------------------------------
0: func1                          1           10018200
1: func2                         10             501894
```

`eprof_print` prints the profiling data of all the instances. The output shows

- Profiler instance ID
- Profiler instance label
- Number of times the instance was invoked (i.e., number of times `eprof_start` and `eprof_stop` pair was called)
- Average code execution time in microseconds from call to `eprof_start` to `eprof_stop`

eProf Implementation

In this section we discuss the implementation of eProf.

```
    /*** eprof.c ***/
#include <stdio.h>
#include <sys/time.h>
```

`MAX_INSTANCE` defines the total number of profiler instances supported by eProf. You can change this value to support more profiler instances.

```
#define MAX_INSTANCE 5
```

eProf data structures include `eprof_curr`, which holds the current timestamp and is populated by function `eprof_start`. `eprof_diff` stores the difference in the timestamps recorded by `eprof_stop` and `eprof_start`. `eprof_calls` stores the number of times the `eprof_start` – `eprof_stop` pair has been called for a given instance. Finally `eprof_label` stores the instance label. It is populated by function `eprof_alloc`.

Listing 8.9   eProf Usage

```
/* prof.c */

#include <pthread.h>

/*
 * eProf header file. The source code of various eProf interfaces
 * is in eprof.c
 */
#include "eprof.h"
#define MAX_LOOP 10  // loop count

/*
 * This function runs in a context of a different thread. Here we
 * profile the time taken to execute the main loop of the
 * function
 */
void func_1(void * dummy){
  int i;
  /*
   * Allocate a profiler instance. Assign a name to this it -
   * 'func1'
   */
  int id = eprof_alloc("func1");

  /*
   * Start the profiler. Argument is the instance id returned
   * using eprof_alloc
   */
  eprof_start(id);

  /* We profile this loop */
  for (i = 0; i < MAX_LOOP; i++){
    usleep(1000*1000);
  }

  /*
   * Stop the profiler. We print the profiling results at the end
   * of the program
   */
  eprof_stop(id);
}

/*
 * In this example we profile each iteration of the loop. This
 * function is called by main
 */

void func_2(void){
  int i;
  /* Allocate the profiler instance */
  int id = eprof_alloc("func2");

  /*
   * As you can see we call the eprof_start and eprof_stop pair
   * multiple times. The profiler records the total number of
```

Listing 8.9   eProf Usage (continued)

```
   * times this pair has been called and then shows results on an
   * average basis
   */
  for (i = 0 ; i < MAX_LOOP; i++){
    /* Start the profiler */
    eprof_start(id);
    usleep(500*1000);
    /* Stop the profiler */
    eprof_stop(id);
  }
}

/*
 * The main application. It creates a thread the runs function
 * func_1. It then calls func_2 and then waits for thread to
 * terminate. Finally it prints the profiling results
 */
int main(){
  pthread_t thread_id;

  /*
   * Initialize eProf. It should be done once during program
   * startup
   */
  eprof_init();
  /* Create thread that runs function func_1 */
  pthread_create(&thread_id, NULL, func_1, NULL);
  /* Run function func_2 */
  func_2();
  /* Wait for thread to exit */
  pthread_join(thread_id, NULL);
  /* Print the results */
  eprof_print();
  return 0;
}
```

```
/* Stores the current timestamp. Filled in eprof_start */
long long int eprof_curr[MAX_INSTANCE] ;
/*
 * timestamp(eprof_stop) - timestamp(eprof_start).
 * Populated in eprof_stop
 */
long long int eprof_diff[MAX_INSTANCE] ;
/*
 * Number of times the {eprof_start,eprof_stop} pair has
 * been called
 */
long eprof_calls[MAX_INSTANCE] ;
/* Instance label */
char * eprof_label[MAX_INSTANCE] ;
```

get_curr_time is the core of eProf. It records the current timestamp. To achieve high precision in the profiler result it is necessary that this function be implemented using a high-resolution clock source. Some of the options are:

- Use hardware counters such as Time Stamp Counter (TSC) on Pentium. get_curr_time could be implemented using TSC as below.

```
static unsigned long long get_curr_time()
{
    unsigned long long int x;
    __asm__ volatile("rdtsc" : "=A"(x));

    /* convert x to microseconds */

    return x;

}
```

- Use High-Resolution POSIX Timers (HRT) if available. Refer to Chapter 7 for their usage.
- If your target provides support for high-resolution hardware timers then they could be used. Generally interfaces to access hardware timers may not be available in user space. You can use the kapi driver as explained in Chapter 6 to export its interfaces to user space.
- Finally if no hardware clock source is available then use gettimeofday to get the current timestamp. The precision of gettimeofday is determined by the system clock. So if the value of HZ is 100, the precision is 10 msecs. If the value of HZ is 1000, the precision is 1 msec.

```
/* Returns the current timestamp */
static unsigned long long get_curr_time(){
  struct timeval tv;
  gettimeofday(&tv,NULL);
  return tv.tv_sec*1000000 + tv.tv_usec;
}
```

eprof_init initializes the various data structures.

```
/* Initialize */
void eprof_init () {
  int i;
  for (i=0; i<MAX_INSTANCE; i++) {
    eprof_diff[i] = 0;
    eprof_curr[i] = 0;
    eprof_calls[i] = 0;
    eprof_label[i] = NULL;
  }
}
```

eprof_alloc allocates a profiler instance. It checks a non-NULL entry in eprof_label and returns the corresponding index.

```
int eprof_alloc(char *label) {
  int id;
  for (id = 0; id < MAX_INSTANCE &&
                  eprof_label[id] != NULL; id++)
```

```
              ;
    if (id == MAX_INSTANCE)
      return -1;
    /* Store the label and return index */
    eprof_label[id] = label;
    return id;
  }
```

eprof_start records the current timestamp in eprof_curr.

```
  void eprof_start(int id) {
    if (id >= 0 && id < MAX_INSTANCE)
      eprof_curr[id] = get_curr_time();
  }
```

eprof_stop stores the timestamp difference between self and eprof_curr in eprof_diff. Recall that eprof_curr is populated in eprof_start. It also keeps track of the number of times the profiler instance has been invoked in eprof_calls.

```
  void eprof_stop(int id) {
    if (id >= 0 && id < MAX_INSTANCE) {
      eprof_diff[id] += get_curr_time() - eprof_curr[id];
      eprof_calls[id]++;
    }
  }
```

eprof_free frees up the entry in eprof_label.

```
  void eprof_free(char *label){
    int id;
    for (id = 0; id < MAX_INSTANCE &&
                   strcmp(label,eprof_label[id]) != 0; id++)
         ;
    if (id < MAX_INSTANCE)
      eprof_label[id] = NULL;
  }
```

eprof_print is more of a formatting function. It prints the profiling data of all the profiler instances.

```
  void eprof_print () {
    int i;
    printf ("\neProf Result:\n\n"
        "%s %.15s %20s   %10s\n"
      "-------------------------------------------------\n",
          "ID", "name", "calls", "usec/call");
    for (i=0; i<MAX_INSTANCE; i++) {
      if (eprof_label[i]) {
        printf ("%d: %.15s %20d", i, eprof_label[i],
                                  eprof_calls[i]);
        if (eprof_calls[i])
          printf(" %15lld", eprof_diff[i] / eprof_calls[i]);
```

```
        printf ("\n");
    }
  }
}
```

8.7.2 OProfile

OProfile is a profiling tool for Linux. It has the capability to capture the performance behavior of the entire system including the kernel, shared libraries, and applications. It can also be used in profiling kernel modules and interrupt handles. It runs transparently in the background collecting information at a low overhead.

In this section we discuss the OProfile usage in the Linux 2.6 kernel. For this you need to rebuild the kernel with the CONFIG_OPROFILE option set. You also need to cross-compile OProfile for your target. Please follow the cross-compiling instructions in Section 8.2 and the OProfile installation instructions available at http://oprofile.sourceforge.net to set up OProfile for your target.

OProfile uses various hardware performance counters to record various events such as CPU cycles, cache misses, TLB flush, and so on. In architectures that don't have performance counters, OProfile uses the RTC clock interrupt to collect samples. If the RTC clock is also not available then OProfile falls back to timer interrupt. You can also forcibly enable the timer interrupt mode by passing oprofile.timer = 1 on the kernel boot command line. Also note that various events such as the TLB flush, cache miss, and so on that are generally associated with performance counters are not available in RTC/timer-interrupt mode.

In this section we profile a video player application, FFmpeg™ (http://ffmpeg.sourceforget.net) using OProfile on a PC. The idea of this exercise is to give you a quick start with OProfile. For the complete OProfile usage refer to http://oprofile.sourceforge.net. The following steps are followed to profile ffmpeg. Note that you need root permission to execute OProfile commands.

1. *Set up the Oprofile*: We don't want to profile the kernel.

    ```
    # opcontrol --no-vmlinux
    ```

2. *Start the profiler*:

    ```
    # opcontrol -start
    Using default event: GLOBAL_POWER_EVENTS:100000:1:1:1
    Using 2.6+ OProfile kernel interface.
    Using log file /var/lib/oprofile/oprofiled.log
    Daemon started.
    Profiler running.
    ```

3. *Start the application*:

    ```
    # cd /usr/local/bin
    # ./ffplay_g /data/movies/matrix.mpeg &
    ```

Listing 8.10   OProfile Output

```
# opreport -l ./ffplay_g
CPU: P4 / Xeon with 2 hyper-threads, speed 2993.82 MHz
(estimated)
Counted GLOBAL_POWER_EVENTS events (time during which
processor is not stopped) with a unit mask of 0x01 (count
cycles when processor is active) count 100000
samples    %         symbol name
120522    28.8691    synth_filter
68783     16.4758    mpeg_decode_mb
36292      8.6932    ff_simple_idct_add_mmx
24678      5.9112    decode_frame
15623      3.7422    MPV_decode_mb
15514      3.7161    put_pixels8_mmx
14861      3.5597    clear_blocks_mmx
             ............. .
             ............. . .
```

4. *Collect samples:* Listing 8.10 shows the command to collect the samples along with output. The first column of the output is the total number of samples taken in the function and the second column shows the relative percentage of total samples for the function. As GLOBAL_POWER_EVENTS represents the CPU time, so we can say that the function synth_filter has utilized 28.8 percent of total CPU time whereas function mpeg_decode_mb has utilized 16.5 percent of total CPU time during video playback.

5. *Get the annotated source:* Application should be compiled with debug on. In this example, the annotated source files for all the samples collected are created in the /usr/local/bin/ann folder. mpegaudiodec.c and mpeg12.c contain the annotated source for symbols synth_filter and mpeg_decode_mb functions, respectively. Refer to Listing 8.11 for details.

6. *Get the complete system performance report:*

```
# opreport --long-filenames
CPU: P4 / Xeon with 2 hyper-threads, speed 2993.82 MHz
(estimated)
Counted GLOBAL_POWER_EVENTS events (time during which
processor is not stopped) with a unit mask of 0x01
(count cycles when processor is active) count 100000
GLOBAL_POWER_E...|
  samples|        %|
------------------
223651 73.9875 /no-vmlinux
22727   7.5185 /lib/tls/libc.so.6
15134   5.0066 /usr/bin/local/ffplay_g
7329    2.4246 /usr/bin/nmblookup
        ....... . .
        ....... . .
```

7. *Shut down the profiler:*

```
# opcontrol --shutdown
```

Listing 8.11   OProfile Output with Associated Source

```
# opannotate --source --output-dir=/usr/local/bin/ann ./ffplay_g
# vim /usr/local/bin/ann/data/ffmpeg/libavcodec/mpegaudiodec.c

                :static void synth_filter(MPADecodeContext *s1,
                :              int ch, int16_t *samples, int incr,
                :              int32_t sb_samples[SBLIMIT])
    179  0.0407 :{ /* synth_filter total: 126484 28.7945 */
                ......
     75  0.0171 :   offset = s1->synth_buf_offset[ch];
     89  0.0203 :   synth_buf = s1->synth_buf[ch] + offset;
                ......
   1097  0.2497 :   p = synth_buf + 16 + j;
  38956  8.8685 :   SUM8P2(sum, +=, sum2, -=, w, w2, p);
   1677  0.3818 :   p = synth_buf + 48 - j;
  41582  9.4663 :   SUM8P2(sum, -=, sum2, -=, w + 32, w2 + 32, p);
                ......

# vim /usr/local/bin/ann/data/ffmpeg/libavcodec/mpeg12.c

                :static int mpeg_decode_mb(MpegEncContext *s,
                :              DCTELEM block[12][64])
    296  0.0674 :{ /* mpeg_decode_mb total:  72484 16.5012 */
                :   int i, j, k, cbp, val, mb_type, motion_type;
    155  0.0353 :   const int mb_block_count = 4 + (1<< s-
                               >chroma_format)
                ......
    257  0.0585 :   if (s->mb_skip_run-- != 0) {
     74  0.0168 :       if(s->pict_type == I_TYPE){
                ......
                :       /* skip mb */
      2 4.6e-04 :       s->mb_intra = 0;
    114  0.0260 :       for(i=0;i<12;i++)
     54  0.0123 :           s->block_last_index[i] = -1;
     51  0.0116 :       if(s->picture_structure == PICT_FRAME)
                ......
```

8.7.3 Kernel Function Instrumentation

In the last two sections we discussed methods for profiling user-space applications. In this section we discuss Kernel Function Instrumentation (KFI), a tool to profile kernel functions.[5]

KFI can be used to measure time taken by any kernel function. It is based on the function instrumentation and profiling feature of GCC, the -finstrument-functions[6] GCC flag. KFI is available in the form of a kernel patch and set of utilities for the 2.4 and 2.6 kernels. The kernel patch adds support for generating profiler data and utilities are used for postanalysis of the profiler data. Download them from www.celinuxforum.org. Apply the kernel patch and enable the CONFIG_KFI option in the kernel build. During kernel configuration you can also decide to do *KFI static run* if you want to measure kernel boot time and time taken by various kernel functions during boot. This is achieved by enabling the KFI_STATIC_RUN config flag. In this section we discuss *KFI dynamic run*; that is, we collect profiling data when the kernel is up and running. Please follow instructions in README.kfi, which is part of the KFI package, for steps to do a static run.

KFI Toolset

Before going into usage of KFI we must understand various tools that are part of the KFI toolset. The KFI toolset consists of three utilities: kfi, kfiresolve, and kd. kfi triggers profiling data collection in the kernel. kfiresolve and kd examine the collected data and present it to the user in a readable format.

You need to cross-compile the kfi program for your target. The various kfi commands are:

```
# ./kfi
Usage: ./kfi <cmds>
commands: new, start, stop, read [id], status [id], reset
```

- new: Start a new profiling session. Each session is identified by a run-id.
- start: Start profiling.
- stop: Stop profiling.
- read: Read the profiler data from the kernel.
- status: Check the status of your profiling session.
- reset: Reset KFI.

Most of the time you may not want to profile the complete kernel. You may just want to profile interrupt handlers or some specific kernel functions. KFI provides filters to do selective profiling. You need to set appropriate filters before starting a profiler session. To set up filters you need to modify the kfi program. The source code of the kfi program is located in file kfi.c and structure definitions are in kfi.h.

Every profiling session is associated with a struct kfi_run that contains all the necessary details for the session.

```
typedef struct kfi_run {
    ...
  struct kfi_filters filters;
    ...
} kfi_run_t;
```

The filters can be specified by setting fields appropriately in structure kfi_filters_t.

```
typedef struct kfi_filters {
  unsigned long min_delta;
  unsigned long max_delta;
  int no_ints;
  int only_ints;
```

```
    void** func_list;
    int func_list_size;
       ...
} kfi_filters_t;
```

The various fields of `kfi_filters_t` are:

- `min_delta`: Don't profile functions with execution time less than `min_delta`.
- `max_delta`: Don't profile functions with execution time greater than `max_delta`.
- `no_ints`: Don't profile functions that execute in interrupt context.
- `only_ints`: Profile functions that execute in interrupt context.
- `func_list`: Profile functions given in the list.
- `func_list_size`: If `func_list` is valid then `func_list_size` contains the number of entries in `func_list`.

In `kfi.c`, `myrun` is a structure of type `kfi_run_t`.

```
struct kfi_run myrun = {
  0, 0,
  { 0 },
  { 0 },
  { 0 }, /* struct kfi_filters_t filters */
  myrunlog, MAX_RUN_LOG_ENTRIES, 0,
  0,
  NULL,
};
```

As you can see, all the fields of its filter members are set to zero. You need to change `filters` members as per your need. For example, assume you need to profile the `do_fork` kernel function. The following steps should be performed to set up the appropriate filter.

1. Open `System.map` file of your kernel and locate `do_fork`.

   ```
   ....
   c0119751 T do_fork
   ....
   ```

2. Define `func_list`.

   ```
   void *func_list[] = {0xc0119751};
   ```

3. Modify `filters` member of `myrun`.

   ```
   struct kfi_run myrun = {
      ...
     { 0,0,0,0,func_list,1 },
      ...
   };
   ```

4. Recompile `kfi.c` and generate `kfi`.

Other filters can be set similarly. The generated profiler data can be examined using two phython scripts `kfiresolve` and `kd`. We discuss their usage in the next section.

Using KFI

In this section we discuss a KFI dynamic run with an example. We profile the `do_fork` kernel function. All the changes mentioned in the previous section to set up function-based filters are done. Our setup is a KFI-enabled 2.6.8.1 kernel running on a 2.8 GHz P4 machine. Our sample program is:

```
/* sample.c */
#include <sys/types.h>
#include <sys/stat.h>
#include <fcntl.h>

int main(int argc, char *argv[]){
  int i;
  printf("Pid = %d\n", getpid());
  for (i = 0; i < 2; i++){
  if (fork() == 0)
    exit(0);
  }
}
```

The steps are:

1. Create device node.

    ```
    mknod /dev/kfi c 10 51
    ```

2. Reset `kfi` to ensure fresh KFI start-up.

    ```
    ./kfi reset
    ```

3. Create a new KFI session.

    ```
    # ./kfi new
    new run created, id = 0
    ```

    Note that if you get a memory allocation failure error when executing this command then set MAX_RUN_LOG_ENTRIES in `kfi.h` to some lesser number.

4. Start profiling.

    ```
    # ./kfi start
    runid 0 started
    ```

Listing 8.12   KFI Sample Run

```
Kernel Instrumentation Run ID 0

Logging started at 2506287415 usec by system call
Logging stopped at 2506609002 usec by system call

Filters:
    1-entry function list
    no functions in interrupt context
    function list

Filter Counters:
No Interrupt functions filter count = 0
Function List filter count = 57054552
Total entries filtered = 57054552
Entries not found = 0

Number of entries after filters = 4


  Entry    Delta    PID      Function      Called At
--------  --------  -----    --------      ---------------
 137565     82      3982     do_fork       sys_clone+0x4a
 138566     22      4050     do_fork       sys_clone+0x4a
 138661     21      4050     do_fork       sys_clone+0x4a
 320729     70      3982     do_fork       sys_clone+0x4a
```

5. Run application.

    ```
    # ./sample
    Pid = 4050
    ```

6. Stop profiling.

    ```
    ./kfi stop
    runid 0 stopped
    ```

7. Read profiler data from kernel.

    ```
    ./kfi read 0 > sample.log
    ```

8. Postprocess data.

    ```
    ./kfiresolve.py sample.log /boot/System.map > sample.out
    ```

File `sample.out` contains the profiler result. All the timings are measured in microsecond units. In the output shown in Listing 8.12, `Entry` is the time when the function was entered and `Delta` is the time taken by the function. In the output, entries corresponding to PID 4095 are from our application. The other two entries corresponding to PID 3982 are from the shell.

You can also use `kd` to analyze profiler data.

```
# ./kd sample.out
Function                        Count  Time    Average  Local
--------------------------      -----  ------- -------  -------
do_fork                            4    195       48     195
```

Porting KFI

KFI is architecture independent. The core of KFI is the `kfi_readclock` function that returns the current time in microseconds.

```
static inline unsigned long __noinstrument kfi_readclock(void)
{
  unsigned long long t;
   t = sched_clock();
  /* convert to microseconds */
  do_div(t,1000);
  return (unsigned long)t;
}
```

`kfi_readclock` calls `sched_clock`, which is generally defined in `arch/<your-arch>/kernel/time.c`.

```
/*
 * Scheduler clock - returns current time in nanosec units.
 */
unsigned long long sched_clock(void)
{
   return (unsigned long long)jiffies * (1000000000 / HZ);
}
```

The above implementation of `sched_clock` is architecture independent and returns a value based on jiffies. On many embedded platforms the resolution of jiffies is 10 msec. Thus to have better precision in profiler results you should provide a better `sched_clock` based on some hardware clock source with at least microsecond-level resolution. For example, `sched_clock` is implemented using the timestamp counter in x86 processors with TSC support.

```
unsigned long long sched_clock(void)
{
  unsigned long long this_offset;

   .....

  /* Read the Time Stamp Counter */
  rdtscll(this_offset);

  /* return the value in ns */
  return cycles_2_ns(this_offset);
}
```

Alternatively you can write your own version of `kfi_readclock` if you do not want to use `sched_clock` as its clock source. One such implementation is included in the patch for PPC.

```
static inline unsigned long kfi_readclock(void)
{
  unsigned long lo, hi, hi2;
  unsigned long long ticks;

  do {
    hi = get_tbu();
    lo = get_tbl();
    hi2 = get_tbu();
  } while (hi2 != hi);
  ticks = ((unsigned long long) hi << 32) | lo;
  return (unsigned long)((ticks>>CLOCK_SHIFT) &
                                      0xffffffff);
}
```

Notes

1. The techniques have remained almost the same across the 2.4 and 2.6 versions.
2. The TOPDIR is a build variable and is used to get the base kernel source directory throughout so that the build is independent of the base directory location.
3. For multithreaded programs link with libdmallocth.a. For C++ programs link with libdmallocxx.a and for multithreaded c++ programs link with libdmallocthcxx.a.
4. Though a sore point with many kernel developers, Linus feels that debuggers fix the symptoms rather than offering a cure.
5. You can also use OProfile for kernel profiling.
6. GCC expects the user to define two functions: `__cyg_profile_func_enter` and `__cyg_profile_func_exit`. These functions are added at the entry and exit of a function, respectively, by GCC when the `-finstrument-functions` flag is used. KFI defines these two functions in which it collects the profiling data.

Chapter 9

Embedded Graphics

In an attempt to provide a better user experience, electronic products these days provide a graphical user interface. The complexity of the interface depends on the product and its usage scenario. For instance, consider these devices: a DVD/MP3 player, a mobile phone, and a PDA. A DVD/MP3 player requires some form of primitive interface that is capable of listing the CD/DVD contents. Creating playlists and searching tracks would be the most complex of operations that can be done on a DVD/MP3 player. Obviously this is not sufficient for a mobile phone. A mobile phone has more functionality. The most complex requirement is in the PDA. One should be able to run almost all applications such as word processors, spreadsheets, schedulers, and the like on a PDA.

One might have various questions regarding graphics support on embedded Linux.

- What comprises a graphics system? How does it work?
- Can I use Linux desktop graphics on embedded systems as is?
- What are the choices available for graphics on embedded Linux systems?
- Is there a generic solution that can address the entire range of embedded devices requiring graphics (i.e., mobile phone to DVD player)?

This chapter is outlined to answer these questions.

9.1 Graphics System

The graphics system is responsible for

- Managing the display hardware
- Managing one or more human input interface(s), if necessary

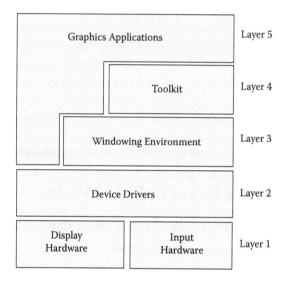

Figure 9.1   Graphics system architecture.

- Providing an abstraction to the underlying display hardware (for use by applications)
- Managing different applications so that they co-exist and share the display and input hardware effectively

Regardless of operating systems and platforms, a generic graphics system can be conceptualized into different module layers as shown in Figure 9.1. The various layers are:

- Layer1 is the graphics display hardware and the input hardware, the essential hardware components in any graphics system. For example, an ATM kiosk has a touchscreen as both its input interface and display hardware, a DVD player has video output on the TV, and a front panel LCD has its display hardware and a remote control as input interface.
- Layer2 is the driver layer that provides interfacing with the operating system. Each operating system has its own interfacing mechanism and device manufacturers try to make sure that they provide drivers for all popular OSs. For example, the NVIDIA® driver cards ship with video drivers for Linux and Windows.
- Layer3 consists of a windowing environment that is a drawing engine responsible for graphics rendering and a font engine responsible for font rendering. For example, drawing engines provide line, rectangle, and other geometric shape-drawing functionalities.
- Layer4 is the toolkit layer. A toolkit is built over a particular windowing environment and provides APIs for use by the application. Some toolkits are available over multiple windowing environments and thus provide application portability. Toolkits provide functions to draw complex controls such as buttons, edit boxes, list boxes, and so on.
- The topmost layer is the graphics application. The application need not always use a toolkit and a windowing environment. With some minimum

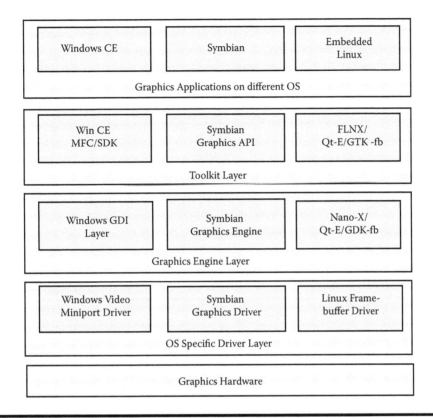

Figure 9.2   Graphics layers across operating systems.

abstraction or glue layer it might be possible to write an application that directly interacts with the hardware via the driver interface. Also some applications such as a video player require an accelerated interface to bypass the graphics layer and interface with the driver directly. For such cases the graphics system provides special interfacing such as the famous Direct-X in Windows. Figure 9.2 compares layers across various operating systems.

The chapter progressively discusses each layer in detail with respect to embedded Linux.

9.2 Linux Desktop Graphics—The X Graphics System

The X Windowing System provides Linux desktop graphics. We use this as a case study to understand the layered architecture of a complete graphics solution.

The X system is primarily written for the desktop computer. Desktop graphic cards follow predefined standards, VGA/SVGA. Input devices such as the mouse and keyboard input drivers also have standards. Hence a generic driver handles the display and input hardware. The X system implements a driver interface necessary to interact with PC display hardware. The driver interface isolates the rest of the X system from hardware-specific details.

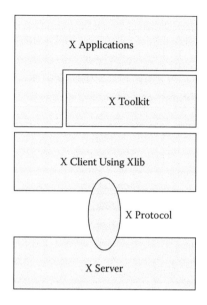

Figure 9.3   X toolkit architecture.

The windowing environment in X has a client/server model. X applications are clients; they communicate with the server and issue requests and also receive information from the server. The X server controls the display and services requests from clients. Applications (clients) only need to know how to communicate with the server, and need not be concerned with the details of rendering graphics on the display device. This commutation mechanism (protocol) can work over any interprocess communication mechanism that provides a reliable octet stream. X uses sockets for the same: the result, X Protocol. Because X is based on sockets it can run over a network and can be used for remote graphics as well. X-clients use APIs provided by the X windowing system to render objects on the screen. These APIs are part of a library, X-lib, which gets linked with the client application.

The *X-Toolkit* architecture is shown in Figure 9.3. It comprises APIs that provide windowing capabilities. Controls such as list boxes, buttons, check boxes, edit boxes, and the like are also windows built over the X-lib primitives and a collection of such libraries is called a *widget/toolkit*. The toolkit makes the life of the application programmer easy by providing simple functions for drawing controls. With multiple clients connecting to the server, there arises a need to manage different client windows. The X server provides a *window manager*, another X client, but a privileged one. The X architecture provides special functions for the window manager to perform, actions such as moving, resizing, minimizing or maximizing a window, and so on. For more details you can check the X11 official site, http://www.x.org.

9.2.1 Embedded Systems and X

X is highly network oriented and does not directly apply over an embedded system. The reasons why X cannot be used in an embedded system are listed in the following.

- X has mechanisms for exporting a display over a network. This is not required in an embedded system. The client/server model is not aimed at single-user environments such as the one on embedded systems.
- X has many dependencies such as the X font server, X resource manager, X window manager, and the list goes on. All the above increase the size of X and its memory requirements.
- X was written to be run on resource-full giant Pentium processor machines. Hence running X as-is on power/cycle savvy embedded microprocessors is not possible.

The requirements for a graphics framework an on embedded system are:

- Quick/near real-time response
- Low on memory usage
- Small toolkit library (footprint) size

Many modifications have been done to X, and microversions are available for running on embedded platforms. Tiny-X and Nano-X are popular and successful embedded versions based on the X graphics system. We discuss Nano-X in Section 9.6.

9.3 Introduction to Display Hardware

In this section we discuss various graphics terminologies and also generic graphics hardware functions.

9.3.1 Display System

Every graphics display system has a video/display controller, which is the essential graphics hardware. The video controller has an area of memory known as the *frame buffer.* The content of the frame buffer is displayed on the screen.

Any image on the screen comprises horizontal scan lines traced by the display hardware. After each horizontal scan line the trace is moved down in the vertical direction, and traces the next horizontal scan line. Thus the whole image is composed of horizontal lines scanned from top to bottom and each scan cycle is called a *refresh.* The number of screen refreshes that happen in a second is expressed as the *refresh rate.*

The image before being presented on the screen is available on the frame buffer memory of the controller. This digital image is divided into discrete memory regions called *pixels* (short for pictorial elements). The number of pixels in the horizontal and vertical direction is expressed as the *screen resolution.* For instance, a screen resolution of 1024 × 768 is a pixel matrix of 1024 columns and 768 rows. These 1024 × 768 pixels are transferred to the screen in a single refresh cycle.

Each pixel is essentially the color information at a particular (row, column) index of the display matrix. The color information present at a pixel is denoted

Table 9.1   RGB Color Formats

Format	Bits	Red	Green	Blue	Colors
Monochrome	1	—	—	—	2
Indexed—4 bit	4	—	—	—	2^4 = 16
Indexed—8 bit	8	—	—	—	2^8 = 256
RGB444	12	4	4	4	2^12
RGB565	16	5	6	5	2^16
RGB888	24	8	8	8	2^24

using a color representation standard. Color is either represented in the RGB domain, using Red, Green, and Blue bits, or in the YUV[1] domain, using luminance (Y) and chrominance (U and V) values. RGB is the common representation on most graphic systems. The bit arrangement and the number of bits occupied by each color results in various formats listed in Table 9.1.

The number or range of color values to be displayed determines the number of bytes occupied by a single pixel, expressed by the term *pixel width*. For example, consider a mobile display unit of resolution 160 × 120 with 16 colors. The pixel width here is 4 bits per pixel (16 unique values best represented using 4 bits), in other words a ½ byte per pixel. The frame buffer memory area required is calculated using the formula

Frame Buffer-Memory = Display Width * Display Height * Bytes-per-pixel.

In the example discussed above the required memory area is 160 × 120 × (½) bytes. Most frame buffer implementations are linear, in the sense that it is a contiguous memory location, similar to an array. The start byte of each line is separated by the constant width of the bytes, called the *line width* or *stride*. In our example, 160 * (½) bytes is the line width. Thus the location of any pixel (*x, y*) = (line_width * *y*) + *x*. Figure 9.4 illustrates the location of pixel (40, 4), which is marked in bold.

Now, look at the first three entries in Table 9.1. They are different from the remaining entries, in the sense that they are *indexed color formats*. Indexed formats assign indices that map to a particular color shade. For example, in a monochrome display system, with just a single bit, two values (0 or 1), one can map 0 to red and 1 to black. Essentially what we now have is a table with color values against their indices. This table is called a *Color LookUp Table (CLUT)*. CLUTs are also called *color palettes*. Each palette entry maps a pixel value to a user-defined red, green, and blue intensity level. Now, with the CLUT introduced, note that the frame buffer contents get translated to different color shades based on the values in the CLUT. For instance, the CLUT can be intelligently used on a mobile phone to change color themes as shown in Figure 9.5.

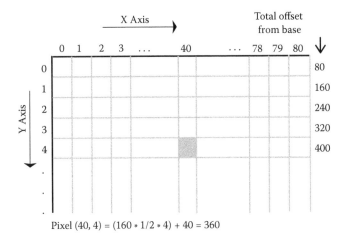

Pixel (40, 4) = (160 * 1/2 * 4) + 40 = 360

Figure 9.4 Pixel location in a linear frame buffer.

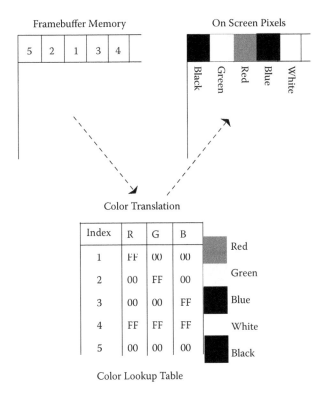

Figure 9.5 CLUT mapping.

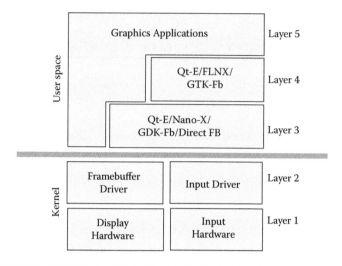

Figure 9.6   Embedded Linux graphics system.

9.3.2 Input Interface

An embedded system's input hardware generally uses buttons, IR remote, touchscreen, and so on. Standard interfaces are available on the Linux kernel for normal input interfaces such as keyboards and mice. IR remote units can be interfaced over the serial interface. The LIRC project is about interfacing IR receivers and transmitters with Linux applications. The 2.6 kernel has a well-defined input device layer that addresses all classes of input devices. HID (Human Interface Device) is a huge topic and discussing it is beyond the scope of this chapter.

9.4   Embedded Linux Graphics

The previous section discussed hardware pertaining to embedded systems. In the next sections we cover in depth the various embedded Linux graphics components. Figure 9.6 provides a quick overview of the various layers involved.

9.5   Embedded Linux Graphics Driver

The first frame buffer driver was introduced in kernel version 2.1. The original frame buffer driver was devised to just provide a console to systems that lack video adapters with native text modes (such as the m68k). The driver provided means to emulate a character mode console on top of ordinary pixel-based display systems. Because of its simplistic design and easy-to-use interface, the frame buffer driver was finding inroads in graphics applications on all types of video cards. Many toolkits that were essentially written for traditional X window systems were ported to work on a frame buffer interface. Soon new windowing environments were written from scratch targeting this new graphics interface on Linux. Today, the kernel frame buffer driver is more of a video hardware abstraction layer that provides a generic device interface for graphics applications. Today almost all graphical applications on embedded Linux systems make use of the kernel frame buffer support for graphics display. Some of the reasons for wide usage of the frame buffer interface are:

- Ease of use and simple interface that depend on the most basic principle of graphics hardware, a linear frame buffer
- Provides user-space applications to access video memory directly, immense programming freedom
- Removes dependency on legacy display architecture, no network, no client-server model; simple single-user, direct display applications
- Provides graphics on Linux without hogging memory and system resources

9.5.1 Linux Frame Buffer Interface

The frame buffer on Linux is implemented as a character device interface. This means applications call standard system calls such as open(), read(), write(), and ioctl() over a specific device name. The frame buffer device in user space is available as /dev/fb[0-31]. Table 9.2 lists the interfaces and the operations. The first two operations on the list are common to any other device. The third one, mmap, is what makes the frame buffer interface unique. We go slightly off track now to discuss the features of the mmap() system call.

The Power of mmap

Drivers are a part of the kernel and hence run in kernel memory, whereas applications belong to user land and run in user memory. The only interface available to communicate between drivers and applications is the file operations (the fops) such as open, read, write, and ioctl. Consider a simple write operation. The write call happens from the user process, with the data placed in a user buffer (allocated from user-space memory) and is passed over to the driver. The driver allocates a buffer in the kernel space and copies the user buffer to the kernel buffer using the copy_from_user kernel function and does the necessary action over the buffer. In the case of frame buffer drivers, there is a need to copy/DMA it to actual frame buffer memory for

Table 9.2 Frame Buffer Interface

Interface	Operation
Normal I/O	Open, read, write over /dev/fb
Ioctl	Commands for setting the video mode, query chipset information, etc.
Mmap	Map the video buffer area into program memory

User Space Application

Repeat seek/write

| Open (device name) | → | Seek (offset) | → | Write (bytes) |

| Driver open, Init Hardware | Seek to Buffer Offset | Write/DMA to Framebuffer |

Kernel Driver

Figure 9.7   Repeated seek/write.

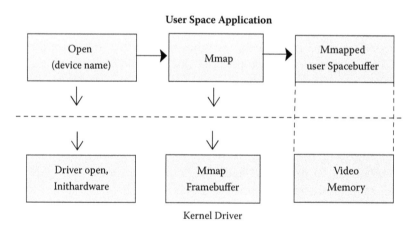

User Space Application

| Open (device name) | → | Mmap | → | Mmapped user Spacebuffer |

| Driver open, Inithardware | Mmap Framebuffer | Video Memory |

Kernel Driver

Figure 9.8   mmaped write.

output. If the application has to write over a specified offset then one has to call seek() followed by a write(). Figure 9.7 shows in detail the various steps involved during the write operation.

Now consider a graphics application. It has to write data all over the screen area. It might have to update one particular rectangle or sometimes the whole screen or sometimes just the blinking cursor. Each time performing seek(), followed by a write() is costly and time consuming. The fops interface provides the mmap() API for use in such applications. If a driver implements mmap() in its fops structure then the user application can directly obtain the user-space memory-mapped equivalent of the frame buffer hardware address. mmap() implementation is a must for the frame buffer class of drivers.[2] Figure 9.8 shows the various steps when mmap is used.

All frame-buffer applications simply call open() of /dev/fb, issue necessary ioctl() to set the resolution, pixel width, refresh rate, and so on, and then finally call mmap(). The mmap implementation of the driver simply maps the whole of the hardware video frame buffer. As a result the application gets a pointer to the frame buffer memory. Any changes done to this memory area are directly reflected on the display.

To understand the frame buffer interface better we set up the frame buffer driver on the Linux desktop and write a sample frame buffer application.

Setting Up Frame Buffer Driver

The Linux kernel must be booted with the frame buffer option to use the frame buffer console and to init the frame buffer driver. Pass the vga=0x761 command line option during the kernel boot.[3] The number represents a resolution mode of the card; for a complete listing on what the number means, refer to Documentation/fb.txt under the Linux kernel source directory. If the kernel boots with the frame buffer mode enabled, you will immediately notice the famous tux boot image on the top-left portion of your screen. Also kernel prints will be displayed in high-resolution fonts. To confirm further, just cat some file onto /dev/fb0. You will see some garbage on the screen. If that did not work, then you might have to compile frame buffer support into your kernel and then try again. For further assistance on setting up the frame buffer device refer to the frame buffer HOWTO available at http://www.tldp.org/.

Now we discuss data structures and ioctls that provide the frame buffer user-space interface. Generally graphics devices have support for multiple resolution and modes. For example, a single device might have the following configurable modes.

- *Mode 1:* 640 × 480, 24-bit color, RGB 888
- *Mode 2:* 320 × 480, 16-bit color, RGB 565
- *Mode 3:* 640 × 480, monochrome, indexed

The fixed parameters in a particular mode are reported by the device driver using the fb_fix_screeninfo structure. In other words, the fb_fix_screeninfo structure defines the fixed or unalterable properties of a graphics card when set to work in a particular resolution/mode.

```
struct fb_fix_screeninfo {
  char id[16];                    /*Identification string ex
                                    "ATI Radeon 360"*/
  unsigned long smem_start;       /*Start of frame buffer
                                    memory*/
  __u32 smem_len;                 /*Length of frame buffer
                                    memory*/
  __u32 type;                     /*one of various FB_TYPE_XXX
                                    */
  __u32 visual;                   /*one of FB_VISUAL_XXX*/
```

```
    ...
    ...
    __u32 line_length;         /*length of a line in bytes*/
    ...
    ...
};
```

smem_start is the physical start address of the frame buffer memory of length smem_len. Fields type and visual indicate the pixel format and color mode. The FBIOGET_FSCREENINFO ioctl is used to read the fb_fix_screeninfo structure.

```
    fb_fix_screeninfo fix;
    ioctl(FrameBufferFD, FBIOGET_FSCREENINFO, &fix)
```

The fb_var_screeninfo structure contains the alterable features of a graphics mode. One can use this structure and set up the required graphics mode. The important structure members are:

```
struct fb_var_screeninfo {
    __u32 xres;            /*visible X, Y resolution*/
    __u32 yres;
    __u32 xres_virtual; /*virtual resolution*/
    __u32 yres_virtual;
    __u32 xoffset;      /*offset from virtual to visible
                          resolution*/
    __u32 yoffset;
    __u32 bits_per_pixel; /*Number of bits in a pixel*/
    __u32 grayscale;      /*!= 0 Graylevels instead of
                            colors*/
    ...
    ...
    struct fb_bitfield red; /*bitfield in fb mem if true
                              color*/
    struct fb_bitfield green;
    struct fb_bitfield blue;
    struct fb_bitfield transp; /*transparency level*/
    __u32 nonstd;              /*!= 0 Nonstandard pixel
                                format*/
    ...
    ...
};
```
The structure fb_bitfield above details the length and bit offset of each color in a pixel.

```
struct fb_bitfield {
    __u32 offset;   /*beginning of bitfield*/
    __u32 length;   /*length of bitfield*/
    __u32 msb_right; /*!= 0 : Most significant bit is
                       right*/
};
```

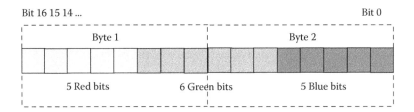

Figure 9.9   RGB565 pixel format.

Recall the different color modes that were discussed, RGB565, RGB888, and so on, and the `fb_bitfield` elements represent the same. For example, a single RGB 565 pixel is of 2 bytes' width and has the following format as shown in Figure 9.9.

- `red.length =5`, `red.offset = 16` → 32 pure red shades
- `green.length = 6` and `green.offset = 11` → 64 pure green shades
- `blue.length = 5` and `blue.offset = 5` → 32 pure blue shades
- pixel length is 16 bits or 2 bytes → 65536 shades in total.

Fields `xres` and `yres` represent the X and Y resolution of the visible screen. Fields `xres_virtual` and `yres_virtual` indicate the virtual resolution of the card, which might be greater than visible coordinates. For example, consider the case where the visible Y resolution is 480, whereas the virtual Y resolution is 960. Because only 480 lines are visible it is necessary to indicate which 480 lines out of the 960 are to be made visible on the screen. The `xoffset` and `yoffset` field is used for this purpose. In our example if `yoffset` is 0, then the first 480 lines will be visible or, if `yoffset` is 480, the last 480 lines are made visible. By just changing the offset value programmers can implement double buffering and page flipping[4] in their graphics applications.

`FBIOGET_VSCREENINFO` ioctl retrieves the `fb_var_screenifno` structure and `FBIOSET_VSCREENINFO` ioctl sets a configured `fb_var_screeninfo` structure.

```
fb_var_screeninfo var;
/* Read the var info */
ioctl(FrameBufferFD, FBIOGET_VCREENINFO, &var);

/* Set 1024x768 screen resolution */
var.xres = 1024; var.yres = 768;
ioctl(FrameBufferFD, FBIOSET_VCREENINFO, &var);
```

The next important structure in frame buffer programming is the `fb_cmap` structure.

```
struct fb_cmap {
    __u32 start;    /* First entry*/
```

```
    __u32 len;      /* Number of entries */
    __u16 *red;     /* Color values    */
    __u16 *green;
    __u16 *blue;
    __u16 *transp; /* transparency, can be NULL */
};
```

Each color field red, green, and blue is an array of color values of length len. Thus the structure represents a color map table or CLUT, where the color value for any index n is obtained by looking up the table at red[n], green[n], blue[n], where start < n < len. transp field is used to indicate the level of transparency,[5] if required and is optional.

The FBIOGETCMAP ioctl is used to read out the existing color map table and FBIOPUTCMAP ioctl programs/loads a new color map table/CLUT.[6]

```
/* Read the current color map */
fb_cmap cmap;
/* Initialize cmap data structure */
allocate_cmap(&cmap, 256);
ioctl(FrameBufferFD, FBIOGETCMAP, &cmap);


/* Change the cmap entries and load 8 bit indexed color map */
#define RGB(r, g, b) ((r<<red_offset)|
                       (g << green_offset)|
                       (b << blue_offset))

/* Setup offset for RGB332 mode */
red_offset = 5; green_offset = 2; blue_offset = 0;
for(r=0;r<3;r++) {
  for(g=0;j<3;g++) {
    for(b=0;b<2;b++) {
      q=RGB(r, g, b);
      cmap.red[q]=r;
      cmap.green[q]=g;
      cmap.blue[q]=b;
    }
  }
}


/* Finally load the CLUT */
ioctl(FrameBufferFD, FBIOPUTCMAP, &cmap);
```

Now, we are ready to write our frame buffer *Hello world* program. Listing 9.1 plots a single white pixel in the middle of the screen.

The first step is obvious enough: open the frame buffer device /dev/fb0, with O_RDWR (read/write). The second step is to read the device information structures. The frame buffer device has two important structures: fixed and variable. Fixed information is read-only: read using FBIOGET_FSCREENINFO ioctl. The fb_fix_screeninfo structure includes frame buffer device identification, information about the pixel format supported by this device, and

Listing 9.1   Sample Frame Buffer Example

```
/* File: fbs.c */

#include <stdio.h>
#include <stdlib.h>
#include <fcntl.h>
#include <errno.h>
#include <string.h>
#include <unistd.h>
#include <asm/page.h>
#include <sys/mman.h>
#include <sys/ioctl.h>
#include <asm/page.h>
#include <linux/fb.h>

/* Device Name like /dev/fb */
char *fbname;
/* handle to fb device */
int FrameBufferFD;
/* fixed screen information */
struct fb_fix_screeninfo fix_info;
/* configurable screen info */
struct fb_var_screeninfo var_info;
/* The frame buffer memory pointer */
void *framebuffer;
/* function to plot pixel at position (x,y) */
void draw_pixel(int x,int y, u_int32_t pixel);

int main(int argc, char *argv[])
{

  int size;
  u_int8_t red, green, blue;
  int x, y;
  u_int32_t pixel;

  fbname = "/dev/fb0";

  /* Open the framebuffer device in read write */
  FrameBufferFD = open(fbname, O_RDWR);
  if (FrameBufferFD < 0) {
    printf("Unable to open %s.\n", fbname);
    return 1;
  }

  /* Do Ioctl. Retrieve fixed screen info. */
  if (ioctl(FrameBufferFD, FBIOGET_FSCREENINFO, &fix_info) < 0) {
    printf("get fixed screen info failed: %s\n",
    strerror(errno));
    close(FrameBufferFD);
    return 1;
  }

  /* Do Ioctl. Get the variable screen info. */
if (ioctl(FrameBufferFD, FBIOGET_VSCREENINFO, &var_info) < 0) {
    printf("Unable to retrieve variable screen info: %s\n",
```

Listing 9.1   Sample Frame Buffer Example (continued)

```
strerror(errno));
    close(FrameBufferFD);
    return 1;
}

/* Print some screen info currently available */
printf("Screen resolution: (%dx%d)\n",
                          var_info.xres,var_info.yres);
printf("Line width in bytes %d\n", fix_info.line_length);
printf("bits per pixel : %d\n", var_info.bits_per_pixel);
printf("Red: length %d bits, offset %d\n",
                    var_info.red.length,var_info.red.offset);
printf("Green: length %d bits, offset %d\n",
                var_info.red.length, var_info.green.offset);
printf("Blue: length %d bits, offset %d\n",
                    var_info.red.length,var_info.blue.offset);

/* Calculate the size to mmap */
size=fix_info.line_length * var_info.yres;

/* Now mmap the framebuffer. */
framebuffer = mmap(NULL, size, PROT_READ | PROT_WRITE,
                            MAP_SHARED, FrameBufferFD,0);
if (framebuffer == NULL) {
  printf("mmap failed:\n");
  close(FrameBufferFD);
  return 1;
}

printf("framebuffer mmap address=%p\n", framebuffer);
printf("framebuffer size=%d bytes\n", size);

/* The program will work only on TRUECOLOR */
if (fix_info.visual == FB_VISUAL_TRUECOLOR) {
  /* White pixel ? maximum red, green & blue values */
  /* Max 8 bit value = 0xFF */
  red = 0xFF;
  green = 0xFF;
  blue = 0xFF;


  /*
   * Now pack the pixel based on the rgb bit offset.
   * We compute each color value based on bit length
   * and shift it to its corresponding offset in the pixel.
   *
   * For example: Considering a RGB565, the formula will
   * expand as:-
   * Red len=5, off=11 : Green len=6, off=6 : Blue len=5, off=0
   * pixel_value = ((0xFF >> (8 - 5) << 11)|
   *       ((0xFF >> (8 - 6) << 6) |
   *      ((0xFF >> (8 - 5) << 0) = 0xFFFF // White
   */
  pixel =   ((red >> (8-var_info.red.length)) <<
                            var_info.red.offset) |
```

Listing 9.1   Sample Frame Buffer Example (continued)

```
  ((green >> (8-var_info.green.length)) <<
                                 var_info.green.offset) |
               ((blue >>(8-var_info.blue.length)) <<
                                 var_info.blue.offset);

  }else {
    printf("Unsupported Mode.\n");
    return 1;
  }

  /* Obtain center of the screen */
  x = var_info.xres / 2 + var_info.xoffset;
  y = var_info.yres / 2 + var_info.yoffset;

  /* Plot the pixel at x,y */
  draw_pixel(x,y, pixel);

  /* Release mmap. */
  munmap(framebuffer,0);
  close(FrameBufferFD);
  return 0;
}

void draw_pixel(int x, int y, u_int32_t pixel)
{

  /*
   * Based on bits per pixel we assign the pixel_value to the
   * framebuffer pointer. Recollect the matrix indexing method
   * described for the linear framebuffer.

   * pixel(x,y)=(line_width * y) + x.
   */


  switch (var_info.bits_per_pixel) {

    case 8:
      *((u_int8_t *)framebuffer + fix_info.line_length * y +x) =
          (u_int8_t)pixel;
      break;

    case 16:
      *((u_int16_t *)framebuffer +fix_info.line_length/2 *y +x) =
          (u_int16_t)pixel;
      break;

    case 32:
      *((u_int32_t *)framebuffer + fix_info.line_length/4*y +x) =
          (u_int32_t)pixel;
      break;

    default:
      printf("Unknown depth.\n");
  }
}
```

addresses for memory mapping the frame buffer. The variable screen information is read/write retrieved using the FBIOGET_VSCREENINFO ioctl and set using the FBIOSET_VSCREENINFO ioctl. The fb_var_screeninfo structure describes the geometry and timings of the current video mode. The next step is to mmap the hardware buffer into our application's process space using the mmap() system call.

Now we are ready for plotting our pixel. We take care of the various bit depths and pixel-packing schemes. The fb_var_screeninfo structure provides the bit length and offsets of individual color channels. Finally, using the property (pixel (x,y) = (line_width * y) + x) of the linear frame buffer, we plot the single pixel. So much for getting one pixel!

9.5.2 Frame Buffer Internals

The kernel provides a frame buffer driver framework (implemented in drivers/vieo/fbmem.c and drivers/video/fbgen.c). This framework provides for easy integration of the actual frame buffer hardware driver into the kernel. All board-specific frame buffer drivers register to this interface in the kernel. The framework provides APIs and defines data structures to hook up the hardware-dependent code. The skeleton of any driver that uses this framework looks like the following.

- Fill up driver operations structure struct fb_ops.
- Fill up frame buffer fixed info struct fb_fix_screeninfo.
- Fill up driver information structure struct fb_info.
- Initialize hardware registers and video memory area.
- Allocate and initialize color map struct fb_cmap, if necessary.[7]
- Register the fb_info structure with driver framework using register_framebuffer.

We have already discussed the fb_fix_screeninfo, fb_var_screeninfo, and fb_cmap structures. Hence, we look into the other two driver structures, fb_ops and fb_info. The important fields of struct fb_ops are function pointers to operations like open, close, read, write, and ioctl. Many of them are handled generically by the framework. So unless there is a need to do something special for your hardware there is no need to define most of these fields. For example, blanking a screen, fb_blank, and setting color register, fb_setcolreg, are hardware-specific routines. These need to be filled up if your hardware supports them and handled accordingly. Descriptions of the various structure members of struct fb_info can be found in include/linux/fb.h.

struct fb_info is the most important structure as it is the single hook point for all the other data structures. The driver registers with the kernel with a pointer to the driver-specific fb_info structure. The important fields in this structure are:

```
struct fb_info {
   …
   …
   struct fb_var_screeninfo var;    /*Current variable
                                      screen information*/
   struct fb_fix_screeninfo fix;    /*The fixed screen
                                       information */
   …
   …
   struct fb_cmap cmap;             /*Current Color map*/
   struct fb_ops *fbops;            /*Pointer to fb_ops
                                      structure */
   char *screen_base;               /*Video memory base
                                      address (virtual)*/
   …
   …
};
```

The field `screen_base` is the video memory base address, a pointer to the actual frame buffer hardware memory. But it is to be noted that the hardware address has to be io-remaped before providing the address to the kernel. Once the data structures are ready the driver should register with the kernel by calling `register_framebuffer`.

```
int register_framebuffer(struct fb_info *fb_info);
```

To summarize, the driver needs to fill

- `fb_info.fix`: Fixed information on screen area and type.
- `fb_info.var`: Variable information on screen resolution and pixel depth for the current mode.
- `fb_info.fb_ops`: Function pointers for frame buffer operations; use only when hardware-specific handling is required.
- `fb_info.screen_base`: Video memory base (virtual) address, exposed to user applications via mmap.
- `fb_info.fb_cmap`: Set up the color map entries, if necessary.
- `fb_ops.fb_blank`, `fb_ops.fb_setcolreg`: Set up hardware-specific fb_ops entries, if necessary.
- And finally call `register_framebuffer(&fb_info)`.

For an idea on writing a simple frame buffer driver you can look at `drivers/video/vfb.c`, the virtual frame buffer example in the kernel. One can also look at the other driver source code to get an idea of the driver coding details. Now we discuss a sample Linux 2.6 kernel frame buffer driver.[8] Tables 9.3 and 9.4 list the specification/data sheet details of our hypothetical graphical hardware: Simple Frame Buffer (SFB) device.

Let's first fill the hardware-specific macros for this driver. The rest of the code is generic and hardware independent. All the hardware-related details are in Listing 9.2. Listing 9.3 is a simple skeleton frame buffer driver that would work with any hardware, provided Listing 9.2 is updated accordingly.

Table 9.3   SFB Hardware Details

Parameter	Value
Video memory start address	0xA00000
Video memory size	0x12C000
Video memory end address	0xB2C000
Max X resolution	640
Max Y resolution	480
Min X resolution	320
Min Y resolution	240
Color formats	32-bit, true color, RGBX888, MSB 8 bits don't care 16-bit, high color, RGB565 8-bit, indexed color, palette programming required
Palette present	Yes, 256 hardware color index registers
Palette register start	0xB2C100
Mode register	0xB2C004
Resolution register	0xB2C008. High 2 bytes are Y resolution and low 2 bytes are X resolution

Table 9.4   Mode Register

Value in Register	Mode of the Card
0x100	RGB X888
0x010	RGB 565
0x001	8-bit, indexed mode

9.6 Windowing Environments, Toolkits, and Applications

Applications written directly over the frame buffer interface do exist, but only simple ones. As the GUI gets complex with more shapes and controls, there is a need for abstraction. Libraries/API layers that make GUI programming simple and easy have been in existence on desktop platforms for many years. These libraries abstract the driver interface over simpler APIs that make sense for a graphics application programmer. These libraries are essential in all windowing environments. A generic windowing environment consists of:

Listing 9.2 Frame Buffer Driver Hardware-Specific Definitions

```
/* sfb.h */

#define SFB_VIDEOMEMSTART 0xA00000
#define SFB_VIDEOMEMSIZE  0x12C000
#define SFB_MAX_X              640
#define SFB_MAX_Y              480
#define SFB_MIN_X              320
#define SFB_MIN_Y              240


/* No transparency support in our hardware */
#define TRANSP_OFFSET          0
#define TRANSP_LENGTH          0


/*
 * Hardware has 0 to 255 (256) programmable color pallete
 * registers
 */
#define SFB_MAX_PALETTE_REG256
#define SFB_PALETTE_START   0xB2C100


/* Mode register and modes */
#define SFB_MODE_REG        0xB2C004
#define SFB_8BPP                0x1
#define SFB_16BPP               0x10
#define SFB_32BPP               0x100


/* Resolution register */
#define SFB_RESOLUTION_REG 0xB2C008


/*
 * The different bits_per_pixel mode (8/16/24/32) is hardware
 * specific. Hence the mode needs to be correspondingly handled.
 * SFB hardware supports only 8, 16 and 32 bit modes,  Check for
 * validity of modes and adjust accordingly
 */

static inline int sfb_check_bpp(struct fb_var_screeninfo *var)
{
  if (var->bits_per_pixel <= 8)
    var->bits_per_pixel = 8;
  else if (var->bits_per_pixcl <= 16)
    var->bits_per_pixel = 16;
  else if (var->bits_per_pixel <= 32)
    var->bits_per_pixel = 32;
  else
    return -EINVAL;
  return 0;
}

static inline void sfb_fixup_var_modes(struct fb_var_screeninfo *var)
{
  switch (var->bits_per_pixel) {

    case 8:
      var->red.offset = 0;
```

Listing 9.2 Frame Buffer Driver Hardware-Specific Definitions (continued)

```
              var->red.length = 3;
              var->green.offset = 3;
              var->green.length = 3;
              var->blue.offset = 6;
              var->blue.length = 2;
              var->transp.offset = TRANSP_OFFSET;
              var->transp.length = TRANSP_LENGTH;
              break;

          case 16:  /*RGB565*/
              var->red.offset = 0;
              var->red.length = 5;
              var->green.offset = 5;
              var->green.length = 6;
              var->blue.offset = 11;
              var->blue.length = 5;
              var->transp.offset = TRANSP_OFFSET;
              var->transp.length = TRANSP_LENGTH;
              break;

          case 24:
          case 32:   /* RGBX 888 */
              var->red.offset = 0;
              var->red.length = 8;
              var->green.offset = 8;
              var->green.length = 8;
              var->blue.offset = 16;
              var->blue.length = 8;
              var->transp.offset = TRANSP_OFFSET;
              var->transp.length = TRANSP_LENGTH;
              break;
      }
      var->red.msb_right = 0;
      var->green.msb_right = 0;
      var->blue.msb_right = 0;
      var->transp.msb_right = 0;
}
/* Program the hardware based on user settings */
static inline sfb_program_hardware(struct fb_info *info)
{
    *((unsigned int*)(SFB_RESOLUTION_REG)) =
        ((info->var.yres_virtual & 0xFFFF) << 0xFFFF) |
        (info->var.xres_virtual & 0xFFFF)

    switch(info->var.bits_per_pixel) {

        case 8:
            *((unsigned int*)(SFB_MODE_REG)) =  SFB_8BPP;
            break;

        case 16:
            *((unsigned int*)(SFB_MODE_REG)) =  SFB_16BPP;
            break;
```

Listing 9.2 Frame Buffer Driver Hardware-Specific Definitions (continued)

```
case 32:
    *((unsigned int*)(SFB_MODE_REG)) =  SFB_32BPP;
    break;
  }
}
```

- An interface layer for low-level drivers, such as the screen and input drivers
- A graphics engine for drawing objects on the screen
- A font engine that is capable of decoding one or more font file formats and rendering them
- APIs that provide access to the various features exported by graphics and font engines

Recall we discussed X as a windowing environment used on Linux desktops. X-lib is the API layer provided by the X windowing environment. GUI toolkits are also libraries built over windowing environments to overcome some disadvantages of the lower library.

- Windowing environment libraries are platform-specific. For instance, application code written over X-lib is almost impossible to port to Windows. Most toolkits are available on multiple platforms and hence make porting possible. Qt is a cross-platform toolkit available on various platforms such as Qt/Windows (Windows XP, 2000, NT 4, Me/98/95), Qt/X11 (X windows), Qt/Mac (Mac OS X), and Qt/Embedded (embedded Linux).
- APIs exported by windowing environment libraries perform simple tasks. Toolkits implement many GUI components/objects and provide APIs for them. For example, toolkits provide APIs for commonly used dialog boxes such as File-Open, File-Print, Color Selection, and so on.
- Native widgets are too simple and applications cannot change the way a widget looks when they use windowing libraries. Toolkits provide theme support and widgets that are often loaded with features such as 3-D look and feel, animation, and so on.
- Most important of all, toolkits provide GUI designers or Rapid Application Development (RAD) tools. RAD tools are GUI builders that offer a point-and-click interface for tasks such as widget placement or callback definitions. Qt provides Qt Designer. Glade is used for Gtk programming.

Toolkits are not always advantageous. Some of them bloat up your code heavily, in return for the huge feature set that they carry along. There are lots of options available when it comes to embedded Linux windowing environments/toolkit combinations. Table 9.5 lists the popular ones.

A major advantage of the Linux toolkit is that it provides a simulation environment on the PC. Applications can be developed and prototyped on the desktop, thus decreasing developing time and simplifying debugging. In this section we discuss the Nano-X windowing environment.

Listing 9.3   Generic Frame Buffer Driver

```
/* sfb.c */

#include <linux/module.h>
#include <linux/kernel.h>
#include <linux/errno.h>
#include <linux/string.h>
#include <linux/mm.h>
#include <linux/tty.h>
#include <linux/slab.h>
#include <linux/vmalloc.h>
#include <linux/delay.h>
#include <linux/interrupt.h>
#include <asm/uaccess.h>
#include <linux/fb.h>
#include <linux/init.h>

static char *videomemory =   VIDEOMEMSTART;
static u_long videomemorysize = VIDEOMEMSIZE;
static struct fb_info fb_info;

/* Set up some default screeninfo*/
static struct fb_var_screeninfo sfb_default __initdata = {
   .xres =            SFB_MAX_X,
   .yres =            SFB_MAX_Y,
   .xres_virtual = SFB_MAX_X,
   .yres_virtual = SFB_MAX_Y,
   .bits_per_pixel = 8,
   .red =             { 0, 8, 0 },
   .green =           { 0, 8, 0 },
   .blue =            { 0, 8, 0 },
   .activate =        FB_ACTIVATE_TEST,
   .height =          -1,
   .width =           -1,
   .left_margin =   0,
   .right_margin = 0,
   .upper_margin = 0,
   .lower_margin = 0,
   .vmode =           FB_VMODE_NONINTERLACED,
};

static struct fb_fix_screeninfo sfb_fix __initdata = {
   .id =              "SimpleFB",
   .type =            FB_TYPE_PACKED_PIXELS,
   .visual =          FB_VISUAL_PSEUDOCOLOR,
   .xpanstep =      1,
   .ypanstep =      1,
   .ywrapstep =     1,
   .accel =           FB_ACCEL_NONE,
};

/* Function prototypes */
int sfb_init(void);
int sfb_setup(char *);
```

Listing 9.3   Generic Frame Buffer Driver (continued)

```
static int sfb_check_var(struct fb_var_screeninfo *var,
                           struct fb_info *info);
static int sfb_set_par(struct fb_info *info);
static int sfb_setcolreg(u_int regno, u_int red, u_int green,
                           u_int blue, u_int transp,
                           struct fb_info *info);
static int sfb_pan_display(struct fb_var_screeninfo *var,
                             struct fb_info *info);
static int sfb_mmap(struct fb_info *info, struct file *file,
                      struct vm_area_struct *vma);

/*
 * Define fb_ops structure that is registered with the kernel.
 * Note: The cfb_xxx routines, these are generic routines
 * implemented   in the kernel. You can override them in case
 * your hardware provides accelerated graphics function
 */
static struct fb_ops sfb_ops = {
  .fb_check_var    = sfb_check_var,
  .fb_set_par      = sfb_set_par,
  .fb_setcolreg    = sfb_setcolreg,
  .fb_fillrect     = cfb_fillrect,
  .fb_copyarea     = cfb_copyarea,
  .fb_imageblit    = cfb_imageblit,
};

/*
 * Recollect the discussion on line_length under the Graphics
 * Hardware section. Line length expressed in bytes, denotes the
 * number of bytes in each line.
 */
static u_long get_line_length(int xres_virtual, int bpp)
{
  u_long line_length;
  line_length = xres_virtual * bpp;
  line_length = (line_length + 31) & ~31;
  line_length >>= 3;
  return (line_length);
}

/*
 * xxxfb_check_var, does not write anything to hardware, only
 * verify based on hardware data for validity
 */

static int sfb_check_var(struct fb_var_screeninfo *var,
                           struct fb_info *info)
{
  u_long line_length;
  /* Check for the resolution validity */
  if (!var->xres)
    var->xres = SFB_MIN_XRES;
  if (!var->yres)
    var->yres = SFB_MIN_YRES;
```

Listing 9.3   Generic Frame Buffer Driver (continued)

```
if (var->xres > var->xres_virtual)
    var->xres_virtual = var->xres;
  if (var->yres > var->yres_virtual)
    var->yres_virtual = var->yres;

  if (sfb_check_bpp(var)) return -EINVAL;

  if (var->xres_virtual < var->xoffset + var->xres)
    var->xres_virtual = var->xoffset + var->xres;
  if (var->yres_virtual < var->yoffset + var->yres)
    var->yres_virtual = var->yoffset + var->yres;

  /*
   * Make sure the card has enough video memory in this mode
   * Recall the formula
   * Fb Memory = Display Width * Display Height * Bytes-per-pixel
   */
  line_length = get_line_length(var->xres_virtual,
                                    var->bits_per_pixel);
  if (line_length * var->yres_virtual > videomemorysize)
    return -ENOMEM;

  sfb_fixup_var_modes(var);
  return 0;
}

/*
 * This routine actually sets the video mode. All validation has
 * been done already
 */

static int sfb_set_par(struct fb_info *info)
{
   sfb_program_hardware(info);
   info->fix.line_length = get_line_length(
                               info->var.xres_virtual,
                               info->var.bits_per_pixel);
   return 0;
}

/*
 * Set a single color register. The values supplied are already
 * rounded down to the hardware's capabilities (according to the
 * entries in the var structure). Return != 0 for invalid regno.
 */

static int sfb_setcolreg(u_int regno, u_int red, u_int green,
                            u_int blue, u_int transp,
                            struct fb_info *info)
{
   unsigned int *palette = SFB_PALETTE_START;

   if (regno >= SFB_MAX_PALLETE_REG)     //no. of hw registers
     return 1;
```

Listing 9.3   Generic Frame Buffer Driver (continued)

```
  unsigned int v = (red << info->var.red.offset) |
                        (green << info->var.green.offset) |
                        (blue << info->var.blue.offset) |
                        (transp << info->var.transp.offset);

    /* Program the hardware */
    *(palette+regno) = v;
    return 0;
 }


/* Driver Entry point */
 int __init sfb_init(void)
{
   /* Fill fb_info structure */
   fb_info.screen_base = io_remap(videomemory, vidememory);
   fb_info.fbops = &sfb_ops;
   fb_info.var = sfb_default;
   fb_info.fix = sfb_fix;
   fb_info.flags = FBINFO_FLAG_DEFAULT;

   fb_alloc_cmap(&fb_info.cmap, 256, 0);

   /* Register the driver */
   if (register_framebuffer(&fb_info) < 0) {
     return -EINVAL;
   }

   printk(KERN_INFO "fb%d: Sample frame buffer device
                      initialized \n", fb_info.node);
   return 0;
}

static void __exit sfb_cleanup(void)
{
   unregister_framebuffer(&fb_info);
}

module_init(sfb_init);
module_exit(sfb_cleanup);

MODULE_LICENSE("GPL");
```

9.6.1 Nano-X

The Nano-X project is an open source project available under MPL/GPL licenses. It provides a simple but powerful embedded graphic programming interface. The prime features in Nano-X that make it suitable as an embedded Windowing environment are listed below.

- Developed from scratch targeting embedded devices, accounting for various constraints such as memory and footprint. The entire library is less than 100 K and only uses 50 to 250 K of runtime memory.

Table 9.5   Popular Windowing Environments

Name	License	Comments
Nano-X www.microwindows.org	GPL/MPL	Windowing environment providing Win32- and X11–like APIs, targeting embedded systems.
FLNX www.fltk.org	LGPL	FLTK toolkit ported over Microwindows
MiniGUI www.minigui.com	LGPL	Compact graphic user interface support system for Linux. MiniGUI defines some Win32-like APIs for the applications; provides a small windowing system support library
DirectFB www.directfb.org	LGPL	A thin library that provides hardware graphics acceleration, input device handling and abstraction, integrated windowing system with support for translucent windows, and multiple display layers
PicoGUI www.picogui.org	LGPL	A new graphic user interface architecture designed with embedded systems in mind; includes low-level graphics and input, widgets, themes, layout, font rendering, network transparency
Qt/Embedded *www.trolltech.com/products/ embedded/index.html*	QPL GPL	C++-based windowing system for embedded devices, provides most of the Qt API
GTK+/FB www.gtk.org	LGPL	Frame buffer port of the popular GTK+ windowing system.

- The architecture of Nano-X allows for adding different types of display, mouse, touchscreen, and keyboard devices. This is done by providing a separate device driver interface layer. This makes porting to any hardware platform simple.
- Nano-X implements two popular APIs: a Microsoft Windows-based API layer and an X-lib such as the Nano-X API layer. This reduces the API learning time.
- The screen driver layer has support for all possible pixel formats such as 1, 2, 4, 16, 24, and 32 bits per pixel, and hence is portable to any device right from monochrome LCDs to true-color OSDs.
- It provides highly configurable and component-selectable architecture. For instance, one can add or remove support for any image or font library almost instantaneously.

Nano-X Architecture

Nano-X architecture is highly modular and has primarily three layers. These are:

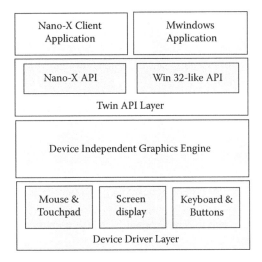

Figure 9.10   Nano-X windowing system architecture.

- Device driver layer
- Device-independent graphics engine
- API layer (Nano-X and Microwindows)

Figure 9.10 explains the Nano-X architecture.

The lowest-level device driver layer has an interface for various devices such as the screen over frame buffer, touchpad, mouse, and keyboard. This layer allows for adding any new hardware device to Nano-X without affecting the rest of the layers.

The core of Nano-X is the graphics engine that implements graphics routines for line, circle, and polygon draw. It also supports image drawing from various formats such as JPEG, BMP, and PNG. This layer also comprises the font engine responsible for rendering fonts and drawing text on the screen. The font engine supports both true-type and bitmapped fonts.

Nano-X supports two different API layers. Both the API layers run on top of the core graphics engine and the device driver. One set is very similar to the X Lib APIs and hence is referred to as Nano-X. Another API layer is similar to the Microsoft Win32 and WinCE APIs and hence is called Microwindows. Due to this dual API support, programmers of both the X and WIN32 SDK worlds are at great advantage and require little or no learning curve. The Nano-X API layer is based on the X framework and essentially has a client/server model. *Nano-X server* is a separate process that runs the server code. The application, the *Nano-X client*, runs as a separate process and is linked against a special library that provides for the UNIX/IPC socket communication with the server. There is also the option of linking the client and the server together to form a single application. This speeds things up by removing the IPC.

Microwindows API on the other hand is based on the Win32 SDK model. Microwindows essentially has a message-passing mechanism very similar to its Windows counterpart. Most windowing objects and methods have the same structures as in Windows SDK. Please refer to the architecture document available from http://www.microwindows.org/.

Getting Started with Nano-X

1. *Obtain latest source code:* At the time of this writing the latest version is Nano-X v0.91 and is available at ftp://microwindows.censoft.com/pub/.
2. *Compile:* Untar the sources (say /usr/local/microwin). cd to directory src/Configs/. This directory consists of preconfigured config files for various platforms. Choose and copy a suitable one for your platform and copy to microwin/src/config. Every item in the config file has a good amount of comment. That will give you an idea of the configuration flexibility that microwindows provides. For getting started we compile it for the i386. Enable the X11 option by setting X11=Y. This will ensure that we can run Nano-X as just another X11 application. The font engine of Nano-X supports a wide variety of font file formats including true-type (outline) fonts and bitmap fonts. The font engine uses external libraries such as Freetype-1, Freetype-2, and the like to provide support for TTF files. Choose a font-rendering system that is available on your PC, most likely Freetype-2. Finally compile using make in the microwin/src directory.
3. *Run demo:* After the compilation is complete, start the demo program in the directory microwin/src by running ./demo2.sh. This script starts off the Nano-X server and some sample client programs.

The src/demos directory contains a number of sample programs at various difficulty levels. One must go through at least a few of them to get acquainted with Nano-X programming.

Building a Sample Nano-X Application

Listing 9.4 is a simple Nano-X application that just draws a box.
Compile the program using the command

```
#gcc simple.c -o simple
            -I$(MICROWINDIR)/src/include  -lnano-x
```

We need to start the Nano-X server before starting the application.

```
#nano-X &; simple
```

Any Nano-X client application must call GrOpen() first to connect to the Nano-X server. After the connection is successful, the application creates a window of size 200 by 100 at the pixel location (100,100) using the function GrNewWindow(). The border specified for the window is 5 pixels wide, with border color as red and window fill color as white. Next the window is displayed on the screen using the GrMapWindow(). Mapping the window to

Listing 9.4   Sample Nano-X Application

```
/* nano_simple.c */

#define MWINCLUDECOLORS
#include <stdio.h>
#include "nano-X.h"

int main(int ac,char **av)
{
  GR_WINDOW_ID w;
  GR_EVENT event;

  if (GrOpen() < 0) {
    printf("Can't open graphics\n");
    exit(1);
  }

  /*
   * GrNewWindow(GR_ROOT_WINDOW_ID, X, Y, Width, Height,
   * Border, Windowcolor, Bordercolor);
   */

  w = GrNewWindow(GR_ROOT_WINDOW_ID, 100, 100, 200, 100, 5, WHITE,
                    RED);

  GrMapWindow(w);

  /* Enter event loop */
  for (;;) {
    GrGetNextEvent(&event);
  }

  GrClose();
  return 0;
}
```

the screen is followed by the all-important "event loop" of the program. The call to `GrGetNextEvent()` checks if there is a mouse, keyboard, or GUI event available to be read. Though the sample application does not handle any events, applications will have to react in response to these various events accordingly. For more information on programming using Microwindows refer to the various tutorials at http://www.microwindows.org.

Nano-X Toolkit

Simple GUI applications don't require any toolkit and should not be a problem to write in Nano-X. In this section we discuss the toolkit options available over Nano-X.

FLTK (Fast Light Tool Kit) has a port for Nano-X called FLNX. FLTK provides C++ abstraction over Nano-X APIs. FLTK also provides a GUI designer called Fluid that can be used to design GUI forms. The Nano-X/FLTK combination is proven and tested; many embedded applications have successfully employed this combination. For instance, the ViewML browser is an HTML browser implemented using the same combination.

NXLIB (Nano-X/X-lib Compatibility Library) allows X11 binaries to run unmodified using the Nano-X server. This means that many full-featured applications that run on the X-server would run on the Nano-X server as well with little or no modifications. The NXLIB is not a complete replacement of X-lib, because it provides only a subset of X-lib APIs. NXLIB will help reduce porting time of huge applications that were written using other toolkits built over X-lib. For example, a program written using Gtk-X will run on Nano-X without many code changes.

9.7 Conclusion

The chapter addressed various queries about graphics systems and their architecture and options available on Linux embedded systems. One question remains unanswered: is there a generic solution that can address the entire range of embedded devices requiring graphics, that is, mobile phones to DVD players?

The Linux frame buffer provides a solution for all types of devices. If the application is simple enough as in the case of a DVD player, then programmers can use the frame buffer interface along with a tiny windowing engine such as Nano-X and get the whole system up and running. The mobile phone solution requires a lot of programs such as calendar, phone book, camera, and the like to run over a user-friendly menu-driven GUI, which can be implemented using a toolkit such as Qt/Embedded or FLNX. Smart phones using Qt are already available on the market at the time of this writing.

Notes

1. YUV is more commonly employed in video encoding/decoding systems.
2. Note that this is not required in non-MMU operating systems such as VxWorks or uClinux because the whole memory address space is one flat area. In the flat-addressing model any process can address any memory space, regardless of kernel or user.
3. You can edit /etc/lilo.conf or grub.conf boot loader configuration files to achieve the same.
4. Double buffering and page flipping are graphics techniques in which the image is drawn to an off-screen (nonvisible) buffer. A simple pointer swap between visible and nonvisible buffers renders the image on the screen.
5. The transparency field is also called the alpha channel. We add a new mode to the list of known modes, the 32-bit RGBA8888 mode, where A stands for the alpha channel (8 bits).
6. Loading a new CLUT or color map is referred to as palette programming.
7. Not all hardware supports storing color map tables.
8. There is a small difference between the frame buffer drivers in the 2.4 and 2.6 kernels. The 2.4 frame buffer info structure directly stores pointers to the console driver data; the 2.6 removed this dependency separating the console from the graphic interface completely.

Chapter 10

uClinux

A new version of Linux ported to an M68k processor was released in January 1998. The major difference in this release from standard Linux was that this variant of Linux was running for the first time on a processor without an MMU. This variation of Linux is widely known as uClinux.[1] Until then, MMU-less processors used to run only commercial or custom-made RTOSs. The possibility of running Linux on such processors means a major design and development advantage. This chapter tries to address some queries related to running Linux on MMU-less processors.

- Why use a separate Linux for MMU-less systems?
- What tools are required to build and run uClinux on an embedded system?
- What are the changes involved at the various levels such as kernel, user space, file system, and so on?
- Will applications compiled for standard Linux run on uClinux?
- What are the application porting guidelines from Linux to uClinux?

10.1 Linux on MMU-Less Systems

Standard Linux primarily runs on general-purpose processors that have inbuilt hardware support for memory management in the form of an MMU. The MMU essentially provides the following major functions.

- Address translation using TLB[2]
- Demand paging using page faults
- Address protection using protection modes[3]

Linux is tightly integrated with virtual memory implemented using an MMU and hence was never meant for MMU-less processors. As Linux had this dependency on MMU, it was necessary to restructure some portions of the virtual memory management code in the kernel. The idea of running Linux on MMU-less processors and the impact of the changes on the then-stable Linux 2.0 kernel was not clear to everyone. Hence a new project was started to support Linux on MMU-less processors, the uClinux project (http://www.uclinux.org).

The uClinux project provided a Linux that was capable of running on MMU-less processors. Although uClinux has always focused on Linux for systems without an MMU, support for MMU-capable processors has always remained as is. uClinux adds support for MMU-less processors to the kernel, but removes nothing in the process, a small but important point that is often overlooked when discussing uClinux. It is to be noted that uClinux is capable of running on systems with an MMU too, but the chapter is concerned only with uClinux running on MMU-less systems.

10.1.1 Linux Versus uClinux

On a regular Linux system, a user process can be defined as a program in execution. Every program is an executable file stored in the file system; it is either stand-alone (statically linked) or dynamically linked with shared libraries. Virtual memory allows the allocation of private memory space for every process. However on uClinux, because there is no MMU, you will have doubts as to whether there are separate programs in uClinux or will it be similar to a traditional flat-memory OS where the OS and applications form one single image. In this section we look in detail at the differences between uClinux and Linux.

Process Address Space and Memory Protection

In standard Linux, applications are user processes that execute in private address space called the process address space. The MMU provides for memory protection and hence no application can corrupt any other application's address space. MMU also provides for virtual memory (VM) and each application is capable of addressing the maximum virtual memory limit[4] irrespective of the system's physical memory limit.

On the other hand, uClinux without VM applications cannot run in individual virtual process address space. Hence address space allocations across applications are shared from the available memory. The lack of MMU means there is no way to implement memory protection and hence all processes share a single global memory space. Because all processes share the same memory space, a process can corrupt another process' data. This is a major drawback with which uClinux developers will have to live.

User Mode and Kernel Mode

The user mode/kernel mode memory protection in a Linux system is realized by efficiently using MMU along with the processor operating modes. uClinux does have kernel and user-space applications because of lack of MMU and no memory protection. This means that any user-space application can corrupt kernel memory or even cause a system crash.

Demand Paging and Swapping

In an MMU-enabled processor, one can program page fault handlers. Linux uses the page fault handler[5] to implement demand paging and swapping. Because page fault handlers cannot be set up on an MMU-less processor it means that there can be no demand paging and swapping. Although uClinux has a common memory space for the kernel and applications, it allows an application image to be different from the kernel. Thus the application and the kernel can be kept as separate programs on the file system and can be loaded separately. uClinux achieves this by cleverly tweaking the toolchain (compilers, linkers, etc.) and the loaders that are necessary for program execution. uClinux has its own development toolchain. As a matter of fact, a major portion of porting uClinux to a new platform is to get the toolchain working. Once the toolchain is available, getting the applications to work on uClinux becomes a surprisingly easy effort. Discussing the changes required for porting a toolchain is beyond the scope of this chapter; rather this chapter focuses on how uClinux strives to maintain the same environment as regular Linux for the developers.

The design challenges involved in running a Linux platform on an MMU-less processor and keeping the platform as close as possible to the existing system are many and complex. In this chapter we try to point out a few of those design challenges and how uClinux engineers have solved them, explaining the basics involved in each approach.

The rest of this chapter is divided into two parts.

- The first part (Sections 10.2 to 10.6) discusses in detail the concepts behind uClinux, outlines the building blocks, and describes the modifications done to Linux to be able to run on an MMU-less system.
- The second part details a guideline for porting applications to uClinux. If you are interested in only porting applications and not bothered about system internals, then you can skip these sections and move on to Section 10.7.

10.2 Program Load and Execution

Standard Linux applications are linked with absolute addresses. In other words the compiler and linker build the applications with the assumption that each application has the complete virtual memory address range available.

We write a small program on the x86 to get an idea of how the different segments are organized in the address space available.[6]

```
int data1=1; //will go to .data section
int data2=2; // will also go to .data section
int main(int argc, char *argv[]) // .text
```

```
{
  int stack1=1; // program stack
  int stack2=2; // program stack
  char *heap1 = malloc(0x100); //heap allocation
  char *heap2 = malloc(0x100); //again from heap

  printf(" text    %p\n", main);
  printf(" data    %p %p\n", &data1, &data2);
  printf(" heap    %p %p\n", heap1, heap2);
  printf(" stack   %p %p\n", &stack1, &stack2);
}

Program Output:

text    0x804835c
data    0x80494f0 0x80494f4
heap    0x8049648 0x8049750
stack   0xbfffe514 0xbfffe510
```

The program output makes things clear on where a section is located and
in which direction a particular segment grows. The stack is near the top of
the PAGE_OFFSET (0xC000_0000) and grows downwards. Text is located
closer to the bottom of the memory (libraries have some regions reserved
below), followed by the data section. After the end of data (i.e., initialized
data + bss), heap allocation starts and grows above towards the growing stack.
What happens when heap and stack meet? In this case the page fault hander
posts signal SIGSEGV to the program. Figure 10.1 shows the standard Linux
application memory map.

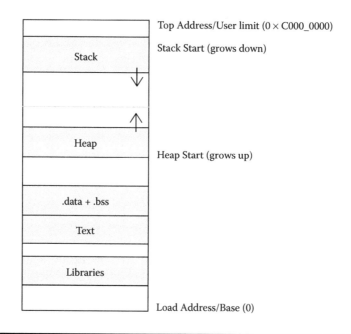

Figure 10.1   Linux application memory map.

Start multiple instances of the program and the output will be in the same range for all instances of the application. This is made possible because of MMU, which aids in providing a separate virtual address space for each process. The application deals only with the virtual address. The kernel virtual memory software and MMU hardware map the virtual address to the actual physical address.

Now in the absence of VM individual virtual address space cannot be created for each program. Hence in uClinux applications are forced to share all the available address space as one huge contiguous physical chunk. Programs are loaded in an available free chunk of memory, at any arbitrary memory location. Recall that on MMU-enabled systems this arbitrary location will get mapped to virtual address zero in the process' map. Unlike standard Linux, this means that the start address of a program is unknown (rather than an arbitrary address) and the addressing used in the instructions cannot be absolute.[7] The uClinux loaders take up this additional job of patching a program at start-up based on the start address available. The compilers and linkers also need to interop with the loader to assist in the same. uClinux has two different methods to solve this unknown address problem.

10.2.1 Fully Relocatable Binaries (FRB)

The binary is compiled with the text starting at zero address. The toolchain generates fixed non-Position Independent Code (PIC). To aid the loader to load the image at any arbitrary address, the linker adds a relocation table at the end of the data segment. The entries in the relocation table point to locations in the file that are in need of a fix-up. The loader copies the text and data segments to RAM and runs through the relocation table, patching each entry by adding the start address of the particular segment available at load time.

10.2.2 Position Independent Code (PIC)

In this case the compiler generates position independent code using program counter–relative text addresses.[8] Relative addressing requires hardware support, instructions that are capable of interpreting PC-relative addressing modes. All data is referenced using a table called the Global Offset Table (GOT). The GOT is placed at the start of the data segment and contains address pointers to data used in the code. The size of the GOT is limited in some architectures such as the m68k.

eXecute In Place (XIP)

PIC mode also comes in handy in implementing eXecute-In-Place (XIP). Unlike the relocation case where text and data both need to be copied to RAM before execution (for patching jumps and calls), there is nothing that needs to be patched for a PIC-based binary file. The program can start execution once the data segment has been set up.[9] XIP leverages this property and runs the

Table 10.1   FRB versus PIC

Fully Relocatable Binary	Position Independent Code
XIP not possible.	XIP possible.
Multiple instances of the same program result in wastage of memory as text segments need to be copied to RAM for every instance.	With XIP the text segment is shared across multiple instances without allocating RAM.
Start-up time is high as relocations need to be patched up before start-up.	Less start-up time.
Works for all targets.	PIC requires target support (relative addressing mode).

text *as is* directly from flash/ROM in place. Multiple instances of the program just create new data segments and the text segment is actually shared across all instances. Table 10.1 summarizes the differences between FRB and PIC.

10.2.3 bFLT File Format

The standard Linux execution file format is ELF. uClinux introduces a new file format that is designed with the following design goals.

- Simplify the application load and execute process.
- Create a small and memory-efficient file format (ELF headers are large).
- Create a file format that will help solve problems in loading programs in an MMU-less system.
- Provide for storing the relocation table for FRBs or GOT in case of PIC binaries.

The file format used in uClinux is binary FLAT (bFLT). uClinux compilers and linkers have special flags that help generate a relocation or PIC-based bFLT file. The uClinux kernel also has a new loader that can interpret the bFLT headers. Following is the 64-byte bFLT header structure, present at offset 0 of any bFLT file.

```
struct flat_hdr {
  char magic[4];
  unsigned long rev;          /* version */
  unsigned long entry;        /* Offset of first executable
                                 instruction with text
                                 segment from beginning of
                                 file */
  unsigned long data_start;   /* Offset of data segment from
                                 beginning of file */
  unsigned long data_end;     /* Offset of end of data
                                 segment from beginning of
                                 file */
  unsigned long bss_end;      /* Offset of end of bss segment
                                 from beginning of file */
```

```
/*
 * It is assumed that data_end through bss_end forms the
 * bss segment.
 */

  unsigned long stack_size;   /* Size of stack, in bytes */
  unsigned long reloc_start;  /* Offset of relocation
                                 records from beginning of
                                 file */
  unsigned long reloc_count;  /* Number of relocation
                                 records */
  unsigned long flags;
  unsigned long filler[6];    /* Reserved, set to zero */
};
```

The magic string in any bFLT file is the 4-byte ASCII sequence 'b','f','l','t' or 0x62, 0x46, 0x4C, 0x54. rev identifies the version number of the file. Entry indicates the start offset of the text segment from the beginning of the file. This is generally 0x40 (64), the size of this header. Immediately following the text is the data segment and the size of the data segment is stored in data_start and data_end. The bss segment starts at data_end and runs through bss_end. The bFLT header stores the stack size allocated for the application in the stack_size.[10] Later we show why we need to specify stack size.

The fields reloc_start and reloc_count provide information about the relocation start offset and the number of relocation entries. Recall that each relocation entry is a pointer to an absolute address that needs to be patched. The new address for an entry is calculated by adding the base address of the relevant segment to the absolute address pointed by an entry.

The kernel bFLT file loader is implemented in the file linux/fs/binfmt_flat.c. The core function is load_flat_binary. This function is responsible for the loading and execution of a bFLT file on a uClinux system. The function reads the header and allocates necessary memory. Based on the entries in the flags field, the amount of memory allocated for a PIC binary will be the size of stack and data (including GOT). If it is a non-PIC binary then it is the size of stack, data (including relocation table), and text. It also maps in the necessary text segments and marks the pages executable. The file format also allows for a gzip compressed text section, which is indicated using the flags field. In this case the loader takes care of decompressing the text sections in RAM as well. Once all the sections are mapped in, we are ready for the relocations. Figure 10.2 shows the sections of a bFLT file and Figure 10.3 shows the flat file when loaded in memory. Note that the stack falling into bss will result in a system crash as there is no fault handler.

10.2.4 Loading a bFLT File

The flat file format loading is handled in the function load_flat_file. The steps in the load procedure are as follows.

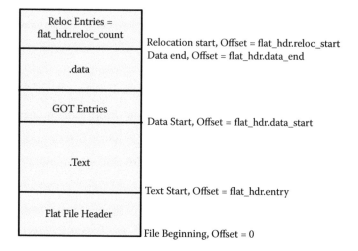

Figure 10.2   bFLT file sections.

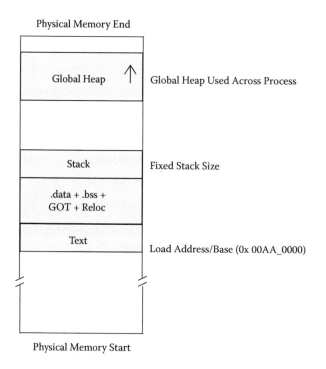

Figure 10.3   bFLT file loaded in memory.

1. First the function reads in various fields of the header and calculates the required memory and type of loading required.

```
text_len   = ntohl(hdr->data_start);
data_len   = ntohl(hdr->data_end) - ntohl(hdr->data_start);
bss_len    = ntohl(hdr->bss_end) - ntohl(hdr->data_end);
stack_len  = ntohl(hdr->stack_size);
```

```
   if (extra_stack) {
     stack_len += *extra_stack;
     *extra_stack = stack_len;
   }
   relocs     = ntohl(hdr->reloc_count);
   flags      = ntohl(hdr->flags);
   rev        = ntohl(hdr->rev);


      ...
      ...
   /*
    * calculate the extra space we need to map in
    */
   extra = max(bss_len + stack_len, relocs *
                        sizeof(unsigned long));
```

2. The loader then maps sections of the file into RAM or from the flash based on flags set in the file header. For instance, if the file has compressed data or text sections, then the loader needs to read the file into memory and decompress those sections first. Listing 10.1 indicates each logical step in this process.

3. The loader sets up the process task structure with details about location of stack, data, and text.

```
current->mm->start_code = start_code;
current->mm->end_code = end_code;
current->mm->start_data = datapos;
current->mm->end_data = datapos + data_len;
```

4. Finally it performs relocations as shown in Listing 10.2.

The check for the presence of GOT is made using the `flags` variable set up earlier from the bFLT file header. Also note that `datapos` is the start of the GOT table offset after mapping the file into memory. Now the loader needs to patch every entry present in the GOT. The `calc_reloc` function does the necessary address patching as shown in the following snippet.

```
static unsigned long
calc_reloc(unsigned long r, struct lib_info *p, int curid,
          int internalp)
{
    ...
    ...
  if (r < text_len)     /* In text segment */
    addr = r + start_code;
  else                  /* In data segment */
    addr = r - text_len + start_data;

  return addr;
}
```

The calculation is simple. If the address to be relocated is within the text segment then the start address of the text segment is added to it. Otherwise

Listing 10.1   bFLT Loader

```
...
if ((flags & (FLAT_FLAG_RAM|FLAT_FLAG_GZIP)) == 0) {
  ...

/*
 * ROM Mapping case: Map from the file for XIP
 */
textpos = do_mmap(bprm->file, 0, text_len, PROT_READ|PROT_EXEC,
                                              0, 0);

  ...

/*
 * Allocate memory for data, stack and relocation sections. Note
 * that this is done for Shared libraries also
 */
realdatastart = do_mmap(0, 0, data_len + extra +
                    MAX_SHARED_LIBS * sizeof(unsigned long),
                        PROT_READ|PROT_WRITE|PROT_EXEC, 0, 0);

  ...
  ...

/*
 * Read .data section from file in to memory, decompress if
 * necessary
 */
#ifdef CONFIG_BINFMT_ZFLAT
if (flags & FLAT_FLAG_GZDATA) {
  result = decompress_exec(bprm, fpos, (char *) datapos,
                data_len + (relocs * sizeof(unsigned long)), 0);
}else
#endif
{
result = bprm->file->f_op->read(bprm->file, (char *) datapos,
              data_len + (relocs * sizeof(unsigned long)), &fpos);
}

  ...
  ...
} else {
/*
 * RAM Mapping case: Allocate memory for all (text, data, stack,
 * reloc)
 */
textpos = do_mmap(0, 0, text_len + data_len + extra +
                    MAX_SHARED_LIBS * sizeof(unsigned long),
     PROT_READ | PROT_EXEC | PROT_WRITE, 0, 0);
  ...
  ...

/*
 * Read .text, .data sections from file in to RAM, decompress if
 * necessary
```

Listing 10.1   bFLT Loader (continued)

```
*/
if (flags & FLAT_FLAG_GZIP) {
  result = decompress_exec(bprm, sizeof (struct flat_hdr),
            (((char *) textpos) + sizeof (struct flat_hdr)),
            (text_len + data_len + (relocs * sizeof(unsigned long))
            - sizeof (struct flat_hdr)), 0);

  ...


result = bprm->file->f_op->read(bprm->file, (char *) textpos,
                                text_len, &fpos);

  ...
```

the address is in the data segment and hence relocation is done based on the
start address of the data segment. After fixing up the GOT entries, the relocation
table entries are run through and fixed up using the `calc_reloc` function.
We take an example to understand the finer details of relocation.

FRB Case

Write a sample.c file with just an empty main function.

```
Sample.c
main {}
```

Compile and create a flat file. Refer to Section 10.7.1 on how to compile
FRB files with the correct compiler options. Let the output file be `sample`
and the symbol file be `symbol.gdb`. The flat file header is dumped using
the `flthdr` program.

```
#flthdr sample
  Magic:       bFLT
  Rev:         4
  Entry:       0x48
  Data Start:  0x220
  Data End:    0x280
  BSS End:     0x290
  Stack Size:  0x1000
  Reloc Start: 0x280
  Reloc Count: 0x1c
  Flags:       0x1 ( Load-to-Ram )
```

The output can be directly related to the bFLT header described previously.
Because this is a relocatable binary, note the `Load-to-RAM` flag set in the
header. Also `Reloc Count` is 0x1C; that is, 28 relocation entries for a dummy
main file have been created. To solve the mystery let's look at the symbol
file `symbol.gdb`.

Listing 10.2   Relocations Done by Loader

```
/* Check for GOT and do relocations in GOT */

if (flags & FLAT_FLAG_GOTPIC) {
   for (rp = (unsigned long *)datapos; *rp != 0xffffffff; rp++) {
      unsigned long addr;
      if (*rp) {
         addr = calc_reloc(*rp, libinfo, id, 0);
         if (addr == RELOC_FAILED)
            return -ENOEXEC;
         *rp = addr;
      }
   }
}


/* Run through relocation entries and patch them as well */

for (i=0; i < relocs; i++) {
   unsigned long addr, relval;

   /* Get the address of the pointer to be relocated (of course,
    * the address has to be relocated first).
    */
   relval = ntohl(reloc[i]);
   addr = flat_get_relocate_addr(relval);
   rp = (unsigned long *) calc_reloc(addr, libinfo, id, 1);

         …
         …

   /* Get the pointer's value.   */
   addr = flat_get_addr_from_rp(rp, relval, flags);
   if (addr != 0) {
      /*
       * Do the relocation.   PIC relocs in the data section are
       * already in target order
       */
      if ((flags & FLAT_FLAG_GOTPIC) == 0)
         addr = ntohl(addr);

      addr = calc_reloc(addr, libinfo, id, 0);

         …
         …

   /* Write back the relocated pointer.   */
   flat_put_addr_at_rp(rp, addr, relval);
}
```

```
# nm sample.gdb
  00000004 T _stext
  00000008 T _start
  00000014 T __exit
  0000001a t empty_func
```

```
0000001a W atexit
0000001c T main
00000028 T __uClibc_init
0000004a T __uClibc_start_main
000000ba T __uClibc_main
000000d0 T exit
   ...
   ...

00000214 D _errno
00000214 V errno
00000218 D _h_errno
00000218 V h_errno
0000021c d p.3
   ...
   ...
00000240 B __bss_start
00000240 b initialized.10
00000240 B _sbss
00000240 D _edata
00000250 B _ebss
00000250 B end
```

The listing shows the various symbols in the file. As any application needs to link with libc, so in the symbol dump all the symbols except the `0x1c T main()` are from the libc, in this case uClibc. The libc data and text have relocation points in them indicated by the relocation table: 28 reloc entries.

Now add code to the `sample.c` file.

```
Sample.c

int x=0xdeadbeef;
int *y=&x;

main () {
  *y++;
}
```

Once again compile and dump the file header.

```
#flthdr sample

  Magic:        bFLT
  Rev:          4
  Entry:        0x48
  Data Start:   0x220
  Data End:     0x280
  BSS End:      0x290
  Stack Size:   0x1000
  Reloc Start:  0x280
  Reloc Count:  0x1f
  Flags:        0x1 ( Load-to-Ram )
```

Note the increase in relocation count from 0x1c to 0x1f; two additional relocation entries are created. In the new `sample.c` the reference to the address of variable x in y creates a relocation entry in the data section. Also the increment to the contents of y creates a relocation entry in the text section.

Using nm on `sample.gdb` we get addresses of x and y as follows.

```
...
00000200 D x
00000204 D y
...
```

The relocation table entry for y is added. The table has entry 204 that needs to be relocated. Also the address pointed to by 204 (i.e., 200) should be relocated. This is what is achieved in Listing 10.2. Following is a simpler interpretation of the relocation code.

Do a dump of the `sample` using `od`. We dump only the relocation table here starting at byte offset 280 as specified by the flat header.

```
#od -Ax -x sample -j280

   000280 0000 1e00 0000 2400 0000 2c00 0000 3600
   000290 0000 4000 0000 4600 0000 6400 0000 6c00
   0002a0 0000 7600 0000 7e00 0000 8c00 0000 9e00
      ...
```

Now note the second nonzero entry 0x2400. The steps involved in relocations are:

- Step 1:

```
relval = ntohl(reloc[i]);
addr = relval;
```

0x2400 has to be converted to host byte order and it is 0x0024.

- Step 2:

```
rp = (unsigned long *) calc_reloc(addr, libinfo, id, 1);
```

This means entry 0x0024 has to be relocated. calc_reloc will return the relocated address at runtime based on the start address of text (because 0x24 < text_len).

- Step 3:

```
addr = *rp;
```

The content of (start_of_text + 0x0024) for the sample file is actually the address of y 0x204, which has to be relocated.

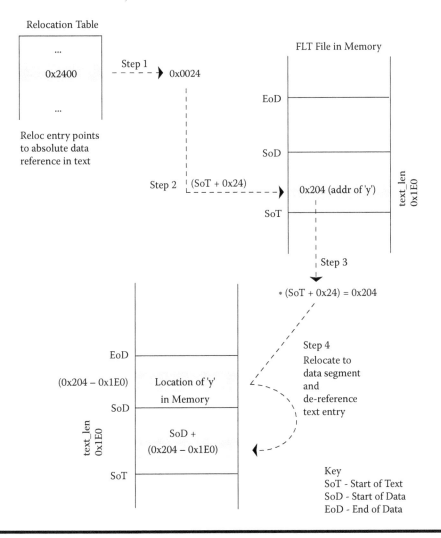

Figure 10.4   Flat file relocation.

- Step 4:

```
addr = calc_reloc(addr, libinfo, id, 0);
*rp=addr;
```

`calc_reloc` for 0x204 and write the actual entry in memory.

To summarize, Figure 10.4 shows the various steps involved in relocation. A similar entry will be created for the text reference also.

PIC Case

Again take a `sample.c` file with just empty `main`.

```
Sample.c
main {}
```

Compile the program with PIC enabled and examine the code generated.

```
#flthdr sample
```

```
  Magic:          bFLT
  Rev:            4
  Entry:          0x48
  Data Start:     0x220
  Data End:       0x2e0
  BSS End:        0x2f0
  Stack Size:     0x1000
  Reloc Start:    0x2e0
  Reloc Count:    0x2
  Flags:          0x2 ( Has-PIC-GOT )
```

Note that there are only two relocation entries and the `flags` field indicates the presence of GOT. Recall that GOT is present at the beginning of the data section with the last entry indicated by −1. We use `od` to examine the bits of the flat file to see the presence of GOT.

```
#od -Ax -x sample

  000000 4662 544c 0000 0400 0000 4800 0000 2002
  000010 0000 e002 0000 f002 0000 0010 0000 e002
  000020 0000 0200 0000 0200 1342 678b 0000 0000
     ...
     ...
  000220 0000 0000 0000 0000 0000 0000 0000 6802
  000230 0000 7c02 0000 a002 0000 aa01 0000 7402
  000240 0000 6002 0000 6c02 0000 7002 0000 2001
  000250 0000 8802 0000 6402 0000 2800 0000 1c00
  000260 0000 0000 0000 0000 0000 0000 0000 c800
  000270 0000 0000 0000 0001 0000 4400 0000 0000
  000280 ffff ffff 0000 0000 0000 0000 0000 0000
  000290 0000 0000 0000 0000 0000 0000 0000 0000
     ...
```

Note the beginning of GOT at 0x220 as indicated by `Data Start: 0x220` and the end of GOT at 0x280 by a value 0xFFFFFFFF, a total of 16 valid (nonzero) GOT entries. All these GOT entries are for standard libc symbols.

Now we add our lines back in `sample.c`, compile, and dump the flat header.

```
Sample.c

int x=0xdeadbeef;
int *y=&x;

main () {
  *y++;
```

```
}

#flthdr sample
   Magic:        bFLT
   Rev:          4
   Entry:        0x48
   Data Start:   0x220
   Data End:     0x2e0
   BSS End:      0x2f0
   Stack Size:   0x1000
   Reloc Start:  0x2e0
   Reloc Count:  0x3
   Flags:        0x2 ( Has-PIC-GOT )
```

We immediately notice the increase in `Reloc` count by 1. This relocation is for the x address in y. The reference of y in the text has created a GOT entry as expected. We take the od dump of `sample`.

```
000220 0000 0000 0000 0000 0000 0000 0000 7002
000230 0000 8402 0000 a002 0000 b601 0000 7c02
000240 0000 6802 0000 7402 0000 7802 0000 2c01
000250 0000 9002 0000 6c02 0000 3400 0000 1c00
000260 0000 6402 0000 0000 0000 0000 0000 0000
000270 0000 d400 0000 0000 0000 0c01 0000 5000
000280 ffff ffff 0000 0000 0000 0000 0000 0000
```

We have a total of 17 GOT entries, that is, one extra entry. We need to identify the one GOT entry that corresponds to y. Do `nm sample.gdb` and spot the variables as before.

```
   ...
00000260 D x
00000264 D y
   ...
```

The bold entry in the GOT table above shows the entry for y.

The loader in Listing 10.2 checks for the GOT flag and relocates the GOT entries first and then proceeds to fix the relocation entries. Figure 10.5 shows how the GOT entry gets relocated.

We sum up our discussion for this section.

- uClinux uses bFLT (Binary FLAT) file format.
- bFLT is either FRB or PIC.
- FRB has absolute references to both data and text, relocation entry points to locations that need to be fixed by the loader.
- PIC employs relative text addressing and hence requires platform support. Data references in text are done using GOT. GOT has data pointers that are fixed up by the loader.
- XIP provides for running files from flash, thus saving on the text space otherwise occupied in RAM.

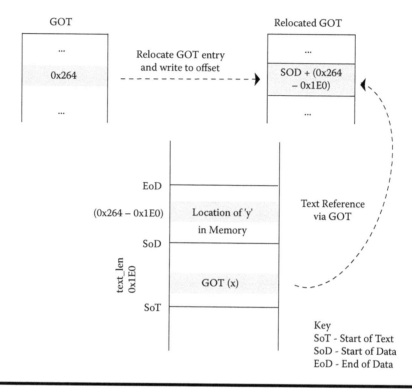

Figure 10.5   GOT entry relocation.

10.3 Memory Management

In this section we understand the changes done in the kernel and libc with respect to memory management in uClinux. We divide our discussions based on the two memory sections, heap and stack.

10.3.1 Heap

Memory Allocation

`malloc`, `realloc`, `calloc`, and `free` are the library calls used for heap allocation/deallocation. The base function is `malloc` and we need to understand how `malloc` works in standard Linux and why it cannot be used in uClinux.

The `malloc` provides for dynamic heap allocation in a process. It essentially uses the low-level system calls `sbrk()`/`brk()` to manage the size of process address space. `sbrk()` adds memory to the end of the process address space thus increasing the size. `brk()` on the other hand can set an arbitrary size to the process space. These are effectively used by the `malloc/free` library calls to allocate/deallocate memory for the application, respectively. Process space on standard Linux is virtual address space and hence adding more memory is simply done by tweaking the virtual memory structures in the kernel, which provides the necessary mapping to the physical address. So

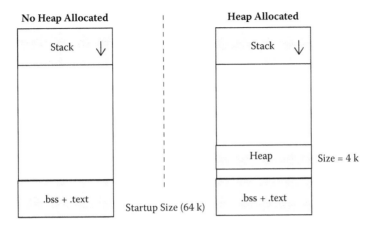

Figure 10.6   Heap allocation.

malloc simply increases the VM size and free reduces the VM size as necessary. For example, consider an application of size 64 K (including bss size) with an initial heap size of 0. This uses up 0 to 64 K in virtual memory (total VM size = 64 K + stack size) as shown in Figure 10.6.

Now, let us assume the application calls malloc(4096). This would increase the VM size to 68 K as shown in Figure 10.6. The actual physical memory gets allocated only at the actual usage time in the page fault handler.

In uClinux without VM it is not possible to add or alter the limits of the process address space. Hence we are forced to provide alternate solutions. The alternate solution should allow for very little or no change while porting an application to uClinux. So simple ones such as no heap available on uClinux, preallocating all required memory using static arrays, providing fixed size heap, and so on, are all ruled out. These will require huge porting efforts and even redesigning a majority of the applications, which is not desirable.

The solution in uClinux is provided by using a systemwide pool of free memory for heap allocation across all processes. Because all processes allocate from the same pool, a single process can allocate all the available memory and result in a systemwide memory crunch. This a system-level disadvantage on any MMU-less design.

The simplest malloc implementation uses direct calls to mmap() / munmap(). All memory required is requested directly using the kernel memory allocator. The implementation is given below.

■ Call mmap() system call to obtain memory from the kernel memory pool.

```
void * malloc(size_t size) {
    ...
    result = mmap((void *) 0, size, PROT_READ | PROT_WRITE,
                     MAP_SHARED | MAP_ANONYMOUS, 0, 0);
    if (result == MAP_FAILED)
      return 0;
```

Listing 10.3   uClinux mmap Implementation

```
do_mmap_pgoff() {

   ...
   ...

  if (file) {
    error = file->f_op->mmap(file, &vma);
    if (!error)
      return vma.vm_start;

    ...
  }

   ...

  tblock = (struct mm_tblock_struct *)
            kmalloc(sizeof(struct mm_tblock_struct),GFP_KERNEL);
   ...
   ...
  tblock->rblock = (struct mm_rblock_struct *)
   kmalloc(sizeof(struct mm_rblock_struct), GFP_KERNEL);

   ...
   ...
  result = kmalloc(len, GFP_KERNEL);
   ...
   ...

  /* Reference counting */
  tblock->rblock->refcount = 1;
  tblock->rblock->kblock = result;
  tblock->rblock->size = len;

   ...
   ...


  /* Attach block to list of blocks in task struct */
  tblock->next = current->mm->context.tblock.next;
  current->mm->context.tblock.next = tblock;
  current->mm->total_vm += len >> PAGE_SHIFT;

  return (unsigned long)result;

}
```

```
      return(result);
    }
```

- Call `munmap()` to return the used memory.

The problems with this approach become evident from its implementation as shown in Listing 10.3, where mmap is hooked to the kernel memory allocator, kmalloc, to get free memory. The returned memory is maintained in a link-list of pointers for bookkeeping purposes. The bookkeeping is necessary so that the system can keep track of the memory allocated by a particular process and therefore these are linked to the process structure so that it can be freed up when the process exits. The `tblock` and `rblock` data structures amount to 56-byte overhead per allocation. Applications that need small `malloc` chunks will obviously waste memory.

Also `kmalloc` returns memory chunks of a size rounded to the nearest power of 2, limited to a maximum size of 1 MB. For example, an allocation request of 1.5 K (1536) will result in wastage of 0.5 K (512), as the closest power of 2 available is only 2 K (2048). Thus the allocator is very inefficient and limited.

The 56-byte overhead can be reduced by making the `malloc` API more intelligent. For example, one can either group allocations or allocate larger chunks and then manage those chunks using smaller data structures. Also the problem has been addressed in the 2.6 kernel and the `rblock` and `tblock` structures have been removed. The second problem needs a rewrite of the kernel memory allocation scheme. A modified kernel allocation method is available in the uClinux kernel. This helps reduce the overhead in memory allocations. The new `kmalloc` uses power-of-2 allocation for memory requests up to 1 page size (e.g., 4 KB or 4096 bytes) and for sizes above 1 page, it rounds to the nearest page boundary. For example, consider allocating 100 K using standard `kmalloc`. This will result in an allocation of 128 K and wastage of 28 K. But using the new `kmalloc`, it is possible to allocate an exact 100 K.

uClibc provides three different `malloc` implementations. We list each of their advantages and disadvantages.

- `malloc-simple [uClinux-dist\uClibc\libc\stdlib\malloc-simple]`:

```
malloc(size_t size) {
    …
    …
    result = mmap((void *) 0, size, PROT_READ | PROT_WRITE,
                    MAP_SHARED | MAP_ANONYMOUS, -1, 0);

    if (result == MAP_FAILED)
      return 0;
    return(result);
}
```

  This is the simplest form of `malloc` used in uClinux. It is simple one-line implementation with fast and direct allocations. The disadvantage is the 56-byte overhead, which is evident when used by applications that require a large number of small-size mallocs.
- `malloc [uClinux-dist\uClibc\libc\stdlib\malloc]`: In this implementation, `malloc` has an internal heap allocated in the static area. The function `malloc_from_heap()`, based on the requested size, decides whether to allocate from this static area or to fall back on `mmap`. In this approach small-size requests do not have allocation overhead issues as allocations happen from the internal heap. The implementation is shown in Listing 10.4.

Listing 10.4   uClibc malloc Implementation Using Heap

```
HEAP_DECLARE_STATIC_FREE_AREA (initial_fa, 256);
struct heap __malloc_heap = HEAP_INIT_WITH_FA (initial_fa);

void * malloc(size_t size) {
    ...
    ...
  mem = malloc_from_heap (size, &__malloc_heap);
  if (unlikely (!mem))
  {
  oom:
    __set_errno (ENOMEM);
    return 0;
  }
  return mem;
}

static void *
malloc_from_heap (size_t size, struct heap *heap){

/* First try to allocate from internal heap area */
  __heap_lock (heap);

  mem = __heap_alloc (heap, &size);

  __heap_unlock (heap);

  /* on failure call mmap */
  if (unlikely (! mem)) {
    /* We couldn't allocate from the heap, */
    block = mmap (0, block_size, PROT_READ | PROT_WRITE,
                  MAP_SHARED | MAP_ANONYMOUS, 0, 0);
  }

}
```

- `malloc-standard [uClinux-dist\uClibc\libc\stdlib\`
  `malloc-standard]`: This is the most complex of all `malloc` implementations and is used in the standard libc call. Essentially, the `malloc` library
  maintains small-size allocations internal to itself by using bins of various
  sizes. If an allocation request falls in a particular bin size, then a bin is
  removed from the free list and marked as used (until it is freed or the
  application exits). If the allocation request size is larger than the available
  bin size or if all bins are used up, then the library calls `mmap` provided
  the allocation size is greater than a threshold size. This threshold size is
  adjusted so that the allocation overhead due to `mmap` is minimized. Otherwise `brk` is used to increase the process heap size and on failure, it
  finally falls back on `mmap`. In this approach very efficiently managed bins
  reduce the allocation overhead added by `mmap` but this solution is available
  only on MMU-based systems.

Memory Fragmentation

The amount of free memory available does not guarantee the same amount of allocatable memory. For example, if a system has 100 K free memory, it does not necessarily mean that a `malloc(100K)` will be successful. This arises due to a problem called *memory fragmentation*. The available memory may not be contiguous and hence the allocation request cannot be met. The systems allocation process begins only at a page boundary. A free page is requested from the available free list and added to the used list. Any subsequent memory request that fits inside the remaining space is given away from the same page. And once a page is marked as used it can be returned to the system free list only when all allocations using the page have been freed.

For example, let us assume a program allocated 16, 256-byte allocations. Assuming zero overhead in the allocation scheme, this matches a single page size; in our case 4 K = 16*256. Now unless and until the application frees all 16 pointers, the page that is used cannot be freed. Thus there might be a situation when there is enough memory available on the system, but still not sufficient to service the current allocation.

Defragmenting Memory

In standard Linux, all user-space applications use virtual addresses. Defragmenting memory is simpler in the sense that one has to alter the process' virtual mappings to point to new physical locations. Even if the actual physical memory location has changed, programs still use the virtual address and are able to run seamlessly even after the relocation. This becomes impossible without VM.

There is no solution for defragmentation on uClinux and developers need to be aware of the situation and avoid it by altering memory allocation patterns of the applications.

10.3.2 Stack

The program stack on standard Linux systems grows on demand. This is made possible by an intelligent page fault handler. The stack grows downwards from the top of the user-space data segment. The growing stack is only limited by the program's own growing heap that grows in the opposite direction starting from the end of bss.

On MMU-less systems there is no way to implement a page fault handler and hence on-demand stack growth is not possible. The only solution uClinux offers here is fixed stack size. This stack size is specified at the time of compilation and stored as a part of the application's executable image.

As seen in the previous section, the bFLT header has an entry called `stack_size` to store the amount of stack to be reserved by the loader at program start-up. For now it is with the developers to make a good guess of the maximum stack size for a required program and make it available at the time of binary image creation.

10.4 File / Memory Mapping—The Intricacies of `mmap()` in uClinux

Memory regions in Linux are mapped into the process address space using the `mmap()` system call. The mapped region is controlled using protection flags such as `PROT_READ` and `PROT_WRITE` and the usability specified either private or shared mapping using `MAP_PRIVATE` and `MAP_SHARED` flags. For example, the loader maps text regions of a shared library as read-only, shared (`PROT_READ` and `MAP_SHARED`) regions in the application's process space.

`mmap()` internally fills up VM data structures that describe the property of each region mapped and leaves the rest to the page fault handler. Using the fault condition and the flags in the VM data structures the page fault handler does the necessary action. For example, it might allocate fresh pages if it finds the region valid and page entries missing. Or it might choose to expand the region if the region is marked expandable (such as stack).

In uClinux, without the page fault handler the `mmap` functionality provided is very primitive. The following two forms of `mmap` cannot be implemented due to lack of MMU. We discuss the reason briefly here.

- `mmap(MAP_PRIVATE, PROT_WRITE)` is not implemented. This type of mapping creates a writable mapping of the file in the process virtual address area. This means that pages have to be allocated at the time of write and maintained per process, and the process alone (private) sees the changes. The page fault handler takes care of allocation of pages as and when written by the process and thus only those pages of the file modified by the process are allocated.

- `mmap(MAP_SHARED, PROT_WRITE, file)` is not implemented. Standard implementation in Linux for this type of `mmap` call creates shared memory pages across processes and writes to the area will get synced onto the disk. Pages mapped as above trigger a page fault the first time the page is written to and are marked as dirty. Later the kernel writes dirty pages to disk and marks them ready for the next fault handling in case of a later write.

Both the above require a working page fault handler, available only on MMU hardware. Hence in uClinux this cannot be implemented. In uClinux, the implementation of `mmap` is the `do_mmap_pgoff()` function in the kernel. `do_mmap_pgoff()` for the MMU-less case does the following.

1. Checks validity of protection and map flags for the cases that are not implemented.

```
...
if ((flags & MAP_SHARED) && (prot & PROT_WRITE) && (file)) {
  printk("MAP_SHARED not supported (cannot write mappings
         to disk)\n");
  return -EINVAL;
```

```
}
if ((prot & PROT_WRITE) && (flags & MAP_PRIVATE)) {
  printk("Private writable mappings not supported\n");
  return -EINVAL;
}
...
```

2. If a file pointer is provided and if the file operations of the file support the mmap function, then the file specific mmap is called.

```
...
if (file &&  file->f_ops->mmap)
  file->f_ops->mmap(file, &vma);
return vma.vm_start;
...
```

3. If no file pointer is provided then it allocates the requested memory from the kernel memory allocator using kmalloc.

```
...
...
result = kmalloc(len, GFP_KERNEL);
...
...
```

10.5 Process Creation

Process creation in Linux is done using the fork() system call. fork() creates a new child process for the caller. Once fork returns, the parent and child are two independent entities having individual PIDs. Theoretically what fork() needs to do is to create an exact replica of all the parent process data structures including memory pages private to the parent process. In Linux this duplication of the parent's memory pages is postponed. Instead the parent and child share the same pages in memory until one of the two attempts to modify the shared pages. This approach is called COW (Copy on Write). Now let us see how fork() achieves this. We discuss the Linux 2.6 implementation of fork. In Linux 2.4 the APIs called are different but the functionality is still the same.

1. Allocate a new process task structure for the child.

```
p = dup_task_struct(current);
```

This will create a new task structure, and copy some pointers from current.

2. Get a PID for the child process.

```
p->pid = alloc_pidmap();
```

3. Copy file descriptors, signal handlers, scheduling policies, and so on from
   the parent to the child process.

```
/* copy all the process information */
    ...
    ...
// Copy file descriptors
if ((retval = copy_files(clone_flags, p)))
  goto bad_fork_cleanup_semundo;
if ((retval = copy_fs(clone_flags, p)))
  goto bad_fork_cleanup_files;

// Copy signal handlers
if ((retval = copy_sighand(clone_flags, p)))
  goto bad_fork_cleanup_fs;

// Copy signal information
if ((retval = copy_signal(clone_flags, p)))
  goto bad_fork_cleanup_sighand;

// Copy memory pages
if ((retval = copy_mm(clone_flags, p)))
  goto bad_fork_cleanup_signal;
    ...
    ...
```

4. Add the child to the scheduler's queue and return.

```
    ...
    ...
/* Perform scheduler-related setup */
sched_fork(p);
    ...
    ...

if (!(clone_flags & CLONE_STOPPED))
  wake_up_new_task(p, clone_flags);
else
  p->state = TASK_STOPPED;
    ...
    ...
```

This will change the process state to TASK_RUNNING and insert the process
into the runnable process list maintained in the scheduler.

Once fork returns, the child process is a runnable process and will be
scheduled as per the scheduling policy of the parent. Note that only the data
structures of a parent are copied in the fork. Its text, data, and stack segments
are not copied. fork has marked those pages COW for later on-demand
allocation.

In step 3 the copy_mm() function essentially marks pages of the parent
as shared read-only between the parent and the child. The read-only attribute
ensures that the memory contents cannot be modified as long as they are

shared. Whenever either of the two processes attempts to write into this page, the page fault handler identifies a COW page using a special check of the page descriptors. The page corresponding to the fault is duplicated and marked writable in the process that attempted the write. The original page remains write protected until the other process attempts a write, during which this page is marked writable only after making sure that it is no longer shared with any other process.

As seen above, process duplication in Linux done via COW is implemented using the page fault handler and hence uClinux does not support `fork()`. Also it is not possible for parent and child to have a similar virtual address space as expected from `fork`. Instead of using `fork()` to create a child process, uClinux developers suggest the usage of `vfork()` along with `exec()`. The `vfork()` system call creates a child process and blocks execution of the parent process until the child exits or executes a new program. This will ensure that the parent and child need not share memory pages.

10.6 Shared Libraries

The dynamic linker that takes care of shared library loading is extensively based on MMU and virtual addressing. A shared library gets loaded in RAM when an application uses it for the first time. Other programs using the same library that start later (but before the first app exits) get the text location mapped into their virtual address spaces. In other words only one copy of the library text is present in physical memory. All future references are just virtual entries that point to this single physical copy. Also note that only text is shared; data still needs to be allocated per process. The shared pages are freed when the last application using the library exits.

Without MMU it is not possible to map the same physical memory into individual process address space. Hence uClinux employs a different method to implement shared libraries.

10.6.1 uClinux Shared Library Implementation (libN.so)

As we have already seen, uClinux uses the bFLT format for executables. The uClinux kernel loader does the job of loading the application into the available memory location by setting up necessary data and code sections. Also recall that if the bFLT file being loaded has XIP capabilities then the kernel loader will reuse the text segment across multiple instances of the application, and set up individual data sections for respective instances. This XIP support is used as the base for implementing a shared library in uClinux. If text is not XIPable then shared libraries can't work. This is because shared text pages cannot exist in memory without support from MMU. Hence the idea is to store them in a common place (flash) and all programs access directly from the same location.

There are a few different types of shared library implementations on uClinux. We discuss the m68k implementation of shared libraries that uses bFLT files, popularly known as the libN.so method. In this method, shared libraries are binary bFLT files, but those that contain a specific library ID in them. This requires changes in the compiler as well as the loader. Each symbol referenced in an executable has the specific library ID added to it. When the loader has to resolve a symbol, it looks up the reference using the ID contained in the symbol and thus identifies the required library. For making the lookup simple, shared library names follow a particular pattern. A library that has ID=X, has the name `libX.so`. Hence the loader simply loads the file `/lib/libX.so` when it has to resolve a symbol with ID=X in it.

The compiler generates a separate GOT and data segment for the application and for each library. When the program is loaded it is ensured that the individual data segments (of the shared libraries) are available at fixed offsets from the base. The unique identification number allotted per library is used to determine the offset to locate a particular data segment. The application also has to use the same referencing method using an id, and the id value 0 is reserved for the application.

The shared library support in the kernel is component selectable using the flag `CONFIG_BINFMT_SHARED_FLAT`. The primary structure to support shared library support in uClinux is the following `lib_info` structure.

```
struct lib_info {
  struct {
    unsigned long start_code;   /* Start of text segment */
    unsigned long start_data;   /* Start of data segment */
    unsigned long start_brk;    /* End of data segment */
    unsigned long text_len;     /* Length of text segment */
    unsigned long entry;        /* Start address for this
                                   module */
    unsigned long build_date;   /* When this one was
                                   compiled */
    short loaded;               /* Has this library been
                                   loaded? */
  } lib_list[MAX_SHARED_LIBS];
};
```

The macro `MAX_SHARED_LIBS` is defined to 4 if `CONFIG_BINFMT_SHARED_FLAT` is set or else it defaults to value 1. This structure is used to hold the list of the libraries loaded per application. Though the theoretical limit for the maximum number of libraries is 255 − 1, the kernel defines it at 4, enabling the use of 3 shared libraries per application. The ID at value 0 is used to refer to the application being loaded. The symbol resolution of an application using a shared library is done from within the `calc_reloc` function shown in Listing 10.5.

Note the extraction of id from the value to be relocated r, using id = (r >> 24) & 0xff. Modifications in the linker enable the padding of the id value into the high byte of the symbol address. For example, if a symbol foo

Listing 10.5   Shared Library Symbol Resolution

```
static unsigned long
calc_reloc(unsigned long r, struct lib_info *p, int curid,
           int internalp)
{
    …
    …


#ifdef CONFIG_BINFMT_SHARED_FLAT
  if (r == 0)
     id = curid;        /* Relocs of 0 are always self referring */
  else {
     id = (r >> 24) & 0xff;   /* Find ID for this reloc */
     r &= 0x00ffffff;         /* Trim ID off here */
  }

  if (id >= MAX_SHARED_LIBS) {
     printk("BINFMT_FLAT: reference 0x%x to shared library %d",
                                              (unsigned) r, id);
     goto failed;
  }

  if (curid != id) {
     …
     …
  }else if ( ! p->lib_list[id].loaded &&
        load_flat_shared_library(id, p) > (unsigned long) -4096) {
     printk("BINFMT_FLAT: failed to load library %d", id);
     goto failed;
  }
     …
     …
#else
        id = 0;
#endif
     …
     …
}
```

is undefined in the application, but defined in the library with ID=3, then
that particular symbol in the application will have an entry of the form
0x03XX_XXXX = (0x03FF_FFFF | address of foo() in lib3.so). Thus all
symbols external to the application will have the id corresponding to the
library in its high byte.

The actual loading of the library into program memory takes place inside
the function load_flat_shared_library. This function loads the file /
lib/libX.so using the regular binary flat file loader function
load_flat_file by passing the corresponding id=X[11] value. The binary flat
file loader maintains the lib_info.lib_list[] array to track all files being
loaded, including the application that is loaded at location 0. The loader
ensures that all unresolved/external symbols required for execution are made
available.

The above-explained implementation is the one that is most widely used in m68k-based processors and was contributed by Paul Dale. There are other implementations of shared library available in uClinux. XFLAT from Cadenux is another shared library implementation used widely on ARM processors. FRV-uClinux also has an implementation of shared library. Each implementation has been done with different design goals, addressing variant concerns.

10.7 Porting Applications to uClinux

In this section we discuss the steps necessary to create uClinux programs and shared libraries and what points should be considered before porting an application from standard Linux to uClinux.

10.7.1 Creating uClinux Programs

uClinux executables are in binary flat file format. The regular ELF file is not supported on uClinux. The uClinux toolchain provides a special tool to convert an ELF file to a bFLT file. Not all ELF files can be converted into BFLT. For this the code generated has to be position independent. uClinux has two variants of position-independent binaries: the fully relocatable binaries and the PIC binaries. A list of compiler commands for creating different forms of the bFLT file using the m68k toolchain is listed below.

Creating Fully Relocatable Binaries

- Compile the file. This will create `sample.o`.

```
m68k-elf-gcc -m68000 -Os -g -fomit-frame-pointer -m68000
-fno-common -Wall   -Dlinux -D__linux__ -Dunix
-D__uClinux__ -DEMBED -nostdinc
-I/home/sriramn/work/uclinux/uClinux-dist/include
-I/home/sriramn/work/uclinux/uClinux-dist/include/include
-fno-builtin -c -o sample.o sample.c
```

- Link and create `flt` file. This step will create executable `sample` and symbol file `sample.gdb`.

```
m68k-elf-gcc -m68000 -Os -g -fomit-frame-pointer -m68000
-fno-common -Wall   -Dlinux -D__linux__ -Dunix
-D__uClinux__ -DEMBED -nostdinc
-I/home/sriramn/work/uclinux/uClinux-dist/include
-I/home/sriramn/work/uclinux/uClinux-dist/include/include
-fno-builtin -Wl,-elf2flt -Wl,-move-rodata -nostartfiles
/home/sriramn/work/uclinux/uClinux-dist/lib/crt0.o
-L/home/sriramn/work/uclinux/uClinux-dist/lib o sample
 sample.o -lc
```

Creating PIC Binaries

- Compile the file.

```
m68k-elf-gcc -m68000 -Os -g -fomit-frame-pointer -m68000
-fno-common -Wall   -Dlinux -D__linux__ -Dunix
-D__uClinux__ -DEMBED -nostdinc
-I/home/sriramn/work/uclinux/uClinux-dist/include
-I/home/sriramn/work/uclinux/uClinux-dist/include/include
-fno-builtin -msep-data -c -o sample.o sample.c
```

- Link and create flt file.

```
m68k-elf-gcc -m68000 -Os -g -fomit-frame-pointer -m68000
-fno-common -Wall   -Dlinux -D__linux__ -Dunix
-D__uClinux__ -DEMBED -nostdinc
-I/home/sriramn/work/uclinux/uClinux-dist/include
-I/home/sriramn/work/uclinux/uClinux-dist/include/include
-fno-builtin -msep-data -Wl,-elf2flt -Wl,-move-rodata
-nostartfiles
/home/sriramn/work/uclinux/uClinux-dist/lib/crt0.o
-L/home/sriramn/work/uclinux/uClinux-dist/lib -o testhw1
 sample.o -lc
```

- Note that –msep-data forces –fPIC internally. And –elf2flt is passed to the linker forcing a conversion from ELF to bFLT format. Also –msep-data enables XIP.
- To alter the stack size of a bFLT file use the command

```
elf2flt -s <stack _size> test.flt
```

- To compress the file (all but the headers) use

```
elft2flt -z -o test.flt test.elf
```

Compressed images are not XIPable as they need to be decompressed in RAM before execution.

10.7.2 Creating Shared Libraries in uClinux

Shared libraries in uClinux are normal bFLT files, created using special compiler flags. The compiler flags help identify the symbol references using a fixed library ID number. The steps required to create and use a shared library are listed below. In this example we use a.c and b.c to create a shared library libtest.

```
File: a.c
void a()
{
```

```
  printf("I am a\n");
}

File: b.c
void b()
{
  printf("I am b\n");
}
```

- Compile the individual files. Note that we use the flag –mid-shared-library.

```
m68k-elf-gcc  -Wall -Wstrict-prototypes -Wno-trigraphs
-fno-strict-aliasing  -Os -g -fomit-frame-pointer
-m68000 -fno-common -Wall -fno-builtin -DEMBED
-mid-shared-library -nostdinc
-I/home/sriramn/work/uclinux/uClinux-dist/include
-I/home/sriramn/work/uclinux/uClinux-dist/include/include
-Dlinux -D__linux__ -D__uClinux__ -Dunix -msoft-float
-fno-builtin a.c -c -o a.o

m68k-elf-gcc  -Wall -Wstrict-prototypes -Wno-trigraphs
-fno-strict-aliasing -Os -g -fomit-frame-pointer -m68000
-fno-common -Wall -fno-builtin -DEMBED -mid-shared-library -
nostdinc -I/home/sriramn/work/uclinux/uClinux-dist/include -
I/home/sriramn/work/uclinux/uClinux-dist/include/include
-Dlinux -D__linux__ -D__uClinux__ -Dunix  -msoft-float
-fno-builtin b.c -c -o b.o
```

- Create the archive.

```
m68k-elf-ar r libtest.a a.o b.o

m68k-elf-ranlib libtest.a
```

- Create the binary flat file library with proper library id (here we use 2, libc has id =1). Note the addition of file uClibc/lib/main.o for a dummy main function and option -shared-lib-id=2.

```
m68k-elf-gcc -nostartfiles -o libtest -Os -g
-fomit-frame-pointer -m68000 -fno-common -Wall
-fno-builtin -DEMBED -mid-shared-library -nostdinc
-I/home/sriramn/work/uclinux/uClinux-dist/include
-I/home/sriramn/work/uclinux/uClinux-dist/include/include
-Dlinux -D__linux__ -D__uClinux__ -Dunix -Wl,-elf2flt
-nostdlib -Wl,-shared-lib-id,2
/home/sriramn/work/uclinux/uClinux-dist/uClibc/lib/main.o
-Wl,-R,/home/sriramn/work/uclinux/uClinux-dist/lib/libc.gdb
-lc -lgcc -Wl,--whole-archive,libtest.a,--no-whole-archive
```

- Remove start-up symbols. As we need to be able to use the library with another application, start-up symbols that get added via C runtime linking such as _main, _start, and the like have to be removed. It is done by using the following command.

```
m68k-elf-objcopy -L _GLOBAL_OFFSET_Table_ -L main -L __main
-L _start -L __uClibc_main -L __uClibc_start_main
-L lib_main -L _exit_dummy_ref
-L __do_global_dtors -L __do_global_ctors
-L __CTOR_LIST__ -L __DTOR_LIST__
-L _current_shared_library_a5_offset_
libtest.gdb
```

■ Install the library in the rootfs under the proper name.

```
cp libtest.gdb romfs/lib/lib2.so
```

Do nm on this symbol file to analyze the symbols created.

```
#nm libtest.gdb | sort
  0100001c A __assert
  01000098 A isalnum
  010000b8 A isalpha
  010000d8 A isascii

     ...

     ...
  010355c4 A __ti19__pointer_type_info
  010355d0 A __ti16__ptmd_type_info
  010355dc A __ti19__builtin_type_info
  020000cc T a
  020000e4 T b
  02000100 D __data_start
  02000100 D data_start
```

Note the presence of 01xxxxxx symbols from libc (lib1.so) and the symbols of our library lib2.so starting with 02xxxxxx.

10.7.3 Using Shared Library in an Application

Now we see how to use the created library with an application. The linker needs to be informed about the external references in the application, so that it can mark them as shared library references in the generated bFLT file. To compile the program we need to do the following two steps.

```
File: use.c

extern void a();
extern void b();

main()
{

  a();
  b();

}
```

- Compile use.c (note shared-library-id=0).

```
m68k-elf-gcc -m68000 -Os -g -fomit-frame-pointer -m68000
-fno-common -Wall   -Dlinux -D__linux__ -Dunix
-D__uClinux__ -DEMBED -nostdinc
-I/home/sriramn/work/uclinux/uClinux-dist/include
-I/home/sriramn/work/uclinux/uClinux-dist/include/include
-fno-builtin -mid-shared-library -mshared-library-id=0 -c
-o use.o use.c
```

- Link use.c with libc and libtest.

```
m68k-elf-gcc -m68000 -Os -g -fomit-frame-pointer -m68000
-fno-common -Wall   -Dlinux -D__linux__ -Dunix
-D__uClinux__ -DEMBED -nostdinc
-I/home/sriramn/work/uclinux/uClinux-dist/include
-I/home/sriramn/work/uclinux/uClinux-dist/include/include
-fno-builtin -mid-shared-library -mshared-library-id=0
-Wl,-elf2flt -Wl,-move-rodata -Wl,-shared-lib-id,0
-nostartfiles
/home/sriramn/work/uclinux/uClinux-dist/lib/crt0.o
-L/home/sriramn/work/uclinux/uClinux-dist/lib -L. -o use
use.o -Wl,-R,
/home/sriramn/work/uclinux/uClinux-dist/lib/libc.gdb -lc
-Wl,-R,libtest.gdb -ltest
```

Again we do an nm on use.gdb to notice the presence of the library.

```
#nm use.gdb | sort
  00000004 T _stext
  00000008 T _start
  00000014 T __exit
  0000001a t empty_func
  0000001c T main
    …
    …
  00000260 B end
  00000260 B _end
  0100001c A __assert
  01000098 A isalnum
  010000b8 A isalpha
  010000d8 A isascii
  010000ec A iscntrl
    …
    …
  010355d0 A __ti16__ptmd_type_info
  010355dc A __ti19__builtin_type_info
  020000cc A a
  020000e4 A b
```

After understanding the steps necessary to create uClinux programs, you should also understand various uClinux limitations before porting applications from standard Linux to uClinux.

10.7.4 Memory Limitations

uClinux does not provide a dynamic stack. Executables have a predefined stack size set at compile time using `elf2flt`. Programmers should avoid huge allocations on the stack. Instead use the heap or if the requirement is not dynamic, move it to the bss section.

C++ programs use `malloc` even for built-in data-type declarations via the new operator. Many C++ applications have had problems running on uClinux. The lack of MMU and a wise `malloc` results in an unsolvable memory fragmentation issue, rendering the system useless. Hence C++ is not recommended on an MMU-less system. Redesign any application that has to allocate small chunks of `malloc` or if possible write application-specific allocation methods that will internally manage a preallocated memory region.

10.7.5 mmap Limitations

uClinux `mmap()` is very primitive in its functionality and programs that depend on the behavior of `mmap()` might fail. So we present here a list of `mmap()` calls that will fail, and those that work along with the limitations if any.

- Write-enabled, shared file mapping is not possible on uClinux.

  `mmap(MAP_SHARED, PROT_WRITE, file)`

- Any write-enabled, private mapping is not supported on uClinux.

  `mmap(MAP_PRIVATE, PROT_WRITE, file or nofile)`

- Unprotected shared mapping on a nonfile descriptor returns the requested size. It is similar to MMU systems, but memory is direct kernel address. `mmap(MAP_SHARED, 0, nofile, size)` allocates `size` memory from the kernel allocator.

10.7.6 Process-Level Limitations

There is no `fork()` call implemented in uClinux. So to make programs (that require `fork()`) work one needs to supplement the call to `fork()` using a call to `vfork()` followed by an `exec()`. The child process should not modify the data of the parent until an `exec()` is called. Listing 10.6 shows a normal Linux program using `fork()` and how it can be ported to uClinux.

10.8 XIP—eXecute In Place

In standard Linux, programs are usually loaded and executed from system memory. The loader loads sections of text from the storage medium (disk or flash) in the memory. More pages get demand paged when required by the page fault handler. In case of uClinux as page fault handling is not possible,

Listing 10.6   Porting Applications to uClinux

```
/* Sample program on standard Linux */

/* fork.c */
#include <stdio.h>
#include <unistd.h>
#include <stdlib.h>
#include <string.h>
#include <sys/types.h>

int main(int argc, char *argv[])
{
  pid_t pid;
  /*
   * When fork returns -1, implies fork failed no child process
   * created pid of child process in parent's thread of execution
   * 0 in child's thread of execution
   */
  if ((pid = fork()) < 0) {
    printf("Fork() failed\n");
    exit(1);
  }else if (pid != 0) {
    /* Parent code */
    printf("Parent exiting.\n");
    exit(0);
  }
  /* Child code */
  printf("Starting child...\n");
  while (1) {
    sleep(2);
    printf("...Child running\n");
  }
}


/* Above application can be ported to uClinux */

/* vfork.c */
#include <stdio.h>
#include <unistd.h>
#include <stdlib.h>
#include <string.h>
#include <sys/types.h>

int main(int argc, char *argv[])
{
  pid_t pid;
  int c_argc = 0;
  char *c_argv[3];
  char child=0;

  /* Indentify child, we use the magic argument argv[1]=child */
  if (argc > 2 && !strcmp(argv[1],"child")) child=1;

  /* use vfork(), return values similar to fork() */
```

Listing 10.6   Porting Applications to uClinux (continued)

```
if (!child) {
    if ((pid = vfork()) < 0) {
        printf("vfork() failed\n");
        exit(1);
    } else if (pid != 0) {
      /* Parent code */
      printf("Parent exiting.\n");
      exit(0);
    }

    /*
     * Invoke the child exec here. We pass the special argument to
     * identify the child
     */
    c_argv[c_argc++] = argv[0];
    c_argv[c_argc++] = "child";
    c_argv[c_argc++] = NULL;
    execv(c_argv[0], c_argv);

    /* Note that if successful, execv never returns */
    printf("execv() failed\n");
    exit(1);

  }else { // Child code
    printf("Starting child...\n");
    while (1) {
      sleep(2);
      printf("...Child running\n");
    }
  }

}
```

the whole of the text section has to be directly read into RAM by the loader. The flat file loader allocates memory for the size of the text along with the stack, data, and relocation table.

In a system tight on memory uClinux provides an alternative, XIP. With XIP it becomes possible to execute code from the storage device without having to load it in the RAM. The loader directly uses a pointer to the storage memory and this saves on the allocation otherwise done for the text section. Note that data and stack still need to be allocated for execution. XIP has some limitations or design requirements. We list those here.

10.8.1 Hardware Requirements

■ *Processor support for PIC:* XIP is possible only if the processor has support for generating position-independent code. It should be able to do PC-relative addressing. This is required to avoid (hard) references to addresses in the text. In the absence of PIC, the generated code will have address offsets from zero and the loader will have to patch the addresses based on the load address and hence will require the load of text to RAM, defying the purpose of XIP.

- *NOR flash only:* There are two types of flash devices, NOR and NAND, both employed widely in embedded systems. NOR flash allows for random read access to all its sectors and is readable just like SRAM. NAND on the other hand requires programming of some control registers to read from its memory. Usually a flash driver is required to read contents from NAND flash. When the program is being executed from flash it means the instruction pointer or program counter is simply incremented to fetch the next instruction pointing to the next word in flash memory. It will not be possible to run driver code to fetch the next instruction. Hence only NOR flash is suitable for XIP.

10.8.2 Software Requirements

- File system support: ROMFS (can't use CRAMFS or JFFS2). The file system used in conjunction with XIP should be raw and cannot be compressed. If the files are compressed, then they need to be decompressed into pages allocated from RAM. Hence this rules out any file system that tries to use compression. It is good design to put all XIP executables in a ROMFS partition and have CRAMFS, JFFS2 partitions for other compressed files based on system requirements.

10.9 Building uClinux Distribution

In this section we discuss how to build uClinux distribution. The build procedure for uClinux is fairly simple. The build system is well integrated and controlled by the GNU make system. The top-level build integrates the following.

- Platform/vendor selection
- Kernel version selection and build
- C library selection and build
- Building support libraries (libmath, libz, etc.)
- Selection of user applications (Busybox, Tinylogin, etc.)
- Building the root file system
- Making the final ROM/flash image for the target

We run through the various steps and the menu configurations. Download the latest tar from http://www.uclinux.org. Untar the distribution under a directory.

```
#tar jxvf uClinux-dist-20041215.tar.bz2
```

This untars the distribution files under the `uClinux-dist` directory. The steps to build the distribution are:

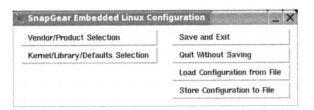

Figure 10.7   make xconfig.

Figure 10.8   Vendor/product selection.

1. *Build configuration:* Go to the distribution directory and issue

```
make config (or)
make menuconfig (or)
make xconfig
```

It prompts the top-level menu. Figure 10.7 shows the top-level menu for
`make xconfig`.

2. *Choose platform:* The Vendor/Product Selection menu lists all the platforms
on which uClinux is available. Choose a suitable vendor and product from
the available list. Figure 10.8 shows the Vendor/Product Selection menu
for `make xconfig`.

3. *Kernel/Library selection:* The Kernel/Library Selection menu is shown in
Figure 10.9. uClinux distribution supports three versions of Linux kernels:
2.0, 2.4, and 2.6. Based on features required and project needs choose a
suitable kernel. uClinux provides three options for the C library: glibc,
uClibc, and uC-libc. uC-libc is an old version of uClibc. uClibc is written

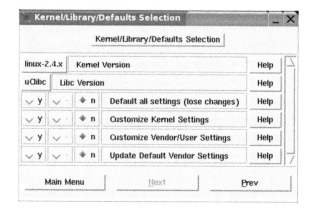

Figure 10.9   Kernel/library selection.

Figure 10.10   Application selection.

for embedded systems and hence is most suitable. uClibc will be sufficient for most systems. Set *Customize Kernel Settings* to y if you need to modify the kernel configuration. Set *Customize Vendor/User Settings* to y if you need to modify the user-space applications and support libraries.

4. *User-space configuration:* Setting *Customize Vendor/User Settings* to y provides the user-space configuration menu. This menu provides options to choose the applications that you need on the target. The libraries required for the build can also be selected. The menu is shown in Figure 10.10.

5. *Dependency and build:*

```
# make dep
# make
```

6. This completes the build procedure. The build procedure will make all files and place the final ROM/flash image in the images directory.

Notes

1. uClinux is pronounced as in you-see Linux and stands for Micro(μ)Controller Linux.
2. TLB stands for Translation LookUp Buffer, a hardware lookup table used for translating physical address to virtual address and vice versa.

3. Processors provide different modes of protection such as Intel's Real mode, Protected mode, and so on. Each mode can be programmed to address a different range of memory addresses.
4. The virtual memory limit on 32-bit (x86) machines is 4 GB.
5. In fact most of the virtual memory features of Linux-like page cache, COW, and swap have portions implemented in the page fault handler.
6. Each application on x86 is capable of addressing a 4-GB virtual address range. 1 GB of this space is reserved for the kernel area and the remaining 3 GB are available for the user area of the application.
7. This problem is called the unknown address problem.
8. For example, a function call will use "call 0x500" meaning call the function located at PC+0x500 or "jmp 0x20" meaning branch to location PC+0x20.
9. Note that for this the data and text segments must be separated using appropriate compiler arguments.
10. Stack size can be set at the time of conversion of ELF to an FLT file.
11. Note that during execution of a flat binary exec() uses the same function with id=0.

Appendix A

Booting Faster

Fast booting is an important system requirement in most of the embedded systems. As Linux is gaining a strong foothold in the embedded systems market, it is becoming increasingly important for a Linux-based embedded system to boot up as fast as possible. However, decreasing the boot time for an embedded Linux system is not a trivial task due to the following reasons.

- If we define turn-on state as a state in which the basic services (depending on the system functionality) are available, then different embedded systems have different requirements for the turn-on state. Let us analyze a router and a handheld device for defining the turn-on state. For a router the turn-on state becomes effective when the router has configured all the network interfaces, started all the required network protocols, and has configured the various routing tables. However, for a handheld this state is effective when a windowing system and the input/output devices are available for the user. Unlike the router the network connectivity stack initialization is not a must for reaching the turn-on state for the handheld; rather the networking stack can be initialized at a later point in time. Throughout this section the boot-up time refers to the time taken by the system to reach the turn-on state after it is powered on.
- Linux has evolved with the desktop and server market for which the boot-up time is not an important requirement. On the desktops and servers, Linux takes as much as a few minutes to come up; this is totally unacceptable for embedded systems.
- As processing power of embedded systems increases, the software on embedded systems too has increased manyfold. More software stack simply means more boot-up time.

Decreasing the boot-up time hence is a customized process for an embedded system. This section explains some of the generic techniques for cutting

Table A.1   Linux Boot Stages

State	Description	Time-Consuming Activities
Bootloader	The boot loader does the POST, starts a screen for user interaction, and downloads a Linux kernel to memory for initialization.	POST, locating a kernel, copying it to memory, uncompressing the kernel.
Kernel turn-on	Kernel needs to initialize the hardware, set up the various subsystems and the drivers, mount a root file system, and transfer the control to user space.	Driver initialization, file system mounting.
User-space turn-on	Start the various services on the system.	Services getting started sequentially, services getting started that can be deferred to later, loading of kernel modules.

down on the boot-up time. However, each of the techniques normally has a tradeoff with respect to memory or speed; those are also discussed. The boot-up time for a Linux-based system can be divided into three stages as shown in Table A.1.

Techniques for Cutting Down Bootloader Initialization

- *POST:* Power-on self test can be done only during a cold boot operation; during warm boot it can be skipped and hence can cause decreased boot-up time.
- *Locating, uncompressing, and downloading the kernel memory:* This step can be one of the most time-consuming operations as it may take between 500 msec and 1 sec depending on the size of the kernel. The larger the size of the kernel the more will be the time to uncompress and copy it to memory. If the kernel is a part of a Linux file system stored on the flash, then locating the kernel and parsing the file headers (such as ELF headers) can be time consuming. Storing the kernel image in a raw partition can circumvent it. To avoid uncompression the file can be stored in uncompressed format but that would be at the expense of expensive flash storage space. To avoid copying the kernel to memory, the kernel can be XIPed. eXecute In place is a method by which the kernel is executed directly out of flash. XIP is discussed in detail in Chapter 10. Other than cutting down start-up time the other benefit of XIP is that it conserves memory because the kernel's text section is not copied to memory. However, the disadvantages of using XIP are:
  - XIP slows the execution time of the kernel because it is executed out of flash.

- Because the XIPed image cannot be compressed that would mean that you would want more flash for storing the uncompressed image.
- Using a kernel XIP would require changes to the flash driver code because operations such as flash erase and write cannot be done when the kernel is executed out of flash. The changes to the flash driver would typically be copying a portion of it to RAM and executing it with interrupts disabled. However this is not required if the kernel is XIPed from a flash that has only a read-only file system such as CRAMFS.
- However, if XIP is too expensive an operation then it is imperative that the kernel image should be kept as small as possible to avoid the copying time. Some additional tricks can be used to cut down copying time such as using DMA to transfer the image from the flash to the memory.

Tuning Kernel for Decreased Boot-Up Time

- *Disabling kernel prints:* If the kernel prints are directed to a serial console (which is a slow device) then the prints can cause a huge delay while the kernel is initialized. To avoid this kernel prints can be disabled using the kernel command line option `quiet`. However, the messages can be viewed later by the `dmesg` command.
- *Hard coding the `loops_per_jiffies` value within the kernel:* As already explained in Chapter 2, the kernel initialization includes invoking the function `calibrate_delay()` to calculate the value of `loops_per_jiffies`. Depending on the processor architecture this can take up to 500 msec. If the process frequency can be known at the time of compiling the kernel, then this value can be hard-coded inside the kernel or else a command line option can be added to the kernel to pass the value of this variable when the kernel is downloaded.
- *Cutting down driver initialization time:* Different drivers have different initialization times. This can be caused by spins in the driver. Also probing for hardware devices on certain buses such as PCI can cause increased boot-up time. Tweaking the initialization time in such cases would mean changes to the drivers such as presetting them with values already known at the time of building the kernel.
- *Using the proper root file system:* Different file systems have different initialization times. The boot time for journaling file systems such as JFFS2 is extremely high because they scan the entire flash during the initialization for searching the records. Read-only file systems such as CRAMFS and ROMFS have shorter initialization times.

Tuning User Space for Decreased Boot-Up Time

- *Module loading:* The more the number of kernel modules, the more time is taken to load the modules. In case there are many kernel modules then making them into a single module can effectively decrease the module loading time.

■ *Starting the services concurrently:* As explained in Chapter 2, the system RC scripts are used to turn on the system services, which are started sequentially. Considerable improvement can be found by starting the services in parallel. However, if that is done care should be taken regarding dependency between services.

Measuring Boot-Up Time

There are lots of methods to measure system boot-up time. In this section we discuss *Instrumented printks* to measure boot time. The patch can be downloaded from www.celinuxforum.org. The patch adds support for displaying timestamps along with `printk` output. Apply the patch to the kernel and enable *Show timing information on printks* under *Kernel hacking*. Compile and boot the new kernel. A sample output is shown in Listing A.1.

The core of the patch is the `sched_clock` function. As discussed in Chapter 8, high precision during measurement is achieved if the BSP provides better support for the `sched_clock` function.

Listing A.1   Sample Instrumented Printk Output

```
[4294667.296000] Linux version 2.6.8.1 (root@amol) (gcc version
                 3.2.2 20030222 (Red Hat Linux 3.2.2-5)) #4 Wed
                 Mar 9 15:22:08 IST 2005
[4294667.296000] BIOS-provided physical RAM map:
[4294667.296000] BIOS-e820: 0000000000000000 - 000000000009fc00
                 (usable)
[4294667.296000] BIOS-e820: 000000000009fc00 - 00000000000a0000
                 (reserved)
[4294667.296000] BIOS-e820: 00000000000e6000 - 0000000000100000
                 (reserved)
[4294667.296000] BIOS-e820: 0000000000100000 - 000000000ef2fc00
                 (usable)

        ...
        ...

 [4294671.443000] Dentry cache hash table entries: 32768 (order:
                 5, 131072 bytes)
[4294671.444000] Inode-cache hash table entries: 16384 (order: 4,
                 65536 bytes)
[4294671.570000] Memory: 237288k/244924k available (2099k kernel
                 code, 6940k reserved, 673k data, 172k init,
                 0k highmem)
[4294671.570000] Checking if this processor honors the WP bit
                 even in supervisor mode... Ok.
[4294671.570000] Calibrating delay loop... 5488.64 BogoMIPS
        ...
        ...
```

Appendix B

GPL and Embedded Linux

Linux and most of the open source applications, libraries, drivers, and so on are distributed under GNU GPL. In earlier days companies were reluctant to move to embedded Linux because of its GPL licensing. They feared that moving to Linux might force them to make their intellectual property public. As time passed companies gained more insight into GPL and they realized that proprietary software can always be kept safe with embedded Linux.

In your design you may decide to use some open source applications in the product. You should not assume that all the open source software comes under GPL. Apart from GPL there are other licenses such as Mozilla Public License (MPL), Lesser GPL (LGPL), Apache License, BSD License, and so on.[1] We highly recommend that you contact an open source legal advisor and clarify that you are not violating any of the licenses.

In this appendix we discuss how proprietary software can be kept safe with Linux. First we discuss the user-space applications and then the kernel.

User-Space Applications

Linus Torvalds made a clarification regarding user-space programs that run on Linux.

> *This copyright does *not* cover user programs that use kernel services by normal system calls - this is merely considered normal use of the kernel, and does *not* fall under the heading of "derived work."*[2]

It means that you can write a code from a fresh code base and use services of Linux and keep your code proprietary. It does not come under GPL and you need not release the source code either. But you must make sure that you are not using any GPL software accidentally in your user-space programs. The following points should be taken care of.

- You must not use source code of any program under GPL in your application.
- You must not link your application with any GPL library either statically or dynamically. You can link your application with LGPL libraries. Most of the key libraries in Linux such as libc, pthreads, and so on are released under LGPL. You can link LGPL libraries in your program with no obligation to release the application's source code.

It's allowed to use IPC mechanisms between GPL and non-GPL programs. For example, you can download the DHCP server released under GPL and write your own DHCP client. You are not obliged to release your DHCP client under GPL. However, any modifications done by you to any GPL application and that use the IPC mechanisms to work around GPL are very dangerous. You must take advice from an attorney in such cases.

Note that GPL only applies when it comes to distributing a program or a product. You can use any GPL programs, drivers, and so on in any manner you want as long as it's for internal use and not for distribution. For example, you can use open source debuggers and profilers for debugging your proprietary programs. You can also make modifications to them without releasing any code as long as they are for internal use.

Thus, user applications can always be kept proprietary in Linux. You only need to take some precautions while developing applications.

Kernel

There is a general opinion that loadable kernel modules using standard exported kernel interfaces can be kept safe and need not come under GPL. For example, you can have proprietary device drivers implemented as a Linux kernel module and need not release the source code of the driver provided you use standard interfaces exported by the kernel. However, this is one of the gray areas and you should consult your attorney.

Listing B.1 shows an excerpt from mail from Linus Torvalds to the kernel mailing list regarding his view on loadable kernel modules and GPL.

Thus the following points should be taken care of.

- Consult your attorney to find out whether you can use loadable kernel modules to protect your proprietary software.
- Any modifications done to the Linux kernel come under GPL.
- In the kernel do not export any nonexported kernel interface to support your loadable module.
- Any changes done to the kernel in the form of a kernel patch come under GPL.

Points to Remember

- As a manager of a project you should make sure that the developers understand GPL and other licenses involved in the project.
- During development, the developers should take care when using a piece of software (in the form of a library or some source code) available on the Net for their project. They should not accidentally violate any licenses involved. As rightly said, prevention is better than cure.
- One point where you must take care is software patent violation. It is possible that you are using some off-the-shelf source code that is violating some software patent. These violations are very difficult to catch and you should be extremely careful.

Listing B.1   Linus Torvalds' Mail Regarding GPL and Binary Kernel Modules

From: Linus Torvalds

Subject: Re: Linux GPL and binary module exception clause?

Date: 2003-12-03 16:10:18 PST

….

And in fact, when it comes to modules, the GPL issue is exactly the same. The kernel _is_ GPL. No ifs, buts and maybe's about it. As a result, anything that is a derived work has to be GPL'd. It's that simple.

Now, the "derived work" issue in copyright law is the only thing that leads to any gray areas. There are areas that are not gray at all: user space is clearly not a derived work, while kernel patches clearly _are_ derived works.

But one gray area in particular is something like a driver that was originally written for another operating system (i.e. clearly not a derived work of Linux in origin). At exactly what point does it become a derived work of the kernel (and thus fall under the GPL)?

THAT is a gray area, and _that is the area where I personally believe that some modules may be considered to not be derived works simply because they weren't designed for Linux and don't depend on any special Linux behavior.
   Basically:

- Anything that was written with Linux in mind (whether it then _also_ works on other operating systems or not) is clearly partially a derived work.
- Anything that has knowledge of and plays with fundamental internal Linux behavior is clearly a derived work. If you need to muck around with core code, you're derived, no question about it.

Listing B.1   Linus Torvalds' Mail Regarding GPL and Binary Kernel Modules (continued)

Historically, there's been things like the original Andrew filesystem module: a standard filesystem that really wasn't written for Linux in the first place, and just implements a UNIX filesystem. Is that derived just because it got ported to Linux that had a reasonably similar VFS interface to what other UNIXes did? Personally, I didn't feel that I could make that judgment call. Maybe it was, maybe it wasn't, but it clearly is a gray area.

Personally, I think that case wasn't a derived work, and I was willing to tell the AFS guys so.

Does that mean that any kernel module is automatically not a derived work? NO! It has nothing to do with modules per se, except that non-modules clearly are derived works (if they are so central to the kernel that you can't load them as a module, they are clearly derived works just by virtue of being very intimate - and because the GPL expressly mentions linking).

So being a module is not a sign of not being a derived work. It's just one sign that _maybe_ it might have other arguments for why it isn't derived.

Notes

1. http://www.gnu.org/philosophy/license-list.html has the complete list. GPL license can be downloaded from http://www.fsf.org/licensing.
2. See the COPYING file in kernel sources.

Index

9 780849 340581